The New
History of Florida

A March Day in St. Augustine, Florida (1885)

The New History of Florida

Edited by
Michael Gannon

Gainesville **University**
Tallahassee **Press**
Tampa **of**
Boca Raton **Florida**
Pensacola
Orlando
Miami
Jacksonville

A Florida Sesquicentennial Book

08 07 06 05 04 03   8 7 6 5 4 3

Library of Congress Cataloging-in-Publication Data
The new history of Florida / edited by Michael Gannon.
        p.   cm.
        "A Florida sesquicentennial book"—T.p. verso.
        Includes bibliographical references and index.
        ISBN 0–8130–1415–8 (alk. paper)
        1. Florida—History.   I. Gannon, Michael, 1927– .
F311.5.N49 1996   95-11055
975.9-dc20   CIP

The University Press of Florida is the scholarly publishing agency
for the State University System of Florida, comprised of Florida
A&M University, Florida Atlantic University, Florida International
University, Florida State University, University of Central Florida,
University of Florida, University of North Florida, University of
South Florida, and University of West Florida.

University Press of Florida
15 Northwest 15th Street
Gainesville, FL 32611
http//:www.upf.com

Dedicated to two of our colleagues
who participated in the preparation of this book

Herbert J. Doherty, Jr.
1926–1993

George E. Pozzetta
1942–1994

Contents

Illustrations

Introduction

On 3 March 1945, one hundred years to the day after President John Tyler signed the congressional resolution admitting Florida as the twenty-seventh state of the American Union, the Honorable Claude D. Pepper, senator from Florida, rose in the Library of Congress to present an address on the Centennial of Statehood. After rehearsing numerous events of Florida's recorded history, Senator Pepper exalted "the land of five flags and four successive civilizations; the land of color and the sunshine of life; the land of the faithful farmer and worker; the land of Osceola and Bloxham and Broward and William Jennings Bryan and Thomas A. Edison, of Plant and Flagler; the land where St. Augustine still keeps her stately vigil of nearly four centuries over a continent which has truly become what the conquistadors held it to be, 'the hope of the old world.'"[1]

On 3 March 1995 similar ceremonies took place in Washington, in Tallahassee, and at various sites throughout the State of Florida, to observe Florida's *Sesquicentennial*—150 years as a state. On that date fifty more remarkable years of membership in the American Union were memorialized by speakers, both old and young, many of whom, like the late Alabama-born Claude Pepper, were recent immigrants to the Sunshine State from other parts of the country and the world.

On yet another 3 March, in 1513, over four and three-quarter centuries ago, the Spaniard Juan Ponce de León weighed anchor in Añasco Bay on the southwestern coast of Puerto Rico and steered the prows of his three small vessels toward the legendary island of Bimini. In Easter Week of that year he and his companions stumbled upon the shore of what he called *La Florida*, the first permanent geographic name of European origin to be etched upon the maps of this continent. With Juan Ponce's voyage began the formal history of Florida, which may be remarked to be the oldest recorded history of any of the American states.

By 1565, one year following the death of Michaelangelo and the birth of William Shakespeare, a Spanish city would be founded on the coast of that Florida. Named St. Augustine, it bears today the mantle of first permanent European settlement in North America and oldest city in the United States. Founded forty years before Jamestown and fifty-five years before Plymouth, St. Augustine in its "stately vigil" reminds us that, as one contributor to this volume writes, looking back even farther, to Juan Ponce: "More than three centuries of sunrises and sunsets lay between the first and final appearances of the Spanish flag in Florida. It will be the twenty-second century before the same can be said about the flag of the United States" (chapter 9).

A twenty-one-year British interregnum and 174 years as U.S. territory and state fill out Florida's recorded history, as detailed in the pages of this book. But no history of Florida should fail to take into account the story of a people who possessed no written history, who instead passed down their knowledge of the past from generation to generation by oral tradition and left, in the form of their artifacts, a buried record under Florida's soil. Archaeologists today are mining the riches of that record in every part of Florida and by that means are pushing back in time our understanding of this state's first human inhabitants, who entered the peninsula and Panhandle about 10,000 years ago. They were the people who were already here. Tragically, in the early and middle decades of the eighteenth century, as a result of European-introduced diseases and slaving raids by English forces from South Carolina and Georgia, Florida's first natives became extinct.

The history of Florida that is preserved in documents has been told many times, in comprehensive and specialized books, journal articles, conference papers, and special reports. It is a body of work that has drawn admiration from scholars and readers in every part of the country. When we consider comprehensive histories, as this volume aspires to be, we think of such models as *Ensayo Cronológico para la historia general de la Florida, 1512–1722,* by Andrés González de Barcía (pseudonym Gabriel de Cardensa z Cano), published in Madrid, Spain, in 1723; *History of Florida from Its Discovery by Ponce de León in 1512 to the Close of the Florida War in 1842,* by George R. Fairbanks, published in Jacksonville, Florida, in 1871; *Florida Land of Change,* by Kathryn Trimmer Abbey [Hanna], published in Chapel Hill, North Carolina, in 1941; and *A History of Florida,* by Charlton W. Tebeau, published in Miami in 1971, updated in 1980. Numerous other titles might be joined to these, all of which have laid the foundation on which this work is based.

During the past quarter century there has been a veritable efflorescence of historical research activity directed at uncovering the major details of Florida's long past, in the course of which a galaxy of specialists emerged to match the best company of state historians to be found in any other part of the country. With such an extraordinary amount of new information at hand, and with such an impressive corps of scholars to write it down, the editor of this book saw an eminently appropriate way to observe Florida's Sesquicentennial: to persuade these scholars to join in composing a new one-volume history of Florida. Such a volume would provide a documented, reliable, up-to-date source for the use and reading pleasure of the general public, teachers, students, and fellow historians, both professional and avocational.

To that end, the projected contributors accepted an invitation to meet for an editorial planning session in Gainesville on 25 April 1993, under the sponsorship of the Institute for Early Contact Period Studies of the University of Florida. At that meeting Dr. George Bedell, director of the University Press of Florida, personally commissioned the work and urged its publication during the sesquicentennial year. The contributors jointly established how they would proceed, agreeing on the varying length of chapters, how each chapter would mesh with those chapters preceding and following it, how certain subjects would be treated thematically rather than chronologically, and how even small details, such as endnotes, bibliographies, and illustrations, would be handled. Each chapter would be new work, written especially for this volume, presenting in compact fashion the most recent findings and interpretations in each specialist's field; in four cases two specialists would combine their knowledge and skills in the writing of single chapters.

Following that editorial conference, two historians were added to the team. Sadly, two of the participants in the meeting died before being able to see their work in print. This volume is dedicated to them.

Readers of *The New History of Florida* will observe that most of the twenty-two chapters of this book follow upon each other chronologically, e.g., "Fortune and Misfortune: The Paradoxical Twenties" (chapter 16) is followed by "The Great Depression" (chapter 17) which in turn is followed by "World War II" (chapter 18). Certain subject areas, however, overlap several or numerous time periods, and these are treated thematically. Thus, chapter 10, "Free and Slave," treats African societies in Florida from the sixteenth to the middle of the nineteenth century. Similarly, chapter 11, "Florida's Seminole and Miccosukee Peoples," follows those peoples from their first arrival in Florida during the early eighteenth century as far as the 1990s. In this way, certain subjects of special interest are not broken up into segmented time periods but are studied in one continuous, connected form.

The editor expresses his gratitude to all the contributors, who have approached this project as a labor of love and have made his task easy by submitting wonderfully organized and elegantly written manuscripts. Anyone would be honored to work in their company. He thanks Dr. Bedell, who championed the publication of this volume; Dr. Walda Metcalf, editor-in-chief of the press, whose fine hand (and wit) gilded the lily; Judy Goffman, copyeditor; the editor's secretary, Ms. Myrna Sulsona, who brought order to the process with her usual skill and patience; Ms. Barbara Smerage, who ably transferred the final edited copy to computer disk; and Ms. Joan Morris and Ms. Joanna Norman, of the Photographic Collection, Florida State Archives, Tallahassee, who provided most of the book's illustrations.

Through the editor all the contributors thank their colleagues who read their manuscripts before submission and offered constructive suggestions for their improvement.

Here, then, is the grand story of Florida—as best we know it—presented in Florida's 10,000th year of human habitation, 483d year of recorded history, and 151st year of American statehood.

Michael Gannon
Editor

Note

1. *Florida's Centennial, Library of Congress, March 3, 1945. An Address by the Hon. Claude Pepper, Senator from Florida, on the Occasion of Ceremonies Opening the Florida Centennial Exhibition at the Library of Congress Together with a Catalog of the Exhibition* (Washington: U.S. Government Printing Office, 1946), p. 11.

1 Original Inhabitants

Jerald T. Milanich

What is now the state of Florida was first settled by humans whose ancestors had entered North America from eastern Asia during the Pleistocene era, the Great Ice Age, about 12,000 years ago. Sea levels as much as 350 feet lower than present—because of huge amounts of water were tied up in Ice Age glaciers—exposed a large land bridge between Siberia and Alaska across what is now the Bering Strait. Hunter-gatherers in search of game and other foods easily crossed this land bridge which connected Asia and North America and was at least as wide as the distance from Orlando to New York City.

These early hunter-gatherers are called Paleoindians, and they entered Florida around 10,000 B.C., about the same time that they moved into other parts of what is now the United States. Evidently their nonsedentary life-style and a new world filled with plant and animal foods never encountered previously by humans enabled—perhaps encouraged—them to colonize the Americas quickly. Campsites of the Paleoindians are found across North America from Alaska to south Florida.

Some archaeologists argue that the Paleoindian migration was preceded by even earlier movements of people from Asia across the Siberia-Alaska land bridge into the Americas. But as yet the evidence for such a pre-Paleoindian presence in North America is tenuous. Certainly in Florida, the Paleoindians were the first human residents.

At the time of the Florida Paleoindians, the same lowered seas that created a transcontinental bridge across the Bering Strait gave Florida a total landmass about twice what it is today. The Gulf of Mexico shoreline, for instance, was more than 100 miles west of its present location. During the Paleoindian period Florida also was much drier than it is today. Many of our present rivers, springs, and lakes were not here, and even groundwater levels were significantly lower. Plants that survived were those that could grow in the dry, cool conditions. Scrub vegetation, open grassy prairies, and savannahs were common.

Sources of surface water, so important to Paleoindians and to the animals they hunted for food, were limited. The Paleoindians sought water in deep springs, like Little Salt Spring in Sarasota County, or at watering holes or shallow lakes or prairies where limestone strata near the surface provided catchment basins. Such limestone deposits are found from the Hillsborough River drainage north through peninsular Florida into the Panhandle. Paleoindians hunted, butchered, and consumed animals at these watering holes, leaving behind their refuse, artifacts that can be studied and interpreted by modern archaeologists.

Today, with higher water levels, many of these catchment basins are flowing rivers, like the Ichetucknee, Wacissa, Aucilla, and Chipola. Paleoindian camps with bone and stone weapons and tools, including distinctive lanceolate stone spear points, are found in deposits at the bottoms of these rivers, as well as at land sites nearby. With the stone tools are found bones of the animals the Paleoindians hunted, some exhibiting butchering marks. A number of the animal species hunted by Paleoindians became extinct shortly after the end of the Pleistocene epoch, perhaps in part because of human predation. They include mastodon, mammoth, horse, camel, bison, and giant land tortoise. Other of the animals that provided meat for the Paleoindian diet—deer, rabbits, raccoons, and many more—continue to inhabit Florida today.

After about 9,000 B.C., as glaciers melted and sea levels rose, Florida's climate generally became wetter than it had been, providing more water sources around which the Paleoindians could camp. But as the sea rose, coastal areas were flooded and the Florida landmass was reduced. Less land and larger human populations may have influenced the later Paleoindians to follow a less nomadic way of life. They moved between water sources less frequently, and their camps were occupied for longer periods of time. Archaeological sites corresponding to these larger late Paleoindian camps have been found in the Hillsborough River drainage near Tampa, around Paynes Prairie south of Gainesville, near Silver Springs, and at other locations in northern Florida.

Paleoindian sites, relatively common in the northern half of the state

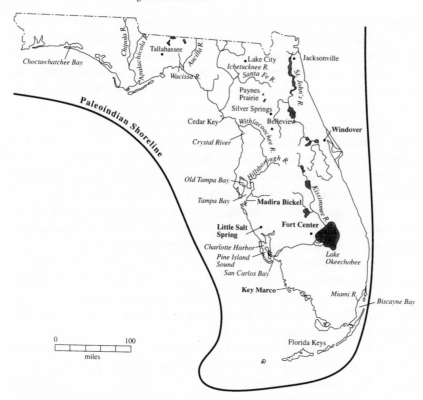

Archaeological sites (in bold) and other Florida locations mentioned in chapter 1.

in the region of surface limestone strata, also occur in smaller numbers in southern Florida. Paleoindian artifacts have been found as far south as Dade County.

Over time the tool kits of the Paleoindians changed as people altered their lifeways to adjust to the new environmental conditions that confronted them. They began to use a wider variety of stone tools, and many of the stone points originally used to hunt the large Pleistocene animals were no longer made. These changes were sufficient by 7500 B.C. for archaeologists to delineate a new culture, the early Archaic.

The environment of the early Archaic peoples was still drier than our modern climate, but it was wetter than it had been in earlier times. Early Archaic peoples continued to live next to wetlands and water sources and to hunt and gather wild foods.

One remarkable early Archaic period site is the Windover Pond site in Brevard County, which contains peat deposits in which early Archaic people interred their dead. Careful excavations by Glen Doran and David Dickel of Florida State University revealed that during the period between 5,000 and 6,000 B.C. human burials were placed in the peat in the bottom of the shallow pond. The peat helped to preserve an array of normally perishable artifacts and human tissues, including brains, from which scientists have recovered and studied genetic material.

Artifacts recovered by the excavation team included shark teeth and dog or wolf teeth which had been attached with pitch to wooden handles for use as tools. Other tools were made from deer bone and antler, from manatee and either panther or bobcat bone, and from bird bone. Bone pins, barbed points, and awls were found preserved in the peat, along with throwing stick weights made from deer antler. The weights were used with a handheld shaft to help launch spears; the earlier Paleoindians probably also used throwing sticks.

Animal bones found in the pond, presumably from animals eaten by the people who lived there, were from otter, rat, squirrel, rabbit, opossum, duck and wading birds, alligator, turtle, snake, frog, and fish. Remains of plants, including prickly pear and a wild gourd fashioned into a dipper, were also preserved.

A well-developed and sophisticated array of cordage and fiber fabrics and matting lay in the Windover Pond peat. Fibers taken from Sable palms, saw palmettos, and other plants were used in twining and weaving. The early Archaic people of Florida, like the people that preceded them and those that would follow, had an assemblage of material items—tools, woven fabrics, and the like—well suited to life in Florida.

After 5,000 B.C. the climate of Florida began to ameliorate, becoming more like modern conditions, which were reached by about 3,000 B.C. The time between 5,000 and 3,000 B.C. is known as the middle Archaic period. Middle Archaic sites are found in a variety of settings, some very different from those of the Paleoindians and early Archaic periods, including, for the first time, some along the St. Johns River and the Atlantic coastal strand. Middle Archaic peoples also were living in the Hillsborough River drainage northeast of Tampa Bay, along the southwest Florida coast, and in a few south Florida locales. And middle Archaic sites are found in large numbers in interior northern Florida. The presence of a larger number of surface water sites than had been available in earlier times provided many more locales for people to inhabit.

It is clear that during the middle Archaic period Florida natives took advantage of the increased number of hospitable areas. Populations increased significantly. The people practiced a more settled way of life and utilized a larger variety of specialized tools than their ancestors had done.

By 3,000 B.C., the onset of the late Archaic period, essentially modern environmental conditions were reached in Florida, and expanding populations occupied almost every part of the state. Wetland locales were heavily settled. Numerous late Archaic sites have been found in coastal regions in northwest, southwest, and northeast Florida and in the St. Johns River drainage. Such sites, representing the remains of villages, are characterized by extensive deposits of mollusks—snails and mussels at freshwater locations and oysters along the coasts—which represent the remains of thousands of precolumbian meals. At both marine and freshwater settlements fish and shellfish were dietary staples, as they were for many generations of later native Floridians.

Late Archaic groups probably lived along most if not all of Florida's coasts, but many of their sites have been inundated by the sea rise that continued throughout the Archaic period as Pleistocene glaciers melted. This is certainly true around Tampa Bay, where dredging has revealed extensive shell middens that today are under water. It is also likely that Paleoindian and early and middle Archaic sites have been covered by the rising sea.

Slightly before 2000 B.C. the late Archaic villagers learned to make fired clay pottery, tempering it with Spanish moss or palmetto fibers. Sites with fiber-tempered pottery, some associated with massive shell middens, are distributed throughout the entire state down to the Florida Keys.

By the end of the late Archaic period at 500 B.C., many new types of fired clay pottery were being made by regional groups. Because different groups made their ceramic vessels in specific shapes and decorated then with distinctive designs, archaeologists can use pottery as a tool to define and study specific cultures. Often those cultures are named for modern geographical landmarks where their remains were first recognized. In some instances we can trace, albeit incompletely, the evolution of these regional cultures from 500 B.C. into the sixteenth and seventeenth centuries when European powers sought to colonize Florida. We can correlate the precolumbian archaeological cultures with native American groups described in colonial-period European documents.

Each regional culture with its distinctive style of pottery tended to live within one major environmental or physiographic zone. Each developed an economic base and other cultural practices that were well suited to that particular region and its various habitats and resources.

Like their Archaic and Paleoindian ancestors, the people associated with these post–500 B.C. regional cultures made a variety of stone tools as well. Today examples of those tools are found throughout Florida, although they are more numerous in regions where chert—a flintlike stone—was mined from limestone deposits and fashioned into spear and arrow points, knives, scrapers, and a variety of other tools.

East Florida—including the St. Johns River drainage from Brevard County north to Jacksonville, the adjacent Atlantic coastal region, and the many lakes of central Florida—was the region of the St. Johns culture. Like the Late Archaic groups that preceded them, the St. Johns people made extensive use of fish and shellfish and other wild foods. They hunted and collected the foods that could be found in the natural environment where they lived.

By 100 B.C. or shortly after, the St. Johns people were constructing sand burial mounds in which to inter their dead. Each village had a leader or leaders who helped coordinate activities, such as communal ceremonies. Villagers most likely were organized into a number of lineages or other kin-based groups, each of which probably had a name and distinctive paraphernalia or other symbols of membership.

When a village grew too large for its residents to be supported easily by local economic resources, one or more lineages broke away, establishing a new village nearby. Traditions and shared kinship and origins served to tie old and new villages together. Such a social system probably was present in nearly all of Florida at this same time.

Although squashes and gourds probably were grown in gardens even in the late Archaic period, it was not until A.D. 750 or even later that some of the northerly St. Johns peoples began to cultivate corn. Food production, in conjunction with hunting, collecting, and fishing, could support larger human populations. Many more post–A.D. 750 St. Johns villages are known than earlier sites, reflecting this population increase.

Agriculture, important to native groups in the central portion of peninsular Florida and the eastern panhandle, led to changes in lifeways. After about A.D. 1000 some of the St. Johns groups living along the northern St. Johns River constructed large sand mounds to serve as bases for temples or for residences in which their leaders lived. Larger populations, a desire to understand and try to control such things as agricultural fertility and rainfall, and the need for more social cooperation in order to maintain fields and protect territory stimulated the development of more complex forms of political organization and new beliefs and ceremonial practices.

With the coming of agriculture village leaders were replaced by chiefs and religious figures, who exercised control over the people and sought to bridge the gap between the villagers and the supernatural. Often these chiefly and religious officials were associated with special objects and symbols, visible reminders of their power. Through alliances or the threat of military force, some chiefs sought to extend their political power and increase the territory under their aegis. At times such leaders controlled outlying villages and their chiefs, receiving respect and tribute from those chiefs as symbols of their allegiance.

Many villages of the St. Johns region, some with large mounds, were inhabited in the early sixteenth century when Europeans first entered the interior of east Florida and traveled up the St. Johns River. From that period on, we have written records left by those Europeans which offer firsthand descriptions of the early colonial-period descendants of the St. Johns people. Those descendants include many eastern groups speaking the Timucuan language who lived along and near the St. Johns River and its tributaries, groups with names like Saturiwa, Utina, and Acuera.

In northwest Florida and the interior of northern Florida and along the Gulf coast from Cedar Key north, the earliest post–500 B.C. regional culture was called Deptford. Especially numerous in locales adjacent to the salt marshes and tidal streams of the Gulf coast are village sites and fishing camps characterized by the distinctive Deptford pottery (decorated with check-stamped and grooved surface designs applied by using carved wooden or clay paddles to malleate the surface of the ceramic vessels before they were fired). Smaller hunting camps are found inland.

In the Panhandle after about A.D. 100, increased use of interior wetland and forest resources, especially the rivers and lakes in Gadsden, Leon, and Jefferson counties, led to the development of the Swift Creek culture out of the Deptford culture. Swift Creek, with its distinctive pottery stamped with geometric designs, was related to the Santa Rosa–Swift Creek culture that followed Deptford in the western Panhandle at about the same time. Influenced by cultures to the north of Florida, the ideology of the late Deptford and Swift Creek cultures was associated with a rich variety of ceramic, shell, stone, and even copper items, some traded into the state from the north. Many of these objects display stylized animal motifs representing the same species important to later native Floridians as well.

Like the Deptford people who preceded them, the Swift Creek and Santa Rosa–Swift Creek built sand mounds in which they interred their deceased relatives. Swift Creek villages are found in the interior of

A late-sixteenth-century engraving offers a European view of Florida Indian chief Saturiwa and his wife going for a walk by their village on the south bank of the St. Johns River near its mouth. The chief and his wife are both tattooed, a sign of their high status, and they are wearing shell beads. Feather cloaks and tanned and painted animal hides also were worn. Male villagers typically wore breechcloths, and women dressed in skirts skillfully woven from Spanish moss. The men's hair was pulled up and tied.

eastern northwest Florida, evidence that people were moving into that region, perhaps a result of continuing population increase.

The Weeden Island culture and its coastal and inland regional variants appeared after about A.D. 300 from Sarasota County north along the Gulf coast to Alabama as well as in the interior of north and northwest Florida. Weeden Island, named for a site on Old Tampa Bay in Pinellas County excavated in the early 1920s, emerged out of local Deptford, Swift Creek, Santa Rosa–Swift Creek, and related cultures that were present in that large area.

Weeden Island villages, often with burial mounds and other mounds in association, are found in a variety of environments and geographical locations from Crystal River to near Lake City to Tallahassee and beyond to Pensacola. In each area villagers practiced distinctive lifeways, but they shared many aspects of Weeden Island ideology and social and political organization.

One Weeden Island variant culture was the Cades Pond culture of Alachua County and the western portion of Putnam County. Cades Pond peoples lived in villages adjacent to extensive wetlands—lakes, wet prairies, marshes, and the like—where they could fish and gather water birds and a wide variety of other wetland-dwelling animals. They also hunted in the adjacent forests and collected acorns, hickory nuts, and persimmons. Numerous Cades Pond mounds are known, some with Weeden Island pottery. Like the Swift Creek people in northwest Florida, Cades Pond villages took advantage of the resources in the interior away from the coast to establish settlements.

Weeden Island variant cultures also are found around Tampa Bay (the Manasota culture) and along the north peninsular Gulf Coast. In those regions people continued to practice the same patterns of subsistence as did their late Archaic ancestors. Like the villagers in other Weeden Island cultures they built mounds and manufactured and traded for ornate ceramic vessels and other objects displaying a rich array of symbols important to their beliefs. The ceramic complex associated with mounds is the defining characteristic of these cultures.

Cultivation of corn appeared among the northern Weeden Island cultures after about A.D. 800, about the same time it did in the St. Johns region. In the eastern portion of northwest Florida maize agriculture became particularly important to aboriginal subsistence, providing—after A.D. 1000—the economic base for the development and elaboration of the Fort Walton culture, which eventually stretched from the Aucilla River west through the Panhandle. Fertile inland locales—especially the Tallahassee Hills zone of Leon and Jefferson counties and the upper Apalachicola River Valley—supported a number of large Fort Walton villages, some with mounds built as platforms on which to erect the temples and residences of chiefs and religious leaders. The Lake Jackson Mounds, in a state park near Tallahassee, is one such site.

Fort Walton was the largest and most politically complex precolumbian culture in Florida. Separate political units—each consisting of a number of villages, village chiefs and other officials, and outlying agricultural homesteads, all united under a paramount chief—vied with one another for power and territory. The Apalachee natives encountered by Spanish expeditions in the early colonial period were the descendants of precolumbian Fort Walton populations. West of the Fort Walton region in the western Panhandle, influences from the north, from cultures in Alabama, provided the impetus for the development of the Pensacola culture. Pensacola villages and mounds are

Line drawing of a copper breastplate excavated at Lake Jackson, a Fort Walton archaeological site in Leon County. The figure depicted is probably a person dressed in the costume of a bird.

found clustered around the coastal bays from Choctawhatchee Bay west. The Pensacola people probably practiced agriculture, but it was not as extensive as the cleared-field farming of the Fort Walton culture.

Agriculture also was added to the economic system of the late Weeden Island–period culture of north Florida, which occupied the region east of the Aucilla River, north of the Santa Fe River, and west of the St. Johns River drainage. Named the Suwannee Valley culture, the people of this post–A.D. 750 culture also never practiced agriculture as extensively as did Fort Walton farmers. The descendants of Suwannee Valley populations are the various western Timucua-speaking groups of Madison, Suwannee, Hamilton, and Columbia counties who witnessed the passage of the Hernando de Soto expedition in 1539. They include, among others, the Aguacaleyquen, Napituca, and Uzachile.

Farther south in north-central Florida from the Santa Fe River down to Belleview in Marion County, another culture replaced the Weeden Island–period Cades Pond culture around A.D. 600. The Alachua culture represents a migration of a new population into Alachua and western Marion counties from the river valleys of southern Georgia. It is uncertain if this intrusive culture was associated with farming when it first appeared in north-central Florida, but by about A.D. 1250, if not before, we are certain that maize was being cultivated.

Early in their history in Florida, the Alachua villages expanded westward into Levy and Dixie counties, although they apparently did not live on the coast itself, where villagers continued to make their livelihood from the marine environments. The Potano Indians, a Timucua-speaking native group, are the descendants of the Alachua population.

Around Tampa Bay, a huge estuary capable of supporting large populations, the Weeden Island–period culture developed into the Safety Harbor culture after about A.D. 900. Safety Harbor sites are found along the Gulf coast from Charlotte Harbor north to the Withlacoochee River in Citrus County. The Safety Harbor people on Tampa Bay probably were not farmers, but the villagers just north of Tampa Bay did grow corn, though it was not as important to their diet as it was in northwest Florida.

Safety Harbor sites, some with huge heaps of shellfish as well as mounds and village areas, once dotted the shoreline of Tampa Bay, but many were destroyed around the turn of the century when the shell was mined to build roads. Today only a few of these large sites exist, such as the one at Madira Bickel state park.

Small, triangular stone points were used by the Safety Harbor people to tip arrows. Similar points—suggesting bow and arrow use—are common in the contemporary Fort Walton, Suwannee Valley, and Alachua cultures in northern Florida.

The colonial-period Uzita, Mocoso, Pohoy, Tocobaga, and possibly the Ocale Indians all were Safety Harbor groups, and at least some of them—those living from Tampa Bay north—spoke Timucua. Like other north Florida native societies, all of these people of the Tampa Bay region people were in contact with Spanish expeditions in the sixteenth century.

The lifeways of the various regional cultures of southern Florida also were well established by 500 B.C., the end of the late Archaic period. Although some beliefs and symbols were shared with the agricultural cultures farther north in Florida, the nature of the south Florida precolumbian cultures reflects their reliance on coastal and freshwater wetlands for their subsistence.

The vast savannah around Lake Okeechobee, called by Florida natives Lake Mayaimi, was the home of the Belle Glade culture. By as early as 400 B.C., shortly after the end of the late Archaic period, the Belle Glade peoples evidently grew small amounts of maize. But the practice seems to have been abandoned by A.D. 500 or so, possibly because of increasingly wet conditions. The Belle Glade peoples built a remarkable series of villages, each containing mounds and earthen embankments and other earthworks, some in geometric shapes. They also dug ditches and canals. One such complex site is Fort Center in Glades County, where numerous wooden carvings of animals were found preserved in a pond.

Belle Glade villagers continued to live around the lake and in the Kissimmee River drainage into early colonial times. The wetlands and savannahs provided them with a rich assortment of fish, birds, turtles, alligator, and other animals, as well as plants. The Belle Glade culture was one of the most distinctive in all of Florida.

Along the mangrove coasts and estuaries of southeast Florida, the coasts of the Ten Thousand Island region, and the coast of Monroe County north of the Florida keys, a distinctive regional culture developed. Hunter-gatherers, these Glades culture people lived by fishing, gathering shellfish, and collecting plants and other animals. Numerous Glades sites also are found in the Everglades and other areas of interior Florida south of the Okeechobee Basin.

Glades archaeological sites once blanketed the shores of the Florida Gold Coast; where huge precolumbian shell heaps once dotted Biscayne Bay, today there are high-rise buildings. Scattered sites are still visible in a few places, such as along the Miami River.

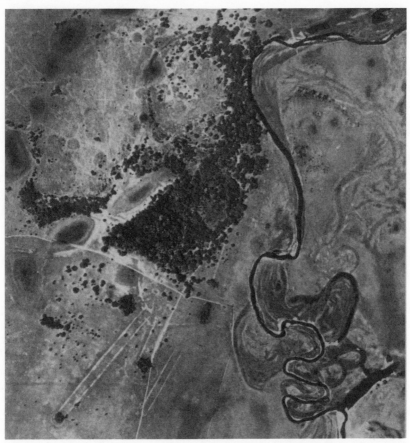

Aerial photograph showing the linear embankments and other earthworks, including a circular ditch, at Fort Center, a Belle Glade culture archaeological site in the Lake Okeechobee Basin. The site covers approximately one mile along the creek bank (north is to the right).

At Key Marco, a site on Marco Island excavated in the late nineteenth century, archaeologists recovered nets, net floats, and other fishing gear along with beautifully carved and painted wooden masks and animal figurines and depictions, providing us with a glimpse into the rich culture of these precolumbian coastal dwellers. These southern Florida native peoples used bows and arrows along with a variety of other tools made of shell and wood. Stone is not as common in southern Florida as it is farther north, and the precolumbian peoples used other raw materials for their artifacts.

In Dade County the colonial-period descendants of the Glades populations were the Tequesta natives. To the north were groups like the Boca Ratones and Santaluces, names given the natives by the Spaniards.

Another coastal-oriented culture, the Caloosahatchee, occupied the southwest coast from Charlotte Harbor south into Collier County. The largest shell mounds in Florida are found there today, as well as large and small shell heaps on nearly every coastal island and the adjacent mainland, especially in Charlotte Harbor, Pine Island Sound, and San Carlos Bay.

The extensive shell middens contain the remains of hundreds of thousands of native meals: fish, sharks, oysters, *Busycons,* and other mollusks. The size and contents of the mounds attest to the antiquity of the Indian cultures of the region and their reliance on marine resources.

The Caloosahatchee peoples, ancestors of the Calusa Indians, also built mounds of shell and earth to serve as the bases for temples. They dug ditches and canals similar to those of the Lake Okeechobee Basin, a region to which they were connected by the Caloosahatchee River, a canoe highway.

These were the major native cultures of precolumbian Florida. When Juan Ponce de León sailed the coastline in 1513 the native population numbered 350,000, including 50,000 Apalachee, 150,000 Timucua speakers, and 150,000 other people in the western Panhandle and central and southern Florida. But as we shall see in subsequent chapters, the European presence brought diseases and slaving raids that severely reduced and ultimately destroyed Florida's original inhabitants. By the late eighteenth century, they were no more.

Bibliography

Carr, Robert S., and John G. Beriault. "Prehistoric Man in South Florida." In *Environments of South Florida: Present and Past,* 2d ed., edited by P. J. Gleason, pp. 1–14. Miami Geological Society Memoir 2. Coral Gables, 1984.

Daniel, I. Randolph, Jr., and Michael Wisenbaker. *Harney Flats: A Florida Paleo-Indian Site.* Farmingdale, N.Y.: Baywood Publishing Co., Inc., 1987.

Doran, Glen H., and David N. Dickel. "Multidisciplinary Investigations at the Windover Site." In *Wet Site Archaeology,* edited by B.A. Purdy, pp. 263–89. Caldwell, N.J.: Telford Press, 1988.

Dunbar, James S. "Resource Orientation of Clovis and Suwannee Age Paleoindian Sites in Florida." In *Clovis: Origins and Adaptations,* edited by R. Bonnichsen and K. Turnmier, pp. 185–213. Corvallis: Center for the First Americans, Oregon State University, 1991.

Gilliland, Marion S. *The Material Culture of Key Marco, Florida.* Gainesville: University of Florida Press, 1975.

Goggin, John M. *Space and Time Perspectives in Northern St. Johns Archeology, Florida.* Yale University Publications in Anthropology No. 47. New Haven, 1952.

Griffin, John W., Sue B. Richardson, Mary Pohl, Carl D. McMurray, C. Margaret Scarry, Suzanne K. Fish, Elizabeth S. Wing, L. Jill Loucks, and Marcia K. Welch. *Excavations at the Granada Site,* vol. 1 of *Archaeology and History of the Granada Site.* Tallahassee: Florida Division of Archives, History and Records Management, 1985.

Jones, B. Calvin. "Southern Cult Manifestations at the Lake Jackson Site, Leon County, Florida: Salvage Excavation of Mound 3." *Midcontinental Journal of Archaeology* 7 (1982):3–44.

Marquardt, William H., ed. *Culture and Environment in the Domain of the Calusa.* Institute of Archaeology and Paleoenvironmental Studies, Monograph 1. Gainesville: Florida Museum of Natural History, 1992.

Milanich, Jerald T. *Florida Indians and the Invasion from Europe.* Gainesville: University Press of Florida, 1995.

———. *Archaeology of Precolumbian Florida.* Gainesville: University Press of Florida, 1994.

Milanich, Jerald T., Ann S. Cordell, Vernon J. Knight, Jr., Timothy A. Kohler, and Brenda J. Sigler-Lavelle. *McKeithen Weeden Island: The Culture of Northern Florida, A.D. 200–900.* Orlando: Academic Press, 1984.

Purdy, Barbara A. *The Art and Archaeology of Florida's Wetlands.* Boca Raton: CRC Press, 1991.

———. *Florida's Prehistoric Stone Tool Technology.* Gainesville: University of Florida Press, 1981.

Sears, William H. *Fort Center: An Archaeological Site in the Lake Okeechobee Basin.* Gainesville: University Presses of Florida, 1982.

Widmer, Randolph E. *The Evolution of the Calusa: A Nonagricultural Chiefdom on the Southwest Florida Coast.* Tuscaloosa and London: University of Alabama Press, 1988.

Willey, Gordon R. *Archeology of the Florida Gulf Coast.* Smithsonian Miscellaneous Collections No. 113. Washington, 1949.

2 First European Contacts

Michael Gannon

The first encounters between the indigenous peoples of Florida and the Europeans who traveled the Atlantic in the wake of Christopher Columbus occurred nearly five centuries ago. The documents and maps are unclear on the point, but it appears that the initial contacts preceded the famous voyage of Juan Ponce de León in 1513 by a number of years. After the turn of the sixteenth century, Spain launched an ever-widening circle of voyages from bases in the Caribbean Sea. Some of those were slaving expeditions in search of island natives to replace the native laborers of La Española and, later, the Isla de Cuba, where, owing to the Spaniards' introduction of harsh work practices and European diseases, indigenous populations were rapidly collapsing. Probably one or more of those expeditions happened upon the Florida peninsula, which may account for the hostility that the natives demonstrated toward Juan Ponce upon his arrival there, as well as for his discovery on the lower Gulf Coast of "an Indian who understood the Spaniards." In any event, the historian can speculate what must have been the wonderment, perhaps terror, that passed through the original Floridians' minds when they beheld the ultimate artifact of European technology, the sailing ship, with its huge hull, masts and shrouds, spread canvas sails, and white, bearded seamen.

Tantalizing suggestions of those first contacts appear in maps and charts as early as 1502, the date of a Portuguese world map known by the name of its owner, Italian nobleman Alberto Cantino. Where it depicted the Spanish Caribbean discoveries, there appears a narrow landmass that is possibly the Florida peninsula but is more likely the coast of Central America. More striking, a map of the islands and shores of the New World was published in 1511 by Peter Martyr (Pietro Martire d'Anghiera), an Italian priest-humanist in the Spanish court of Fernando II of Aragón. Drawn from oral and written reports of navigators, this map shows a long shoreline "to the north" of Cuba which he labeled "Isla de beimeni parte" (Island of Bimini). With the Grand Bahama Bank directly abutting them, the land features of Bimini, and what appear to be keys descending from them, could be Florida.

It was this island of Bimini that Juan Ponce de León was authorized to seek in an *asiento* (charter) issued him by the Spanish Crown on 23 February 1512. Born to a noble family in Valladolid, Juan Ponce at age nineteen shipped to the Caribbean on Columbus's second voyage in 1493, and, after New World seasoning, he conducted the conquest of Puerto Rico in 1506–7, becoming its governor in 1509. In 1512 he was deposed on a technicality by Columbus's older son, Diego Colón, and, finding himself wealthy and with time on his hands, he accepted an asiento to discover and conquer the land "to the north" called Bimini. According to legend, Bimini contained a fountain of waters that rejuvenated old men, the so-called fountain of youth. It should be emphasized that those mythical waters were not mentioned in Juan Ponce's charter from Fernando II, which was meticulously detailed in its specification of the expedition's purpose and goals. Nor were they mentioned in any first-hand report or narrative, although the one extant detailed source for Juan Ponce's voyage of 1513—historian Antonio de Herrera y Tordesillas, who in 1601–15 published a chronicle of Spanish New World explorations—states that on the return end of that voyage, Juan Ponce sent one of his ships into the Lucayan, or Bahama, chain to search for "that celebrated fountain which the Indians said turned men from old men [into] youths."[1] This probably was a gloss by Herrera based on an unsubstantiated account by Peter Martyr. Probably more important to Juan Ponce were gold and the glory of conquest, the lust for which drove all conquistadors of the period.

On 3 March 1513, Juan Ponce left Añasco Bay on the western side of Puerto Rico with two caravels and a bergantina. Notable among the crews and passenger list were thirty-eight-year-old Antón de Alaminos, the most experienced pilot in the islands; two women, Beatriz and Juana Jiménez, who probably were related; two African freemen, Juan Gárrido and Juan González [Ponce] de León; and two unnamed native Taíno seafarer-guides from Puerto Rico.

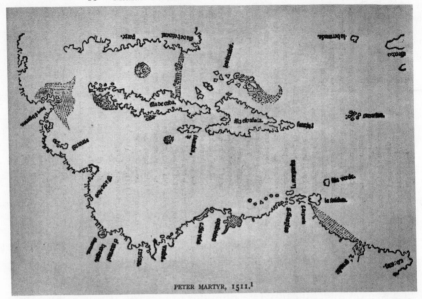

PETER MARTYR, 1511.[1]

Map of the Caribbean published by Peter Martyr in 1511. The landmass to the north of Cuba is named *isla de beimeni parte*. Its placement, and what appear to be keys descending from it, have led some historians to speculate that it is a depiction of Florida, drawn from navigators' reports, two years before the voyage of Juan Ponce de León.

Alaminos set a course of northwest a quarter by north that took the three ships seaward up the eastern edge of the Lucayans as far as the northernmost charted island of San Salvador (the Lucayan Guanahaní that was Columbus's first landfall in 1492), which they reached after eleven days. They were at sea again on the same base compass heading, but in unknown waters, on Sunday the twenty-seventh when the crews and passengers observed the feast of Easter. That day, too, they sighted an island, which probably was Eleuthera. From that point, as indicated by a recent resailing of the route to test the prevailing winds and currents, Alaminos took a new heading of west-northwest through the New Providence Channel and passed well below the southern cape of Great Abaco and the whole of Grand Bahama. This course placed the vessels out of the sight of land for the next six days. When they crossed the three-knot Gulf Stream the Spanish hulls were carried north faster than they shouldered west, with the result that on 2 April they made landfall on what turned out to be the Florida shoreline. The most recent study contends that they were at a point just south of Cape Canaveral, probably near Melbourne Beach, where they anchored in eight *brazas* (forty-four feet) of water.[2]

Herrera describes what followed: "And thinking that this land was an island, they called it *La Florida,* because it was very pretty to behold with many and refreshing trees, and it was flat, and even: and also because they discovered it in the time of Flowery Easter [*Pascua Florida*], Juan Ponce wanted to agree in the name, with these two reasons."[3]

Juan Ponce went ashore to take formal possession of the "island," but there is no indication in the record that he encountered people indigenous to the site. After remaining in the region for six days, he raised anchor on 8 April and sailed south along a featureless coastline. On 21 April he made his second great discovery, though it is doubtful that he and Alaminos realized its dimensions at the time: the Florida Current, or Gulf Stream. That current had made itself felt when the three ships crossed it going west in the first days of April, but now, at a cape north of Lake Worth Inlet, which Juan Ponce named Cabo de las Corrientes (Cape of the Currents), it faced him head-on and with such force that his ships were propelled backward even though they had wind abaft the beam. One, the bergantina, was swept out to deep water. Anchoring north of the cape, Juan Ponce and some of his men rowed ashore in a longboat to make contact with natives they sighted on shore. The encounter did not go well. The native party assaulted the Spaniards with clubs and arrows, rendering one seaman unconscious and wounding two others. Herrera states that Juan Ponce had not wished to do the natives harm but was forced to fight in order to save both his men's lives and their boat, oars, and weapons, which their assailants sought to seize. No cause for the natives' violence is given in the record, whether it was provoked by earlier visits of slaving expeditions, or by the natives' own long tradition of intertribal warfare, or by simple fear of these strange creatures from another world.

Regaining his ships, Juan Ponce put in at Jupiter Inlet to take on firewood and water, only to be attacked again by a larger party of sixty men. This time he seized a warrior for use as a guide. He would remain anchored in the river until rejoined by the bergantina. And somewhere along this river, which he named La Cruz (The Cross), he planted a quarry-stone cross, inscribed, with what words we do not know, in the manner of other Spanish or Portuguese explorers of the period who erected a stone *patrón,* or standard, to identify their claims.

Finally navigating the Cape of the Currents by hugging the shore, Alaminos navigated southward to Key Biscayne, which Juan Ponce named Santa Marta, and, on Friday, 13 May, to one of the Keys, possibly Key Largo, which he named Pola, its derivation and meaning unclear. Rounding the Keys as a body, Juan Ponce named them Los

Mártires (Martyrs), "because viewed from afar the rocks as they rose up seemed like men who are suffering."[4] From Key West he sailed west a short distance and then proceeded north to explore the reverse side of his "island," making a Gulf Coast landfall, it is thought, at San Carlos Bay, off the deep mouth of the Caloosahatchee River, and anchoring near the southeast tip of Sanibel Island. There he found firewood and fresh water, careened one of his ships, and had two belligerent encounters with natives of the Calusa nation, whose chief, Carlos (as the Spaniards pronounced and wrote his name), resided on Estero Island. The Calusa attacked the anchored ships in canoes. One Spaniard and at least four natives died in these actions, leading Juan Ponce to give Sanibel its first European name, Matanzas (Massacre). After nine days in the vicinity, a decision was made to return to Puerto Rico. Accordingly, Alaminos laid a course that took the ships south-southwest, which caused them, on 21 June, to come upon waterless keys that Juan Ponce named Las Tortugas (Turtles), where the crews provisioned the vessels with, among other land and sea species, 160 loggerhead turtles. Following a brief reconnaissance of the Cuban coastline west of Havana, the expedition made for Puerto Rico. Two of the three ships reached it in mid-October. The third ship, with chief pilot Alaminos aboard, Juan Ponce had dispatched into the Lucayans to search again for the elusive Bimini; that ship would arrive in Añasco Bay four months later.

In 1514, Juan Ponce sailed to Spain where he secured a revised royal asiento naming him *adelantado* (self-financing conqueror and direct representative of the king) and governor of the islands of Bimini and Florida. He was delayed for seven years in executing the contract by the death of his wife and his need to raise their two young daughters. During that interim, however, La Florida did not lack for Spanish visitors, including slavers, such as Pedro de Salazar during a voyage of 1514–16. In 1517, Alaminos, now chief pilot for Francisco Hernández de Córdoba, took refuge in San Carlos Bay when Córdoba's expedition returned eastward from its voyage to Yucatán. And two years later, Alaminos again, this time for Alonzo Alvarez de Pineda, put into the same bay for its firewood and drinking water during an expedition that established that Florida was not an island after all but a peninsula attached to a huge continent. Pineda fixed its western juncture to the mainland at a feature he named after the Holy Spirit—Río de Espíritu Santo; this could have been either the Mobile River and Bay, the Mississippi River, or Vermillion Bay, Louisiana.

His own interest in Florida no doubt requickened by news of Hernán

Juan Ponce de León (ca. 1460–1521). The left side of this seventeenth-century engraving represents Juan Ponce and his expedition of 1521 in combat with the Calusa natives at Florida's San Carlos Bay.

Cortés's astonishing discoveries in México, Juan Ponce wrote to the emperor Carlos V (Carlos I, king of Spain) on 10 February 1521 expressing his intention to establish a permanent town, a fort, and missions in the Florida he still thought was an island. On the twenty-sixth of that month he sailed out of Puerto Rico in two ships loaded down with 200 male and female settlers, parish priests and missionary friars, horses and domestic animals, seeds, cuttings, and agricultural implements. The site of his landing in Florida is not known with any certainty, though it has been widely assumed it was in the same San Carlos Bay region that twice had brought back his former pilot, Alaminos. In any event, the natives of that site were no more receptive to strangers than were those Juan Ponce had encountered eight years before. They attacked the Spaniards as they debarked, as they erected buildings, and as they planted their crops and tended their cattle. When Juan Ponce himself received a painful, suppurating arrow wound in his thigh, he ordered the frustrated and fearful colonists to withdraw to Cuba. There, in July, he died from his infection.

By the mid-twenties La Florida was the name given by Spain to the southeastern quarter of what is now the United States. Much of its Atlantic coastline was probed by slaving expeditions during the decade, and one loquacious captive from Winyah Bay, South Carolina, came into the hands of Lucas Vázquez de Ayllón, a royal judge in La Española. Persuaded by the captive, who was given the name Francisco de Chicora, that South Carolina was a land of almonds, olives, and figs—a new Andalucía?—Ayllón sought and received a charter to settle the "Land of Chicora," as he called it. In 1526 he sailed from La Española in six ships carrying 600 colonists, including women and children, three Dominican friars, African slaves, and a number of Carolina captives, including Chicora. After pausing for a short time on the Carolina shore, which, it turned out, bore little resemblance to Andalucía, Ayllón led the party south to the more inhabitable Georgia coast, probably to Sapelo Sound, where on 29 September he established a town named San Miguel de Gualdape (St. Michael of Gualdape, the latter half of the name being the native appellation for the site). It was the first named European settlement in what is now the United States, antedating Pensacola (1559), Fort Caroline (1564), and St. Augustine (1565), though the last-named would be the first permanent settlement. San Miguel lasted fewer than two months, owing to famine, disease, and cold temperatures. Taking advantage of a mutiny among the Spaniards, black slaves deserted and some found freedom in nearby native societies. About 150 survivors, including the Dominican friar Antonio de Montesinos, first priest in the hemisphere to defend the human rights of America's indigenous people, made their way by ship to various ports in the Antilles. Ayllón was not among the survivors.

Next in line to test himself against La Florida was the red-bearded, one-eyed, deep-voiced Pánfilo de Narváez, whose last official mission, in 1520, was to arrest the rogue conquistador Cortés in México. He failed in that, as he would also fail in Florida, where he arrived from Spain on 14 April 1528, near Tampa Bay, with a license to settle and govern a vast principality that ranged along the Gulf littoral from coastal northern México (Amichel) to the Florida peninsula and as far inland as he could control. Carlos V had conferred on him the lofty titles adelantado, governor, and captain general, but no mortal could confer on him common good sense. Foolishly, on landing he dispatched his ships that carried all his food, wine, and supplies, not to mention ten wives destined never to see their spouses again, with the order to rendezvous with him at an indeterminately defined harbor to the north. Though the ships' masters found a harbor that corresponded to Narváez's description, they did not locate the land party, and they cruised in search of them for nearly a year before, finally, sailing to New Spain (Mexico) with their (one supposes) grieving women and depleted cargoes.

Meanwhile, Narváez with 300 men and 40 horses marched northward up the peninsula, toward the chiefdom of Apalachee, around present-day Tallahassee, which, the Tampa Bay natives had assured Narváez, possessed "gold and plenty of everything we wanted." These are the words of surely the most notable member of the party, Alvar Núñez Cabeza de Vaca, treasurer and provost marshal. Fourteen years later, as one of only four survivors of this ill-starred expedition, he would publish a lengthy account of the adventure, thus allowing us to know what happened to the doomed procession.[5]

Cabeza de Vaca's description of the Florida interior is the first we have. The land was flat and sandy, he wrote, with numerous lakes and trees fallen into them. Together with tall stands of pine, there were cypress, oaks, cedars, and other varieties of trees. Animals sighted included deer, bears, and panthers. Wildfowl were abundant. In Apalachee, which the army reached after fifty-six days of marching, there was native-planted maize in the fields ready for harvest.

Although the army encountered Timucua speakers at various points along their route, and were sometimes trailed by them at a distance, it was in Apalachee that they had their first prolonged contacts, most of them violent. The hostility of the Apalachee should not have surprised the Spaniards since Narváez had seized a principal village with its maize stores and held their chief hostage. Cabeza de Vaca paid tribute to their warrior skills, particularly in archery. The men were wonderfully built, he recorded: "Tall and naked, at a distance they appear giants"—an understandable observation since the Spaniards were a good three to four inches shorter in stature—but skeletal remains indicate that six-footers were rare. "Their bows," he wrote, "are as thick as an arm, seven feet long, shooting an arrow at 200 paces with unerring aim." After a day of battle with the Apalachee, some of the soldiers "swore they had seen two oak trees, each as thick as the calf of a leg, shot through and through by arrows, which is not surprising if we consider the force and dexterity with which they shoot. I myself saw an arrow that had penetrated the base of a [hardwood] tree for half a foot in length."[6]

After a month in the region, despairing of finding their ships, enfeebled by illness, down to the last food rations, and continually harried by Apalachee archers, Narváez's men followed their leader to a bay on the Gulf (probably in the vicinity of present-day St. Marks) where they began construction of barges in which to effect an escape by following the coast to refuge in the Spanish settlement at Río Pánuco in Mexico. Although no one among them knew anything about ship construction, desperation lent invention. Killing a horse every third day for food, they fashioned the flayed and tanned leg hides into fresh water bags and used deerskins and hollowed logs to make a bellows with which they operated a forge for melting down their swords, stirrups, spurs, and crossbow iron into saws, axes, and nails. The horses' manes and tails became ropes. Yellow pine trees were split into planks, and pitch for caulking them was drawn from longleaf pine and mixed with palmetto oakum. The men sewed their shirts together to make patchwork sails and shaped cypress logs into oars. On 22 September, after six weeks of work, 242 survivors of the original land party of 300 boarded five rough-hewn thirty-foot-long craft and set out to sea. As a final gesture they christened their embarkation site Bahía de Caballos, Bay of the Horses.

Cabeza de Vaca related the sad consequences. After passing the coasts of Florida, Alabama, Mississippi, and Louisiana, the barges capsized in a violent storm in November and eighty survivors were cast up on an island, either Galveston, Follet's, or Matagorda, off the coast of Texas. As they learned later, Narváez perished in a separate incident. By the following spring, their number was reduced by illness, exposure, and starvation to fifteen. Eventually, there were only four, who managed to eke out an existence as healers, traders, and slaves among the tribes indigenous to southern Texas. In September 1534, those four set out on foot across Texas toward the Sonora Valley. Their two-year-long convoluted trek, in which they crossed the continent from the Gulf to the Pacific, brought them eventually to Mexico City on 24 June 1536, where Cabeza de Vaca related his incredible story to the Spanish viceroy. His three companions were Alonso del Castillo Maldonado, Andrés Dorantes, and the latter's black Moorish servant, Estévan. Behind them the wilderness of La Florida had returned to the private use of its original inhabitants nearly eight years before.

Next to Ponce de León's, the name most closely associated in the public's mind with Florida's early contact period is that of Hernando de Soto. He arrived on Florida's Gulf Coast in 1539 and set out on an overland reconnaissance that would penetrate Florida and nine other states of the American South, covering nearly 4,000 miles over four years' time. Nothing about de Soto, from his landing site, to his treatment of the natives, to his route of march, has escaped controversy, down to and including the present.

Born in the barren Spanish province of Extremadura, whence many New World conquistadors came, de Soto went to Central America in 1513–14 under the ruthless Pedro Arias de Ávila (Pedrárias Dávila). He received further schooling in the grim arts of subjugation as a

Hernando de Soto (1497?–1542). An engraving from *Retratos de los Españoles Ilustres con un Epítome de sus Vidas* (Madrid: Imprenta real, 1791).

lieutenant to his fellow Extremaduran Francisco Pizarro during the looting of Incan Peru in 1532–35. Returning to Spain in 1536, immensely rich, he married Isabel de Bobadilla, third daughter of Pedrárias Dávila, and sought permission from Carlos V to become a conquistador in his own right. As for territory, his preferences were for what later became Ecuador and Guatemala. Instead, Carlos V awarded him La Florida, the vast geographical region previously awarded Narváez and Ayllón, with the titles of adelantado, captain general, and governor over any 200 leagues of coast he could "conquer, pacify and populate." At the same time, the king made him governor of Cuba, where he would establish a base, requisition additional supplies, and organize his expedition. In the elaborate terms of his asiento, dated 20 April 1537, de Soto was enjoined to recruit, arm, supply, and transport the Florida army entirely at his own cost, which he did so well that, by his departure from Seville on 7 April 1538, he had spent his entire fortune and was heavily in debt. But no matter: the gold he was certain to find in Florida would replenish the chests.

De Soto spent half a year at Havana in prudent preparation for the Florida campaign, determined to avoid the mistakes of Narváez about which he had learned from Cabeza de Vaca. Thus, he insisted on adequate provisioning and reliable intelligence. In pursuit of the latter, he sent a trusted aide, Juan de Añasco, with fifty men in three small ships to reconnoiter the Florida Gulf Coast. A guide for navigators, compiled by Alonso de Chaves at Seville probably in 1537, indicated that there were two favorable harbors, Bahía de Juan Ponce to the south, and Bahía Honda (Deep Harbor) to the north.[7] When de Soto made his landing it would be at Bahía Honda, according to one of the expedition's chroniclers. Añasco returned with four native captives to serve as guides and interpreters.

The expedition set out from Havana on 18 May 1539 in five large and four smaller vessels. On board were over 600 soldiers, twelve priests, two women, servants and slaves, 223 horses, numerous mules and war dogs, and a herd of swine. About half the force was from Extremadura; fifteen were Portuguese. The ships made landfall on 25 May and five days later disembarked all of their horses and most of their men. Where was this done? Of all the questions raised by students of the Florida discovery period, none has been more argued for the past half-century than this one. In 1939, a U.S. De Soto Expedition Commission chaired by Dr. John R. Swanton determined that the de Soto landing site was Tampa Bay.[8] Numerous other studies since have concluded that the descriptions given in the documents, as well as de Soto's route of march, favored either Charlotte Harbor[9] or Pine Island Sound–Caloosahatchee River, or San Carlos Bay, all to the south. In 1989 a State of Florida de Soto Trail Committee, relying on the recently republished Chaves guide, on the accounts given by the original de Soto chroniclers, and on correlations of the expedition narratives with an archaeological list of known native encampments greatly expanded since 1939, decided that a Tampa Bay landing best fit the evidence.[10]

According to this last view, which remains provisional, de Soto made his initial landing at Piney Point and finally made camp at a native village, Uzita, which the 1989 findings place at the northern side of the mouth of the Little Manatee River. A cavalry patrol from that site into the interior flushed out a Spanish survivor of an expedition sent from Cuba eleven years earlier to discover, if possible, what had happened to Pánfilo de Narváez. Juan Ortíz by name, he had lived as a tribal native in the region for years. Now his providential rescue provided de Soto with an interpreter who spoke indigenous tongues and Spanish, but as the army encountered different linguistic groups on its march, his facility as a translator and as a geographer would diminish.

The march into the interior began on 15 July. Mindful of Narváez's fateful error, de Soto left all his supplies on board four ships in the harbor, guarded by forty cavalry and sixty infantry, with firm orders not to sail until he sent men to guide the vessels to a precisely known anchorage to the north. The long overland procession of people, horses, mules, and long-legged Spanish range pigs then entered the vastness of Florida's forests, rivers, bogs, and sandhills. The last feature was discovered just three days into the march, in the vicinity of Zephyrhills and Lumberton, where one man died of thirst and others barely survived the absence of springs, streams, or standing water. The next day, near Dade City, the army found its first cornfields. Though he had crossed a smaller river, the Alafia, by constructing a bridge, and had successfully though painfully negotiated the wetlands of the Cove of the Withlacoochee in eastern Citrus County, on 26 July de Soto met his first serious test at the strong currents of the Withlacoochee River itself, not far from Inverness. There the army stretched a rope from bank to bank and managed to wade across, losing one horse to the currents.

On 29 July the army found itself in the major Timucuan province of Ocale, believed to have occupied what now is southwest Marion County. Here and at the province of Acuera, north of Leesburg on or near the Ocklawaha River, the Spaniards commandeered the natives' standing crops and food stores. Then, leaving the main body of the army at Ocale, de Soto led a reconnaissance force through Levy and

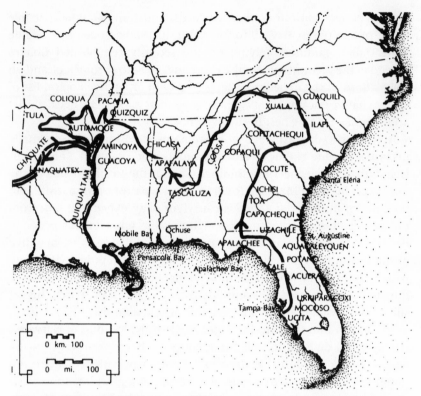

The route of Hernando de Soto's expedition through La Florida, which at the time embraced the entire region shown here. Place-names along the march are the principal native chiefdoms encountered. Also shown here are the future settlements of Tristán de Luna (Ochuse) and of Pedro Menéndez de Avilés (St. Augustine and Santa Elena).

Alachua counties, passing on Gainesville's west side (the native Potano) and reaching the Santa Fe River, which the advance party bridged on 17 August. Here the unity of the force was rent by disagreements of some kind, not recorded, but perhaps rising out of plain frustration: the El Dorado of their dreams must never have seemed less real than it did among the swamps and pines of Florida. The soldiers named the river Santa Fe las Discordias, the River of Discords.

De Soto camped across the river at a moderately sized village named Aguacaleyquen and dispatched eight horsemen to lead forward the main body still in Ocale. At Aguacaleyquen, abandoned by its inhabitants, de Soto found their hidden maize stores. Later, he captured seventeen natives, seized their chief, and held his daughter hostage. To this behavior may be added other, worse, violations that characterized de Soto's peregrinations through the Florida chiefdoms, all of them in direct violation of the king's ordinance to observe "good treatment and conversion" of the natives: some natives he summarily executed for offenses real or perceived; others he mutilated (e.g., cutting off noses or hands) as a warning of what would be done to all if he was not granted free passage through a village or a province; still others he enslaved and shackled to serve the marching army as bearers. By such actions he showed that he had not forgotten the intimidating and violent approach to indigenous societies learned under Pedrárias in Panama and Nicaragua. Ostensibly the actions were authorized by a formal theological proclamation, the *Requirimiento*, which was read aloud in Spanish to the uncomprehending natives. Some probable cultural explanations can be offered for this harsh conduct. First, the Spanish captains' actions to control New World natives were to a large measure an extension of the Reconquista, the struggle to regain control of Iberia from the Muslims, concluded in 1492. A cult of military violence nourished over many centuries carried over into the circum-Caribbean, of which Florida was a part. Second, Roman Catholic theology in Spain was still uncertain about the moral standing of the native Americans, whose existence was not accounted for in holy scripture. Were they fully developed human beings with souls? Or were they a lower species that might justifiably be exploited and enslaved? The question would not be resolved in the natives' favor until Carlos V's promulgation of the so-called New Laws in 1542, the year of de Soto's death. It may be added that, though de Soto's entourage included twelve priests, none appears to have had the vision and moral courage of Ayllón's friar Montesinos where treatment of the natives was concerned.

In their turn, the Florida natives gave back as good as they got, from Tampa Bay, where the aborigines raked the army with cane arrows tipped with fishbones, crab claws, or stone points, until de Soto's withdrawal northward into Georgia from Apalachee. All along the line of march, native archers, darting from woodland cover, killed Spanish dispatch riders or stragglers, set ambushes, or fired volleys into night-time bivouacs. Brave native hostage-guides coolly led the army into ambushes, though it meant certain death for the hostage, probably at the jaws of war dogs. The Spaniards marveled at the velocity and accuracy of the arrows discharged against them by the natives' tall, stiff bows. This would be particularly so in Apalachee, where the projectiles were said to have penetrated horses lengthwise nearly from chest to tail, and de Soto watched one captured archer place an arrow through two coats of Milán chain steel from eighty feet back. The best defense, the Spaniards eventually learned, for their horses as well as for themselves, was to wear quilted fabric three or four fingers thick under the chain mail.

From Tampa Bay through Apalachee, de Soto enjoyed only one stand-up fight in open country where the massed cavalry charge for which he was equipped held the advantage. It took place at Napituca, near Live Oak, in mid-September. Anticipating an ambush, de Soto stationed his cavalry in woods surrounding two flooded limestone sinkholes and charged the warriors of the district when they betrayed their intent. Many natives were lanced in the field. Others threw themselves into the ponds where they treaded water until exhausted. Eventually captured, these and other natives of the region later rose up against their captors, which caused de Soto to execute all the mature warriors among them.

From Napituca the Spaniards traveled almost due west, seeking the province of Apalachee, where Narváez's men had found abundant crops. On 25 September they bridged the River of the Deer, as they named the Suwannee, and six days later, they came to Agile, the first town that was subject to the Apalachee. It was not until 3 October, when they made a difficult crossing of the flooded Aucilla River, that they encountered the Apalachee proper. The natives put up a fierce armed resistance and burned their crops and villages as they drew back before the foreigners' advance. Thirty-eight miles farther west, on 6 October, de Soto entered Anhaica, the main town of Apalachee, where he decided to make his winter camp. Near the coast on Apalachee Bay his men found the remains, including horse skulls, of Narváez's camp of eleven years before. With a known anchorage, de Soto sent a party of cavalrymen south to lead forward the ships, supplies, and men left at Tampa Bay. On 25 December the camp celebrated the first Christmas in what is now the United States.

The Anhaica encampment site, discovered by archaeologist B. Calvin Jones in 1987, is the one undisputed location associated with de Soto in the army's entire four-year march, thanks to the excavation there of a pig mandible (de Soto introduced the pig to North America), an iron crossbow point, iron nails, chain mail, and dated copper coins. All other locations on the line of march, in present-day Florida and beyond, are still contested. The Spaniards' stay at Anhaica was beset by almost constant guerrilla warfare, with the result that, by the date of their departure north into Georgia, on 3 March 1540, numerous bones of man and horse alike remained behind under the Apalachee sun.

It would be tedious to detail the remainder of the expedition outside present-day Florida, which seems to the reader of the surviving chronicles to be an aimless, feckless wandering in search of the same gold, silver, and gems that de Soto had found in Peru. No known attempt was made to map the interior, to record flora and fauna, to understand the polities and cultures of the native societies encountered, to evangelize, or to forge alliances. Suffice it to say that the Spaniards marched northeast through Georgia into South and North Carolina, turned west through a corner of Tennessee, then south through the northwest corner of Georgia, finding plentiful corn and game at Coosa (east of Carters, Georgia) but just missing the gold fields at Dahlonega. They passed southwest into Alabama where the army's supplies were ravaged in a day-long battle, disastrous for both sides, with the warriors of Chief Tascaluza at Mabila; the Mabila lost perhaps as many as 3,000 men. In the aftermath of the battle de Soto made a fateful decision not to avail himself of provisions awaiting him by prearrangement on ships at Pensacola Bay lest his dispirited men seize the ships and desert the enterprise.

"From that day," wrote one of the chroniclers, who interviewed survivors, "as a disillusioned man whose own people have betrayed his hopes . . . he went about thereafter wasting his time and life without any gain, always traveling from one place to another without order or purpose."[11] Those subsequent meanderings took the army northwest into Mississippi where they wintered in 1540–41 among the hostile Chickasaw near Tupelo, to whom they lost more men, horses, and over 300 pigs. Sometime in May 1541 they discovered the great river Mississippi and crossed it on flatboats a few miles south of Memphis on 19 June. Another difficult winter (1541–42) was spent in Arkansas, where the men suffered greatly from cold temperatures, sickness, and malnutrition; several died, including the interpreter Juan Ortíz.

In March 1542, de Soto led the survivors back through southern Arkansas to the Mississippi, where, on 21 May, the would-be conquistador himself died of an unidentified disease and was secretly interred in the bed of the river. Campmaster Luis Moscoso de Alvarado succeeded to command and led the army in an overland attempt to reach New Spain, but by October they got no farther than the Trinity River in eastern Texas. There, with no further signs of maize-cultivating natives, they were forced back to the Mississippi, which they reached in December. They constructed seven keeled boats and boarded them on 2 July in an attempt to escape downriver to the Gulf. A sail and seven oars on each vessel provided propulsion, which was desperately needed on two occasions when riverbank warriors in canoes pursued them with arrows. After successfully reaching the mouth of the Father of

Waters, the tiny fleet pressed westward along the Gulf beaches and headlands toward the Spanish settlement at Río Pánuco, where they landed on 10 September 1543.

Fully four years and four months since setting out from the port of Havana, and after 3,700 miles of travel by land and water, 311 survivors clambered ashore to the embrace of their countrymen. Behind them, they had left the whitened bones of half their original number, including de Soto's; all their horses and pigs; their only plunder, poor-quality freshwater pearls they had found at Camden, South Carolina, but had lost to fire at Mabila; and all their dreams of Incan gold and Mexican magnificence. None of the chartered goals established by the king had been met: behind them stood no settlement or hospital, no mine or farm, no presidio or mission, no flag, no cross. The most significant practical result of what may be called that extended armed raid was the damage inflicted on the southeastern native populations. Dozens of chiefdoms, overstressed and humiliated by de Soto, went into decline or collapsed. And in the wake of the *entrada* thousands of native people lay dead and dying, not from the sword but from the introduction of Old World pathogens against which the aborigines had no acquired immunities—smallpox, measles, and typhoid fever, among others. That "microbial invasion" had begun many years before with the first slavers or with the crews of Juan Ponce, but de Soto's men unwittingly reinforced it on their long, doubly tragic death march through the interior of La Florida.

Then, six years later, there came a Dominican friar's brief humanitarian intervention that startles with its courage and magnanimity. In the spring of 1549, Fray Luis Cáncer de Barbastro set sail in an unarmed vessel from Veracruz, Mexico, bound for the same La Florida in order to win the friendship of its native people by peaceful means alone. Cast in much the same mold as Montesinos and the other, current, great Dominican "defender of the Indians," Fray Bartolomé de las Casas, Cáncer had earlier participated in the pacification and conversion of the seemingly intractable inhabitants of Guatemala, causing that former "province of war" now to be called by his Mexican countrymen the "province of true peace." With Cáncer sailed three other Dominican friars, a Spanish lay brother, a captured Florida native woman interpreter named Magdalena, sailors, and a pilot, Juan de Arana, who had been given strict orders to avoid any harbor where Spaniards had earlier spread the terror of their arms. Whether through perversity or ignorance, Arana delivered his passengers to Tampa Bay.

Contact with the natives was almost immediate. Cáncer made several friendly entreaties to them, and his touching references to the aborigines in a journal he kept on board ship display a genuine concern for their welfare. But news soon arrived by the surprising agency of one Juan Muñoz, one of de Soto's soldiers who had been captured in that locale ten years before, that one of the priests and the lay brother had been killed, that a ship's sailor was being held captive, and that Magdalena, having divested herself of Christian clothing, had deserted to her people. On 26 June, Cáncer took a boat from the ship to the beach where, with a crucifix in hand, he fell on his knees in prayer. A group of natives approached. One of them took away his hat. Another crushed his head with a club.

The province of Florida would remain for now a province of war. But at one shining moment in 1549 it witnessed the spiritual gallantry of a guileless messenger of peace, whose name should be writ large in the pantheon of Floridian and American heroes. Culturally and politically what was most significant about Cáncer's sacrifice was that it demonstrated Spain's commitment in Florida to the New Laws of 1542, a commitment that would be played out on a larger scale in the next Spanish undertaking.

After yet another decade passed without a permanent Iberian presence in La Florida, which by that date was the name given to coastal territory that ranged from the Florida Keys to Newfoundland, Spain was determined to launch another settlement effort. The reasons were various. The Gulf shore and the Atlantic coast of Spanish-claimed Florida were vulnerable to French or English interlopers. Indeed France was advancing its own claim to the Atlantic coast: French fishermen were already going ashore along the Carolina coast to smoke their fish and mend their nets. And pirate ships, French and English alike, were threatening the Gulf and Atlantic trade, particularly the routes of the treasure ships, which departed Mexican ports twice each year heavily laden with gold, silver, and gems and sailed via Havana up the Canal de Bahama (Strait of Florida) as far as Bermuda, where they followed the westerlies to Sevilla in Spain. For the protection of the plate fleets it was decided that Spain needed effective occupation of two anchor sites, Pensacola Bay, with its deep harbor, on the Gulf and what was then called Punta de Santa Elena (Point of St. Helen, probably Tybee Island, Georgia), on the Atlantic. The latter was to be the principal settlement, with town lots, a plaza, church, and stronghouse.

Among the other concerns of Spain at the time were protection of shipwrecked sailors along the Gulf and Atlantic shores and missionary evangelization, now long delayed, of the aborigines. The bishop of Cuba weighed in with still another concern: so few native Cuban women remained as eligible wives for Spanish soldiers that a male on that island was lucky if he could find a wife eighty years old, and Florida, he argued, ought to be an excellent source of young brides.

The new King Felipe II ordered a large Florida expedition to be mounted out of Mexico. To lead it Luis de Velasco, viceroy of New Spain, chose an army colonel, Don Tristán de Luna y Arellano, veteran of the Francisco Vázquez de Coronado expedition into the southwestern corner of the North American continent that had been conducted contemporaneously with de Soto's entrada (the two expeditions being at one point only 300 miles apart in the winter of 1541–42). Three Florida sites now were to be occupied: Pensacola Bay, known as native Ochuse or Spanish Polanco; de Soto's Coosa in northwest Georgia; and Santa Elena, which was thought, erroneously, to be only 120 miles east from Coosa overland. Eventually, it was envisioned, a string of Spanish settlements would link the three sites. Besides their primary mission of preempting French designs on the region, Velasco and Luna hoped to convert the natives to Christianity—for which purpose five Dominican priests and one lay brother joined the expedition—and to find gold, silver, mercury, and precious gems, an aspiration never far from the Spanish mind. To assist Luna in his travels Velasco provided him with a map of the de Soto march.

One 11 June 1559, Luna departed San Juan de Ulúa on the Mexican Gulf Coast in thirteen ships of varying tonnage. His expedition numbered 200 foot soldiers, 200 cavalrymen with 240 horses in slings, 100 craftsmen and tradesmen, a number of de Soto campaigners who knew the Florida interior, a native woman interpreter from Coosa whom the de Soto survivors had brought to Mexico with them, 100 Mexican warriors, and about 900 colonists, including married men, wives, and children. The last category of passengers would prove to be more a burden than an advantage, since the land toward which they headed had too little food and too much hardship for untested civilians. The bishop of Cuba would later comment that, instead of indolent and undisciplined men from New Spain, the expedition should have recruited hardworking peasants from the mountains of León in Old Spain.

After an unexpectedly long voyage, during which about 100 horses died, and after several false sightings, the fleet entered Pensacola Bay (Ochuse) on 14 August. Luna named the bay Bahía Filipina del Puerto Santa María, after Felipe II and the Virgin Mary, and immediately set to work laying out a settlement; exactly where it is not known, although two recent estimates are Gulf Breeze or Tartar Point. We know that there were few natives in the region, which meant few food crops, and that Luna dispatched two search parties, one by land and one by the Escambia River, to hunt for villages and food to the north. The patrols returned empty-handed.

Disaster struck on 19 September in the form of a hurricane that, besides killing an unknown number of colonists, sank or ran aground all but three of the expedition's ships. Half the supplies, including personal belongings, were lost. Worse, most of the food was still on board one of the ships that went down, and what food had already been unloaded was spoiled by the storm's downpour. The lot of nearly 1,500 people was now desperate.

In this extremity Luna had the wit to send two surviving frigates to Havana for food, and another overland patrol north for the same reason, before experiencing the first of a number of physical and mental breakdowns that would afflict him throughout his Florida command. When he recovered, he acted on a promising report from the northern patrol and, except for fifty men, moved his starving coastal colony inland to the eighty-hut native town of Nanipacana, about 100 miles up the Alabama River. There the Spaniards found that the inhabitants had decamped with most of their food stores. A 100-man patrol sent north from Nanipacana, to which Luna appended the name Santa Cruz (Holy Cross), found no better prospects. Meanwhile, the settlers were reduced to eating acorns, tree leaves, and wild roots. Remembering the de Soto survivors' tales of Coosa and its fertile fields, Luna then dispatched 150 foot soldiers and 50 cavalrymen to find that bountiful chiefdom. After three months, during which they subsisted on blackberries, acorns, and the leather of their shoes, while their horses became so famished they could hardly walk three miles a day, the travelers came upon the principal town of Coosa.

It was not the Coosa described by de Soto's men who were in the party. Those men were astonished to find that the populous and wealthy society they had encountered twenty years before had declined to a comparatively few huts and fields. The demographic collapse was attributed to the depredations of "a certain captain," i.e., de Soto; even so, the natives who remained willingly shared their food with the new invaders. During the three months the Spanish detachment remained in the region the Coosa asked them to assist their forces in subjugating a nearby troublesome tribe, the Napoochie. The Spaniards agreed to cooperate. Except for that single act of warfare, the behavior of Luna's men toward the aborigines of La Florida was pacific and correct, in keeping with the spirit of the New Laws.

Meanwhile, three supply ships from Mexico put in at Ochuse, and the famished colonists at Nanipacana fled south to claim the provisions, leaving behind a note to that effect for the Coosa command, which returned to Nanipaca in October 1560. From Ochuse a number of women, children, and invalids returned to Mexico on the supply ships. Besides food and clothing those ships had brought urgent royal and viceregal orders for Luna to establish a presence at Santa Elena without further delay. Accordingly, in July or August 1560, Luna directed sixty soldiers and three Dominicans to sail around the peninsula to that Atlantic coastal site. On the voyage the ships encountered foul weather, and the attempt was abandoned. At Ochuse the remaining colonists soon exhausted their new rations and were reduced to eating their leather, grass, and shellfish. Mutinous in mood, they engaged in endless wrangling and insubordination, a situation that was aggravated by Luna's occasional mental seizures and deliriums. The inevitable rebellion was averted by the skillful intervention of two Dominican friars and by the arrival, in April 1561, of a new governor to relieve Luna, the alcalde mayor of Veracruz, Ángel de Villafañe. Luna sailed to Spain by way of Havana to answer charges of dereliction. The commander of the fleet on which he took passage was Pedro Menéndez de Avilés (see chapter 3).

Villafañe bore orders identical to those last given to Luna: settle Santa Elena at once. Leaving seventy or eighty men behind at Ochuse, he sailed first to Havana to pick up horses and additional supplies. There, not surprisingly, about half his force deserted. With the remainder he followed the Florida current north to what his pilots believed to be Santa Elena. The four extant documents on the voyage are unclear, even contradictory, on what happened at that site, wherever it was. They agree, however, in stating that Villafañe made no settlement there. Instead, he continued north by ship exploring capes, inlets, and rivers as far as 35° north, or Cape Lookout, North Carolina; he lost two small ships and twenty-five men in a storm and, discouraged, returned to Havana, where more of his men disappeared into the local population. In the bitter denouement of the Luna-Villafañe undertaking, the detachment left at Ochuse was rescued and brought home to Mexico,

At the viceregal capital a "pained and saddened" Velasco pondered a communication from Felipe II reporting the opinion of Menéndez de Avilés that La Florida's shoreline was too low and sandy, her countryside too poor in resources, and her harbors too barred and shallow to permit practicable settlement. For that reason, the report concluded, there was no cause to fear that the French would establish themselves there or attempt to take possession.[12]

Notes

1. Antonio de Herrera y Tordesillas, *Historia general de los hechos de los Castellanos en las Islas y tierra firme del mar Océano* 4 vols. in quarto (Madrid, 1601–15), 1:249. [*Note:* The diminutive form Juan Ponce was used by the first Spanish chroniclers of the period of exploration.—M.G.]
2. Douglas T. Peck, "Reconstruction and Analysis of the 1513 Discovery Voyage of Juan Ponce de León," *Florida Historical Quarterly* 71, no. 2 (October 1992):133–54; Peck, *Ponce de León and the Discovery of Florida: The Man, the Myth, and the Truth* (St. Paul, Minn.: Pogo Press, 1993), pp. 36–39.
3. This is the translation by James E. Kelley, Jr., in his "Juan Ponce de León's Discovery of Florida: Herrera's Narrative Revisited," *Revista de Historia de América* 111 (January–June 1991):42. I have altered Kelley's rendering of Pascua as "Passover" to "Easter."
4. Ibid.
5. Alvar Núñez Cabeza de Vaca, *La "Relación" o "Naufragios" de Alvar Núñez Cabeza de Vaca,* ed. Martin A. Favata and José B. Fernández (Potomac, Md.: Scripta Humanística, 1986). See also new translations in Charles Hudson and Carmen McClendon, eds., *Forgotten Centuries* (Athens: University of Georgia Press, 1994), and in John H. Hann, "Translation of the Florida Section of the Álvar Núñez Cabeza de Vaca Accounts of the 1528 Trek from South Florida to Apalachee led by Pánfilo de Narváez," MS, Florida Bureau of Archaeological Research, Tallahassee.
6. John Francis Bannon, intro., *The Narrative of Alvar Núñez Cabeza de Vaca,* trans. Fanny Bandelier, with Oviedo's version of the lost joint report translated by Gerald Theisen (Barre, Mass.: Imprint Society, 1972), p. 27.
7. Alonso de Chaves, *Quatri Partitu en Cosmographia practica, y por otro nombre Espejo de Navegantes* (Madrid, 1537; reprint, Madrid, 1983); Luys Hernández de Biedma, "Relation of the Island of Florida . . . 1539," ed. and trans. John E. Worth, in Lawrence A. Clayton, Vernon James Knight, Jr., and Edward C. Moore, eds., *The De Soto Chronicles: The Expedition of Hernando De Soto to North America in 1539–1543,* 2 vols. (Tuscaloosa: University of Alabama Press, 1993), 1:225.
8. John R. Swanton, ed., *Final Report of the United States De Soto Expedition Commission,* U.S. House of Representatives Doc. 71, 76th Cong., 1st sess. (Washington: Government Printing Office, 1939); reprint, with an introduction by Jeffrey P. Brain (Washington: Smithsonian Institution Press, 1985).
9. Louis D. Tesar, "The Case for Concluding that De Soto Landed Near Present-Day Fort Myers, Florida: The Conclusions Presented by Warren H. Wilkinson Reviewed," *Florida Anthropologist* 42, no. 4 (December 1989):

276–79, and Lindsey Williams, "A Charlotte Harbor Perspective on de Soto's Landing Site," ibid., 280–94. See also Rolfe F. Schell, *De Soto Didn't Land at Tampa* (Ft. Myers Beach: Island Press, 1966).

10. Jerald T. Milanich and Charles Hudson, *Hernando de Soto and the Indians of Florida* (Gainesville: University Press of Florida, 1993).

11. Garcilaso de la Vega, the Inca, *La Florida,* trans. Charmion Shelby, in *The De Soto Chronicles,* ed. Clayton, Knight, Moore, 2:357–58.

12. See the transcript, "Paracer que da a S.M. el Consejo de la Nueva España, en virtud de su Real Cédula [fecha en Madrid a 23 de Septiembre de 1561] que sigue, sobre la forma en que estava la costa de la Florida, y que no convenía aumentar la Población," Buckingham Smith Collection (New York Public Library), vol. 1561–93, p. 11.

Bibliography

Avellaneda, Ignacio. *Los Sobrevivientes de la Florida: The Survivors of the de Soto Expedition.* Edited by Bruce Chappell. Research Publications of the P.K. Yonge Library of Florida History, no. 2. Gainesville: University of Florida Libraries, 1990.

Badger, R. Reid, and Lawrence A. Clayton, eds. *Alabama and the Borderlands: From Prehistory to Statehood.* Tuscaloosa: University of Alabama Press, 1985.

Bishop, Morris. *The Odyssey of Cabeza de Vaca.* New York: Century Co., 1933.

Curren, Caleb, Keith J. Little, and Harry O. Holstein. "Aboriginal Societies Encountered by the Tristán de Luna Expedition." *Florida Anthropologist* 42, no. 4 (December 1989):381–95.

Devereux, Anthony Q. *Juan Ponce de León, King Ferdinand and the Fountain of Youth.* Spartanburg, S.C.: The Reprint Company, Publishers, 1993.

Dobyns, Henry F. *Their Number Become Thinned: Native American Population Dynamics in Eastern North America.* Knoxville: University of Tennessee Press, 1983.

Eubanks, W. S., Jr. "Studying De Soto's Route: A Georgian House of Cards." *Florida Anthropologist* 42 (December 1989):369–80.

Gannon, Michael V. *The Cross in the Sand: The Early Catholic Church in Florida, 1513–1870.* Gainesville: University of Florida Press, 1965.

Hanke, Lewis. *The Spanish Struggle for Justice in the Conquest of America.* Philadelphia: University of Pennsylvania Press, 1949.

Henige, David. "The Context, Content, and Credibility of La Florida del Ynca." *The Americas* 43 (July 1986):1–23.

Hoffman, Paul E. "Nature and Sequence of the Spanish Borderlands." In *Native, European, and African Cultures in Mississippi, 1500–1800,* edited by Patricia K. Galloway. Jackson: Mississippi Department of Archives and History, 1991.

———. *A New Andalucia and a Way to the Orient: The American Southeast during the Sixteenth Century.* Baton Rouge: Louisiana State University Press, 1990.

Lyon, Eugene. "Spain's Sixteenth Century North American Settlement Attempts: A Neglected Aspect." *Florida Historical Quarterly* 59, no. 3 (January 1981):275–91.

Milanich, Jerald T., and Susan Milbrath, eds. *First Encounters: Spanish Explorations in the Caribbean and the United States, 1492–1570.* Gainesville: University of Florida Press, 1989.

O'Daniel, V[ictor] F[rancis], O.P. *Dominicans in Early Florida.* New York: United States Catholic Historical Society, 1930.

Priestley, Herbert Ingram. *The Luna Papers: Documents Relating to the Expedition of Don Tristán de Luna y Arellano for the Conquest of La Florida in 1559–1561.* 2 vols. DeLand: Florida State Historical Society, 1928.

Quinn, David B. *North America from Earliest Discovery to First Settlements: The Norse Voyages to 1612.* New York: Harper & Row, 1977.

Sauer, Carl O. *Sixteenth-Century North America: The Land and the Peoples as Seen by the Europeans.* Berkeley: University of California Press, 1971.

Swagerty, William R. "Beyond Bimini: Indian Responses to European Incursions in the Spanish Borderlands, 1513–1600." Ph.D. dissertation, University of California, Santa Barbara (Ann Arbor, Mich.: University Microfilms International, 1982).

Thomas, David Hurst, ed. *Columbian Consequences: Archaeological and Historical Perspectives on the Spanish Borderlands East.* Washington: Smithsonian Institution Press, 1990.

Tió, Aurelio. "Número Conmemorativo del Cuadringentisexagésimo Aniversario del Descubrimiento de la Florida y Yucatán." *Boletín de la Academia Puertoquena de la Historia* 2, núm. 8 (30 June 1972).

Weber, David J. *The Spanish Frontier in North America.* New Haven: Yale University Press, 1992.

Weddle, Robert S. *Spanish Sea: The Gulf of Mexico in North American Discovery, 1500–1685.* College Station: Texas A&M University Press, 1985.

3 Settlement and Survival

Eugene Lyon

Despite the poor opinion of Florida held at the Spanish Court and the belief that the French were equally uninterested in settling there, the situation was about to change dramatically. A brief look at France in this period helps to explain why.

After the middle of the sixteenth century, France was rent by internal dissension between its crown and groups of powerful nobles. Those conflicts, which had come to a head in 1560, were worsened by religious differences between Catholics and Protestants that often erupted into violence. The intervention of other nations such as Spain in these internal wars further destabilized France. Queen Catherine de Medicis, acting as regent for her minor sons, Francis and Charles, temporized with the various factions and married her daughter to King Felipe (Philip) II of Spain, but she was also influenced by Gaspard de Coligny, *seigneur* of Châtillon, a Protestant noble and admiral of France.

Despite internal troubles, France continued its Atlantic policy. When the Treaty of Cateau-Cambrésis (1559) ended the last war with Spain, the parties had not agreed upon the vital issue of the right of nations to settle in the Americas, leaving the matter in an ambiguous state. While Spain insisted that the papal donations gave her exclusive rights to North America, the French maintained that unsettled areas were free for anyone to sail to and colonize. Thus, beginning in 1562, with the support of the French Crown, Coligny dispatched three royal expeditions to what France called Nouvelle France (New France), on the southeast coast of what is now the United States. Like Coligny himself, many of the leaders and mariners on those voyages were Calvinist Protestants from the ports of Normandy and Brittany.

An able captain, Jean Ribaut, commanded the first expedition, which made landfall near the present site of St. Augustine in the spring of 1562 and erected a marble column bearing the French arms near the mouth of the St. Johns, which he called the River May. Proceeding northward, he discovered Port Royal harbor and planted a colony there, guarded by a fortification called Charlesfort. But when he returned to Europe, Ribaut was arrested and detained in England; that and continuing disturbances in France prevented the sending of reinforcements to Port Royal until April 1564. That year proved to be one of heavy European traffic to and from Florida.

The Spaniards had learned belatedly of Ribaut's settlement the year before, and Philip II licensed Lucas Vázquez de Ayllón the younger to settle Florida but he never sailed. Then the Cuban governor sent an expedition to probe the French base. Arriving at Port Royal in late May, the Spaniards found that the discouraged Frenchmen had already deserted the place, leaving behind among the Indians one young man, Guillaume Rouffi. They returned to Havana, bearing Rouffi and the news of the failed French colony.

Meanwhile, on 22 April 1564, René de Laudonnière sailed from LeHavre with a full-fledged expedition of colonization, and somehow his departure escaped immediate Spanish attention. The French ships were laden with livestock, supplies, and tools for husbandry and Indian trade. There were artisans, women and children, and Protestant nobles from France and Germany. Once in Florida, the Frenchmen did not settle again at Port Royal; instead, they built Fort Caroline inside the mouth of the St. Johns, overlooking the river. At first, the colony prospered as Laudonnière set out to explore the interior of New France. He established generally good relations with the Native Americans in the nearby Timucua and Mocama groupings. Believing that the great river was the highway to the exploitation of peninsular Florida, he dispatched an expedition upriver, perhaps as far as Lake George. Guillaume Brouhart, one of those who made the river voyage, reported that the Indians there were powerful warriors and skilled bowmen who lived in a fruitful land of maize and grapevines, rich in nuts, fruits, deer and small game.

Supplies soon ran short in Fort Caroline, and not enough food could be obtained from the natives. A series of mutinies and desertions began. Eleven men fled in a small craft, and then in December 1564, seventy

The French Fort Caroline was founded in 1564 by René Goulaine de Laudonnière a short distance inside the mouth of the St. Johns River, which the French called "Rivière de Mai." This drawing, by Jacques le Moyne de Morgues, who accompanied Laudonnière, was published by Théodor de Bry in 1591. Laudonnière was relieved of command by Jean Ribaut in 1565. The fort was captured by Pedro Menéndez de Avilés in the same year and renamed San Mateo.

men captured Laudonnière and forced him to authorize their departure in two vessels. All the deserters headed for the booty they hoped to gain in the Spanish Caribbean. Instead, their adventure led to the capture of some of their number and the unmasking of the French colony. After corsairing and raiding in Cuba and Hispaniola, two groups of the Frenchmen were captured by the Spaniards; only one small ship returned to Fort Caroline. But word had now been sent to Madrid, and Philip II was made aware of the French settlement.

In the meantime, the French Crown had prepared to send Jean Ribaut to reinforce Fort Caroline with a sizable fleet. The report of a skilled Spanish spy, Dr. Gabriel de Enveja, gave Philip II a full account of the ships, soldiers, and supplies being readied in Dieppe for the Florida voyage. More than 500 arquebusiers and their munitions, together with many dismounted bronze cannons, were loaded aboard. Ribaut himself went armed with royal decrees making him "captain-general and viceroy" of New France.

But by this time, Philip II had already granted a contract to a new Florida adelantado, Pedro Menéndez de Avilés. Even though the news of Laudonnière's fort impelled the Spanish king to add royal aid to Menéndez's effort, private motivations in the Florida conquest remained significant. Like other would-be Spanish conquerors, Pedro Menéndez had contracted with his king and had been promised the offices and titles of governor, captain general, and adelantado. Under his agreement, Menéndez was obliged to found two cities and was charged with seeing that the natives were converted to the Roman Catholic faith. If successful in his enterprise, Menéndez would receive a large land grant and the title of marquis to go with it. His jurisdiction was immense, extending from Newfoundland to the Florida Keys and, after 1573, westward to Mexico.

In the days of Emperor Charles V, Menéndez had come to royal attention for his daring deeds in the Bay of Biscay against French corsairs. Thereafter, he advanced himself in royal favor while he fought Spain's enemies at sea and on land. The young seaman became renowned for his prompt and decisive actions. For his services to Mary Tudor and young King Philip, the Asturian was awarded a habit in the prestigious Order of Santiago.

Menéndez's exploits and his influence with the Crown aroused the jealousy of the Seville merchants and the associated Crown agency, the Casa de Contratación (House of Trade). He was jailed by Casa officials in 1563 for alleged smuggling but succeeded in having his case transferred to court. Thereafter, when the urgencies of the Florida matter came to the Crown's attention early in 1565, Menéndez was available to serve as adelantado. Before he learned of the existence of Fort Caroline, Menéndez disclosed his interest in the fabled Northwest Passage and the route to the riches of the Orient, when he told the king of his geographic and strategic beliefs about Florida:

> If the French or English should come to settle Florida . . . it would be the greatest inconvenience, as much for the mines and territories of New Spain as for the navigation and trade of China and Molucca, if that arm of the sea goes to the South Sea, as is certain. . . . By being masters of Newfoundland. . . . Your Majesty may proceed to master that land. . . . It is such a great land and [situated] at such a good juncture, that if some other nations go to settle it . . . it will afterwards be most difficult to take and master it.
>
> And they must go directly to Cape Santa Elena, and, with fast ships discover all the bays, rivers, sounds and shallows on the route to Newfoundland. And to provide settlers, in the largest number possible, for two or three towns in the places which seem best . . . and after seeking

out the best ports, having first explored inland for four or five leagues, to see that it might have a good disposition of land for farming and live-stock-raising. And each town would have its fort to defend against the Indians if they should come upon them, or against other nations.[1]

Menéndez expected the Florida enterprise to prove profitable to himself and to the Crown. He anticipated the development of agriculture, stock-raising, fisheries, and forest resources for naval stores and ship-building. Menéndez also hoped to profit from the ships' licenses granted to him. He planned to utilize waterways that he believed connected with the mines of New Spain and the Pacific and those he thought crossed Florida from the Atlantic to the Gulf.

In his Florida venture, the kinship alliance that supported the adelantado was made up of seventeen families from the north of Spain, closely tied by blood and marriage. Members of this coterie pledged their persons and their fortunes to sustain their leader's efforts, and they hoped to acquire town and country lands and civil and military offices in Florida. These partners in Menéndez's enterprise thus shared his vision of enlarged estate and advanced standing before their sovereign. The existence of this familial territorial elite explains much of the dynamism of the Florida enterprise; the adelantado was loyally if not always ably served by his lieutenants and other officials, who held such close connection with him.

At the end of June 1565, Menéndez sailed for Florida with ten ships and more than a thousand men. Other ships departed from the north of Spain, and Menéndez was to receive added support from Santo Domingo. His voyage was beset with storms; several ships were lost before he reached Puerto Rico. He decided to strike out for Florida with the reduced forces he had at hand.

The adelantado arrived at Cape Canaveral in late August 1565. He knew that Jean Ribaut had sailed from Dieppe at the end of May with reinforcements for Laudonnière. The Spaniards had pressed their voyage, hoping to arrive at Fort Caroline before Ribaut. In the event, Menéndez found the French fleet already anchored off the St. Johns bar. After a short but sharp battle, the French put out to sea and Menéndez sailed south to found St. Augustine.

To affirm his king's title to North America, Menéndez took formal possession of all Florida when he landed at St. Augustine on 8 September 1565, officially placing the land and its peoples under Philip II's authority. This action authorized Menéndez to dispense lands to his followers and to make treaties with the natives. The adelantado built his

Pedro Menéndez de Avilés (1519–74), Adelantado de la Florida, Comendador de Santa Cruz de la Zarza, Orden de Santiago. Engraving based on a painting, reproduced from Cesáreo Fernández Duro, *Armada Española* (Madrid, 1895–1903). It was Menéndez who, on 8 September 1565, founded Florida's and the country's first permanent European settlement, St. Augustine.

first fort in Florida around a longhouse given him by Seloy, a local leader of the numerous and powerful Eastern Timucua people.

After Ribaut failed in an attack on the new Spanish colony, a storm struck the French fleet. Sensing that Fort Caroline was weakly defended and that the storm prevented Ribaut from a quick return, Menéndez struck out overland to Fort Caroline. At dawn on 20 September, he attacked the fort, surprised the French defenders, and put most of them to the sword.

Renaming the captured fort San Mateo (St. Matthew), the adelantado left a Spanish garrison there and returned to St. Augustine. Meanwhile, Ribaut's ships had been wrecked along the coast as far south as Cape Canaveral. Two groups of shipwreck survivors, straggling northward along the beaches, reached an inlet of the sea south of St. Augustine. Apprised of this, Menéndez took a body of soldiers there and persuaded many of the Frenchmen, including Ribaut himself, to surrender. Except for a few captives he spared, Menéndez had Ribaut and the rest killed. Thereafter, the little inlet would be called Matanzas, meaning "place of slaughter." Menéndez's actions at Fort Caroline and Matanzas would take their place in history and would tend to overshadow the whole complex story of Spain's colonizing effort in Florida.

Menéndez realized now that his supplies were critically short. He marched south to Cape Canaveral, destroyed a small fort built there by survivors from Ribaut's fleet, met the cacique of Ais, and appointed a Spanish governor for the area. Leaving a contingent of troops there, the adelantado took a small boat for Havana. Once in the Cuban port, he linked up with his forces from Asturias, meeting his nephew, Pedro Menéndez Marqués, and another key lieutenant, Esteban de las Alas. Next the adelantado arranged for supplies to be sent to Florida. Thereafter, meat, corn, cassava, squash, and livestock were regularly dispatched from Cuba and Yucatan to the peninsular garrisons.

Commandeering a ship, Menéndez next sailed for southwest Florida, seeking the outlet of his imagined cross-peninsular waterway. At the chief town of the Calusa, located on Mound Key in Estero Bay, the Spanish leader had an amicable meeting with the cacique Carlos and arranged for the freeing of several captives. Among those was a shipwrecked Spaniard from Cartagena, Hernando de Escalante Fontaneda, who became an interpreter for the Spaniards and later wrote a memoir about his Florida experiences.

Meanwhile, in the Florida garrisons, a harsh winter set in before Menéndez's supply network could begin to function. The garrison left on the east coast rebelled, moved southward, and founded Fort Santa

Sites of settlement and exploration during the period of Spanish expansion in La Florida, 1565–87, are shown here in bold. Spanish claims under the name La Florida extended north to Newfoundland and westward indefinitely from the Atlantic. Other sites in the Caribbean and Gulf of Mexico are shown for reference.

Lucía. Conditions there deteriorated as Indian friendship turned to enmity. The mutinous spirit spread to San Mateo and St. Augustine; it was rooted in the semi-independent nature of the hired soldiers and their captains. By mid-February, mutineers from San Mateo and St. Augustine, looking for a means of escape from Florida, were actively working to complete a half-built ship the French had left on the ways. Several of the captains and noncommissioned officers were also disaffected. After a supply ship entered the port of St. Augustine, the rebels struck. Seizing and confining Don Pedro de Valdés, the adelantado's son-in-law, they captured the ship and prepared to depart. Although Valdés managed to free himself and attacked the mutineers, they sailed away, as did the vessel from San Mateo. Altogether, more than 200 soldiers deserted Florida. Shortly afterward, Menéndez arrived in St. Augustine with the Santa Lucía mutineers whom he had picked up at sea. Having restored order and reinforced the garrisons, he sailed northward in a small craft to explore farther.

He passed the sea islands of the Georgia coast, meeting their native inhabitants and taking possession of each area for the king. That coast looked promising to Menéndez, as the people were numerous and seemed more pacific in nature than the Timucua or their neighbors, the Mocama. At Eastertide of 1566, Menéndez neared the Point of Santa Elena, a place of legendary fertility and plenty, and founded a city on present-day Parris Island. He appointed Esteban de las Alas as regional governor and departed once more for St. Augustine.

The adelantado returned to his first city to find that the fort had been burned by hostile natives and many of the supplies destroyed. He undertook yet another voyage to secure the Cuban supply line; while he was gone, the royal reinforcement fleet arrived in St. Augustine with shiploads of supplies and 1,500 soldiers. One of the companies of newly arrived troops was sent with its captain, Juan Pardo, to strengthen the garrison at Santa Elena.

A powerful incentive for Menéndez and his followers was nonmaterial: as fervent Catholics, they coveted the spiritual merit to be gained by successfully evangelizing Florida's native populations. To further that aim, the adelantado had arranged for members of the Society of Jesus (Jesuits), those noted "shock troops of the Counter-Reformation," to send missionaries to Florida. But the other side of the coin of Spanish–Native American relations was the Spaniards' expectations of native service, to be met through the *repartimientos* and *encomiendas* granted elsewhere in the Spanish Indies. None of these jointly cherished expectations could be realized without satisfactorily resolving the relationships with the present occupants of Florida, whom the Spaniards called Indios. Those diverse peoples, who represented long-established cultures and lived in ordered, hierarchical societies, were spread over the wide reaches of Menéndez's new domains.

By now, the Spaniards had met many of the peoples of Florida: Timucua, Surruque, Ais, Jeaga, Calusa, Tequesta, Mocama, Guale, and Orista. To Menéndez, Indian relations were all of a piece. He meant to establish a benevolent overlordship over them, bringing peace to warring groupings, eradicating heresy and unbelief, and spreading the gospel among them. He planned, conforming to the Jesuit modus operandi, to build a school in Havana to educate the children of their leaders. He also hoped to establish fort-missions in peninsular Florida and Guale and also westward on the route to Mexico. It was for this perceived devotion to his church that the Guale called the adelantado Mico Santamaría, Holy Mary's Chief of Chiefs.

To overcome the language barriers between Europeans and Native Americans, the Spaniards employed interpreters. Those men, usually ransomed Spaniards or Frenchmen who had learned the native languages in captivity, acted also as cultural brokers. They made negotiations possible between the Europeans and the representatives of the diverse indigenous cultures in Florida. Thus it was possible for Menéndez and his lieutenants to negotiate treaties of fealty, tribute, and submission to Philip II. At times, in order to undergird negotiations, the Spaniards took or even exchanged hostages with the Indians. Still, there remained many mutual misunderstandings among the parties to these cultural exchanges.

An example of such misapprehensions was Menéndez's preoccupation with the relationship between the Timucua, who had collaborated in the time of Laudonnière and would again in the time of Dominique de Gourgues. The adelantado believed that the creed of the French Protestants, whom he termed "Lutheran heretics," was at many points similar to the "Satanic" beliefs of the Indians. For that reason, his suspicions continually affected his relationship with the Timucua.

Despite the treaties signed with Florida's native groups, troubles persisted and even multiplied. When the first group of Jesuit missionaries came to Florida in the supply ship *Pantecras,* the ship's pilot missed the St. Augustine harbor entrance, got lost, and put into the inlet near the St. Marys River, now Florida's northeast boundary. There the Jesuit priest Pedro Martínez went ashore in a small boat seeking directions. He and three crewmen were killed by the Mocama, and the Jesuits had their first New World martyr. The surviving missionaries were posted to missions at Tequesta, on the Miami River at Biscayne Bay, and at San Antonio de Padua, built at the main Calusa village at Mound Key on the Gulf. In both places the missionaries were accompanied by a small Spanish garrison. They dedicated themselves to learning the Indian languages and acquainting the Indians with the main symbols and basic beliefs of Christianity, the latter facilitated by the use of some cloth picture books of Christian doctrine developed in Mexico.

But the Spaniards' attempts to impose the Christian religion upon the native people, their claimed right to interfere in native leadership succession, and their propensity to requisition food from Indian stores alienated the Indians, who began to fear for their own survival and for the survival of their cultural identity. Now warfare also broke out at many places in Timucua. Soldier-farmers were killed in cornfields near St. Augustine. Captain Pedro de Andrada and his company were ambushed near Potano in the north-central peninsula; he and many of his soldiers were slain. On the west coast, at the Tampa Bay fort called Tocobaga, the whole Spanish garrison was massacred by natives and the fort was evacuated. To counter the Indians' rapid arrow fire, Menéndez had to change his war tactics; he ordered 500 crossbows for his soldiers and began to dress them in protective padded cotton armor, first used by Spaniards in the conquest of Yucatan and later by de Soto in Apalachee.

On Good Friday of 1568, a French nobleman, Dominique de Gourgues, arrived at the St. Johns River to take revenge upon the Spaniards for the deaths of Jean Ribaut and many of his followers. Guided by Timucua, the attacking Frenchmen and their Indian allies captured the Spanish blockhouses at the river mouth and then took and burned Fort San Mateo. Most of the defending Spaniards had already fled.

Meanwhile, tensions had mounted between Spaniards and the Calusa at Carlos. The attempts of the Europeans to impose their sovereignty and religion finally caused a complete break with the Calusa. Cacique Carlos, the Spaniards believed, planned to kill them all. Captain Francisco de Reinoso forestalled this by executing the Calusa leader and installing an Indian named Philip as his succesor. The Tequesta mission on the lower Atlantic coast had already failed; the Jesuit there had been unable to convert more than one old dying woman to the Catholic faith, and a clash between the soldiers and the Indians led to the withdrawal of the Spaniards.

Painstakingly, on the lower Gulf Coast, the Jesuit priest Juan Rogel gave daily instruction to cacique Philip, his principal people, their wives and children. Many of them learned the prayers, and some of the Christian doctrine coincided with Calusa beliefs, but when the Jesuit pressed the Indians to renounce their own rites, cut their long hair, and burn the images of their deities, they refused. The cacique rejected the proposal that he leave his sister-wife and dismiss his other wives. This dialogue continued, without notable success for the missionaries, until 1569, when both the garrison and the Jesuit mission were withdrawn, and the attempt to evangelize the Calusa ended.

The abandonment of the South Florida forts and missions foreshadowed a general northward relocation of Menéndez's Florida enterprise. Forsaking the effort to exploit the St. Johns River and other inland waterways, the Spaniards evacuated San Mateo and shifted the garrison to a new fort, San Pedro de Tacatacuru, on Cumberland Island. The new fort would anchor the route from St. Augustine to the colony's new center, Santa Elena. The Jesuits, in an attempt to evangelize the Guale and the Orista, moved north with the soldiers.

From Santa Elena the adelantado sent Captain Juan Pardo on two long expeditions westward to the Appalachian mountains. Pardo's mission was to scout fertile lands for future economic development and to find the route to the silver mines of Guanajuato and Zacatecas in Mexico. On his first journey in December 1566, Pardo proceeded into present-day North Carolina, then westward to the foot of the Blue Ridge. There, at a place called Joara, he founded the city of Cuenca and left a garrison in Fort San Juan under Sergeant Hernando Moyano. The lands there, said the Spanish captain, were "as pretty as . . . the best in Spain."[2] At Guatari, near today's Salisbury, North Carolina, Pardo noted a particularly fertile area, where he left four soldiers and a secular priest, the company's chaplain Sebastian Montero, to evangelize the Indians.

When he returned to Santa Elena, Pardo told Menéndez of his inland discoveries, and the adelantado fixed upon the area of Guatari for his own personal land grant, which would undergird his family's future prosperity and make him a marquis. Sent out a second time, in September 1567, Pardo took with him as interpreter the young Frenchman Guillaume Rouffi. He followed much the same route as before, finding rich bottomlands near present-day Asheville. He then went westward across the mountains into eastern Tennessee, to the populous town of Chiaha. After that, concerned about being attacked by powerful Indian groupings, Pardo did not press on to Coosa and Tascaluza, waypoints for him on the road to Mexico. Instead, the Spaniards turned back and returned to Santa Elena.

Now, Menéndez concluded, in order to begin to populate the vast areas of coastal and inland Florida, it was time to begin its serious settlement. From the beginning of his enterprise, the adelantado had planned to import settler-farmers. One of the clauses in his contract required him to establish two towns, to bring livestock, and to carry 500 settlers to Florida. In his first expedition, 138 of his soldiers—carried at his own expense—were craftsmen who represented many of the trades of sixteenth-century Castile. Another 117 of his soldiers were farmers, and 26 brought their wives and children.

In their agreements with the adelantado, the soldier-farmers were promised by Menéndez that he would "give them rations in the said coast and land of Florida, and lands and estates for their planting, farming and stockraising, and divisions of land, in accordance with their service and the quality which each one possesses."[3]

After he expelled the French, established his Florida supply lines, and put down the soldiers' mutinies, Menéndez contracted with one Hernán Pérez, a Portuguese, to bring farmers from the Azores. In his arrangements with this and other settler groups, the adelantado promised to "give them their passage and pay for their freight. Having arrived at this land, I will give them lands and estates for their farms and stockraising, and within two years a dozen cows with one bull, two oxen for plowing, twelve sheep, and the same number of goats, hogs and chickens, and two mares and one farmhand, and a house constructed, with its winepress, and a male and a female slave, and vineshoots to plant."[4] Menéndez then indicated that the settlers would sharecrop with him until the costs incurred were paid out. He added, "I do not have the capability to do this, but I believe that there will be merchants who, once they know how good this land is for cultivation, . . . might wish to put in a part of their wealth in that profitable agricultural enterprise—in order to settle themselves on large *haciendas* of sugar mills, livestock and farms of bread and wine."

This arrangement fell through, but in 1568 Menéndez had the funds in hand to put his plan in motion with settlers from the Iberian peninsula. The potential Florida settlers in Castile were mostly small farmers, *labradores*. Although it had a number of cities, Castile was an essentially agricultural and pastoral area. Most people worked the land, raising sheep and hogs for food, donkeys, mules, and horses to serve as work animals, and cattle. They cultivated gardens and orchards and had widespread wheat, vineyard, and olive plantings. Spanish agriculture was therefore both extensive and intensive. Except for a few fertile plains and the lush green Cantabrian north, Castilians were accustomed to marginal soils and a dry, harsh climate. Water was rare and precious; in the Castilian language, the words for *wealthy* and for *abundant waters* were the same: *caudaloso*. Castilian emigrants to the Americas sought rich and well-watered lands for their husbandry and hoped to find them in Florida.

In the provinces of Extremadura and upper Andalucia, Menéndez recruited a number of farmers who came with their wives and children to Cádiz, where Pedro del Castillo arranged for them to board ship for Florida. After a sharp skirmish with the Casa de Contratación over permission to set sail, Castillo obtained royal permission for two ships, the *Nuestra Señora de la Vitoria* and the *Nuestra Señora de la Concepción,* to

The surnames of many of the first European inhabitants of Florida are given in a four-page document dated 27 September 1568, the first page of which is shown. The document lists the names of 209 farmers, their wives, children, other relatives, and servants from the Spanish province of Extremadura who sailed for Florida in two caravels out of Cádiz in October 1568. The names given in the document are: Sedeño, Martínez Salvatierra, González, Díaz, Martín, Pérez, García, Ruyz Cavallero, Muñoz, Escudero, de Merlo, de Moya, Sánchez, Hernández, Ortíz, Martín Cumplido, Gómez, Oliveros, de Vía, Martín Texada, Olivares, de las Eras, Calvo, Asencio, de la Torre, Rodríguez, de Herrera, de Berrío, Domínguez, Pinto, Rueda, de Sellera Porra, de Segovia, González Dorado, Romero, Martín Silvestre, Serrano, Viejo, Gordillo, Mener, de la Rosa, Ruyz, Alonso, de Olmo, Sigüenza, Tristán, López, and Azaro.

depart. Many of the settlers aboard came from Mérida and the area of Guadalcanal.

In the spring of 1569, the ships reached Florida, and 273 settlers landed in St. Augustine; 193 of these were sent quickly to Santa Elena. Once established there, the settlers built houses, worked at their lands and livestock, engaged in trade, and involved themselves in the city government. On the first of August of that same year, thirty-six households were enumerated in Santa Elena, together with four houses for single men. By October, 327 persons, including the settlers and soldiers, lived there. The families that had come to build their hearths and futures in La Florida were participants in a major transfer of Hispanic culture.

Sixteenth-century Florida society was broadly representative of several regions of the Spanish homeland. It presented a cross section of the trades, crafts, professions, and social strata of early modern Castile. It was a deferential, hierarchical society; goods inventories disclose how real and personal property in Spanish Florida generally mirrored the stratification of the community. Ordinary soldiers and sailors had few possessions, although some had musical instruments and acted as moneylenders. The servant Juan Rodríguez slept on the floor outside his mistress's St. Augustine rooms. At the other end of the social scale, Adelantado Menéndez kept court like a viceroy, with noble retainers and liveried servants. When Menéndez and his wife, Doña María de Solís, moved to Santa Elena in 1571, they shipped luxurious household furnishings: ornate rugs and wall hangings, beds and bedding, and fine table linens and plate. The inventories also describe the sumptuous clothing and elegant accessories imported by the Menéndez family and other noble persons in Florida. The archaeologist Stanley South found the remnants of gold embroidery at Santa Elena, together with jewelry and a fragment from a costly Ming Dynasty porcelain wine ewer. The import lists also feature majolica tableware and food delicacies: dates, almonds, quince-paste, and marzipan. But the class lines evidenced by those goods were tempered by Spanish individualism and by the upward mobility many Florida citizens displayed.

This was, moreover, a corporate society. The Florida immigrants shared many unifying beliefs, traits, and customs, which included their Castilian language. All were communicants of the Tridentine Roman Catholic church; many of the men belonged to one of the Florida confraternities, whose membership cut across social lines. Those laymen organized funerals, marched in processions, and supported their members' widows. The sacramental Mother Church dominated the daily life of Spanish Florida; the very hours and days were numbered by the church bells and the Christian calendar. An inventory of the parish church included a fine painted retable and gilded altar cross. Menéndez's deeds in expelling the French "Lutherans," as all Protestants were called, called forth praise from Pope Pius V. The adelantado then asked the pope for special indulgences for his colonists and soldiers who might die without confession during the events of the conquest.

For their part, the soldiers were the bearers of a long military tradition, formed since the time of Isabel and Fernando. They and their officers were the king's shield against his enemies, but the military had another, darker side; the mutinies of 1566 had been caused by Spanish veterans of wars in Italy and France, who were accustomed, as Menéndez said, to "banquets, booty, and wine."[5]

Qualifying as *vecinos,* or city electors, the citizens of St. Augustine and Santa Elena enjoyed the ancient Castilian municipal liberties. Everyday life was governed by the municipality, which determined prices, established weights and measures, controlled the local court for civil and criminal matters, and regulated the marketplaces.

The surviving body of Florida lawsuits depicts many of the realities of daily life and the prevailing sixteenth-century social climate there. One case, for instance, involved a litigious tailor named Alonso de Olmos, who sued the governor for libel. Olmos claimed that Governor Don Diego de Velasco directed epithets at Olmos's daughter as he ejected her from a religious procession. Moreover, he contended, the governor had also insulted him with the taunt "See the Lutheran going to the synagogue!"[6] In another case, the settlers sued the governor for payment of the clothing, food, and rental owed them; prosperous with goods, the settlers had been extending credit to soldiers and wanted repayment. Velasco was authoritarian in his dealings with the Indians but took care to provide them with the usual gifts and presents.

Documents disclose the vigorous economic life of sixteenth-century Spanish Florida. The farmers from Spain learned to cultivate corn, which was at first imported or bought from the natives; it slowly replaced wheat and cassava as the staple carbohydrate in the colonists' diet. Later, wheat farms would be planted in West Florida. At Santa Elena, archaeologist Stanley South has uncovered ditches from vineyards. Said one witness, "I have planted with my own hands grapevines, pomegranates, orange trees and figs, wheat, barley, onions, garlic and many vegetables that grow in Spain."[7]

One Antonio de Carbajal, describing the richness of Guale and the easy access to inland areas from there, said that "the land of Guale is as fertile as the best land of Spain . . . because he has seen many fruits and plants produced in the said land, and livestock being produced, and the large number of grasslands for the raising of cattle and sheep."[8]

In the cities, peddlers, shoemakers, moneylenders, tavernkeepers, fishermen and hunters, prostitutes, smiths, and carpenters plied their trades. Soldiers' wives operated boardinghouses for unmarried men. Alonso de Olmos made suits of padded cotton armor for the garrison; others worked to make palmetto matchcord. Pedro Menéndez had two ships built in Florida, one near St. Augustine and one at Santa Elena. Silk culture and sugar production never succeeded, but there was substantial export of juniper, oak, and laurel-wood, together with sassafras root bark for medicinal purposes. The production of tar and pitch began. The fur trade with the Indians began, and deerskin boots and jackets were locally made. Commercial documents—the very stuff of trade and business—abound in the Florida records.

In 1569 there occurred a general crisis in Menéndez's finances, strained by his efforts in Florida and worsened by the added costs of bringing in settlers. The adelantado had already filed a suit seeking recompense from the Crown for his ship losses in the Florida expedition and for additional expenses above and beyond those foreseen in his royal contract. Now Menéndez went to Madrid to make his plea before the Council of the Indies for a regular subsidy to support the Florida garrisons. When no immediate action was taken, Menéndez decided to force the issue. He ordered his lieutenants to denude the Florida garrisons of all but 150 men, the number the Crown had in principle agreed to support. In the meantime, difficulties arose with the Jesuit order over Menéndez's control over the missionaries.

Finally, Philip II convened four royal councils—State, Indies, War, and Treasury—and put the Florida matter to them. From that meeting resulted a royal decree, in November 1570, that established a subsidy to undergird the Florida garrisons. Meanwhile, the Jesuits agreed to one more attempt at the difficult Florida mission field: they sent Father Juan Bautista de Segura with other missionaries to the Chesapeake, known to the Spaniards as the Bay of Santa María. Pedro Menéndez Marqués had explored the coasts north of there, all the way to Newfoundland.

For some years, Adelantado Menéndez had been largely absent from Florida, carrying out various royal assignments. Because of stressful events, two of his principal lieutenants, Esteban de las Alas and Pedro de Valdés, had also left Florida. Moreover, after the murder of his favorite daughter, Ana, in Asturias, the adelantado was forced to rethink the succession to his Florida enterprise. His only son, Juan, had been lost at sea. Now Menéndez reconciled with his daughter, Catalina, and the man she had married, Hernando de Miranda. Menéndez also arranged a marriage between his illegitimate daughter, María, and Don Diego de Velasco, the legitimized grandson of the constable of Castile, a high nobleman, and made a dower contract with Velasco to encourage him to serve in Florida.

The new royal subsidy stimulated fresh private efforts. For his part, Menéndez moved his wife and ten other persons in his household to Santa Elena. Velasco also came there as governor with his wife. A new group of settlers came to augment the number of farmers. A list of the new colonists includes "Lorenzo García, native of Puebla del Prior in Badajoz, who has a thin face, is of medium stature, and is missing the little finger of his left hand; he is forty-two years of age."[9]

In February 1571, the Indians of Jacán killed the Jesuit missionaries at the Chesapeake. After word of this reached Santa Elena, Menéndez led a punitive expedition to the site, hanging several Jacán leaders and rescuing a Spanish boy, the son of Alonso de Olmos, who had survived the massacre. After he learned of the missionaries' death, the general of the Society of Jesus terminated their six-year Florida mission.

The tragic end of the Jesuits at the Chesapeake culminated a long list of Indian difficulties that had faced the Spaniards in Florida since 1565. In the Indian River area, at Tequesta, Carlos, and Tocobaga, and among the Timucua peoples, there had been no sustained peace between the Native Americans and the Spanish leaders, soldiers, and settlers. So incensed was Menéndez at the failure of his Indian policies that in 1573 he asked the king's permission to capture rebellious Indians and to sell them as slaves. The king refused the request, but it was apparent that Menéndez's failure to reach a settled peace with many of Florida's indigenous people made it virtually impossible for Spaniards to work the land. In fact, the continual disturbances confined the settlers, and Menéndez himself, to the poorer coastal soils. The Spaniards could not safely reside in the interior, where the land was well suited to pastoral and agricultural enterprise. One by one, the inland garrisons were abandoned.

Back in Spain, while on assignment from the king to assemble a great fleet to reinforce Spanish forces in Flanders, Pedro Menéndez de Avilés fell ill, likely from a typhus outbreak which had swept his fleet. On 17 September 1574, at Santander, he died. His will divided the Florida inheritance: daughter Catalina received the title of adelantado, the

Florida profits, and his entail; daughter María inherited his land grant and the title of marquis.

Catalina's husband hastened to claim his wife's Florida privileges and set sail from Spain late in 1575. Arriving at Santa Elena, Hernando de Miranda deposed Velasco and set to work to ensure his own profits from the enterprise. However, Miranda failed to attend properly to the Florida defenses, and he neglected to give gifts to the natives. He also permitted his lieutenants to abuse the Guale and Orista peoples. Angered, the Indians joined in confederation; by mid-1576, they had killed a number of Spanish officials and soldiers and surrounded Santa Elena itself. Miranda, no leader of men, panicked, evacuated the city, and fled from Florida.

The Council of the Indies removed Miranda as governor and vacated his title of adelantado; they appointed Pedro Menéndez Marqués as the new governor. Henceforth Florida would no longer be a proprietary colony but a crown colony. Menéndez Marqués rebuilt Santa Elena, but after Sir Francis Drake's raid on St. Augustine in 1586 it was finally abandoned—ironically, just as John White, who led Sir Walter Raleigh's third colonizing expedition, landed at Roanoke Island. Thus the Spaniards were poorly positioned to forestall or to combat the English settlements that were later successfully planted to the north of Florida. Pedro Menéndez's dream of a viable colony based on agriculture and commerce had vanished forever.

One man's plaint summed up the experience in Spanish Florida since 1565. "I have served," said Bartolomé Martínez, "in these provinces of Florida . . . since the Adelantado brought me as a soldier, and in this time I have suffered hunger, nudity and much misery, not because the land is so bad as they hold it to be, but due to the poor government it has had, and because their resources were little to conquer so many people and such a great land. I have seen the greater part of the coast of these provinces and thirty leagues around the fort of Santa Elena. What I say to Your Majesty about this land of which all the world says ill, is that it is a marvel of good, because there are most rich lands for tillage and stock-farms, powerful rivers of sweet water, great fertile plains and mountains. . . . And I wish to beg Your Majesty that you might give me some land in it, where I might remain always."[10]

Florida's founding in 1565 was impelled by Hapsburg dynastic strategy and disputes among European powers. But it was also directly linked with the settlement impulse that drove sixteenth-century Spaniards to implant their rich and complex culture in the Americas. After an initial expansion, Spanish Florida became a shrinking empire, struggling with powerful England over the disputed lands to the north of the peninsula.

Only once was serious thought given to abandonment of the peninsula. In 1602 an official inquiry conducted by an administrative investigator from Cuba heard eighteen long-term residents of Florida on the question—soldiers, civilians, and Franciscan friars. Instead of dismantling St. Augustine and transferring the center of Spanish activity farther north on the Atlantic coast, as some in Florida were urging, the official decision was made to keep that center where it was.

The strong desire to settle the peninsula was never completely abandoned. It was revived in the eighteenth century, when farmers from the Canary Islands came to Florida. And St. Augustine, that quintessential survivor city founded by Pedro Menéndez de Avilés, remains today the oldest city of European origin in what is today the United States of America.

Notes

1. Pedro Menéndez de Avilés to the king, no place, no date (probably late February–early March, 1565), from Archives of the Indies, Seville (hereafter AGI), *Patronato* 19; reprinted in Eugenio Ruidíaz y Caravía, *La Florida: su conquista por Pedro Menéndez de Avilés.* 2 vols. (Madrid, 1893), 2:320–26.
2. Narrative of Juan de la Vandera, from Archives of the Counts of Revillagigedo, *Canalejas* 46, reel 105 of microfilm at Flagler College, Center for Historic Research, image 561.
3. Pedro Menéndez to the Crown, St. Augustine, 20 October 1566, AGI *Santo Domingo* 115.
4. Ibid.
5. Ibid.
6. AGI *Escribanía de Cámara* 154-A, fol. 471vto.
7. Bartolomé Martínez to Crown, 17 February 1577, from AGI *Santo Domingo* 125.
8. AGI *Escribanía de Cámara* 154-A, fol. 370.
9. Juan de Abalia to the Crown, 27 June 1573, AGI *Patronato* 257.
10. Bartolomé Martínez to the Crown, Havana, 17 February 1577, from AGI Santo Domingo 125.

Bibliography

Altman, Ida. *Emigrants and Society: Extremadura and America in the Sixteenth Century.* Berkeley: University of California Press, 1989.

Arnade, Charles W. "The Failure of Spanish Florida." *The Americas* 16, no. 3 (January 1960):271–81.

———. *Florida on Trial, 1593–1602.* Coral Gables: University of Miami Press, 1959.

Bennett, Charles E. *Laudonnière and Fort Caroline: History and Documents.* Gainesville: University of Florida Press, 1964.

Bushnell, Amy Turner. *The King's Coffer: Proprietors of the Spanish Florida Treasury, 1565–1702.* Gainesville: University Presses of Florida, 1981.

Deagan, Kathleen. *Spanish St. Augustine: The Archaeology of a Colonial Creole Community.* New York: Academic Press, 1983.

Gaffarel, Paul. *Histoire de la floride Française.* Paris: Firman-Didot et Cie., 1875.

Gannon, Michael V. *The Cross in the Sand: The Early Catholic Church in Florida, 1513–1870.* Gainesville: University of Florida Press, 1965.

———. "The New Alliance of History and Archaeology in the Eastern Spanish Borderlands." *William and Mary Quarterly,* 3d ser., 49, no. 2 (April 1992):321–34.

———. "Sebastian Montero, Pioneer American Missionary, 1566–1572." *Catholic Historical Review* 51, no. 3 (October 1965):335–53.

Hoffman, Paul E. "Diplomacy and the Papal Donation." *The Americas* 30, no. 2 (October 1973):151–83.

———. *A New Andalucia and a Way to the Orient: The American Southeast During the Sixteenth Century.* Baton Rouge: Louisiana State University Press, 1990.

Hudson, Charles. *The Juan Pardo Expeditions: Explorations of the Carolinas and Tennessee, 1566–1568.* Washington: Smithsonian Institution Press, 1990.

Lyon, Eugene. "The Control Structure of Spanish Florida, 1580." MS, Center for Historic Research, Flagler College, 1977.

———. "Cultural Brokers in Sixteenth-Century Spanish Florida." Symposium on "The Provinces of Florida: Defining a Spanish-Indian Society in Colonial North America," Johns Hopkins University, 1987.

———. *The Enterprise of Florida: Pedro Menéndez de Avilés and the Spanish Conquest of 1565–1568.* Gainesville: University Presses of Florida, 1976.

———. "La Visita de 1576 y la Transformación del Gobierno en la Florida Española." *La Influencia de España en el Caribe, la Florida y la Luisiana.* Madrid: Ministero de Cultura, 1983.

———. *Pedro Menéndez de Avilés: A Sourcebook.* Hamden, Conn.: Spanish Borderland Sourcebooks, Garland Publishing Company, 1994.

———. "The Revolt of 1576 at Santa Elena: A Failure of Indian Policy." Paper, American Historical Association, Washington, 1987.

———. *Richer Than We Thought: The Material Culture of Sixteenth-Century St. Augustine.* St. Augustine, Fla.: St. Augustine Historical Society, 1992.

———. *Santa Elena: A Brief History of the Colony.* Columbia: Institute of Archaeology and Anthropology, University of South Carolina, 1984.

———. "Spain's Sixteenth-Century North American Settlement Attempts: A Neglected Aspect," *Florida Historical Quarterly* 59, no. 3 (January 1981): 275–91.

Milanich, Jerald T. "The Western Timuqua: Patterns of Acculturation and Change." In *Tacachale: Essays on the Indians of Florida and Southeastern Georgia During the Historic Period,* edited by Jerald T. Milanich and Samuel Proctor, pp. 59–88. Gainesville: University Presses of Florida, 1978.

Ribaut, Jean. *The Whole and True Discoverye of Terra Florida.* A Facsimile Reprint of the London Edition of 1563. Introduction by David L. Dowd. Gainesville: University of Florida Press, 1964.

4 Republic of Spaniards, Republic of Indians

Amy Turner Bushnell

In 1573 and 1574, Philip II issued three sets of laws for enlarging and governing Spain's American empire: the Ordinances of Pacification, the Ordinances of Patronage, and the Ordinances of the Laying Out of Towns. Together, they marked the end of the High Conquest period in eastern North America, of would-be conquistadors such as Ponce de León, Narváez, and De Soto, and of adelantados such as Ayllón, Luna, and Menéndez de Avilés. Future expansion would be Crown-controlled.

European fighting men were accustomed to band together under a captain for a limited military objective, after which the company would divide the spoils and disband to be free for other ventures. On the edges of Spanish empire, however, captains of conquest were waging continuous war for the sole purpose of taking captives to be sold as slaves. A resolve to end this abuse lay behind the king's new policy of pacification through gifts and conversions. In future, it would not be the military's business to advance the frontier; its mandate was to defend the advancing missionary. As patron of the church, the king was equally determined to reestablish control over the preaching orders to whom Charles V had entrusted the spiritual conquest of the Indians. He would make pastors from the "regular" clergy answer to his bishops as other priests did. Both of these new policies encouraged members of the Franciscan order, especially, to strike out for fresh mission fields.

A third matter on the king's mind was the vital flow of silver from America, threatened by the wild

Chichimeca Indians in northern New Spain and by foreign corsairs in the seaways of the Caribbean and the Gulf Stream. To guarantee the deliveries of silver, the king resorted to a presidial system of fortified outposts and ports. The soldiers and sailors stationed at a *presidio,* like those in a royal *armada,* were regular troops on wages. Unlike conquistadors, they were forbidden to take booty or captives; unlike *encomenderos,* traditional guardians of newly conquered lands, they were not entitled to the tribute or forced services of Indians. In those places where the Indians accepted Christianity, presidios were reinforced by mission provinces and converts provided a buffer zone against invasion and a source of reinforcements, provisions, and labor. Where the Indians rejected Christianity, the frontier did not advance.

Spaniards posted to a "land of constant war," whether as fighting men, missionaries, or bureaucrats, were supported by a subvention known as the *situado,* a transfer of royal revenues from one royal treasury in the Indies to another, for purposes of defense. During the seventeenth century, Florida's situado came from Mexico City, capital of the viceroyalty of New Spain, which also supported presidios on the road to the silver mines of Zacatecas and in selected ports of the Caribbean and the Philippines.

Indians who could not be pacified by the sword, the gift, or the gospel shared certain characteristics. Typically, they were seasonal nomads, indifferent to the sacraments and unwilling to settle down in farming villages on the Mediterranean model. They had a high regard for individual liberty and governed themselves by consensus rather than coercion. Finally, they could not be quarantined from contact with Spain's European rivals.

Every condition that made a pacification difficult was present in Spanish Florida. As a result, the colony would never lose its character as a military outpost. Yet, in the seventeenth century, Florida enjoyed two periods of expansion and a hinterland of productive mission provinces. This was possible because the native societies were diverse. While some Florida peoples were highly nomadic and recognized no authority above the band, others were seasonally agricultural, with paramount chiefs who exercised significant authority. Through these "lords of the land," the *caciques* (chiefs) and *cacicas* (chieftainesses), the Spaniards could implement a Conquest by Contract, establishing an autonomous Republic of Indians to share the land with the Republic of Spaniards, united by their common allegiance to God and the king.

The notarized treaties of peace or trade, acts of homage or submission, records of mission foundings, declarations of just war, and lists of chiefs appearing before the governor that one may find in the archives are evidences of the legal side of pacification. They are the contracts, theoretically voluntary, that the Spaniards called into existence, recorded, and attempted to enforce. But the success of the Conquest by Contract and of the corollary Republics required a degree of isolation from other Europeans that a maritime periphery would find difficult to sustain.

Florida's transformation from an *adelantamiento* to a royal colony was gradual. Slowly, the situado was institutionalized, troops from the armadas were replaced by permanent garrisons, temporary treasury appointments gave way to lifetime offices, and governors began to govern in person rather than through lieutenants. When Santa Elena was abandoned in 1587, the adelantado's dream of a Greater Florida of transcontinental proportions was tabled for the more practical goal of consolidation. Promotional activities ceased, and settlement incentives to farmer families were discontinued.

If the new capital of St. Augustine was to be populated, the soldiers themselves would have to become family men, and Spanish wives were scarce. The answer was mixed marriage. By the turn of the century, half of the women in town were Indians, and many *floridanos,* although they did not advertise it, were *mestizos,* part Indian. Once an increased birthrate had brought the sex ratio closer to equilibrium, consensual unions between the Republic of Spaniards and the Republic of Indians became less common and efforts were made to enforce segregation. Indians could not come to St. Augustine without a pass, and non-Indians traveling on the king's business could stay no more than three days in a native town and had to sleep in the council house. These restrictions did not apply to the Franciscans, who could not leave their posts without permission.

Individuals of African origin added a third ethnic element to the colony. At one time, over fifty black slaves of the king were at work on the wooden fortifications, and numerous private persons owned African domestics. Taking advantage of lapses in security, many of these slaves escaped to live among the Indians or in maroon communities. Free blacks and mulattoes were called *españoles* and occupied the lower social levels of the Spanish community, being Spanish in language, faith, and fealty.

Although Philip II would have preferred it otherwise, the Spanish empire was cosmopolitan and its borders were permeable. By the unwritten rule of "foreigners to the frontiers," St. Augustine was home to several nationalities. Many of the colony's ship captains, pilots, and

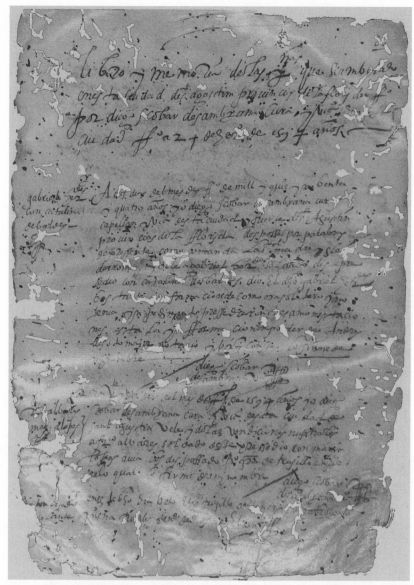

The oldest European document of North American origin preserved in the United States is this page of the surviving Parish Registers of St. Augustine, Florida. Dated 24 January 1594, the first entry records the marriage of Gabriel Hernándes "a soldier of this presidio," and Catalina de Valdés. The officiating priest was the pastor of the parish church and chaplain of the garrison, Diego Escobar de Sambrana. The registers form a continuous record to the present day of Catholic life in the city. The fate of entries from 1565, when the parish was founded, to 1594 is not known.

merchants were Portuguese, often of Jewish background, and a surprising number of the residents were French. In 1607, Governor Pedro de Ybarra reported fifty-six naturalized foreigners: twenty-eight Portuguese, twenty Frenchmen, and, as artillerists, two Flemings and six Germans.

Like the Spanish presidios in North Africa, St. Augustine functioned as a penal colony, a place of exile for unruly officers, trouble-making friars, and sentenced criminals, or *forzados*. Many of the soldiers, too, were "involuntaries," with records as debtors, petty thieves, vagrants, and rioters. Those from New Spain were further stigmatized; their mixed racial heritage was associated in many minds with illegitimacy.

Finally, St. Augustine was a seaside presidio, the only coast guard station along 600 miles of strategic sea lane. After a storm, its vessels scoured the coast for castaways, cargoes, and naval artillery. Their presence reassured voyagers in the Fleet of the Indies, sailing northward on the Gulf Stream sixty miles offshore. When not escorting the Fleet, frigates from the presidio sailed to Havana and Veracruz for supplies, to Spain with dispatches, or to show the flag and trade with the natives in Florida's deepwater harbors, along the inland waterway, and up the St. Johns River.

As advised in the Ordinances of Pacification, the Franciscans who undertook the spiritual conquest of Florida took their "flying missions" directly to the Indians, raising crosses on town plazas, preaching, and inviting the chiefs to come and receive the king's gifts. Once in St. Augustine, the native leaders negotiated alliances of trade and mutual defense and registered a request for friars. In Spanish eyes, these acts made them and their vassals subjects of the king of Spain and Christian neophytes.

Churches and convents rose in the towns of paramount chiefs, giving them access to exotic goods, new means of making war, and spiritual power. From these mission centers, or *doctrinas,* missionaries called *doctrineros* serviced strings of outstations, or *visitas,* in subject towns. To maintain the "divine cult" in all these places, Franciscans relied on the sons of caciques, trained as sacristans, musicians, interpreters, catechists, and overseers. Orphans raised by the missionaries became their gardeners, grooms, and cooks.

The Florida situado underwrote the doctrinas much as it did the presidio. In St. Augustine's 300-man garrison, missionaries and soldiers were budgetarily interchangeable, costing the Crown 115 ducats a year apiece, and, until the number of *religiosos* on the rolls was capped at forty-three, every added friar meant one less soldier. Out of deference

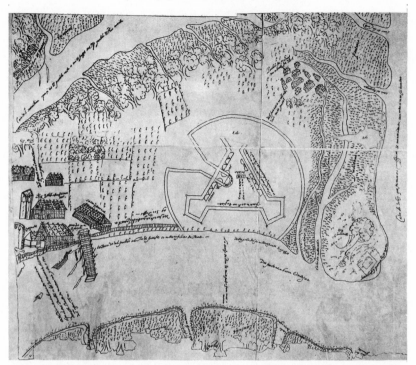

Mapa del Pueblo, Fuerte y Caño de San Agustín. . . . A bird's-eye view of St. Augustine and surrounding area drawn by an unknown cartographer, probably in 1593, shows the principal structures of the town, with vertical board walls and thatched roofs and a wharf extending into the Matanzas River (left); the town's seventh wooden fort (right); and the Indian mission and town of Nombre de Dios (upper right).

to a Franciscan's vow of poverty, his stipend was issued in the form of supplies, called "alms from the king." From other royal funds the friar received a vestment allowance called "habit and sandals" and, if he was an ordained priest, an altar allowance of wine, wheat, and wax. New churches, too, were subsidized. When a town advanced to the status of a doctrina, the Crown made it a 1,000-peso baptismal gift of religious essentials: vestments, linens, images, vessels, parish registers, bells, and an altar stone. The natives prized this sacred treasure and sought to keep it whether or not they had a priest to conduct services.

From 1587 through the 1620s, Spanish efforts created a tier of mission provinces along Florida's east coast and up the north-flowing St. Johns River, with its two districts of Tidewater (Agua Salada) and Freshwater (Agua Dulce). This first wave of expansion, the Nearer Pacifications, added an element of Indian tribute and labor to the support system.

The Timucua chiefs near the presidio were the first to prove their loyalty. During the sixteenth-century wars, don Gaspar Marqués of the town of San Sebastián provided the Spaniards with scouts, porters, couriers, boatmen, and archers. When St. Augustine was temporarily overrun by castaways from the wrecks of five galleons, doña María Meléndez, cacica of Nombre de Dios and wife of a soldier, came to the rescue. The Crown rewarded her timely gift of provisions with 500 ducats worth of red cloth.

By the turn of the century, Governor Gonzalo Méndez Canzo was drafting natives from Guale province in present-day Georgia to rebuild St. Augustine, which had been destroyed by fire and a flood. The laborers received a ration of corn and a daily wage in trade goods. Thereafter, unmarried Indian males came in relays from the provinces to cultivate the soldiers' fields, or *sabanas*, in a labor levy that historians call the *repartimiento*.

Spaniards also made themselves beneficiaries of the Sabana System, which was the native method of public finance. By custom, each planting season the commoners of an Indian town planted one sabana of corn for each of their caciques or cacicas and another for the community as a whole. Now, using new iron adzes and hoes, they cleared and planted other sabanas for the "service of the convent" and the "service of the king." Nor was this their only contribution: often they were pressured to sell the surplus of their harvest to the presidio on credit, in what amounted to a forced loan.

The colony became increasingly dependent on these labor transfers, sanctioned and brokered by the Hispanicized chiefs. As a reward for their services, the rulers of the Republic of Indians were honored with ceremonial staves of office, entertained by the governor, and given gifts of European garments for themselves and cloth, blankets, and tools for their followers. The expense of "regaling" the Indians was the one open-ended fund in the situado.

A nation conquered by the gospel instead of the sword was not supposed to be subject to the labor levy, but all of the Florida pacifications seemed to turn into conquests. Years of Spanish steel, firepower, and scorched earth campaigns were required to divide and conquer the natives of the East Coast, and each chiefdom that rebelled against Spain's overlordship was reconquered and reintegrated under new terms. Meanwhile, undaunted by the Spanish presence, French corsairs continued to trade with the natives for ambergris, a perfume fixative, and sassafras and china root, popular specifics for syphilis. The regions they favored were Ais, above Cape Canaveral, and Guale, on the coast of

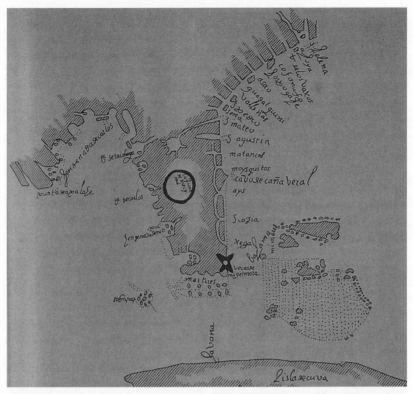

Mapa de la Florida y Laguna de Maymi. . . . (Map of Florida and of the lake of Maymi [Okeechobee]) drawn by an unknown Spanish cartographer during the period 1595–1600, depicts a somewhat squared-off peninsula with a misplaced Okeechobee. It is valuable for its list of place-names, from Santa Elena in the northeast around to Punta de Apalache in the west.

present-day Georgia. In 1596, the Spaniards took action by treaty, turning both Ais and Guale into provinces.

The Guale Rebellion of 1597, best known of the Florida revolts, began with the killing of five friars. The war lasted for six years, during which French corsairs came and went freely in Guale ports. At last, Governor Méndez Canzo defeated the rebel leader Juanillo and sentenced the people of his town, Tolomato, to service a portage near the capital. The province of Ais also rebelled in 1597, with more immediate consequences. A raid on the Ais town of Surruque yielded fifty captives, whom the governor condemned to terms of slavery and distributed among his men. Set free by royal order, the Surruque were relocated where they, too, could make themselves useful to the presidio, but Ais, unlike Guale, did not return to the fold. The Eastern Timucua did their share of rebelling. In 1629, in a spontaneous uprising at the ferry town of San Juan del Puerto, a cacica and her vassals freed her brother from soldiers who were taking him, bound, to St. Augustine. Governor Luis de Rojas y Borja sentenced the cacica to hanging and her confederates to exile and hard labor in Havana, with their ears docked.

War and disease worked in tandem to empty the eastern doctrinas. Between 1613 and 1617, half of the 16,000 converted Indians in Florida and an unknown number of other natives died of a "plague," and other epidemics followed. The colony was further beset by hurricanes and pirates. The great storm of 1622 was responsible for the loss of many ships between the Keys and Bermuda. For years afterward, salvors from St. Augustine haunted the wreck sites, while Dutch and English corsairs lurked near Cape Canaveral to chase their vessels onto the shoals. More than one supply ship trying to escape these enemies ran aground on the St. Augustine sandbar. Coastal Indians traded with the interlopers as they came ashore for wood and water. No help came from the Crown. Instead, the presidio found its reinforcements and matériel diverted to other garrisons. The situado fell years behind. It was a time of short rations and shorter wages. The low point was reached in 1628 when the corsair Piet Heyn captured the entire Fleet of the Indies off the coast of Cuba, with the subsidies for all the Caribbean, including Florida, aboard. Nor did a peace treaty in Europe end hostilities in America, where hundreds of unemployed soldiers and seamen turned to piracy.

Harassed by seaborne enemies and with dwindling resources in capital and labor, the colonists turned their energies inland. Franciscans made dramatic expeditions into new territory, with banners flying and escorts of Indian arquebusiers. There was even a resurgence of interest in Menéndez's Greater Florida. In the 1630s, Governor Rojas y Borja, alone, sent three successive parties of Indians and soldiers to investigate the stories of gold mines, diamonds, and freshwater pearls told by veterans of the Juan Pardo expeditions. Two parties turned back; the third reached fabled Cofitachequi, looted by Hernando de Soto over eighty years earlier. But the Crown refused to countenance a conquest that would push the northern boundary deep into the Appalachian Mountains.

The impulse for the second wave of expansion—the Farther Pacifications, lasting from the 1630s to around 1670—was not a royal initiative but came from within the colony. In the Gulf, floridanos scented opportunities for private trade as well as fresh sources of provisions and labor. Their first step was to "pacify" the Pohoy, Tocobaga, and Calusa who had long dominated the peninsula's Gulf Coast and rivers. Captain Juan Rodríguez de Cartaya made the western watershed safe for Christianity with a gunboat, and the result was the new mission province of Timucua, of which the northern part was sometimes called Timucua Alta, or Yustaga.

In 1633, at long last, Governor Luis de Horruytiner was ready to let the Franciscans carry the Evangel into fertile and populous Apalachee, in the Red Hills surrounding present-day Tallahassee. That province's port, he assured the Council of the Indies, would provide the Fleet with a haven from storms and corsairs, serve as a supply depot for the western missions, and guarantee the food supply for St. Augustine's 500 inhabitants. Boatloads of corn would leave the Apalachee port (San Marcos) and follow the curving coast to a Timucua port (San Martín), where the corn could be transferred to pack animals and taken overland to the capital. Something the governor did not mention was the rapidly growing city of Havana, a short week's sail from the fields of Apalachee.

The populous new provinces replenished the number of peasant farmers and repartimiento laborers in Florida. At the same time, the new ports on Gulf rivers offered outlets for a flourishing coastal trade with Havana in cured deerskins, dried corn and beans, chickens, hogs, and ranch products and drew Caribbean buccaneers into Gulf waters. That the traffic with Cuba was untaxed and unlawful and that foreign vessels were entering the western ports did not trouble caciques or floridanos. Even the friars participated, raising hogs and increasing the size of their sabanas with the object of adorning churches and bringing comfort to convents.

In the middle half of the seventeenth century, royal support for soldiers, friars, and caciques became increasingly irregular. Deeply involved in European wars and peninsular rebellions, Spain could scarcely maintain the centers, much less the peripheries. The situado was stolen by pirates, lost at sea, swamped in red tape, or sequestered by the king's command for more urgent needs. For years at a time it was not paid at all. Although eventually most of the funds would be replaced, their arrival was so unpredictable that the colony learned to rely less on the metropolis and more on its own devices.

During periods of wavering royal support, the demands on Christian Indians rose. When the situado failed to materialize, chiefs who had not received the gifts that reinforced their authority were pressed all the more urgently to have their vassals feed the Spanish. Secondary garrisons were stationed in the provincial capitals of San Luis de

Apalachee, San Francisco de Potano (in Timucua), and Santa Catalina de Guale. Settlements of floridano traders and ranchers grew up around these garrisons, and the provincial settlers, too, expected to be supplied with laborers. Natives in the provinces now had not only caciques and friars to feed but soldiers and "people of quality" as well. Juana Caterina de Florencia, wife of the deputy governor of Apalachee, expected to be supplied with fish, milk, and six women to grind corn.

Because the waters around the peninsula were dangerous and the journey by sea was long, and because cart roads were nonexistent and pack animals scarce, most of the freight between St. Augustine and San Luis was carried on Indian backs. The yearly ration for a Franciscan weighed no less than 1,800 pounds. As the number of friars increased and the supply lines to the western doctrinas lengthened to seventy leagues and longer, more and more burdener-days were required to deliver religious rations, and the packs did not travel back to St. Augustine empty but full of products from the provinces. Two mid-seventeenth-century west coast Indian rebellions would be blamed on burdening, with the friars pointing at the governors and the governors at the friars.

Governor Benito Ruíz de Salazar y Vallecilla, who secured the governorship of Florida in 1645 by promising to build a galleon, marshaled the colony's resources and embarked on a program of economic development. While the king's galleon took shape in the shipyards of Campeche, Yucatan, Salazar y Vallecilla sent the soldiers of the San Luis garrison north into Apalachicola with trade goods to exchange for deerskins. To remedy the shortage of beasts of burden he began to breed mules, and on the border between Yustaga and Apalachee he started a wheat farm.

These enterprises received a series of setbacks. The first was the Apalachee Rebellion of 1647, a kind of civil war between Christian and non-Christian chiefs. No sooner was it suppressed than the colony was stricken with the yellow fever that was sweeping through Caribbean ports. The "black vomit" killed indiscriminately—whites and blacks as well as Indians—and among the many who died was the governor. Development was interrupted a third time by the Timucua Rebellion of 1656, triggered by Governor Diego de Rebolledo's mobilization of the Indian militia after the English capture of Jamaica. Disease, famine, and fugitivism wreaked demographic havoc in central Florida. Outside of Yustaga, Timucua Province had too few inhabitants even to service the transportation network.

St. Augustine itself was badly shaken in 1668 when the privateer

Robert Searles, with a patent issued by the Jamaican governor, sacked the city, killing more than a hundred people in the streets and rounding up everyone who looked African or Indian to be sold as a slave. The colony was too strategic to be abandoned to the English, as many thought it must be. Queen Regent Mariana ordered the viceroy of New Spain to make Florida a priority, bring its situado up to date, increase the Franciscan fund enough to replace the forty-three friars on the rolls with soldiers, and begin sending the Florida treasury an extra 10,000 pesos yearly with which to construct a fort of stone instead of the usual wood. In 1670, the founding of Charleston by settlers from Barbados underscored the urgency of defense measures, and the queen increased the garrison from 300 to 350 men.

Floridanos, who regarded militia service as something for Indians, appropriated a tenth of the billets in the garrison as reserve officers, or *reformados,* who received the pay of a soldier but were exempt from guard duty. They had already naturalized the benefice and lesser positions of the parish, the office of public notary, the two proprietary offices of the treasury—offices so important that those who held them doubled as a municipal council, or *cabildo,* to advise the governor—and its clerkships, and the position of defender of the Indians, which they were seeking to make permanent and salaried.

Among Florida's notable families, the Menéndez Marquéses stood out for their able family strategy. Descended from Juan Menéndez Marqués and María Menéndez y Posada, two close relatives of the sixteenth-century governor Pedro Menéndez Marqués, himself a nephew of Pedro Menéndez de Avilés, the family maintained its position and fortunes for 150 years through marriage, treasury offices, military offices, Cuban commerce, unofficial borrowing from the situado, and cattle ranching. Don Thomás Menéndez Marqués was typical. From his ranch at La Chua in the depopulated savannahs of central Florida, he shipped tallow, hides, and dried beef out the San Martín (Suwannee–Santa Fe) River and down to Havana. Although his brother, father, and grandfather had all been royal officials of the treasury, and he, his son, and his grandson would follow their lead, don Thomás had no compunction about avoiding customs duties. Floridanos honored the king's person, not his regulations, which they did not hesitate to evade or appeal.

All told, the building of St. Augustine's stone fort, the Castillo de San Marcos (Castle of Saint Mark), took twenty-four years and cost the Crown over 138,000 pesos, much of it going for Indian labor in the shellstone quarries on Anastasia Island. Twice as many native workmen were stationed at the capital as formerly; many brought their families and settled down. The influx of money and people caused prices to rise, stimulating agriculture and ranches like don Thomás's La Chua. Even so, there were times when the royal storehouses were empty and governors had to seize the stores of private individuals. It was dangerous to do this to friars or priests, who could quickly close ranks against someone who threatened their prerogatives. Governor Juan Márquez Cabrera alienated the religious establishment throughout his administration (1680–87). In one typical instance, he ordered Captain Francisco de Fuentes, lieutenant governor of Guale, to seize some corn belonging to Father Juan de Uzeda, doctrinero of San José de Zapala, in order to provide rations for refugees from Santa Catalina de Guale who had been asked to build a fort on Sapelo Island. Denied the sacraments for his various offenses, the governor deserted his post. Governor Diego de Quiroga y Losada similarly made an enemy of parish priest Alonso de Leturiondo by exercising eminent domain over his corncrib. The priest responded by padlocking the parish church on the Feastday of St. Mark and doing his part to ruin Quiroga in the lengthy judicial review, or *residencia*, that followed every governor's term of office.

In the late seventeenth century, Florida regained its sixteenth-century reputation as a land of constant war. The provinces came under attack seasonally by pirates and by slave-raiding Indians armed with English firearms in the southeastern version of the proxy war. Yet the new royal funds for fortifications were absorbed by the castillo, with little to spare for the defense of the provinces. When the viceroy of New Spain sent an extra 6,000 pesos with which to build a stone tower on Cumberland Island for the protection of the Guale, Governor Laureano de Torres y Ayala spent it on a seawall for St. Augustine.

North of Apalachee, in the province of Apalachicola, traders from Charleston were replacing the Spanish as buyers of deerskins. Although the Apalachicola were not Christians, as allies and trading partners they had fallen within the Spanish sphere of influence since the 1640s. Florida governors tried to counter the Anglo advance with gifts, warnings, hastily founded missions, and a blockhouse to serve as a trading post, but the lure of English manufactures proved too strong. The Apalachicola moved out of the Spanish orbit and into the English one, to reenter history under the name of Creeks. Between 1680 and 1706, a major part of the Indians in the provinces also withdrew their allegiance, silently deserting their doctrinas for a life of liberty without friars, soldiers, or chiefs who were more Spanish than Indian.

The first to defect were the Guale, whose towns on the sea islands had become magnets for pirates and other predators. The Guale's declining numbers were temporarily masked by a contrary influx of Yamasee moving down the Atlantic coast. By 1696, when the Quaker Jonathan Dickinson passed through Florida, three towns of refugees on Amelia Island were all that remained of Guale province. The last to leave were the Apalachee, who forsook their province after it was invaded by Creeks and Carolinians in 1704 during Queen Anne's War (see chapter 5). Some of the Apalachee fled to Pensacola, refounded in 1698 to counter French influence in the Gulf. Some, under don Patricio de Hinachuba, chief of Ivitachuco, migrated to Timucua, then to the environs of St. Augustine, where they hoped to find safety under the guns of the fort. Others left Apalachee for parts unknown, saying that they would not stay to die with Spaniards.

The kings of Spain had seen themselves as patrons of the Florida Indians and the Indians as wards of the Crown. Royal alms supported their missionaries, royal subsidies regaled their chiefs, and a royal defender of the Indians represented their interests. But wars in Europe, spilling into America, strained the royal revenues and patrimony to the limit. The Spanish elite, floridanos and Spaniards alike, survived the war years by demanding advances of goods and services from people who were in no position to deny them. At such times, the colony survived because it was ideologically reinforced. The "cult of the king" threw a mantle of duty about forced loans and labor, while the "divine cult" taught Indians that they, like women, were natural inferiors.

To many Spaniards, Florida must have seemed a native Utopia. In this maritime periphery of strategic rather than economic importance, the goals of peaceful evangelism were largely met. Indians were not enslaved; their lands were not alienated; their lives were not shortened in mines or workhouses. Territorial expansion observed the forms of the Conquest by Contract. The rulers of the Republic of Indians, mission-trained, channeled the labor and products of Indian peasants to the priests, fighting men, and merchants of the Republic of Spaniards. In exchange, the natives were offered an afterlife in heaven, a sanctuary on earth, and useful tools, plants, and animals.

But pacification, Spain's idealistic design for the mastery of North America, depended on enduring hierarchies and exclusive relationships. The isolation on which it depended was repeatedly breached, giving common Indians a chance to show how little they cared for lords of any kind. When, in the last quarter of the seventeenth century, increasing royal investments and increasing demands on the natives strengthened the colony's center at the expense of its peripheries, the mission hinterland—source of food, labor, and exports—sloughed away, and with it went the comparatively enlightened system of the two Republics.

Bibliography

Andrews, Evangeline Walker, and Charles McLean Andrews, eds. *Jonathan Dickinson's Journal or, God's Protecting Providence.* New Haven: Yale University Press, 1945.

Bushnell, Amy Turner. "How to Fight a Pirate: Provincials, Royalists, and the Defense of Minor Ports During the Age of Buccaneers." *Gulf Coast Historical Review* 5, no. 2 (1990):18–35.

———. *The King's Coffer: Proprietors of the Spanish Florida Treasury, 1565–1702.* Gainesville: University Presses of Florida, 1981.

———. "The Menéndez Márquez Cattle Barony at La Chua and the Determinants of Economic Expansion in Seventeenth-Century Florida." *Florida Historical Quarterly* 56, no. 4 (April 1978):407–31.

———. "The Noble and Loyal City, 1565–1668." In *The Oldest City. St. Augustine: Saga of Survival,* edited by Jean Parker Waterbury, pp. 27–55. St. Augustine: St. Augustine Historical Society, 1983.

———. "Patricio de Hinachuba: Defender of the Word of God, the Crown of the King, and the Little Children of Ivitachuco." *American Indian Culture and Research Journal* 3, no. 3 (1979):1–21.

———. "Ruling the Republic of Indians in Seventeenth-Century Florida." In *Powhatan's Mantle: Indians in the Colonial Southeast,* edited by Peter H. Wood, Gregory A. Waselkov, and M. Thomas Hatley, pp. 134–50. Lincoln: University of Nebraska Press, 1989.

———. "The Sacramental Imperative: Catholic Ritual and Indian Sedentism in the Provinces of Florida." In *Columbian Consequences,* edited by David Hurst Thomas, vol. 2: *Archaeological and Historical Perspectives on the Spanish Borderlands East,* pp. 475–90. Washington: Smithsonian Institution Press, 1990.

———. *Situado and Sabana: Spain's Support System for the Presidio and Mission Provinces of Florida.* Anthropological Papers of the American Museum of Natural History, no. 74; third in the series The Archaeology of Mission Santa Catalina de Guale. New York: AMNH, 1994.

———. "'That Demonic Game': The Campaign to Stop Indian Pelota Playing in Spanish Florida, 1675–1684." *The Americas* 35, no. 1 (July 1978):1–19.

Geiger, Maynard. *The Franciscan Conquest of Florida (1573–1618).* Washington: Catholic University of America, 1937.

George, Paul S., ed. *A Guide to the History of Florida.* Westport, Conn.: Greenwood Press, 1989.

Hann, John H. *Apalachee: The Land Between the Rivers.* Gainesville: University Presses of Florida, 1988.

Hudson, Charles. *The Juan Pardo Expeditions: Exploration of the Carolinas and Tennessee, 1566–1568.* Washington: Smithsonian Institution Press, 1990.

Lockhart, James, and Stuart B. Schwartz. *Early Latin America: A History of Colonial Spanish America and Brazil.* London and New York: Cambridge University Press, 1985.

McAlister, Lyle N. *Spain and Portugal in the New World, 1492–1700.* Minneapolis:University of Minnesota Press, 1984.

Milanich, Jerald T. *Florida Indians and the Invasion from Europe.* Gainesville: University Press of Florida, 1995.

Waselkov, Gregory A. "Seventeenth-Century Trade in the Colonial Southeast." *Southeastern Archaeology* 8, no. 2 (1989):117–60.

Weber, David J. *The Spanish Frontier in North America.* New Haven and London: Yale University Press, 1992.

Worth, John E. *The Struggle for the Georgia Coast: An Eighteenth-Century Spanish Retrospective on Guale and Mocama.* Anthropological Papers of the American Museum of Natural History, no. 75; fourth in the series The Archaeology of Mission Santa Catalina de Guale. New York: AMNH, 1995.

5 The Missions of Spanish Florida

John H. Hann

Missions in Florida, as in other parts of the Spanish New World, sought to spread the knowledge and message of Christ to native peoples. Their goal was to persuade the natives to accept Catholicism and allegiance to the king of Spain. Establishment of missions assumed special importance in the Spanish New World under Pope Alexander VI's grant of exclusive dominion in the New World to Spain's monarchs because the grant was justified by the Crown's assumption of the obligation of preaching Christ's teachings to the natives. The royal contract given to Florida's founder, Menéndez de Avilés, clearly included the obligation to bring clergymen to instruct the natives in the Christian faith.

People may not associate missions with Spanish Florida as readily as they link them with the early Spanish experience from Texas through California. But missions played no less a role in Florida than they did elsewhere in the establishment of Spanish control. During the 138 years of Florida's mission era, 1567 to 1705, missions were attempted or established among at least eleven distinct Indian peoples at about eighty mission centers that served a far greater number of individual villages and hamlets. Almost all of this was the work of Spanish Franciscans. The missions existing simultaneously numbered forty-four by the mid-1630s and probably increased by a few more over the next ten years as new missions appeared among the Apalachee of the Tallahassee region. The number may have begun to contract by 1650, if not before. Twenty thousand Indians had been baptized by

1630, and more than 50,000 others catechized. Only twenty-seven Franciscans were then available to staff the thirty-two missions, which served more than two hundred settlements, sixty of which had churches. Thirty-five Franciscans served 30,000 Christian Indians by 1635. Contraction had definitely set in by 1655, when there were about forty missions. The thirty-six that had friars held only 26,000 Christian Indians by then. A 1656 revolt, the turmoil that followed, and the spread of diseases further hastened the decline.

The relatively successful missions stretched from just south of St. Augustine northward along the coast through Georgia almost to the Savannah River. They reached westward across north Florida to the Apalachicola and extended into parts of south Georgia west of the Okefenokee Swamp. They penetrated central Florida along the St. Johns River for an undefined distance south of Lake George, possibly reached farther south along the Oklawaha, and probably went farthest south in Marion County to the vicinity of the Cove of the Withlacoochee. Apalachee, Guale of the north Georgia coast, and various Timucua-speaking groups constituted the majority of the missionized natives. The Apalachee lived between the Aucilla and Ochlockonee rivers. Timucua-speakers occupied all of north Florida east of Jefferson County, much of the eastern half of Georgia below the Altamaha River, coastal Florida southward to the vicinity of Daytona Beach, and central Florida southward along the rivers for an undefined distance. Tama-Yamasee, Chine, Amacano, Pacara, and Chacato, Mayaca-speakers, and a few Sabacola comprised the remainder. The Tama, from north-central Georgia, migrated to Apalachee to be missionized. Yamasee, also from north-central Georgia, migrated to Apalachee, to coastal Georgia, and to Mayaca-speaking territory along the upper St. Johns River. The Sabacola lived along the Chattahoochee River. The Chine and Chacato migrated to Apalachee from the Florida Panhandle. The Amacano and Pacara, linguistic brothers of the Chine, were living with the Chine on Apalachee Bay's Spring Creek when the Chine mission was established in 1674.

In general, Florida's mission experience paralleled that of other frontier territories of the Iberian New World, but its experience was unique in a number of ways because of various interrelated factors. First, and foremost, soldiers rather than settlers remained the core of most of Florida's Spanish families, even though historian Eugene Lyon has recently revised our image of early Spanish Florida as little more than a bleak and often starving garrison town. The relative lack of settlers and the Crown's close supervision of developments in Florida spared its natives from some of Spain's most exploitative economic institutions. The Crown checked the several attempts to introduce enslavement of the natives. Tribute was not a regular part of the formal Spanish regime in Florida. Spaniards introduced tribute to a degree in an informal sense. In areas where soldiers were introduced some time after the establishment of missions, natives were expected to contribute some of the food those soldiers consumed, although there was no uniform policy in this matter. Similarly, natives carried soldiers' bedding from post to post without pay as a service to the king. The paid labor draft known as the repartimiento was the sole formalized, economically exploitative institution imposed on Florida's natives in general.

Although economic considerations were a factor motivating establishment of missions in Florida, none is known to have become an economic enterprise dominated by friars in the way of the typical California mission. Except for the earliest approaches to coastal natives in the 1560s, missionaries began their work unaccompanied by soldiers and, with few exceptions, at the invitation of elements among the native leaders rather than by thrusting themselves uninvited upon the indigenous societies. By the last years of the sixteenth century, leaders from interior provinces, where no Spanish conquest of the Indians preceded establishment of the mission, began to render obedience to Spain's king and to ask for missionaries.

On the other hand, missions were not the major feature in Spain's initial approaches to Florida's natives that they were in the Spanish domination of Texas and California. The first missionaries were overshadowed by the adelantado, Menéndez de Avilés, and his soldiers or by his governor-successors and their soldiers. With the possible exception of some coastal missions and a few tribes from distant hinterland frontiers, the practice of bringing natives to mission centers at places chosen by the missionaries was not employed in Florida as it was in California. Florida Franciscans established their missions in preexisting villages. In contrast to the Franciscans who established the first missions in New Mexico and Alta or Upper California, Florida's Franciscans did not bring large herds of cattle, horses, or sheep to strengthen their hand in convincing natives to accept their tutelage. There is no evidence that the Spanish authorities induced Florida's Indians to adopt a Spanish-type roster of governor, lieutenant-governor, alcalde, or mayor, and *alguacil*, or peace-officer, for their villages as was done in New Mexico. Except for the installation of the Spanish governor or his lieutenants as supreme authority over each native polity, a traditional roster of native political officials remained largely unchanged and unchallenged. Such differences doubtless were among the reasons that the new faith seemingly held stronger sway over Florida's natives than it did over New Mexico's Pueblo during an equivalent span of time, that Florida's mission structures retained their original simplicity, and that the natives' council house continued to be the mission villages' most impressive and most frequented building.

Members of the Society of Jesus (Jesuits), who made the first mission efforts in Florida, uniformly met resistance, even though the missionaries were accompanied by soldiers. Jesuits are members of a religious society founded in 1534 and devoted to missionary and educational work. They worked briefly at single sites among southwest Florida's Calusa, the Miami area's Tequesta, the Escamacu in the region of Beaufort, South Carolina, and at Tupiqui and one or more other places in Guale. Some of the resistance was doubtless a legacy of de Soto's brutal passage through Florida or was influenced by the natives' contact with the French just before the Jesuits' arrival. But, more fundamentally, the Jesuits met resistance to their message everywhere as soon as they spoke ill of the natives' deities or when they revealed that the natives would have to abandon polygyny, sororal marriage, and other customs on becoming Christians. Soldiers' demands for food and friction with natives also handicapped the Jesuits' efforts. The soldiers' killing of two successive head chiefs and other nobles at Calusa precipitated flight by the rest of the inhabitants, which ended the mission effort among them until late in the seventeenth century. The Jesuits viewed friction or hostilities between soldiers and natives as insuperable obstacles, responsible for their failure.

In reality, from Calusa and Tequesta to Guale and Escamacu, the Jesuits dealt with natives whose confidence in their own value system and worldview had not been shaken sufficiently to make them susceptible to the European Christian message. However much Jesuits might browbeat the Indians with their superior training in rhetoric and logic, they could not move them to abandon their beliefs. Everywhere in Florida, Jesuits made their efforts before the time was right. For the Calusa and other nonagricultural Indians of south Florida, the time would never be right. The Indians' killing of Jesuits who had gone to the Chesapeake Bay region caused withdrawal of the society from Florida in 1572. But their work among the natives had ceased prior to their leaving.

Down to 1595 little is known about the activity of the first Franciscans, who came in 1573. Franciscans were members of the religious community formally called Order of Friars Minor, founded in Italy by

St. Francis of Assisi in 1209. They dedicated themselves especially to preaching in the growing cities of medieval Europe, to missions among non-Christians, and to charitable work. They emphasized humility and were usually referred to as friars, a term derived from the French word for "brother."

In Florida the friars had their earliest success among Salt- and Freshwater Timucua living near St. Augustine and on the St. Johns River in the latter part of the 1570s. Surprisingly, Jesuits appear to have made no effort in those regions despite the Freshwater Timucua's friendship with Menéndez de Avilés from the beginning and despite his friendly relations with some Saltwater Timucua as well. At the start, as Eugene Lyon has noted, a language barrier, a lack of trained missionaries, and unsettled relations with Saltwater Timucua limited religious contact. The Jesuits may have passed over the St. Augustine region initially because one of the first three to arrive was killed by Timucua-speaking Mocama just to the north of the mouth of the St. Johns River when he was stranded on shore with some sailors.

Nombre de Dios is considered the oldest of Florida's enduring missions. Work among its people and the Freshwater Timucua of San Sebastian, just to the south of St. Augustine, appears to have begun around 1577. But people of both villages attended Mass in St. Augustine until 1587, when the first formal missions, known as doctrinas, appear to have been established in both villages. San Juan del Puerto, at the mouth of the St. Johns River, was also founded by 1587. A bridgehead represented by the Franciscans' conversion of a Guale head chief disappeared quickly when that chief was killed by a nephew of another chief whom he had confronted over disrespect for his authority. The Spanish governor's reluctant hanging of the nephew at the insistence of the deceased chief's wife precipitated revolt from Guale north to South Carolina's Escamacu-Orista. The revolt precluded missionary work in that region at least until 1588, when San Pedro Mocama was founded on Georgia's Cumberland Island. Family ties between chiefs of Nombre de Dios, San Juan, and San Pedro may have facilitated mission activity at this date, as had arrival of a new band of friars in 1587. By 1588 at least five missions and a number of outstations, or visitas, existed among Fresh- and Saltwater Timucua.

Arrival of more friars in 1594 permitted a major effort among the Guale. Six friars were working there by 1597. By then friars were making sorties into hinterland Timucua villages whose chiefs had responded favorably to a new governor's invitation to render obedience to his king and to receive gifts the king had sent to those ready to give that obedience. But later that same year, a general uprising of the Guale interrupted the mission effort, as they killed five of their six friars and carried off the sixth one to an inland town to serve his captors as a slave. An imprudent friar's effort to block the rise to head chieftainship of a young Christianized chief who refused to abandon polygyny precipitated the trouble, but the support given the uprising suggests that the discontent involved more than the sexual mores of one individual. The friars' baptism of natives before telling them clearly about the scope of the obligations they were assuming in accepting baptism and about the tribute and labor demands of Spanish civil authorities were factors as well. In the uprising's wake, the governor reduced the maize tribute for the Mocamas to a symbolic six ears for each married Indian. A young Spaniard shipwrecked on Guale's coast in 1595 placed part of the blame on earlier atrocities committed by soldiers on punitive expeditions. The governor's sustained campaign of fire and blood eventually broke the solidarity of the Guales. A majority, coalescing behind a new leader, sued for peace and agreed to capture or kill the rebellion's initial leaders in the inland region where they had taken refuge to escape Spanish retaliation.

Rapid growth resumed in 1607 when arrival of a few new friars made it possible to capitalize on the interest in Christianization shown by some among the hinterland tribes ten years earlier. In that year the friars established the first new missions among Timucua-speakers known as Potano living in the vicinity of Gainesville. Within several years, a friar descending the Santa Fe to the Suwannee established a mission on the Gulf in a village named Cofa at the mouth of the Suwannee. From Potano, friars moved into Columbia County to work among Timucua-speakers identified as Utina. In 1623 friars began to work among other Timucua-speakers known as Yustaga, living between the Suwannee and Aucilla rivers. Friars also resurrected the Guale missions and began work in the remaining Timucua-speaking provinces of mainland south Georgia's coast and hinterland, Acuera along the Oklawaha, and Ocale south of Potano. Two friars began formal missionization of Apalachee in 1633. It was the last of the major mission provinces to be established until late in the century. A mission at Mayaca on the St. Johns River south of Lake George consolidated work done by visiting friars prior to 1602.

Evidence to account for the change of heart that made that expansion possible is fragmentary. In addition to the attraction of the gifts being offered, a series of Spanish successes against French intruders enhanced the Spaniards' image as allies worth cultivating. A personal embassy by

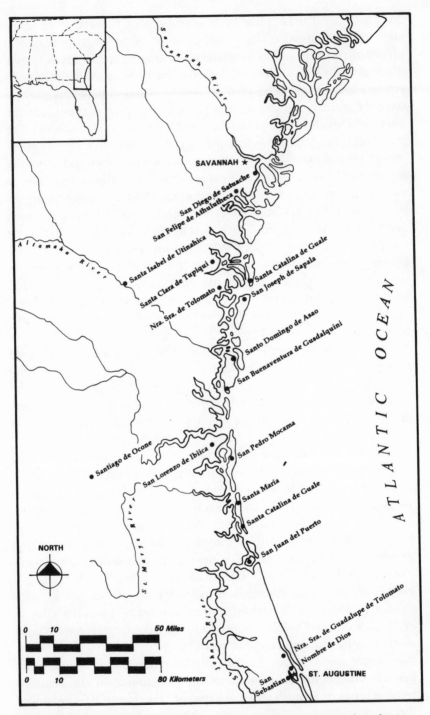

Names and locations of Franciscan missions at St. Augustine and north along the Atlantic Coast in the seventeenth century.

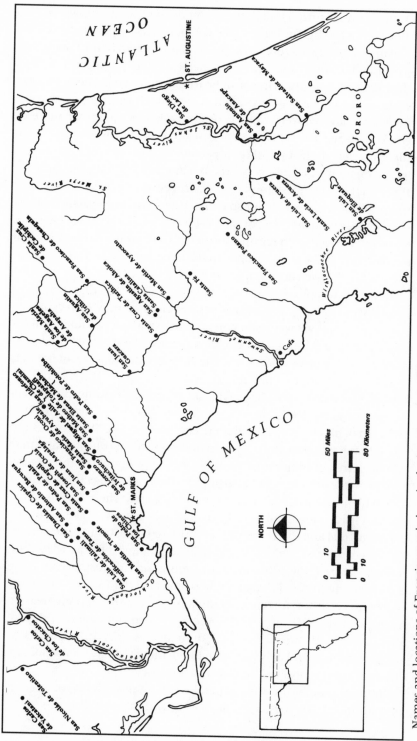

Names and locations of Franciscan missions in the interior of Florida in the seventeenth century.

a leading Christianized Indian from Nombre de Dios may have swayed Utina's most prestigious leader. Use of a mailed fist to punish the killing of Spaniards brought a reversal of hostility on the part of the Potano and Surruque. For some, such as Utina's head chief and Apalachee leaders who asked for friars, the change of heart may have been abetted by loss of faith in the native religious system as a bulwark for their power. Such chiefs may have viewed exotic goods provided by Spaniards and esoteric knowledge and skills Spaniards made available as enhancing the chiefs' prestige in the eyes of their people. That may explain the eagerness of many of the early converts to learn to read and write and the Utina chief's willingness to permit destruction of the idols in five villages under his immediate jurisdiction. The Apalachee leaders' request for friars was motivated in part at least by belief that a Spanish alliance would enable leaders to regain control over their subjects that they had lost. For that and other reasons, Spanish authorities delayed the missionization of Apalachee for a generation.

Florida's missions contrast with those of California in that their friars generally did not alter the natives' settlement pattern, which consisted of a large central village under a head chief, smaller ones under subordinate chiefs, and still smaller chiefless hamlets. Friars established their doctrinas in the head villages, visiting subordinate villages and hamlets to give instructions and building churches in some of the subordinate villages. Some such subordinate villages eventually became missions, at least for a time. In 1602, however, a friar advocated consolidation of the many small hamlets surrounding the coastal missions. There is no indication that it was done, but as populations dwindled consolidation may have occurred in some cases. In Apalachee, best known of the mission provinces, the settlement pattern persisted virtually intact until destruction of the missions in 1704. Guale is the one area where consolidation and extensive moving about of missions is known to have occurred. Between 1604 and the 1670s many Christian Guale from former mainland doctrinas and their subordinate villages moved to the islands off Georgia's coast. Little is known of the timing and circumstances of those moves, except for the Tolomato, whose chief led the 1597 revolt. In the 1620s the governor pressured its inhabitants to move to a site near St. Augustine to provide ferry service and assist in the unloading of ships at St. Augustine. In this earlier period greater security from attacks by Westo and Yuchi probably motivated such moves. A later consolidation on Amelia Island resulted from British attacks.

Florida's inland missions in general were not missions of conquest as were those of the coast to a degree. This difference also sets those missions apart from those of New Mexico and California. Soldiers did not accompany the first friars who began work in the hinterland, following a policy laid down explicitly by the Crown in that era. This seemingly posed no problem for the friars in Utina, but the situation was different in Potano, Yustaga, and Apalachee. Even though Potano's head chief had been baptized in St. Augustine prior to the launching of the formal mission effort in his land, his authority did not suffice to assure the priests a friendly reception. Jeering, jostling, and even threats of bodily harm greeted the friars' first efforts there. The first friars venturing into Apalachee between 1608 and 1612 at the invitation of its most prestigious chief were twice forced to leave because of the unruliness of Indians who did not obey their chiefs well. In deferring the effort there, both governor and friars cited a need for soldiers among their reasons for doing so. Yustaga's head chief initially refused friars entry to work in his territory. Even after admitting two friars, for a time he forbade any of his subjects to be baptized. In the hinterland, Spaniards resorted to a degree of compulsion only among the Chacato of the Panhandle, a few months after the launching of missions there, when opposition to the friars' presence developed.

Steady and, at times, spectacular shrinking of the population accompanied spread of the missions, resulting largely from the Indians' exposure to new diseases brought by outsiders. The magnitude of the population loss is unknown because demographic information is scant and usually imprecise. There are no global estimates for any people in the sixteenth century and none for the first three-quarters of the seventeenth century, except for the Apalachee.

The size of Guale's population in the 1560s or later when they began to be Christianized is among the least known. The only data recorded are that more than 1,200 had been baptized by 1597, that Guale were more populous in 1602 than the coastal and Freshwater Timucua, and that 756 Guale were confirmed by Cuba's bishop in 1606. There are no indications of the size of individual villages until 1675.

For coastal and Freshwater Timucua in the 1560s there are offhand statements about the numbers of warriors whom leaders assembled on several occasions. Based on those statements, demographer Henry Dobyns suggested a total Saltwater population of 7,500 to 10,000 for that era. In 1602, friars provided precise figures on the Christian population of each of the three Saltwater missions of that period (San Pedro 792, San Juan 500, Nombre de Dios 200) and, in the case of San Pedro, figures for its individual subordinate villages. The figures for San Pedro (500) represented the entire population of Cumberland

Island at that time. Six Freshwater villages on the St. Johns and Mayaca held about 200 Christians in 1602, and Mayaca had about 100 people yet to be baptized. The other Freshwater villages on the St. Johns presumably were still heathen. Most of San Sebastian's people perished in a hurricane shortly before 1602. In 1606 a visiting bishop from Cuba confirmed 1,003 Saltwater Timucua and 315 Freshwater Timucua and Mayaca. On the south Georgia coastal mainland, the 1,100 people in Ycafui's eight villages had been catechized by 1602, but the 700 to 800 in Ibi's five settlements were still heathen. The scant data for the 1560s suggest that the Saltwater and Freshwater Timucua populations had declined drastically by 1602.

Among the hinterland Timucua in this period the data are best for Potano. Early in November of 1607, two friars reported more than 1,000 adult baptisms among the Potano over the previous year. The friar who launched the work in four settlements in the vicinity of Gainesville baptized the 400 people of each of two of the settlements and 200 people in a third. Together with the children they were a major portion of the more than 4,000 baptized between mid-1606 and the end of 1607. By then another 1,000-plus were being catechized. Over the next nine years the number of Christianized natives rose to over 16,000, but a series of epidemics beginning in 1614 halved that Christian population and undoubtedly took an equally heavy toll on the non-Christianized who were in contact with them.

We have the fewest data about the size of Utina's population in the mission era and earlier. Hernando de Soto found it to be more populous and better provisioned than lands such as Potano that he had passed through earlier. A remark in 1616 that after the first five years of a friars' work at Tarihica there were 712 living Christian Indians may provide an indicator of Utina mission size. If Tarihica's Christian population lost half its numbers in the 1614–16 epidemics, it would rank with the largest Apalachee mission centers of 1675, as did the head chief's jurisdiction of Ayaocuto with its 1,500 people distributed over five settlements.

Dobyns used a French remark that Yustaga's head chief of the 1560s could put 3,000 or 4,000 warriors in battle to estimate a total population of 15,000 or 20,000. The baptism of 13,000 people during the first twelve years of the friars' work in Yustaga suggests at least that large a population, as does the marked preponderance of Yustaga among western Timucua's surviving population in 1675.

Global estimates made from 1608 to the 1630s placed Apalachee's population during those years at 30,000 to 34,000. Other estimates

An artistic reconstruction of the Franciscan mission church of San Luis de Talimali at Tallahassee. Archaeological excavations reveal that the Apalachee churches were constructed of plank and thatch. The dimensions of this particular church in the Florida hinterland, 110 by 50 feet, make it as large as the seventeenth-century parish church in the capital city of St. Augustine. Artist: John LoCastro; original watercolor, 1993, "Afternoon at Mission San Luis."

from the 1630s placed it at 15,000 or 16,000. A friar gave a late 1640s figure of 20,000. The higher estimates are not inconceivable in view of Apalachee's surviving population of about 10,000 as late as 1675. At the start of missionization in the 1630s that population was distributed over more than forty settlements under the jurisdiction of ten principal chiefs who headed the missions in existence in 1657. Until the 1650s Apalachee was less affected by epidemics than were the other mission territories.

By the 1670s an eleventh Apalachee mission had been established, and the province was host to six or more other peoples who migrated into the province. Three missions were established among the immigrant Chine, Amacano, Pacara, Chacato, and Tama-Yamasee. The sixth group, Tocobaga from the Tampa Bay region, apparently never showed interest in receiving a friar. The Chacato migrants were refugees from one of the last efforts to expand the scope of the missions. In mid-1674, two months after the establishment of the Chine-Amacano-Pacara mission, friars established two missions in the Chacato homeland near Marianna, which ended a year later with the revolt and flight of most of the Chacato. A contemporaneous short-lived third mission on the Apalachicola River served a small band of Sabacola who had migrated downriver from the vicinity of Columbus, Georgia.

Governor Pablo de Hita Salazar gave impetus to the last expansion of the Florida missions. It began with resurrection of missions at Anacape near Welatka and Mayaca to serve Yamasee who had moved to the upper St. Johns River. Friars then moved southward from Mayaca into the lakes district to establish five short-lived missions among the Mayaca-speaking Jororo and the Aypaja by the 1690s. The effort collapsed essentially in 1696–97 when the Jororo of Atoyquime killed their friar and his Guale assistants. A renewed approach to the Calusa in September 1697 ended several months later when Indians stripped the friars of even their clothing and deposited them on Matecumbe Key, where a Spanish vessel eventually rescued them.

The following is a listing of the more enduring missions arranged by province or geographic area. Those marked with a pound sign probably had died out by 1655. Those marked with an asterisk had ceased to exist by 1675 or had merged with another mission. Population statistics are given for most of the missions that existed in 1675 and in 1689. The first figure is the one for 1675.

Coastal Timucua

Nombre de Dios	—	100
San Sebastian#		
San Juan del Puerto	30	125
San Pedro Mocama*		
San Buenaventura de Guadalquini	40	300
San Lorenzo de Ibiica#		
Santiago de Ocone*		

St. Johns and Ocklawaha valleys

San Antonio de Anacape*	—	150
San Diego de Laca or Salamototo	40	200
San Salvador de Mayaca*		
Santa Lucia de Acuera*		
San Luis de Acuera or Avino*		

Guale and other north Georgia missions

Santa Catalina de Guale	140	150
Santo Domingo de Asao or Talaje	30	125
San Pedro or San Felipe de Athuluteca	36	200
Santa Clara de Tupiqui*		
San Diego de Satuache*		
San Joseph de Sapala	50	—
Nra. Sra. de Guadalupe de Tolomato	—	125

Western Timucua

San Francisco de Potano	60	125
Santa Fé	110	180
San Martín de Ayaocuto*		
Sta. Cruz de Tarihica	80	100
San Agustín or/and Sta. Catalina de Ahoica	60	200
Sta. Catalina	80	—
San Juan Guacara	80	150
Sta. Cruz de Cachipile*		
San Agustín de Urihica*		
San Francisco de Chuaquin*		
San Ildefonso de Chamini*		
Sta. María de los Angeles de Arapaha*		
Sta. Isabel de Utinahica#		
San Luis de Eloquale (Ocale)#		
San Pedro y San Pablo de Potohiriba	300	750
Sta. Elena de Machaba	300	500
San Matheo de Tolapatafi	300	250
San Miguel de Asile	40	150

Chacato

San Carlos de Yatcatani	400	150
San Nicolas de Tolentino	100	350

Apalachee

San Lorenzo de Ivitachuco	1200	1000
San Luis de Talimali	1400	1500
Sta. María de Ayubale	800	1200
San Francisco de Oconi	200	400
San Joseph de Ocuia	900	1000
San Juan de Aspalaga	800	250

San Pedro y San Pablo de Patale	500	600
San Antonio de Bacuqua	120	250
San Cosme y San Damián de Cupaica or Escambé	900	2000
San Martín de Tomole	700	650
Sta. Cruz de Capoli or Ychutafun	60	150
Purificación de Tama or Candelaria	300	400
San Pedro de los Chines	300	150

Intervillage migration and flight from Apalachee villages such as To-mole and Aspalaga probably account for some discrepancies in the data from 1675 and from 1689. Evidence for Apalachee in particular indicates that its people were undercounted in 1675. In that year a visiting bishop of Santiago de Cuba confirmed 13,152 Indians, a figure that probably did not include young children. It suggests a population of at least 10,000 in Apalachee, as does a remark by the bishop that he provided long dresses for 4,081 women in Apalachee who were wearing nothing but short skirts that covered them from knees to waist. The standard translation of his letter omitted the detail that identified the women as "from Apalachee."[1] Evidence from the 1680s shows that Guale and Mocama populations also were understated in 1675.

Many of the older missions and their peoples probably disappeared during the years 1649–56 when a series of epidemics devastated the remaining populations of the Guale and Timucua. Another epidemic in 1659 reportedly killed 10,000, many of them probably in Apalachee in view of a remark by the governor that the 1655 smallpox epidemic had left very few Indians in Guale and Timucua. A 1656 revolt among the Potano, Utina, and Yustaga, directed at the governor and his soldiers but not against the friars, also hastened the demise of many missions. An imprudent governor's disrespect for privileges of rank enjoyed by Indian leaders provided a pretext for the revolt, but those leaders' dismay over their steady loss of power and influence as the number of their subjects declined was a more fundamental cause. The governor's relocation of the people of a northern tier of the western Timucuan missions—most of whom had not participated in the revolt—to revive the depopulated rebel missions of southern Utina and Potano that were on the Spanish trail led many of the migrants to flee from mission territory. His policy caused the disappearance of all western Timucuan missions with asterisks in the list.

The establishment of Charleston brought a new threat to the missions. Indians armed by the British of Virginia had attacked missions as early as the 1620s. But the threat intensified in the 1680s from pirates as well as new and closer Indian groups allied with the British, leading ultimately to complete destruction of the missions by 1704–5. The mission Indians' dissatisfaction with Spanish rule intensified as the British threat moved Spain to begin building the stone castillo at St. Augustine in the mid-1670s, increasing the demand for Indian labor and foodstuffs to feed the laborers. British-inspired attacks eliminated all the Georgia coast's missions in the 1680s. Many of the Guale and Yamasee living there migrated to Creek country or to South Carolina. The rest, consisting mainly of Guale, relocated to three mission villages on Amelia Island. The Mocama of Guadalquini moved from St. Simons Island to the north side of the St. Johns River just west of Fort George Island, changing the mission's name to Santa Cruz de Guadalquini. In 1685, Utina Province's Santa Catalina de Ahoica was the first of the remaining hinterland missions to be destroyed. The last perished in the first half of the 1690s, leaving only the four Yustaga missions and two Potano missions in western Timucua territory. Creek struck a Chacato mission on the Apalachicola River in 1695.

South Carolina's governor, James Moore, destroyed the remaining coastal missions and St. Augustine itself in 1702 and put its castillo under siege for a time. That same year, hostile Indians attacked Potano's Santa Fé mission and Apalachee's Ocuia. Just prior to Moore's attack on St. Augustine, a Spanish-led 800-man Apalachee force marching toward the Chattahoochee to retaliate against the Creek for the attacks on Santa Fé and Ocuia was routed at a Flint River crossing in an ambush set by a Creek force moving toward Apalachee. Most destructive of all were two attacks the Creek and the English launched in 1704 that destroyed all but three of Apalachee's twelve surviving missions. At the start of the first attack at least fifty Apalachee warriors went over to the enemy in revolt. Additional Apalachee joined the attackers during ensuing battles. Thirteen hundred Apalachee surrendered, agreeing to leave for South Carolina with a promise that they would not be enslaved. A considerable number who were captured, probably about 1,000, were carried off to Carolina as slaves in what seems to have been the largest slave raid in the South, if not the nation. When the remnant of the Spanish garrison abandoned Apalachee at the end of July 1704, about 400 Apalachee from Ivitachuco under the province's most prestigious chief moved eastward with the soldiers, settling in southern Potano for a short time before continued harassment forced them to move on to the vicinity of St. Augustine. Most surviving inhabitants of the two largest Apalachee missions, San Luis de Talimali and Cupaica, together with the Chacato, migrated to Pensacola and Mobile.

Except for the few who remained at Pensacola, the only mission Indians left in Florida huddled in a few insecure villages under the protective guns of St. Augustine, where disease and continuing raids by Carolinians and their native cohorts steadily reduced their numbers. By 1711, their number had fallen to 401 who lived in seven camps that bore the names of former Guale, Timucua, and Apalachee missions. A native rebellion against the Carolinians in 1715, known as the Yamasee War, removed pressure on Florida's Indians for a time and increased the number of Indians living near St. Augustine. Yamasee, one of the major predator peoples who destroyed the missions, were prominent among the immigrants. The refugees also included Apalachees, who were one of the many native peoples in British territory who participated in the uprising that bears the Yamasee name. By then, the immigrants also included Indians from south Florida who sought to escape English-inspired Creek slave-raiding expeditions that swept as far south as the keys. By 1717, Florida's governor had reorganized and relocated the 946 natives in ten settlements. Three contained about 366 Yamasee speakers. Three Timucua settlements held about 248 people, about 100 of whom were Mocama. Two missions contained 189 Guale. About fifty-four Apalachee lived in the one Apalachee-speaking village or scattered through a number of the other settlements. The tenth settlement held thirty-three Jororo, a Mayaca-speaking south-central Florida people missionized in the 1690s. The rest were natives of other tribes who had not been missionized earlier. Yamasee and Apalachee numbering well over 200 established two villages near the rebuilt Fort St. Mark in Apalachee.

Expansion continued briefly as additional villages were established before 1723. By 1726 sixteen settlements contained 1,011 Indians despite renewal of English-inspired attacks that probably were mainly responsible for reducing the number of Yamasee to 167. But the number of Apalachee grew to 87, probably from immigration from the Creek country. The Guale remained stable at 187, while the Timucua fell to 154. Over the next two years, however, disease and hostilities reduced the population sharply. Decline continued until the British assumed control in 1763. By then few, if any, of Florida's aboriginal peoples remained in their homeland. All of the fewer than 100 Indians living in two villages in the vicinity of St. Augustine chose to depart for Cuba with the Spaniards.

Aside from the introduction of the church at the main village's center and, beside it, the residence of the friar, referred to as a *convento*, and a few Christian symbols such as the cross and bell tower, the missions in

Florida do not seem to have altered the appearance of Florida's aboriginal native villages substantially. In contrast to the round or oval native structures, the two European structures, church and convent, were rectangular and put together with spikes and nails. Church walls were constructed of either vertical planks or wattle and daub, and the latter seem to have been usual for the convent. But the roofs of both European structures followed the native thatch pattern.

The missions brought many changes to the lives of Florida's Indians beyond the obvious ones of religious beliefs and practices. Friars sought to "civilize" the natives in the sense of imposing many European mores on them as well as indoctrinating them in the Christian faith. Friars or other Spaniards introduced the Indians to new cultigens, animal husbandry, and new tools and skills. The process began at baptism, at least, with imposition of a Spanish first name and the friars' insistence that Indian males cut their long hair to conform to Spanish usage. In the economic sphere friars sought to convert Indians from their subsistence economy in which, as a friar phrased it, "they are idle most of the time, the men and the women alike,"[2] to one geared to produce surpluses for export that would enable them to acquire clothing and other goods. Labor itself became an export with introduction of the repartimiento labor system. For most of Florida's missionized Indians, except the Apalachees, the governor imposed that obligation as soon as Indian leaders gave obedience to the king.

The friars banned Indian dances that they considered obscene or that had ties to the Indians' pre-Christian religious practices. Dances that had continued for entire days and nights became shorter. Ultimately, Spaniards banned the Indians' ball game because of its religious associations, violence, and the intervillage hostilities it generated. Christian burial practices supplanted most of those native to the Indians, but archaeologists have found that they continued to bury grave goods with some of the deceased. The Indians' ceremonial wailing for the dead continued for a time at least, possibly because it was practiced by some Europeans.

In many respects, however, Indian society in the mission provinces remained strongly traditional. Leadership positions remained hereditary under a matrilineal system in which rule passed to a deceased chief's nephew (or niece, where female leaders existed) by his eldest sister. Matrilocality, which required that a man live with his wife's family in their village, remained the rule for the ordinary Indian. The council house remained by far the village's most impressive structure. It continued to be built in the traditional way and to serve both as the

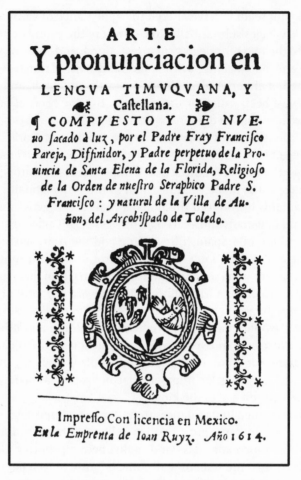

Title page of a dictionary and grammar to the language of the Timucua natives of Florida, compiled by Franciscan missionary Francisco Pareja in 1614.

focus of the community's life and as a place for meeting with Spanish authorities other than the friar. Indians continued to build their houses in their round form, using traditional materials and none of the new iron tools other than the axe. Only in the building of churches and convents did they follow European models and techniques. They continued to use their traditional ceramic vessels to cook, eat, and store food. One distinctive style, known as Leon-Jefferson Ware, found from Potano westward through Apalachee, reached full development during the mission era. Certain vessel forms, known as Colono-Ware, contain direct copies of European pottery features. It is believed they were made for European rather than for Indian use.

Acculturation, the adapting to or borrowing of traits from another culture, was most intense in religious belief and practice. Over time, a substantial segment of Apalachee and Timucua society appears to have embraced Catholicism sincerely. For Timucua, the best indication is that the friars remained at their posts unharmed during the 1656 revolt. There is strong evidence on the faith of the Apalachee from the French who received the exiles at Mobile. The French noted their demand for the sacraments and stated that, in matters religious, the Apalachee were scarcely distinguishable from Europeans who had been Christians for centuries. Only in the gray area of recourse to the shaman as healer are traditional practices with religious overtones known to have survived until the end of the seventeenth century. For all but some from the older generations in Apalachee, and for everyone in western Timucua, the ball game had lost most of its religious overtones by the 1670s.

The Spanish intrusion had its most decisive impact in the material sphere on agriculture in adding many new cultigens and introducing new activities such as raising chickens and hogs, dairy farming, and animal husbandry in general. In contrast to missions in California and elsewhere, chickens, hogs, and cattle belonged to individual Indians or to Indian communities. Disposition of the cattle was controlled by Indian leaders, not the friars, but friars controlled communal plantings of maize, wheat, and other crops in support of the church and feeding of the poor and incapacitated. In Apalachee by 1695 the two keys for the building in which produce was stored were entrusted to the chief and another leading man chosen by the governor's deputy. Export of produce to St. Augustine and Havana increased the area under cultivation and, consequently, the labor performed by ordinary Indians. The degree to which the laborers benefitted, if any, is not known.

For Florida's aboriginal peoples, the coming of the Europeans and adoption of the mission way of life under Spanish auspices were disastrous in the long run. Their population collapse was an inevitable consequence of their encounter with the pathogens of Old World peoples. But in many cases their extinction resulted from preventable human factors: a politically and economically motivated struggle for empire among English, Spanish, and French; the English determination to oust the Spaniards from Florida and eliminate native peoples who had allied with the Spaniards; and the English demand for Indian slaves. Without such human factors, some of the missionized peoples eventually would have acquired immunity to the new diseases and may have survived to the present, as did their Creek neighbors and many southwestern native groups.

Notes

1. Gabriel Díaz Vara Calderón, letter to the Queen, 1675 Archivo General de Indias (Seville), Santo Domingo, 151; microfilm furnished by William H. Marquardt. Cf. Lucy L. Wenhold, ed. and trans., *A 17th-Century Letter of Gabriel Díaz Vara Calderón, Bishop of Cuba, Describing the Indians and Indian Missions of Florida* (Washington: Smithsonian Miscellaneous Collections, vol. 95, no. 16, 1936).

2. Fray Francisco Alonso de Jesus, "1630 Memorial of Fray Francisco Alonso de Jesus on Spanish Florida's Missions and Natives," edited and translated by John H. Hann, *The Americas* 50, no. 1 (July 1993):88.

Bibliography

Boyd, Mark F., Hale G. Smith, and John W. Griffin. *Here They Once Stood: The Tragic End of the Apalachee Missions.* Gainesville: University of Florida Press, 1951.

Gannon, Michael V. *The Cross in the Sand: The Early Catholic Church in Florida, 1513–1870.* Rev. ed. Gainesville: University Presses of Florida, 1983.

———. [pseud. Charles W. Spellman]. "The 'Golden Age' of the Florida Missions, 1632–1674." *Catholic Historical Review* 51, no. 3 (October 1965):354–72.

Geiger, Maynard, O.F.M. *The Franciscan Conquest of Florida (1573–1618).* Washington: Catholic University of America, 1937.

Hann, John H. *Apalachee: The Land Between the Rivers.* Gainesville: University Presses of Florida, 1988.

———. "Demographic Patterns and Changes in Mid-Seventeenth-Century Timucua and Apalachee." *Florida Historical Quarterly* 64, no. 4 (April 1986):371–92.

———. *History of the Timucua Indians and Missions.* Gainesville: University Press of Florida, 1996.

———. "The Indian Village on Apalachee Bay's Río Chachave on the Solana Map of 1683." *Florida Anthropologist* 48, no. 1 (March 1995):61–66.

———. "The Mayaca and Jororo and Missions to Them." In *The Spanish Missions of La Florida,* edited by Bonnie G. McEwan, pp. 111–40. Gainesville: University Press of Florida, 1993.

———. *Missions to the Calusa.* Gainesville: University of Florida Press/Florida Museum of Natural History, 1991.

———. "St. Augustine's Fallout from the Yamasee War." *Florida Historical Quarterly* 68, no. 2 (October 1989):180–200.

———. *Summary Guide to Spanish Florida Missions and Visitas with Churches in the Sixteenth and Seventeenth Centuries.* Washington: Academy of American Franciscan History, 1990 (reprint from *The Americas* 56, no. 4 [April 1990]:417–513, with illustrations added).

———. "Twilight of the Mocamo and Guale Aborigines as Portrayed in the 1695 Spanish Visitation." *Florida Historical Quarterly* 66, no. 1 (July 1987):1–24.

————. "Visitations and Revolts in Florida, 1656–1695." *Florida Archaeology* 7 (1993).

Kessell, John L. *Kiva, Cross, and Crown: The Pecos Indians and New Mexico 1540–1840.* Albuquerque: University of New Mexico Press, 1987 (originally published Washington: National Park Service, U.S. Department of the Interior, 1979).

Lyon, Eugene. *Richer Than We Thought: The Material Culture of Sixteenth-Century St. Augustine.* St. Augustine: *El Escribano,* St. Augustine Journal of History, St. Augustine Historical Society, 1992.

Oré, Luis Jerónimo de. *The Martyrs of Florida (1513–1616).* Translated by Maynard Geiger. New York: Joseph F. Wagner, 1936.

Vargas Ugarte, Ruben. "The First Jesuit Mission in Florida." In *Historical Records and Studies,* edited by Thomas F. Meehan, 35: 59–148. New York: United States Catholic Historical Society, 1935.

Worth, John E. "The Timucuan Missions of Spanish Florida and the Rebellion of 1656." Ph.D. dissertation, University of Florida, 1992.

6 Raids, Sieges, and International Wars

Charles W. Arnade

The arrivals of other Europeans—French, English, Dutch—on the Atlantic Coast during the seventeenth century went basically unchallenged by Spain until 1670, when the English founded the royal colony of Carolina. The next century saw years of wars in the Southeast, which Spain claimed as La Florida. The English and the French challenged Spanish sovereignty in the region. The American natives became a part, and often victims, of that triangular struggle. The English achieved near total victory in 1763, and the First Spanish Period of Florida came to an end.

By the mid-seventeenth century, the French had a thriving colony in Atlantic Canada, and expanded westward and down the Mississippi Valley, looking for its estuary. The English had colonies in what today we call New England and on the mid-Atlantic Coast. The multiple islands of the Caribbean, the location of the original Spanish settlements, also had become targets of the other European powers. Spain had failed to maintain its total hegemony. The English had made the largest conquests, followed by the French and the Dutch. The French were beginning again to scout the Mexican Gulf Coast, including the Florida shores, looking for the mouth of the Mississippi.

In 1670, the English Crown approved the founding of a new colony by settlers coming from their Caribbean islands, mainly Barbados. It became Carolina. It was definitely within what Spain still considered its royal domain and where it had settlements, forts, and missions. The original English proprietary grant of Carolina, dated 1663, was from the southern border of Virginia to the thirty-first parallel, which was just north of St. Augustine, the seat of Spanish Florida. Two years later, the grant was extended south to the twenty-ninth parallel, about where New Smyrna stands today. Spain's protests and diplomatic threats led to a compromise and the signing of the 1670 Treaty of Madrid.

That treaty fixed the boundary between Spanish Florida and the new English Carolina. The Spaniards hoped it would stop private English incursions as well as formal raids south and west, which harassed them and the Spanish-ruled Indians. The treaty designated a border between the two national claims that ran straight west, through territory unknown and unexplored, from south of Port Royal (Barra de Santa Elena in Spanish) on the Atlantic. That was latitude 32° 30″, about ten miles north of the Savannah River, where Hilton Head is located, and the present boundary between South Carolina and Georgia.

France's intentions were less clear. Its penetrations on the Mississippi and along the Mexican Gulf Coast were basically for exploration, in the hope that the Saint Lawrence–Great Lakes and Mississippi networks were connected. Their possession would give France primary control of North America. The three great European powers were establishing strong bases by the mid-seventeenth century, and the Indian nations and tribes were caught between them. It was a foregone conclusion that hostilities would develop and engulf Spanish Florida.

The demarcation line of 1670, observed more on paper than in practice, was only temporary and to some an illusion. As late as 1695, the governor of Carolina, Joseph Blake, would insist to Florida's Governor Laureano de Torres y Ayala that the king of England's authority ran down the coast to twenty-nine degrees. The treaty satisfied for a time the royal offices in Madrid and London, though it was not at all well received in Paris. It did limit the colonization of Carolina south of the Savannah River, but English raiding parties into Spanish Florida, which started in 1660, continued, although with less intensity, after 1670. To be sure, the raids were not Crown approved but originated with Carolina settlers and Indians who fell under English influence or switched from Spanish tutelage. The Spaniards, with their greatest concentration in St. Augustine, failed to make a concerted effort to colonize north to the Savannah River. Spain was in a decline compared to newly dynamic England and France, and Florida had always been a neglected Spanish colony. Would Spain now, in 1670, show greater interest in Florida in view of the new international challenges?

The Spanish population of Florida was never large in this period. Most lived in the garrison city and capital, St. Augustine, where because we lack reliable census data, we rely on varying figures from official reports and correspondence: 1,400 people in 1685; 1,444 in 1689; 1,175 in 1691; and 1,768 in 1702. While the principal employment in the capital was soldiering, a marked degree of agricultural activity was carried on in the interior. For example, in the savannah of La Chua, from which today's county name Alachua derived, extensive cattle ranches were owned and operated by *peninsular* governors and the descendants of prominent creole families such as the Menéndez Marqués line, as well as by various treasury officials. Apalachee had a thriving ranch economy. The combined Espinosa and Sánchez families built up ranches north of St. Augustine in the Diego Plains area. The 1670s and 1680s were years of particularly strong agribusiness. The haciendas in the hinterlands were linked in partnerships with the flourishing mission economy of Apalachee and with seaborne trade conducted, sometimes illegally, out of St. Augustine, the San Martín (Suwannee) River, and Apalachee. Exports from Apalachee to Havana included corn, beans, chickens, hogs, dried meat, hides, and tallow.

Besides St. Augustine there were a few minor forts (all wooden) or military posts, most in the St. Augustine area. Particularly important was the post and fort of San Luis de Talimali, at present-day Tallahassee, in the years 1656–1704. When St. Augustine was invested by Carolinians in 1702 (see below), San Luis was able to dispatch a force of one hundred Spaniards to assist in lifting the siege. A short-lived appendage to San Luis was the small fort San Marcos de Apalachee, on the Gulf Coast, from 1679 to 1682. It was primitive, of wood construction, with a tiny garrison. The fort at St. Augustine proper was the capital's ninth wooden fort. Earlier forts had been destroyed by fire, rot, or the raid by English corsair Francis Drake in 1586. Every governor pleaded for funds for the construction of more solid forts made from stone, but their petitions were to no avail. The only other Spanish presence was the parish church and the outlying missions.

The governor, appointed by the Crown, was usually a military man, always an outsider, and as a rule was disliked by the rest of St. Augustine. To assist in governing the province, there was only a small administrative staff connected with the treasury, and they often resented the governor. There was little in the way of local government, but frequently a cabildo, or town council, did exist.

The most positive development in many years was the building, at long last, of a majestic stone fort, the Castillo de San Marcos, which began in 1672 and took twenty-three years to complete. There is hardly any doubt that the decision to construct the fort was due to the establishment of English Carolina. The Treaty of Madrid failed to stop English intrusions and raids beyond the established 1670 line. And two years

Castillo de San Marcos at St. Augustine, which twice, in 1702 and 1740, saved the city and Spanish Florida from British conquest. In both sieges the thick coquina (shellrock) walls of the fortress proved impregnable, protecting 1,500 soldiers and townspeople for 53 days in 1702 and nearly 2,000 for 38 days in 1740. During the latter attack the grim walls, displaying an unanticipated though fortuitous property, absorbed an intense 27-day British bombardment without shattering from the shot. One frustrated Englishman commented that the native rock "will not splinter but will give way to cannon ball as though you would stick a knife into cheese."

prior to the treaty, in 1668, the English freebooter Robert Searles (alias Davis) had attacked St. Augustine with no warning. He came in the dark of night, at high tide, doing extensive damage, plundering houses and public buildings, including the governor's residence, the monastery, and the church. The records indicate that sixty Spaniards died. Searles freely explored the harbor with the intention of returning. While the raid is usually identified as a pirate attack that had no official English sanction, there are serious doubts about that. The new settlers in Carolina at least tacitly encouraged the raid, the best indication for this being the presence at the time in St. Augustine of the famous Dr. Henry Woodward, who sailed away with Searles. Some claim that the main mission of the surprise attack was not so much to sack St. Augustine as to free Woodward.

Woodward remains one of the most enigmatic English explorers of the period, intimately tied to the history of the Carolina settlement and its challenge to Spanish Florida. He was among the original Carolina settlers and made it his first priority to learn the country and its natives, including their languages. He entered the unknown interior, even beyond the Chattahoochee. Either in the 1660s or in 1685 he appears to have been the first English person to step on the soil of what is today the central Florida Panhandle. Upon his return to the coast, he contacted the Spaniards around their old settlement of Santa Elena near what soon became the 1670 demarcation line. There, apparently, he was captured and carried to St. Augustine, where he was treated by the Spanish governor more as a guest than as a prisoner but was forced to stay. In his residence Woodward learned much about the Spanish status of Florida. It is even said that he might have come voluntarily to survey the Spanish strength. In the end he sailed off with the freebooter Searles.

By the time of the Searles raid, according to historian Luis Arana, the whole of Spanish Florida had only 130 able-bodied soldiers. The majority were stationed at St. Augustine. The required strength was supposed to be 300. They had few armaments, and many of those were unusable. But when Spain appropriated funds to start construction of the new stone fort, over 100 new soldiers were posted to the city. The governor himself journeyed to Havana and hired one of the best military engineers of the Caribbean, Ignazio Daza, to draw up the blueprint and to be in charge of construction. A thoroughly competent military architect, Daza produced a first-rate fortress, the Castillo de San Marcos, that now ranks among the most impressive historical monuments in the United States. The impregnancy of the fort, tested in two notable sieges, confirmed his accomplishment.

The arrival of new personnel and the construction gave St. Augustine a welcome lift from its economic depression. Large paid Indian labor drafts from Guale and Apalachee came to St. Augustine to build the Castillo and to till the soldiers' fields. A certain amount of social tension resulted from the presence and use of the natives. From both Spanish provisioners and mission caciques, the Crown purchased large quantities of corn to feed the workers. Traffic on the interior roads was heavy. The material for the fort was *coquina*, a shell rock, locally quarried. At the turn of the century, St. Augustine was larger, stronger, and probably more dynamic, yet Spanish Florida was still one of the poorest and most tenuous of Spain's colonies in America.

Meanwhile, on the Gulf of Mexico a serious French threat had emerged. While the English were expanding from Carolina into the unchartered West and coming in contact with the southeastern Indians—Creeks, Choctaws, Chickasaws, and Cherokees—the French were expanding all along the Mississippi and its tributaries. It was obvious to French strategists that the mouth of the great river was on the Gulf of Mexico and that its possession was essential for domination.

Their primary thrust was out of today's Canada via the Great Lakes. Explorers René Cavelier, Sieur de La Salle, and Henri de Tonty reconnoitered most of the river, and by 1682 they had apparently reached the southern discharge of the river but could not locate a recognizable estuary.

France had a number of permanent possessions in the Caribbean. In 1684, La Salle, with several ships, sailed through the Spanish sea to find the mouth of the Mississippi from the Gulf side. He failed to do so and landed on the coast of Texas. Trying to reach the Mississippi overland, he perished. Tonty's subsequent search for La Salle was futile. It was clear to the Spaniards that the French were trying to take possession of the lower Mississippi system via the Caribbean. Their efforts were aided by French buccaneers, who probably had the tacit support of the French Crown. They raided the weak Spanish fort San Marcos on the Florida Gulf Coast. It was a small rambling wooden fort, probably built in 1679, at today's St. Marks, that protected the large Apalachee missions. Pensacola Bay, briefly occupied by the Spaniards in 1559–61, had faded from Spanish charts and interests. Mobile Bay, never coveted by Spain, was not yet a target of the French.

In 1682, the same year as the San Marcos raid, the French pirates did something even more daring. They raided the peninsular interior by proceeding up the Río Amajuro (probably the Withlacoochee) either in small boats or by foot along the riverbanks.

It is thought that what the French really were looking for was the source of all the rivers that flowed into the Gulf, wondering whether they were part of the huge Mississippi fluvial system. They realized early on that the European nation that controlled North America's splendid river system would own the continent itself. By the end of the seventeenth century, Spain became aware of this strategic vision. No fewer than eleven Spanish expeditions were dispatched to search for La Salle's settlement and the mouth of the Río de Espíritu Santo, the Mississippi. The first, a search by sea, was conducted out of Apalachee in January 1686. Directed by two experienced Mexican pilots, assisted by Apalachee natives familiar with the coast westward, the expedition failed to find La Salle but did rediscover Pensacola Bay, which excited Spanish interest in the reoccupation of that site. Another search overland was launched from Apalachee in August 1686, but it too missed its target. Finally, in 1689, a Mexican expedition found the abandoned site.

In the minds of Spanish navigators, the deep-water bay at Pensacola was the best in Florida. In 1692 the Crown ordered the viceroy of New Spain to explore and build a fort on the site if it was feasible. Matters took their time. Preliminary explorations were undertaken, but there were diverse opinions on the seriousness of the French threat and the changing relationship of the French and Spanish nations. Also, funds were lacking and key persons in the Spanish administration of the viceroyalty were constantly changing. In 1698 news came to the Spaniards that the French were sending a fleet of their own to occupy Pensacola Bay. Thus energized, in April of that year the Spanish Crown ordered the occupation and fortification of Pensacola as a priority. Indeed, a contingent left France in October 1698. The Spanish fleet also left in October, from Mexico. Arriving first, the Spaniards occupied the bay and started a fortification in November.

In late January 1699, a French naval contingent of five ships arrived in Pensacola Bay within sight of the Spanish fort still being built. France and Spain were at peace, but the situation was tense. Both commanders, the French veteran Pierre le Moyne, Sieur d'Iberville, and the Spanish governor, Andrés de Arriola, while proudly displaying their might, tried to come to a peaceful arrangement. Iberville declared that he had come solely to survey the coast. Arriola said he had strict orders not to permit foreigners into the bay but offered to help find the French another location west of the bay. The French departed and a few days later arrived outside Mobile Bay. In the next weeks the French began the establishment of their new colony at Biloxi. Iberville, its first governor, was succeeded by his capable brother, Jean Baptiste le Moyne, Sieur de Bienville. In the meantime, the Spaniards continued their development of the town, garrison, and wood fort at Pensacola.

So by 1700, the English were established in Carolina and moving into the interior, and the French, having established Louisiana, possessed Mobile Bay and the whole mouth of the Mississippi. The Spaniards, who had occupied Pensacola Bay, were strengthening St. Augustine, extending their mission system to the Apalachicola River, and making a weak attempt to secure the Florida peninsula. Then, suddenly, in Europe there erupted among the three great powers a fierce war that spread rapidly to America. The throne of Spain had become vacant when the feeble Hapsburg king Charles II died. Noting that the king had named a French candidate as heir, the French claimed the throne, but the English would not accept their claim. The resulting War of the Spanish Succession expanded into the colonies and into American history as Queen Anne's War. Florida became a battlefield fought over with an intensity fiercer than any experienced in the past or future.

The union of the Spanish and French dynasties in that conflict brought consternation to the English American colonies, since an alliance of their colonies threatened the English possessions. This was especially true in South Carolina, where James Moore, a tough-minded and ambitious slaveowner, was governor. Having advance information that England would go to war, Moore determined to conquer St. Augustine and its fort before it could be reinforced by French forces. He feared the French and despised, and underestimated, the Spaniards.

As soon as the war started Moore struck against Florida with 1,200 men, half of his force white, half Indian. They came by land and sea and rapidly overran the small Spanish posts north of St. Augustine. By September 1702, Moore occupied St. Augustine, which he had entered with little difficulty. The Spanish governor, Joseph de Zúñiga y Zerda, moved the population of 1,445 into the fort to join the military garrison, which at that time numbered 323 men. To help feed the Spaniards, 163 head of cattle were moved into the moat of the fort. Upon first learning of the coming assault, Zúñiga had dispatched a messenger to authorities in Havana asking that they come to his aid and force Moore to lift the siege. He was optimistic that he could withstand the siege until the relief force arrived but knew that he could not win in open battle with the overwhelming English contingent.

After laying siege to the fort, Moore, too, dispatched a messenger, to English Jamaica, asking for reinforcements. The battle, a celebrated chapter in Florida history, lasted for two months. The Spaniards exhibited remarkable endurance and determination in spite of horribly crowded conditions. Zúñiga's strong leadership, his imposition of discipline and equity in the rationing of food and water, and his maintenance of good sanitary conditions were important factors in keeping up morale and hope.

It became obvious that victory would go to that side whose reinforcements arrived first. When help failed to come from Jamaica, there was a growing awareness among the English that the fort could not be conquered and that the Spaniards would not surrender. English morale slackened, and Moore's ability as a capable military leader was questioned. Christmas brought a decisive present to the Spaniards when help arrived from Cuba. The English rapidly lifted their siege and ordered a retreat, which became something of a rout. Back in South Carolina, Moore had to face severe criticism from which he never recovered. Governor Zúñiga, too, faced an official inquiry as to why he had not presented battle and why he had abandoned the town of St. Augustine, which the Carolinians had totally destroyed, leaving no building standing but the hospital. Zúñiga was vindicated and praised for his costly victory, but St. Augustine was never totally restored by the Spaniards; the parish church was not immediately rebuilt.

The extensive Florida mission system was also a victim of the Carolinian raids. Moore, who had lost his governorship, led a cruel and damaging raid into Apalachee in 1704 (see chapter 5), and the missions there were never restored. Pensacola withstood the aggression but it never became a real town until the English period. It was a shabby village with a rambling wooden fort. The massive fort in St. Augustine remained the only visible symbol of Spanish sovereignty of Florida. The original natives had by and large disappeared. By the end of Queen Anne's War in 1713 the total population of Spanish Florida was at its nadir, probably fewer than 1,000 human beings. Most of Florida appeared depopulated. Then, in 1716 and 1717, Apalachee refugees from the Yamasee War (see below) asked for Spanish protection, and a fifty-soldier force was sent out from St. Augustine to build a wooden blockhouse on Apalachee Bay, south of present-day Tallahassee. Named, like its predecessor in 1679–82, Fort San Marcos de Apalachee, the outpost reestablished a Spanish presence in the hinterland.

Tension between the great powers remained, awaiting the eruption of another war that might again reach international dimensions. In the meantime, England, France, and Spain pursued policies to dominate the large southeastern Indian populations north of Florida, to gain their confidence, even to incite hostilities among them. This cynical manipulation, especially by the English in Carolina, resulted in an Indian uprising in 1715, known as the Yamasee War, that had important consequences in Florida. The Yamasee and other Indian groups, including Apalachee, probably at the instigation of the Creek, rose up against the Carolina settlers, and the war brought much death and destruction to the colony. Initially successful because of the element of surprise, the Yamasees could not overcome the technical superiority of the English. They retreated into Florida to seek the protection of the Spaniards, resettling mainly around St. Augustine. The Apalachee, victims of the English raids during Queen's Anne War and taken by force to English Carolina, also fled English territory posthaste. The repopulation of Florida had begun. Later, Creek from the Chattahoochee and Flint river districts in present-day Georgia and Alabama began pouring into the vacuum that was Florida's interior. It was these Creek immigrants who became the people known as Seminole (see chapter 11).

The Yamasee War reestablished a balance among the three European powers in the Southeast. Spain was strengthened, Carolina was weakened, and France became more apprehensive. The American natives were encouraged by their policy of fueling tension among the three

European nations. The major region of dispute was the unsettled land between the Savannah and the St. Johns rivers, that is, between English Carolina and Spanish Florida, which historian Herbert E. Bolton called the "Debatable Land." Both Spain and England claimed it. Both intermittently made incursions and established a temporary minor presence in it. In one notable example, the English built a blockhouse named Fort King George on the Altamaha River near present-day Darien, Georiga. Despite furious objections by the Spanish, it stood from 1721 to 1727 (requiring reconstruction after a fire in 1725). Each colony protested the other's moves. It was a game of hide-and-seek, but there was no doubt that the English eventually would push south with permanent settlements. If a war were to erupt in Europe, they might even try again to cross the St. Johns and capture St. Augustine.

A short European war erupted in 1719 with consequences for Spanish Florida. In the War of the Quadruple Alliance, the new Bourbon dynasty in Madrid found itself at war with the Bourbon dynasty of France. Like the War of Spanish Succession, it spread to the colonies. Plans of the Spaniards to strike at Charleston by sea from Havana came to nothing, since the French in Louisiana attacked the Spaniards around Pensacola. The Spaniards had to go on the defensive against the French on the Gulf Coast rather than on the offensive against the English on the Atlantic.

French attempts to capture Pensacola were initially successful, but it was recaptured by Spain with the Havana fleet that was originally assigned to take Charleston. A Spanish effort to continue their counterattack and expel the French from Louisiana failed when a promised contingent from Mexico did not materialize. The French then recaptured Pensacola. When the War of the Quadruple Alliance suddenly ended in 1720, the French government in Paris showed little interest in the Gulf of Mexico claims. Originally, the French had wanted to secure the whole Gulf Coast as far as Tampa Bay, or at least to the Apalachicola River. In the end, they returned Pensacola to Spain. The ensuing peace treaty returned boundaries to their antebellum status, but the situation on the Atlantic Coast remained in flux.

The next successful English colony, predictably, was in the debatable land. Less utopian in character than the never-established Azilia, the new colony became known as Georgia, a typical "product of the religious-philanthropic movements of the early eighteenth century" (Crane 1956, 303). Plans for the colony had been formulated in London in July 1730. The colony was founded in February 1733 under the leadership of James Edward Oglethorpe. The initial claim ranged from the

James Edward Oglethorpe (1696–1785), English founder and governor of Georgia, who unsuccessfully laid siege to St. Augustine in 1740.

Savannah River south to the Altamaha River and westward to the Pacific; it crossed not only Spanish Florida but Spanish Texas. A serious confrontation with the Spaniards was inevitable. Oglethorpe soon extended Georgia's claim as far south as the St. Johns River and daringly established a military presence on the coastal islands above the St. Johns. Spain protested vehemently, and what today we call shuttle diplomacy ensued among St. Augustine, Havana, and Frederica, Oglethorpe's capital on St. Simons Island. Madrid sent a special delegate and threatened war. But, bowing to reality in 1737, the governor of Spanish Florida, Francisco del Moral Sánchez, signed an agreement with Oglethorpe according to which the Georgian withdrew north from the St. Johns while sustaining his claim as far as the Altamaha. Spain disallowed Sánchez's action, ordered him to Spain, court-martialed him, convicted him, and, some reports say, executed him.

Spain now prepared for a military expedition against the English presence below 32° 30". St. Augustine was reinforced, and a fleet of up to 7,000 men and 60 ships was made ready in Havana. But the Florida-Georgia conflict was just one dispute between these two world powers and not the most important one. In March 1738, Madrid suddenly ordered the suspension of the planned offensive.

With the tacit approval of London, Oglethorpe continued to increase his power surreptitiously, at the same time wooing the Indians in the interior. He was convinced that armed conflict between England and Spain was inevitable. When war was declared he wanted to be ready to strike immediately and capture St. Augustine. In October 1739, the two nations did begin hostilities in what became known as the War of Jenkins's Ear, caused by trade controversies in the Caribbean. In May 1740, Oglethorpe attacked Florida by land and by sea. A more competent leader than Moore in 1702, he directed a trained force of Georgia and South Carolina militia. The principal question was whether he could overpower and conquer the massive Spanish fort at St. Augustine.

History repeated itself in everything but the details. The English campaigns to capture St. Augustine in 1702 and 1740 and thereby conquer Spanish Florida were high points of eighteenth-century Florida history. Yet, while both ended in an English defeat, there were notable differences. In 1740 the English prepared their campaign carefully and hoped to have their military movements supported by English forces from the Caribbean. One major strategy was to establish picket lines of ships that would prevent the Spaniards from dispatching reinforcements of their own from Cuba. Furthermore, in 1740 the English attackers had a much shorter distance to traverse, since they possessed nearly all the Georgia offshore islands.

Oglethorpe's forces were successful in speedily capturing the small Spanish satellite forts north of St. Augustine, including the one held by free blacks, Fort Mose, two miles north of St. Augustine, where a fierce battle took place. However, it soon became obvious that the conquest of

St. Augustine itself, with its massive fort and about 2,500 inhabitants, would be more difficult than expected. The planned coordination with the English Caribbean naval forces did not succeed, and the naval blockade of the southern access routes failed to materialize. Also, the Spanish had a better knowledge of the terrain and the tides, and they had pretty well guessed the English intentions. Furthermore, tensions between the Georgia and South Carolina militias became a serious problem.

The Spanish forces of only about 600 men, led by the able Governor Manuel de Montiano, showed resolution and confidence. Overall, as one student of this attack stated, the governor handled his forces "well and judiciously" (Herson 1993). The Spanish military equipment was superior to what the castillo had in 1702. Consequently, the hardships of the garrison were less intense than those experienced in 1702. But Montiano had to deal with a more competent English leader in the person of Oglethorpe.

The English forces took possession first of the north end of Anastasia Island. They then besieged the town and the fort, but the situation was quite different from that of 1702 when the Carolina forces rapidly conquered the town and forced the inhabitants into the fort. This time the English artillery was too distant to be effective. Ground assaults to reach the fort were all repulsed. While the morale and enthusiasm of the English declined, the confidence of the Spanish increased. Military preparedness and additional construction of defense lines since 1702 proved to be invaluable to the defenders.

By the end of June, Fort Mose was reconquered by the Spaniards, with heavy losses inflicted on the British forces. A week later, the British said openly that the conquest of St. Augustine with its fort would be impossible without massive reinforcements, which in all probability were not available. Indeed, some of the naval forces, basic for the blockade of the inlets, had already been reassigned to places unrelated to the St. Augustine campaign. Instead of conquering the town and fort, the English now strove for a permanent presence close to St. Augustine, especially on Anastasia Island. They hoped such a presence would neutralize the fort and lead eventually to final victory.

On 15 July the British ordered the lifting of the siege of St. Augustine but retained Anastasia Island. Artillery duels between the opposing forces continued and there were some minor English patrol assaults, but the fight went out of the English and dissension among the militias from the different English colonies increased. By August any hope of

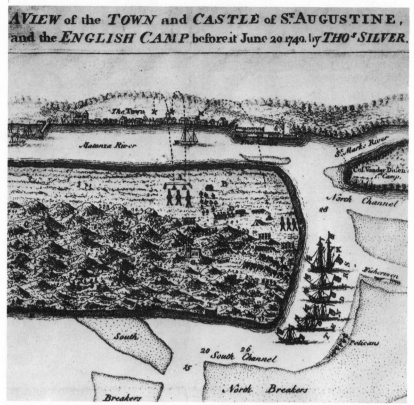

A VIEW of the *TOWN* and *CASTLE* of S:AUGUSTINE, and the *ENGLISH CAMP* before it June 20.1740. by *THO: SILVER.*

This English drawing of the siege of St. Augustine by Governor James Oglethorpe of Georgia in 1740 shows the disposition of the English land and naval forces. From two artillery emplacements, one on Anastasia Island (*center*) and another at Point San Mateo ("Col. Vander Dussen's Camp," *right*), the English lay down a steady barrage of cannon fire against "The Town" and "The Castle." Of the nearly 2,000 Spaniards gathered in the Castillo only two men were killed in the fruitless bombardment, and Oglethorpe's force retired on 20 July.

even a partial English victory had vanished. A South Carolina Assembly report on the 1740 siege states that on 6 August the remaining English forces, having negotiated "the St. Johns River bar set sail for St. Simons Island." Thus, the second British siege of St. Augustine came to an end, and the Castillo de San Marcos remained unconquered. The British report ends on 22 August: "All arrived safely at Charles Town." After Oglethorpe regained his prestige by defeating a Spanish assault on Frederica in 1742, he made a feeble attempt in 1743 to capture St. Augustine by a surprise land attack but failed. Unfortunately, we still lack detailed research on that raid. Soon thereafter he left America, never to return.

Oglethorpe did not destroy Spanish Florida, and the Spaniards could not eliminate Georgia. Encouraged by their victory of 1740, the Spaniards planned a massive assault on Georgia. In May 1742, a large expedition sailed from Cuba to St. Augustine. In July the Spanish forces landed on San Simons Island in order to capture Frederica, the capital of Oglethorpe's Georgia. While moving through marshy terrain toward Frederica, they were forced to battle the determined defenders. In a long, intense engagement the Spaniards suffered a humiliating defeat and many casualties. This encounter, known in history as the "Battle of the Bloody Marsh," assured the permanency of Georgia just as the unsuccessful 1740 siege of St. Augustine destroyed English hopes of conquering Florida by military means.

After Oglethorpe's return to England in 1743 a long stalemate developed as "neither side any longer desired to revive actual hostilities" (Chatelain 1941, 92). Spain maintained vigilance and nominal sovereignty as far as the St. Johns River mouth. St. Augustine with its sturdy, unconquered fort remained the most visible sign of the Spanish presence. Its satellite forts of Mose and Matanzas were strengthened, and the garrison of the main fort was somewhat increased. Yet St. Augustine remained a garrison town with little economic activity, a situation that prevailed in all of Spanish Florida—except that, at mid-century, there were substantial citrus and other exports to the English colonies, and a development company, Compañía de la Habana, introduced Canary Island settlers to St. Augustine. Far to the west, Pensacola, with weak wooden defenses, still was more a village than a town. It was relatively peaceful since the nearby French were not at war with Spain. The greatest threat came from surrounding natives who oscillated between belligerency and submission. Spain kept a tenuous presence on the Gulf Coast. San Marcos de Apalachee continued in existence. The most noted event of the time was the expedition of Francisco María Celi in 1757 to make a careful survey of Tampa Bay, with a view toward establishing a permanent presence there. No settlement resulted, but Celi's report, with an excellent map, is a vital document in the history of Spanish Florida. There was hardly any Spanish presence on the Atlantic Coast south of St. Augustine.

By 1759, according to Michael Gannon, only ten Franciscan priests were left in Florida. They had "lost their jurisdiction over the Indians of St. Augustine" (1965, 82). Their authority had been curtailed in 1746 and given over to the secular clergy. In every respect, Spanish Florida was but a pale image of its former self, which had never been impressive. As the colony entered the 1760s it was particularly vulnerable to manipulation, even by the *madre patria*. Gannon has summarized what happened:

> Eventually Spain would have to yield on paper what it had never yielded on the field of battle. To the north France and England were contending for hegemony over the larger part of the continent: French fur-hunting ranges were pushing eastward from the Mississippi and the Great Lakes while English farmsteads were moving westward from the Atlantic. In the inevitable collision, which we call the French and Indian War (1754–63), Spain, worried about English dominance over the continent, threw in its lot with France in 1761. It was a disastrous decision, for England quickly and easily seized Havana. In the humiliating peace treaty that followed, Spain had to sacrifice Florida in order to regain the rich Cuban port. France lost much more—virtually all of its North American territories, including Canada. Louisiana might have been kept but instead was given in gratitude to Spain. Florida was now English, and the treaty provisions placed the western boundary of Florida at the Mississippi River. (1993, 17)

Bibliography

Arana, Luis Rafael, and Albert Manucy. *The Building of Castillo de San Marcos*. St. Augustine: Eastern National Park Monument Association, 1977.

Arnade, Charles. "Celi's Expedition to Tampa Bay: A Historical Analysis." *Florida Historical Quarterly* 47, no. 2 (July 1968):1–7.

———. "The French and the Suwanee River." In Library Notes of the Friends of the Library of the University of South Florida, Tampa, March 1976.

———. *The Siege of St. Augustine in 1702*. Gainesville: University of Florida Press, 1959.

Bolton, Herbert E. *The Spanish Borderlands: A Chronicle of Old Florida and the Southwest*. New Haven: Yale University Press, 1921.

———, ed. *Arredondo's Historical Proof of Spain's Title to Georgia: A Contribution to the History of One of the Spanish Borderlands*. Berkeley: University of California Press, 1925.

Caruso, John Anthony. *The Southern Frontier*. Indianapolis: Bobbs-Merrill, 1963.

Chatelain, Verne E. *The Defenses of Spanish Florida, 1565 to 1763*. Washington: Carnegie Institution of Washington, 1941.

Crane, Verner W. *The Southern Frontier, 1670–1732.* Ann Arbor: University of Michigan Press, 1929.

Gannon, Michael V. *The Cross in the Sand: The Early Catholic Church in Florida, 1513–1870.* Gainesville: University of Florida Press, 1965.

———. *Florida: A Short History.* Gainesville: University Press of Florida, 1993.

Gold, Robert L. *Borderland Empires in Transition: The Triple Nation Transfer of Florida.* Carbondale: Southern Illinois University Press, 1969.

Herson, James P. "The Oglethorpe Siege of 1740." Paper, Florida Historical Society Annual Meeting, Pensacola, 20–22 May 1993.

Morales Padrón, Francisco. *Manual de Historia Universal. Historia General de América,* vols. 5, 6 (Madrid, 1962).

TePaske, John Jay. *The Governorship of Spanish Florida, 1700–1763.* Durham, N.C.: Duke University Press, 1964.

"The St. Augustine Expedition of 1740: A Report to the South Carolina General Assembly." Introduction by John Tate Lanning. Columbia: Archives Department, 1954.

Weddle, Robert S. *The French Thorn: Rival Explorers in the Spanish Sea, 1682–1762.* College Station: Texas A&M University Press, 1991.

———. *Spanish Sea: The Gulf of Mexico in North American Discovery, 1500–1685.* College Station: Texas A&M University Press, 1985.

7 Pensacola, 1686—1763

William S. Coker

The Sieur de La Salle's 1685 voyage to the Texas coast (see chapter 6) created near-panic among the Spanish officials in New Spain (Mexico). It also prompted Spain to plant a colony on the northern Gulf Coast, although some years passed before it was done.

Eleven expeditions by land and by sea searched for the La Salle colony. The first of the sea expeditions, that of Juan Enríquez Barroto and Antonio Romero in 1686, examined the Bahía Santa María Filipina, the site of the Luna colony of 1559–61. The pilot, Ensign Juan Jordán de Reina, called the bay "the best that I have ever seen in my life." He also noted that the Indians there referred to the bay as Panzacola, a Choctaw word that means "long haired people," because the men and women both wore their hair long.

This was not the earliest reference to Panzacola, also spelled Pansacola. A 1657 report listed Pansacola as a satellite village of San Juan de Aspalaga in the Apalachee area and the name of its cacique as Manuel. Pansacola was also a common surname there. Interestingly, the natives who occupied the Pansacola village in 1657 were Apalachee. It is believed that some Pansacola were in that area at a much earlier period. There were also some Panzacola in the Choctawhatchee and Mobile areas at a later date. But those met by Jordán de Reina in 1686 were a separate tribe. Seven years later, in 1693, Laureano de Torres y Ayala visited Pensacola

Bay and found the Panzacola village abandoned. He reported that these natives had been exterminated by their mortal enemies, the Mobila. About 1725, some forty Panzacola and Biloxi were living on the Pearl River, but whether they were survivors from the Pensacola Bay village is unknown. Little is known about the Panzacola natives after 1725.

Jordán de Reina's glowing report of the Bahía de Panzacola prompted officials to recommend a settlement there to prevent the French from occupying the bay. The viceroy sent Captain Andrés de Pez, one of the advocates of the Panzacola site, to Spain to obtain permission and support for such a settlement. Because of Panzacola's superior harbor, Pez recommended abandoning San Agustín de la Florida (St. Augustine) and making Panzacola the capital of La Florida. For only half of the money spent on St. Augustine, 48,000 pesos annually, he stated, Spain could maintain a fort at Pensacola and have an excellent harbor to go with it. In addition, the Indians at Pensacola (the English spelling) were ready to be converted to Christianity.

The Council of War in Madrid disapproved Pez's plan, but Carlos II, king of Spain, ordered that Panzacola be settled without abandoning St. Augustine. The council acquiesced but directed that first a scientific survey be made of Pensacola Bay.

The viceroy sent two expeditions to Pensacola Bay in 1693. The first, by sea, was headed by Admiral Pez, accompanied by Dr. Carlos de Sigüenza y Gongóra, a noted retired professor from the University of Mexico, and Captain Jordán de Reina. They rechristened the bay Bahía de Santa María de Galve, for the Virgin Mary and the viceroy, the Conde de Galve. The only site still bearing a name given it in 1693 is Punta de Sigüenza (Point Sigüenza), the western end of Santa Rosa Island. After their survey of the bay, Sigüenza joined Pez as one of the staunchest supporters of a settlement there.

Laureano de Torres y Ayala, governor-to-be of St. Augustine, commanded a land expedition that arrived at Pensacola Bay on 2 July 1693. His report indicated that Pensacola was a good port that could easily be fortified but that it lacked building stone.

As a result of these expeditions, a royal order issued on 13 July 1694 directed that Pensacola Bay be occupied and fortified without delay. The initial force was to come from Mexico, but because of a lack of troops and money in Mexico, and the fact that Spain was involved in King William's War (1689–97), nothing was done. There matters rested until 1698.

In that year, two events pushed the Spaniards to occupy Pensacola Bay. Reports indicated that a French expedition led by the Sieur

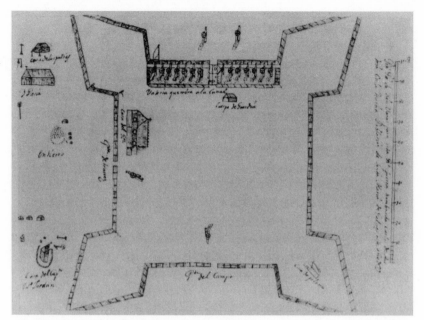

The village of Santa María de Galve, 1698–1722, is shown to the left side of Fort San Carlos de Austria. From top to bottom at left are the rectory, church, cemetery, seven cabins, and the residence of Captain Juan Jordán [de Reina]. The governor's residence was inside the fort. The first known European settlement on the Barrancas coloradas, or Red Cliffs, the village and fort were captured by the French from Mobile and Dauphin Island in 1719 and then abandoned after the Spaniards returned to the site in 1722. Electing to move to Santa Rosa Island, the Spaniards would not occupy the cliffs again until the 1790s.

d'Iberville was preparing to sail for Pensacola Bay. The French had been spurred to action by the plans of Dr. Daniel Coxe of London, who hoped to establish a large settlement of exiled French Huguenots in his province of Carolana (Florida). The Gulf of Mexico was his objective. Spain ordered the viceroy in Mexico to occupy Pensacola Bay without delay. Captain Jordán de Reina, who was in Spain at the time, left immediately for Havana to secure the necessary troops and supplies and sail for Pensacola Bay.

Jordán de Reina reached Pensacola Bay on 17 November 1698 with two ships and sixty soldiers. Four days later, Andrés de Arriola, the appointed governor, who had visited Pensacola Bay in 1695, arrived from Veracruz with three ships and 357 persons. Captain Jaime Franck, an Austrian, was the military engineer. Franck selected a site for the fort near the Barranca de Santo Tomé, which overlooked the entrance to

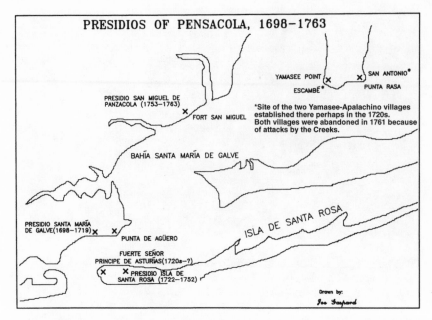

A plan of the Pensacola Bay region in the period 1698–1763 showing the various presidios. Drawn by Joe Gaspard.

the harbor, and began to build. He named the fort San Carlos de Austria, for thirteen-year-old Charles of Austria, later Charles VI of the Holy Roman Empire. Built of pine logs, each side of the planned fort measured 275 feet with a bastion on each corner. Immediate construction was restricted to building the front wall facing the harbor entrance, and there sixteen cannon were mounted to discourage any foreign ships from entering the bay. Neither Arriola nor Franck liked Pensacola, and both wanted to leave as soon as possible.

The situation at Pensacola was far from good. Many of the troops and workers had been released from jails in Mexico and were not desirable settlers. Forty of the criminals deserted soon after their arrival, but most were recaptured. The camp split into factions, and stealing was common. On 4 January 1699, a fire caused by some careless gamblers destroyed a number of buildings, including the main storehouse for provisions, and the garrison there faced the possibility of starvation.

To add to the Spaniards' woes, the anticipated French squadron arrived on 26 January. The commander of the fleet, the marquis de Chasteaumorant, informed Arriola that they were only in search of some Canadian adventurers. But Arriola was not deceived; he was sure that it was d'Iberville's expedition and that it intended to establish a base on the Gulf Coast. Arriola refused permission to enter the harbor, and the French sailed westward. Soon after they departed, Arriola left for Mexico to warn the viceroy about the French and to secure supplies and reinforcements.

Upon arriving at Veracruz, Arriola learned that because the Scots were planning a colony at Darién (Panama) and the Spaniards were preparing an expedition to oust them, no help could be provided him. Reports also reached Mexico that Englishmen were planning a settlement near Pensacola. Fortunately, the Scottish threat was soon over, and Arriola finally secured 100 men from Mexican slums and prisons whom he carried to Pensacola to assist him in driving both the French and English from the Gulf Coast.

Arriola departed Pensacola on 4 March 1700 to accomplish his mission. The so-called Englishmen turned out to be Frenchmen whom Arriola captured and carried to the French at Fort Maurepas (Ocean Springs, Mississippi). The Spaniards were received with great hospitality. Arriola warned, however, that the French fort was in Spanish territory and must be abandoned. The French countered that they had been ordered by their king to establish the fort on the Gulf Coast to prevent the English from doing so and that they could not leave without orders from France. Arriola decided to give up his plans to oust the French and sailed for Pensacola. A hurricane hit en route, and the Spaniards lost all their ships but one. After much suffering, the survivors returned to Fort Maurepas, where, again, they were well treated by the French, who returned them to Pensacola.

The Pensacola garrison suffered constantly from a lack of supplies. Efforts to grow foodstuffs failed in the sandy soil. The garrison engaged in raising sheep and, much later, cattle. An abundant supply of large pine trees enabled them to produce ships' masts for export, but that industry never made Pensacola self-sufficient and the settlement was forced to rely heavily upon outside sources for its survival.

France and Spain had a basic difference in their reasons for being on the northern Gulf Coast. The Spaniards came to prevent the French from settling there. The French came to make money through trade with the Indians and Spaniards. They mistakenly thought they were near the silver mines of northern Mexico, but they also hoped to discover rich mineral deposits in the Mississippi Valley. The one thing Spain and France had in common was to prevent the English from settling on the Gulf Coast.

When the French sold goods at Pensacola, they usually received cash because the Spaniards were most often paid in specie when the situado, or annual subsidy, was received. Unfortunately, it did not always arrive on time, and even when it did, it usually contained only a fraction of the money due the presidio.

The relationship between Spain and France over their Gulf Coast settlements during the early years reflected their differing goals. In 1701, France requested that Spain cede Pensacola to them. In turn, Spain wanted French Louisiana to be placed under the jurisdiction of the viceroy of New Spain. Neither side succeeded in these diplomatic efforts, although the French continued to want Pensacola. Later, they argued over the boundary between Florida and Louisiana: The Spaniards claimed jurisdiction to the east bank of Mobile Bay, while the French held out for the Perdido River and Bay as the boundary. This dispute went on for years, but Spain finally, and not willingly, recognized the Perdido as the boundary.

The death of Carlos II on 1 November 1700 soon brought on the War of the Spanish Succession (Queen Anne's War in the colonies). Carlos II had no children. Before he died, and after much diplomatic maneuvering, he had designated Philip of Anjou, grandson of Louis XIV, as his heir. Other European countries including England, not wanting to see France and Spain united under one crown, formed the Grand Alliance, which declared war on 4 May 1702. These events were to have a direct bearing on Spanish Pensacola and on Mobile, where by 1702 the French had built Fort St. Louis de La Mobile at the mouth of the Dog River. The French at Mobile were much better supplied than were the Spaniards, and, fortunately for the Spaniards, they were generous with what they had. The Spanish garrison would have been forced to abandon Pensacola, or to surrender it to the English, if it had not been for supplies and military support furnished by the French.

After their military success in the Apalachee area in 1704 (see chapter 5), the English and their Indian allies tried several times—unsuccessfully—to capture the Pensacola presidio. They destroyed the fort in the winter of 1704–5, but the French came to the Spaniards' rescue. Between 1707 and 1713, the Anglo-allied Indians, usually led by a few Englishmen, laid siege to Pensacola on several occasions, but help from Mobile forced them to retire. Almost miraculously, the war ended with Pensacola still in Spanish hands.

Some but not much information is available on the priests who served the presidio during its early years. Three priests arrived with Arriola in 1698: Fathers Rodrigo de la Barreda, Alfonso Ximénez de Cisneros, and Miguel Gómez Alvarez. In 1702, Arriola purchased a house from one of the soldiers and converted it into a hospital, Nuestra Señora de las Angustias (Our Lady of Afflictions). Fray Joseph de Salazar, a friar-surgeon, served in this hospital as did several others of the Order of San Juan de Dios. About 1709, the hospital moved inside the fort; and Fray Juan de Chavarria and Fray Felipe de Orbalaes y Abreo served as medico-friars there, but they were gone by 1713. Some gossip about several of the presidio's priests, along with some information about Pensacola's population, was recorded by Father François Le Maire, a visiting priest from Mobile.

Le Maire arrived in Pensacola in 1712 and stayed as acting pastor for three years. He came, he wrote, because two priests had been murdered there in just punishment for the wicked life they led. Nothing more is known about this incident unless it is in some way related to the murder of one priest and the capture of another by enemy Indians in 1711. But Le Maire had more to say about Pensacola.

The fort there, he wrote, was a "land galley," garrisoned by 250 soldiers, who were well known by the Indians for their cowardice. He classified the civil population as "scum" who had escaped torture or execution in Mexico by being sent to Pensacola. These residents, Le Maire observed, were his "fine parishioners." Despite his caustic comments about Pensacola's citizens, Le Maire was an outstanding cartographer, whose significance in North American map-making has only recently been recognized. His map of 1713 is of special interest because of the canal or channel shown on Santa Rosa Island.

The period of peace for Pensacola lasted only from the end of Queen Anne's War in 1713 to the outbreak of the War of the Quadruple Alliance in 1718. Cooperation between Pensacola and Mobile was not as good as it had been during the war years. The French wanted to sell merchandise in Pensacola, but Spain opposed the practice. The result was an extensive contraband trade which was estimated, by 1717, at 12,000 pesos a year. Even so, the French grumbled that they made little money from the Spaniards.

England, Holland, Austria, and France formed the Quadruple Alliance in 1718 to check the ambitions of Philip V of Spain. France declared war on Spain on 9 January 1719. Two days previously, the Company of the Indies had ordered the Sieur de Bienville, the governor of Louisiana, to take possession of Pensacola. On 14 May, the French captured the recently built battery on Point Sigüenza, then crossed the channel to Fort San Carlos de Austria and engaged in a brief cannonade with the fort. Governor Juan Pedro Matamoros de Isla, unaware that France and Spain were at war, quickly surrendered.

The French took their Spanish prisoners to Cuba, where they

planned to leave them. But when they reached Havana, its commander, Captain General Gregorio Guazo Calderón, refused to recognize the French flag of truce on the grounds that the French had attacked Pensacola without proper warning. The Spaniards prepared to recapture Pensacola, and Admiral Alfonso Carrascosa de la Torre, commander of a Spanish fleet of twelve ships and 1,800 men, reached Pensacola on 6 August. When the Spaniards landed, about ninety French soldiers (the numbers vary) deserted to join them. The French officer in charge at the site, the Sieur de Châteaugué, Bienville's brother, still had about 200 soldiers under his command, but they put up such a feeble defense he had no choice but to surrender. The Frenchmen were sent to Cuba for imprisonment in Havana's notorious Moro Castle.

When word reached Mobile that the Spanish fleet was at Pensacola, French troops accompanied by several bands of Indians rushed there but arrived too late. The Chevalier de Noyan, who commanded one of the French-Indian forces, talked with Matamoros de Isla and learned that the next Spanish objective was Mobile and Dauphin Island. Noyan quickly returned to Mobile, and the French prepared to defend the area.

Part of the Spanish fleet led by Captain Antonio de Mendieta quickly set sail for Dauphin Island. After twelve days and nights of frustrating efforts to capture Dauphin Island, and without the arrival of expected assistance from Mexico, the Spaniards finally gave up and departed Mobile Bay on 25 August.

In early September, the French made plans to recapture Pensacola. Bienville led a force of 400 Indians overland, while the recently arrived French fleet under the command of Admiral Desnos de Champeslin left Mobile and reached Pensacola on the sixteenth. Pensacola was well defended because the Spanish *flota* from Havana was still there, but the naval battle that ensued lasted only an hour before the Spaniards gave up. The reinforced Spanish battery at Point Sigüenza put up a stout defense but ran out of ammunition and surrendered. Matamoros de Isla at Fort San Carlos de Austria had planned a strong defense, but fear of Bienville's Indian warriors persuaded him to give up without a fight.

The French sent 625 privateersmen and noncombatants back to Havana in exchange for the French soldiers under Châteaugué. The soldiers and the officers, including Matamoros de Isla, were taken as prisoners to Brest, in France. When the Spaniards departed, the French permitted the Indians to plunder the Spanish presidio. Forty-seven of the Frenchmen who had surrendered to the Spaniards in August were court-martialed. Twelve were hung, the others were sentenced to forced labor. Twelve French soldiers and eight Indians were left at Pensacola under the command of the Sieur Delisle with orders to give token opposition if the Spaniards returned. He was then to destroy what was left of the fort and retreat to Mobile.

A long-awaited Spanish fleet from Veracruz, commanded by Admiral Francisco de Cornejo, finally sailed for Pensacola but went instead to St. Joseph's Bay. There Cornejo was warned that Champeslin and his ships were still at Pensacola. Fearful that he might not succeed in an attack upon the French, Cornejo went to Havana to await reinforcements. Plans to recapture Pensacola continued, but nothing was actually done. By early 1720, peace overtures were under way in Europe.

France planned to keep Pensacola under any circumstances, while Spain demanded its return. For nearly a year they negotiated an end to the war. Finally, France recognized that it would be impossible to obtain Spanish cooperation unless Pensacola was restored to Spain, so, in the treaty of 27 March 1721, France gave up its claim.

Bienville received orders on 6 April 1722 to return Pensacola to Spain. Lieutenant Colonel Alejandro Wauchope, the Spanish governor-to-be of the Pensacola presidio, visited Mobile in June. He carried instructions for the French to return Pensacola and all of the armament and supplies that were there in 1719, but Bienville could not comply with the Spanish demands: The Indians had destroyed virtually everything in the presidio except some cannon, which were buried in the sand.

After some delay, Wauchope reached Pensacola with three ships and an infantry company. Wauchope (also written Wauchop) was a Scotsman who had served in Spain's Irish Brigade. He received possession of the site from Lieutenant Jean Baptiste Rebue (also Reboul) on 26 November. All that remained was one delapidated cabin, a bake oven, and a lidless cistern.

Wauchope's orders called for a canal to be dug across Santa Rosa Island to lower the water level in Pensacola Bay to prevent large enemy ships of war from entering the harbor. An engineer, Don José de Berbegal, accompanied Wauchope to supervise the project. If it proved to be an impractical plan, they were to move the presidio to Santa Rosa Island. The projected fort to be built on Point Sigüenza was to be manned by 150 soldiers of infantry and artillery but supplemented by the garrison from St. Joseph. In February 1723, Captain Pedro Primo de Rivera and men from St. Joseph's Bay were brought to Pensacola. By that date considerable progress had been made in building the new Presidio Isla de Santa Rosa/Punta de Sigüenza about three-quarters of a mile east of Point Sigüenza. The canal across the island was not attempted.

The new presidio consisted of a church, warehouse, powder magazine, quarters for the officers, barracks for the soldiers, twenty-four small buildings for the workmen, convicts, and others, a bake oven, a house for the governor, and a look-out tower sixty feet high.

But for the Spaniards, troubles in Pensacola were far from over. Wauchope had the same basic problem that his predecessors confronted: Supplies for the garrison were uniformly inadequate and late in arriving. Once more, Pensacola turned to its French neighbors for help. Bienville complied with Wauchope's plea for assistance and sent supplies from New Orleans to Pensacola via Mobile. In spite of this help, Wauchope intended to observe royal orders that directed that all contraband French goods arriving for sale at Pensacola were to be burned and those involved punished.

In 1724, Wauchope complied strictly with these orders when a Madame Olivier and others from Mobile visited Pensacola. The madame, it seems, came to visit friends, while her companions brought some goods to sell. The Spaniards seized and burned the boats including the merchandise and put all the Frenchmen except Madame Olivier and her daughter in irons. This was only one of several similar incidents.

If contraband trade was not enough, hostile Indians presented the Spaniards with additional trouble. An attack upon Pensacola by the pro-English Talapoosa in 1727 may well have spelled disaster for the Spaniards had it not been for the Sieur de Périer, governor of Louisiana, who came to the rescue. He warned the Talapoosa that, if they did not cease their attack upon the Spanish presidio, he would turn loose a large force of Choctaw that would destroy them. As a result, the Talapoosa lifted the siege and retreated from Pensacola.

Illegal trade between the French and Spaniards could not be prevented, despite the best efforts of officers like Wauchope. In 1738, the Spanish secretary of state wrote the viceroy of New Spain that he should take action against the commandant and officers at Pensacola unless they stopped trading with the French. Such warnings had little effect, but one policy did affect this trade. In 1743, Louisiana officials forbade French merchants at Mobile and New Orleans to carry merchandise to Pensacola because the Spaniards had not paid their outstanding debts. The Spaniards were thus forced to go to New Orleans for their goods and to pay cash for them.

The year 1743 was important to Pensacola for reasons other than the trade imbroglio. An artist's sketch of the Santa Rosa Island presidio and orders for a report on the remote outpost would be significant in the history of Pensacola.

Dominic Serres, a Frenchman serving on a trading ship that visited Pensacola in 1743, made the sketch of the presidio. He later became a seascape painter in London. When the British learned that Florida was to be traded to Great Britain in 1763, Serres's drawing was published in William Roberts's *Natural History of Florida* (London, 1763). Several of the buildings are identified in the sketch, including the octagonal-shaped church. This drawing is the only existing representation of the island presidio.

On 15 April, the viceroy in Mexico City directed Field Marshal Pedro de Rivera y Villalón to prepare a report on the Pensacola presidio. Rivera had made an extended inspection of the presidios west of Louisiana some years earlier, which had had a strong impact on those fortifications.

In the preparation of his Pensacola study he did not visit the site but relied for his observations on the letters and recommendations of men who had served there. In his report, dated 29 May 1744, Rivera briefly, and with some errors, traced the history of Pensacola's presidios and the ebb and flow of the three-way struggle for Florida among France, Great Britain, and Spain. He noted that the violent storms that had virtually destroyed the presidio on several occasions were an ever-present danger. He also recognized that, in the event of war, the presidio would easily fall prey to an attacking force but that it would cost thousands of pesos to build a more suitable fort, which would then require more manpower. In spite of its problems, Rivera recommended retaining Pensacola but with a reduction in the size of the garrison. He did not have a recommendation on whether the presidio should remain on the island or be moved back to the mainland.

The only part of Rivera's report that seems to have been implemented was the reduction in manpower. In 1750, two companies of infantry were stationed there, only sixty-two men with thirty-six fit for duty. The labor battalion had twenty-four men.

Sometime in the 1740s the Spaniards built a small blockhouse on the mainland which they named Fort San Miguel. Its purpose and that of the small detachment of soldiers stationed there were to help protect the Yamasee-Apalachino Indians living nearby from attacks by British-allied Indians. Located in present-day downtown Pensacola, the little fort was soon to be the site of Pensacola's third presidio.

On 3 November 1752, a hurricane struck Santa Rosa Island. It

In 1743 a Frenchman, Dominic Serres, serving as a seaman on a Spanish merchant ship, made a drawing of the presidio on Santa Rosa Island, the only illustration of the presidio that exists. The view is from the interior of the bay looking south. Notable among the buildings shown is an octagonal-shaped church, the first such building in Pensacola's history. Serres later became famous as a seascape painter for King George III of England.

destroyed all of the buildings except a storehouse and the hospital. Nearly three years later, a fort built of stakes, a warehouse for supplies, and another for gunpowder were located on the site of the old presidio. Some distance to the west were the church, hospital, commandant's quarters, and a camp for the garrison. In August 1755, the buildings were reported to be deteriorating.

The following summer, the Marqués de las Amarillas, the viceroy of New Spain, ordered that the presidio be relocated to the site of Fort San Miguel on the mainland and that it be named the Presidio San Miguel de las Amarillas. A royal order of October 1757 changed the name to the Presidio San Miguel de Panzacola. Although the area had long been familiarly known as Panzacola, it was now officially so recognized. The new presidio was to be manned by 200 soldiers, although it would be some time before that many were in place.

A new commandant, Colonel Miguel Román de Castilla y Lugo, reached Pensacola in early 1757. En route from Veracruz, he had been shipwrecked on Massacre (Dauphin) Island and had lost most of the supplies and some of the troops he was bringing to Pensacola. The soldiers who survived increased the garrison to about 150 men. By August 1757, that number had grown to 180. Still, the new location was in no condition to defend itself in the event of Indian hostilities, which were expected any day. Román de Castilla quickly set about building a new stockade and establishing other defensive measures for the presidio.

The walls of the new stockade, built of vertical pointed stakes, were soon completed except for the one facing the water. The walls eventually measured 365 by 700 feet. Within the stockade were the government house, a church, warehouses, barracks, bake ovens, and a brick house for the governor. Outside the stockade, seven or eight paces distant, was a single line of dwellings for the civilians, officers, and married soldiers.

Except for periodic scares, Pensacola escaped attacks by hostile Indians for several years after Román de Castilla arrived, despite the fact that the French and Indian War swept the hinterland. During that time the number of soldiers increased to 224, including two infantry companies and one of light artillery. Even supplies and provisions arrived more frequently. By the summer of 1760, however, conditions began to deteriorate.

In June, fear of an attack by unfriendly Indians prompted the governor to clear the area around the stockade, destroying the houses and moving the occupants into the fort. If the Indian menace was not enough, in August a hurricane destroyed half of the stockade and blew the roofs off the houses. The Spaniards were unable to secure new cypress bark, so Pensacola's houses went through the winter of 1760–61 without roofs.

The year 1761 was more trying. In February, the Alibama Indians attacked the Spanish Indian village of Punta Rasa on Garçon Point, killing several soldiers and resident Indians. Such attacks continued periodically, and the situation became so alarming that, in May, Román de Castilla moved the friendly Yamasee-Apalachino Indians from the villages on Garçon Point into the stockade. In June, the captain-general of Cuba dispatched two infantry companies of *pardos* (mulattoes) commanded by Captain Vizente Manuel de Zéspedes to Pensacola. In turn, some of the women from Pensacola went to Havana, but about 200 women and children remained. For the most part, the residents were confined to the stockade, although cavalrymen did escort them to the nearby creek for water.

Again, the French came to the rescue. In September, the governor of Louisiana, Chevalier de Kerlerec, sent a representative, M. Baudin, to help establish peace between the Indians and the Spaniards. Baudin succeeded, and the peace accord was signed on 14 September 1761. The Indians agreed to cease their attacks, and arrangements were made for an exchange of prisoners.

The question of why the French were usually successful in such negotiations has a simple answer: They carried on an extensive trade with the Indians, while the Spaniards did not. The French traded guns and provisions for deerskins and other furs, and if they stopped this exchange, the Indians, heavily dependent upon such trade, would suffer. Thus the French exercised great influence among the natives of the area. But for Spanish Governor Román de Castilla, the French solution of the Indian problem came too late.

By the summer of 1761, officials in New Spain replaced the Pensacola governor with an officer who was an experienced Indian fighter, Colonel Diego Ortiz Parrilla. Although opposed to his new assignment, he assumed command on 21 October. The new governor was appalled at the terrible condition of the presidio. He accused Román de Castilla and some of the other officers of gross mismanagement. He also believed Román de Castilla to be involved in illicit trade, which seemed to be confirmed when a British ship belonging to William Walton & Co. arrived later that year. In addition, Román de Castilla and some of the officers owned and operated stores in the stockade which charged exorbitant prices for the goods sold. But the official residencia, the investigation into the former governor's conduct in office, was still not complete by May 1762, when Román de Castilla left Pensacola.

For his part, Ortiz Parrilla spent the next year and more rebuilding the presidio and preparing its defenses in the event that the French and Indian War should again reach Pensacola. Spain finally entered the war in 1762 as an ally of France. As a result, France ceded Louisiana west of the Mississippi River including the Isle of Orleans, to Spain. But Spain quickly lost Havana to the British. When the war ended in February 1763, Spain exchanged La Florida for Havana. Thus Pensacola became a British possession.

In June 1763, a British entrepreneur, James Noble, arrived at Pensacola. He quickly purchased a number of town lots from the departing Spaniards. He also bought all of the lands claimed by the Yamasee-Apalachinos, probably a million or more acres, for $100,000. Later, this purchase from the Indians was disallowed for a lack of proof of his claim.

Finally, on 6 August 1763, British Lieutenant Colonel Augustin Prevost and accompanying troops reached Pensacola. He officially accepted its transfer to Great Britain from Spanish Colonel Ortiz Parrilla. All of the Spaniards, with one exception, and all of the Yamasee-Apalachinos left for Havana and Veracruz in early September. The British were happy with the strategic location that they had acquired

This British plan of the harbor and settlement of Pensacola was made in the year 1763, when Great Britain assumed rule over Florida. It contains a number of inaccuracies.

on the Gulf Coast, but they were sorely disappointed with its ruinous condition.

What had it cost the Spaniards to maintain Pensacola's presidios from 1698 to 1763? Over four and a half million pesos:

Presidio Santa María de Galve (1698–1719)	971,763 pesos
War of the Quardruple Alliance (1719–22)	1,070,284 pesos
Presidio Isla de Santa Rosa (1722–52)	572,505 pesos
Presidio San Miguel de Panzacola (1753–63)	435,826 pesos
Other expenses charged the presidios	1,515,442 pesos
Total	4,565,820 pesos

Excluding expenses for the war of 1719–22, the cost was divided into salaries, 45.9 percent; provisions, 38.9 percent; fortifications, 4.7 percent; matériel, 9.5 percent; other, 1.0 percent.

Spain had accomplished only half of its original objective in occupying Pensacola. With the assistance of the French, it had prevented the British from establishing a base on the Gulf of Mexico for sixty-five years. But it had not accomplished its other major purpose, the ouster of France from Louisiana. The British victories accomplished that ouster, but they also cost Spain Pensacola and all of La Florida.

Bibliography

Coker, William S. "The Financial History of Pensacola's Spanish Presidios, 1698–1763." *Pensacola Historical Society Quarterly* 9, no. 4 (Spring 1979):1–20.

———. "The Village on the Red Cliffs." *Pensacola History Illustrated* 1, no. 2 (1984):22–26.

———. "West Florida (The Spanish Presidios of Pensacola), 1686–1763." In *A Guide to the History of Florida*, edited by Paul S. George, pp. 49–56. New York: Greenwood Press, 1989.

———, et al. "Pedro de Rivera's Report on the Presidio of Punta de Sigüenza, Alias Panzacola, 1744." *Pensacola Historical Society Quarterly* 8, no. 4 (Winter 1975; rev. ed. 1980):1–22.

Cox, Daniel. *A Description of the English Province of CAROLANA, by the Spaniards call'd FLORIDA, And by the French La LOUISIANE.* Introduction by William S. Coker. Gainesville: University Presses of Florida, 1976.

Dunn, William Edward. *Spanish and French Rivalry in the Gulf Region of the United States, 1678–1702: The Beginnings of Texas and Pensacola.* Austin: University of Texas Bulletin, no. 1705, 1917.

Dunn transcripts, 1700–1703. "Autos made upon the Measures taken for the Occupation and Fortification of Santa María de Galve." University of Texas, Austin.

Faye, Stanley. "The Spanish and British Fortifications of Pensacola, 1698–1821." *Pensacola Historical Society Quarterly* 6, no. 4 (April 1972):151–292. Reprinted from the *Florida Historical Quarterly*.

Folmer, Henry. *Franco-Spanish Rivalry in North America.* Glendale, Calif.: Arthur H. Clark Co., 1953.

Ford, Lawrence C. *The Triangular Struggle for Spanish Pensacola, 1689–1739.* The Catholic University of America Studies in Hispanic-American History, vol. 2. Washington, 1939.

Griffen, William B. "Spanish Pensacola, 1700–1763." *Florida Historical Quarterly* 27, nos. 3, 4 (January–April 1959):242–62.

Griffith, Wendell Lamar. "The Royal Spanish Presidio of San Miguel de Panzacola, 1753–1763." Master's thesis, University of West Florida, 1988.

Hann, John H. "Florida's Terra Incognita: West Florida's Natives in the Sixteenth and Seventeenth Century." *Florida Anthropologist* 41, no. 1 (March 1988):61–107.

Holmes, Jack D. L. "Dauphin Island in the Franco-Spanish War, 1719–1722." In *Frenchmen and French Ways in the Mississippi Valley*, edited by John Francis McDermott, pp. 103–25. Urbana: University of Illinois Press, 1969.

Jackson, Jack, Robert S. Weddle, and Winston Deville. *Mapping Texas and the Gulf Coast: The Contributions of Saint-Denis, Oliván, and Le Maire.* College Station: Texas A&M University Press, 1990.

Leonard, Irving A. "Don Andrés de Arriola and the Occupation of Pensacola

Bay." In *New Spain and the Anglo-American West: Historical Contributions Presented to Herbert Eugene Bolton,* edited by George P. Hammond, pp. 81–106. Lancaster, Pa.: Lancaster Press, Inc., 1932.

——, ed. and trans. "The Spanish Re-Exploration of the Gulf Coast in 1686." *Mississippi Valley Historical Review* 22, no. 1 (June 1935):547–57.

Manucy, Albert. "The Founding of Pensacola—Reasons and Reality." *Florida Historical Quarterly* 37, nos. 3, 4 (January–April 1959):223–41.

Rowland, Dunbar, and A. G. Sanders, eds. *Mississippi Provincial Archives: French Dominion, 1701–1743.* 3 vols. Jackson: Press of the Mississippi Department of Archives and History, 1927–29.

Spain. Archivo General de Indias. Testimony of Autos, no. 5, Mexico 633, 1709.

Weddle, Robert S. *The French Thorn: Rival Explorers in the Spanish Sea, 1682–1762.* College Station: Texas A&M University Press, 1991.

8 British Rule in the Floridas

Robin F. A. Fabel

Florida acquired a white population of significant size only after 1763, when the area became British. King George III's empire had benefitted enormously from victory in the Seven Years' War (called the French and Indian War in North America). To retrieve Cuba from its British conquerors, Charles III of Spain reluctantly agreed to hand them the larger, if poorer, province of Florida. In the same region Louis XV of France ceded to Britain all his holdings east of the Mississippi River—chiefly Fort Toulouse and Mobile—except for the "island" on which stood New Orleans. In a gesture shrewder and less generous than might at first appear, Louis gave to Spain that city and all French claims to territory west of the Mississippi.

The British thus acquired more land on or near the Gulf of Mexico than could conveniently be administered as a single unit. They decided to create two Floridas. East Florida comprised most of what is today Florida, except for the Panhandle; it was separated from West Florida by the Apalachicola River. Its northern boundary was the St. Marys River.

The Gulf of Mexico and Lake Pontchartrain formed the southern boundary of West Florida, a much bigger province than East Florida. Its western boundary was the Mississippi and its northern boundary, initially, 31° of latitude. That arbitrary line, decided in ignorance, quickly seemed inadequate, particularly to speculators with an eye on the lush lands around Natchez. Among the men lobbying for an adjustment were George Johnstone, governor-elect of West Florida, and General

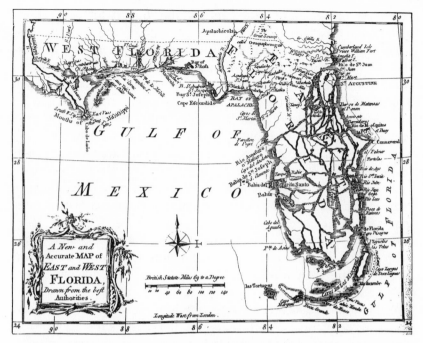

As shown on this 1763 British map, the Florida inherited by Great Britain in that year extended as far west as the Mississippi River. London decided that the territory was so vast that it should be established as two colonies, divided at the Apalachicola River, with capitals at St. Augustine and Pensacola. These were the fourteenth and fifteenth continental British colonies south of Canada. They remained loyal to the British Crown during the American Revolution.

Phineas Lyman, a would-be colonizer. The administration responded in 1764 by setting the new northern boundary of West Florida at a line drawn eastward from the confluence of the Yazoo with the Mississippi, the line of 32° 28″.

Johnstone and his counterpart in East Florida, James Grant, began to govern in 1764. Each avidly sought to increase the population in his province. Only settlers could exploit the supposedly rich economic potential of the Floridas and protect the new provinces from enemies. The Spaniards in Louisiana were seen, correctly, as likely to war again with the British. Other potential enemies were the Amerindians who formed the great majority of the population in the Floridas before the American Revolution. The London government forbade the superintendent of southern Indians, for instance, to mediate an end to the Creek-Choctaw War, which began in 1765. Although the ministry's motive was to deflect Indian hostility from whites, the war probably deterred some would-be immigrants. Others, hungry for land, refused to be scared away.

The crown offered land free but for registration and surveying expenses. Major entrepreneurs who promised to import agricultural laborers could apply for large tracts, tens of thousands of acres. Veterans and immigrants with no other qualification than a family could get smaller acreages. News of these opportunities, together with apocryphal testimony to the healthiness of the climate and optimistic forecasts of the commercial prospects in both Floridas, appeared in papers on both sides of the Atlantic. For a while, in 1763, South Carolinians rushed to claim lands north of the St. Marys River and in East Florida. In London an East Florida Society formed to lobby to secure major land grants for its members.

Obtaining labor posed more problems than obtaining land. White people could be recruited to work as indentured servants on the plantations of others: Andrew Turnbull enlisted over 1,400 individuals from Mediterranean countries to work on his estates at New Smyrna. The difficulty was to make them stay. Governor Grant wrote in 1771, on the eve of his permanent departure from it, that East Florida had a white population of only 288 and 900 black slaves.

West Florida had a greater white population than East Florida, but, even so, whites were a small minority. More of the land granted there was in comparatively small tracts, given according to family size or for service in the Seven Years' War. In the early 1770s, William Gordon, the chaplain at Mobile, guessed the size of the main tribes in West Florida. If one uses a commonly accepted equivalent of three and a half individuals for every warrior, there were, by Gordon's estimate, 1,600 Chickasaw, 10,500 Choctaw, and 15,750 Creek. At about the same time Elias Durnford, West Florida's lieutenant governor, estimated that the province contained only 3,700 white and 1,200 black inhabitants.

The difficulty of getting to the Floridas and the disappointments following arrival inhibited immigration. Merchants found that settling on the Gulf of Mexico did not ensure a brisk trade with Mexico. Farmers found that the soil on the coast and for many miles inland was infertile. The cost of living was dismayingly high. Manufactured goods were understandably expensive, but so, too, was meat of all sorts. Worst of all was the prevalent sickness. Sometimes, as at Mobile, it was the result of polluted water, but more often it was tropical fevers that devastated newcomers, especially if they came straight from the British Isles. In the fall of 1765, for instance, the British 31st Infantry Regiment, around

400 men, landed at Pensacola in perfect health. They were instantly attacked by a "distemper," probably yellow fever. Within three weeks only two officers and twenty enlisted men remained fit for duty: inside six months almost half the regiment was dead.

Betsey Pilot, the wife of one of the regiment's officers who survived this epidemic and who was at the center of social life wherever she lived, wrote an account years later of her time in Pensacola and, after the regiment moved to East Florida, of her experiences in St. Augustine. As a woman's depiction of life in the British Floridas this unique and still unpublished manuscript reveals that women in the British Floridas had to endure at least as many hardships as the men.

After 1763 the regular British Army garrisons in America and the West Indies had twenty regiments, four of them in the Floridas. Soldiers and, to a lesser extent, sailors of the Royal Navy were important components of the population of the ports of St. Augustine, Pensacola, and Mobile. Their pay helped to keep alive languid economies, and the public works that they undertook, like road building, provided amenities useful to all. But their main purpose, one of enormous comfort to potential immigrants, was to guarantee security. A serious deterrent to immigrants wishing to settle West Florida's hinterland occurred when the British government decided in 1768 to withdraw troops from outlying posts at Manchac and Natchez. The abandonment of Fort St. Mark, Apalachee, in a part of East Florida of little interest to settlers, gave more relief than grief to Britons.

Each of the first governors of the British Floridas put a distinctive stamp on his province. Both were Scots, beneficiaries of the patronage of George III's favorite prime minister, the Scottish Earl of Bute. Neither governor was without merit. Both had reputations for martial prowess, and there was a reasonable expectation that combat experience might be useful in the new provinces. There was an anticipation, an unwarranted one as it turned out, that Spanish and French inhabitants of the Floridas might resent British rule, and a fear, almost realized, that a war with Indians might break out.

James Grant had fought Indians in 1760 and 1761. Burning their homes and crops, he had forced the Cherokee to sue for peace essentially by destroying their means of sustenance. Thus achieving victory without high white casualties had earned him great credit in Britain.

Grant was a bon vivant in his habits and feudal in his outlook. He cooperated with the East Florida Society, whose rich, aristocratic members did not themselves intend to live in Florida. Their general aim was to secure large estates in East Florida to be run by resident

James Grant (1720–1806), first governor of British East Florida.

whites overseeing—after it became clear that white indentured servants would not work the land—black slaves.

Influenced by the example of South Carolina, where he had many
friends, Grant was sure that holdings in East Florida could be made
profitable if landowners established large plantations, employed primarily black slaves, and chose the right crops. He made his North
River Plantation thrive by concentrating on indigo. In the year 1774,
three years after Grant had retired from his governorship, his planta-

tion produced 5,400 pounds of indigo, almost a quarter of that year's export from the entire province. Mount Oswald, the plantation of a wealthy absentee Scottish merchant, Richard Oswald, also prospered. He was the province's chief importer of slaves, and blacks comprised the labor force at Mount Oswald. Cultivation of smallholdings by whites was futile, thought Grant. Amelia Island initially was earmarked for settlement by impoverished white Bermudian yeomen. Clearly in the belief that such a scheme had no future, Grant awarded 10,000 acres on the island to an aristocratic crony, the absentee Lord Egmont, to add to the thousands of acres on the St. Johns River that Egmont already possessed.

At a time when more northerly provinces resounded with debate on the Stamp Act, the Townshend duties, and the rights of colonists, Grant believed that providing a forum for public debate in East Florida was neither necessary nor desirable. He congratulated himself on thus averting the political turmoil then distressing Governor Johnstone in Pensacola.

George Johnstone was a professional naval officer. He had seen combat in two major wars but had risen no higher than post captain. He certainly would never have become a colonial governor had it not been for his friendship with John Home. Best known as a dramatist, Home was also Bute's personal secretary when appointments to the Floridas were decided. Detested by English politicians who were furious that the king had entrusted the highest political office in his gift to a Scottish amateur, Bute soon resigned.

His energetic gubernatorial nominee in West Florida stayed on. Johnstone had a touch of the populist about him. In the navy, ratings had liked him, admirals had not. Now, responsible for the distribution of plots of land in Pensacola, the governor held a lottery for the allocation of plots instead of using this power as a way to distribute favors. Johnstone took no lot for himself until 201 of them had been given out. This self-restraint was probably approved, as was, doubtless, his early summoning of a legislature. It should be noted that an elected lower house first convened in Pensacola in November 1766, while East Floridians had to wait until March 1781 for a comparable institution. West Florida's was a popular assembly in several senses. Johnstone widened the franchise specified in his instructions to include leaseholders as well as freeholders. Moreover, the assemblymen were to receive salaries, a practice absent from the British parliament until the twentieth century.

However popular Johnstone may have been initially, he had a gift for making enemies. It was not long before the army officers in his

George Johnstone (1730–1787), first governor of British West Florida.

province were complaining, with reason, of his high-handedness. In addition he and his Irish-born lieutenant governor, Montfort Browne, were soon on dueling terms. When Johnstone, like Grant in East Florida, insisted on collecting stamp duties, he surely lost some friends. In 1766, however, parliament repealed the contentious Stamp Act, and Johnstone's bellicose Indian policy regained him some popularity with the West Florida assembly. It earned him none with the ministry in

London. Johnstone already had permission for a furlough. He left Pensacola in January 1767, never to return.

Throughout the short history of the British Floridas the poor quality of their immigrants posed a problem. Johnstone had anticipated the difficulty before assuming his governorship and had argued, to deaf ministerial ears, for a scheme to attract immigrants of higher caliber, including Norwegians, Dutch, and New Englanders. He was no chauvinist, and a favorite scheme of his, one that again came to little, was to attract from neighboring Louisiana some French, Germans, and Swiss who had already demonstrated their worth as colonists. He preferred them to the Anglo drifters he described as the overflowing scum of the empire. Confirming Johnstone's generalization, in part, is a letter from his lieutenant governor who alleged that three of the few lawyers in West Florida were poor attorneys expelled from other provinces. The opinion of Brigadier General Frederick Haldimand in 1768 echoed Johnstone's: in Pensacola, he wrote, lived none but drunks and idlers, who corrupted newcomers and who would delay for a long time the growth of West Florida.

Similar difficulties plagued East Florida, where in its early days the only two significant settlements outside the capital were the creations of Denys Rolle on the St. Johns River, and Turnbull's on Mosquito Inlet. Those brought to Rollestown included London vagrants, beggars, debtors, and prostitutes. The immigrants to Turnbull's New Smyrna may have been of higher social standing, but they were less docile. Some of them staged a major mutiny shortly after their arrival in 1768. Governor Grant willingly supplied military force to suppress the rising, which involved bloodshed, drunkenness, and the theft of a vessel as a means to flee Florida. Thereafter, Turnbull treated his Mediterranean settlers more like slaves than indentured servants. His settlement endured until 1777, but, overworked and underfed, many New Smyrnans had died in the years 1768–70.

The British Floridas survived initial difficulties and a loss of optimism. By the early 1770s, both had discovered routes to economic viability, despite early misconceptions and failures.

Johnstone's schemes to lure French Louisianans to West Florida and to make the British trading post at Manchac eclipse New Orleans came to nothing. New Orleans remained the region's chief commercial center, and West Floridians developed an illicit, one-sided, highly profitable trade with it. Louisianans had a large demand for manufactures of good quality, above all for textiles. The colony's Spanish rulers could not satisfy it, but British neighbors could. As early as 1769, a Spanish governor complained that 90 percent of the profits of the Louisiana trade went to the British; in 1776, another Spanish official, Francisco Bouligny, placed that number even higher.

West Florida's timber products also brought profit. The demand in the West Indies for the staves and headers used in barrel-making and for the clapboards, cedar posts, and shingles used to build houses was insatiable. For the tar and pitch obtainable from West Florida's conifers the British government paid a bounty.

East Florida, too, produced naval stores. Of more future significance were its exports of oranges and orange juice, but its chief export was indigo. West Florida grew less indigo but exported far more furs and skins, particularly deerskins, to Britain.

Once West Florida's economic viability was proven, there followed a rush to acquire land in its rich Natchez district. The Company of Military Adventurers intended to settle thousands of New Englanders in seventeen townships there. Phineas Lyman, the company's head, wanted to become governor of a new colony carved from the western region of West Florida, with a capital on the Bayou Pierre or the Big Black River. Montfort Browne, a former lieutenant-governor of West Florida, had similar ambitions. Neither got what he wanted, but if the two men had been given more time, they might well have brought in enough settlers to rule out the possibility of Spanish conquest.

Far more likely than war with Spain in the 1760s and early 1770s was an Indian war. The Indians had classic reasons to resent British intrusion into their traditional territories after 1763, when British newcomers first landed in sizable numbers. The British wanted far more land than their Spanish and French predecessors had occupied. Once land was granted, white interlopers almost instantly violated the boundaries that were supposed to separate them from Indian territory. The Indians wanted the goods the white traders brought but did not like receiving short measure or being swindled through the use of rum. The traders, too, it soon appeared, wanted skins in quantities that depleted the traditional hunting grounds. The British colonial authorities deplored the abuse of rum and passed laws severely restricting its sale to Indians but showed themselves as powerless to control their own traders as they were to prevent illegal settlement in Indian territory.

On top of these grievances was the legacy of war. During the Seven Years' War some tribes, especially the Choctaw, had been allies of the French and were suspicious of English professions of friendship. Rumors circulated that, without the French to check them, the English would enslave the Indians in the Floridas.

More than any other single factor in averting a war between Indians and whites in the Floridas was the diplomatic skill of John Stuart. He was superintendent of Indians in the Southern Department from 1762 until his death in 1779. The chief aims of the Indian congresses Stuart organized in the early 1760s were to legalize cessions of territory to the British with clearly defined and well-understood boundaries and to establish mutually agreed on trade regulations. Indians knew and appreciated that Stuart was sincerely concerned that these agreements should be fair to them.

Understanding the southern Indians as well as he did, Stuart realized, when the American Revolution broke out, that recruiting them to war on the revolutionaries could do the Indians much harm and the British little good. Other factors apart, the Indians would have great difficulty in ascertaining the political sentiments of whites they attacked and were almost as likely to kill loyalists as revolutionaries. Stuart knew too that, since only the British, and not the Americans, had any chance of regularly supplying the trade goods on which the tribes had become dependent, the Indians would be unlikely to turn against them. He therefore tried to keep the southern Indians neutral—but in vain.

Despite the calamity that visited the Cherokee in 1776 when, unsupported by British forces and against Stuart's advice, they warred on the Americans, Seminole that same year acted for the loyalists in East Florida.

Stuart quartered in St. Augustine from June 1775 until the spring of 1776, when he moved to Pensacola to enjoy the advantage of its more central location. A strong force of Georgian revolutionaries under Lachlan McIntosh had invaded East Florida, whose very survival was thus placed in doubt. Orders from London in August both to Stuart and to Patrick Tonyn, Grant's successor as governor of East Florida, confirmed that the southern Indians were to be used as allies. Stuart mediated a peace in October between the Choctaw and Creek, ending their decade-long conflict; it was a peace that his masters in England, in pursuit of "Divide and Rule," had previously forbidden him to arrange. The Creek were far from united in their willingness to support the British, but, with the Seminole, some of them did help to repel a second Georgian invasion of East Florida in 1777.

Stuart won over most of the major Creek headmen to the British cause at a congress in Pensacola in May 1778. Chief among them were Emistiseguo and Alexander McGillivray, both strong partisans of the British. In combination with British redcoats and a provincial force, Thomas Brown's East Florida Rangers, the Indians fought effectively, significantly contributing to the return of Georgia to the Crown in 1778.

For three years after Johnstone's departure in 1767, West Florida had poor leadership. Montfort Browne, obsessed with building a new colony on the Mississippi frontier, governed reluctantly amid great unpopularity. A new governor, John Eliot, arrived in 1769 but hanged himself after one month. From 1769 until 1770, Elias Durnford was a caretaker governor. But his successor, Peter Chester, was a professional soldier and a sound administrator.

Frederick Haldimand commanded the British army's southern district from Pensacola—which he detested—from 1765 to 1773. He has been described as the best and most experienced general then in America. It was the War Office in London, not Haldimand, that in 1768 gave the unfortunate order to evacuate the redcoat garrisons from Manchac and Natchez on the Mississippi. The efficient Haldimand nevertheless restored discipline and order into the troops elsewhere in West Florida. The results would still have been evident in 1778, when for the first time the province would be touched by the war. By then Haldimand was gone from Pensacola, but John Stuart was not, and the superintendent had taken precautions against a surprise incursion into West Florida by way of the Mississippi.

The Choctaw sentinels given the permanent watch on the river at Walnut Hills (Vicksburg) were off-duty one winter's day in 1778 when Captain James Willing of the U.S. Navy and six dozen of his men floated past, unobserved, in the armed vessel *Rattletrap*. On 19 February he arrived at an old haunt of his, Natchez, where the defenseless settlers were glad to believe his promise that, in return for their neutrality, he would spare them and their property.

His instructions from the Continental Congress have not survived, but if winning West Floridians to the revolutionary cause was part of his brief, Willing failed. Looting and unobstructed mayhem characterized his career on the lower Mississippi. He greatly embarrassed Bernardo de Gálvez, governor of Spanish Louisiana, by taking his booty to New Orleans. At the time not only were Spain and Britain not at war, but the British had marked armed superiority locally in the presence of frigates on the Mississippi.

The Willing squall soon blew itself out. Most of his men got back to the United States, but Willing himself and the vessel in which he was sailing fell into British hands. The net effect of his expedition was detrimental to his country. One result was the strengthening of the defenses of West Florida. A number of West Floridians volunteered for John Stuart's mounted rangers, while others joined the infantry regiment raised by the Mobile merchant John McGillivray. The British high command, moreover, ordered regulars to regarrison the abandoned forts at Natchez and Manchac and to build a new one at Baton Rouge. Economically, too, there was reason for Governor Chester to be optimistic. Traditionally, the New England colonies had supplied the West Indies with timber and timber products. Congress had forbidden the continuance of that trade, so there was a huge unsatisfied demand for wood products which West Florida could and did help supply.

The principal restraint on optimism was the prospect of war with Spain. Once France was at war with Britain, as occurred in 1778, it was likely that Spain would join its old ally, as it had done in the Seven Years' War. Although he did not want to set an example damaging to the interests of Spain, and so was reluctant to support rebelling colonists, the Spanish monarch, Charles III, was eager to avenge the humiliations and losses that Britain had inflicted on his country in the 1760s. So, even though the act would help the American rebels succeed, Charles declared war on Britain on 21 June 1779.

In theory he had placed both the British Floridas in jeopardy. Although East Florida stuck out like a thumb temptingly close to Spanish Cuba, the authorities there were more interested in British Jamaica, which they never took, and the Bahamas, which they eventually did conquer. West Florida, therefore, became the preferred target. Gálvez, in Spanish Louisiana, calculated that West Florida was vulnerable. Its weak spot was the thinly garrisoned settlements scattered along the lower Mississippi where Willing had met such small resistance. Of particular importance, in that its possession by an enemy would sever the link between West Florida's capital and the settlements in the Natchez district, was the tiny trading center of Manchac, at the junction of the Mississippi River and the Iberville Bayou. Its twenty-three-man garrison could not even delay Gálvez when he appeared with an army nearly 1,000 strong.

Potentially able to hold out longer, Baton Rouge had a garrison of 300. Their commander, Colonel Alexander Dickson, had thirteen cannon within a redoubt protected by a ditch and chevaux-de-frise. It had been hurriedly constructed and would probably have fallen if Gálvez had stormed it with the superior numbers he had at his disposal. He preferred to reduce it with artillery, almost certainly saving lives by using a ruse to site his (comparatively) heavy guns rather than by digging trenches and saps in the conventional way. Baton Rouge fell after a few hours of bombardment. Dickson gave up the entire Natchez district when he surrendered Baton Rouge to Gálvez. He must have reasoned that any further resistance by inhabitants scattered through the province's western area would be futile. Some Natchez residents preparing to defend Fort Panmure disagreed and were furious with him, but his assumption was probably correct.

Gálvez had met with great difficulty in securing cooperation from the Spanish authorities but received better support after his conquests of 1779. In March of the following year, he was able to secure the surrender of Fort Charlotte in Mobile. Its commander was an engineer officer and West Florida's former acting governor, Elias Durnford, who could justly argue that the fort's crumbling walls made prolonged resistance against determined besiegers impossible.

But for an untimely and extremely destructive fall hurricane, Gálvez possibly could have taken West Florida's capital in the same year as Mobile. He had to delay a serious attempt until 1781, when success was not a foregone conclusion. The British Fort George, on a hilltop site, was a great deal stronger than Fort Charlotte, and the breathing space afforded by the hurricane gave Major General John Campbell, the military commander at Pensacola, time for a considerable concentration of loyalists in the town. Had they been used more skillfully and in greater numbers, Britain's Creek and Choctaw allies might have severely damaged Pensacola's Spanish besiegers. With luck, Campbell's coastal batteries could have kept the Spaniards out of Pensacola harbor until relief ships of the British navy arrived from Jamaica to scatter the Spanish transports.

The British enjoyed little luck in 1781, however, in Pensacola or elsewhere. With some justification Sir Peter Parker, who commanded the king's ships at Port Royal, Jamaica, refused to give high priority to the relief of Pensacola. The invasion of Jamaica from nearby Cuba was certainly on the Spanish agenda. Parker well knew that in England, although the fall of Pensacola might be thought unfortunate, the fall of Jamaica would be received as utterly disastrous.

And so, during a siege which lasted from 9 March until 8 May 1781, General Campbell and Governor Chester looked in vain for English sails on the horizon. On 8 May a grenade from a Spanish siege howitzer ignited the powder store in the Halfmoon Redoubt, a key strongpoint in Pensacola's fortification system. Further resistance was useless. After Campbell's surrender, West Florida ceased to be a British province.

Paradoxically, East Florida was becoming stronger in the revolution's later stages. Both Savannah and Charleston had fallen to British arms in the heyday of the southern strategy that the administration of Lord North had pursued from 1778, but neither port proved permanently tenable. After their fall to Patriot arms the loyalist inhabitants, together with Tory refugees from the Georgia and Carolina hinterland, fled to

Bernardo de Gálvez, twenty-seven-year-old Spanish governor of Louisiana, helped the Patriot cause during the American Revolution by capturing British forts in the Mississippi valley, Mobile in March 1780, and Pensacola and the remainder of British West Florida in 1781.

East Florida. As a result, by 1783 its population had ballooned to 17,375. The newcomers were loyal but not submissive. Used to having a representative assembly, they pressured a reluctant Governor Tonyn into summoning one, chiefly so that a slave code could be enacted.

The squabbles of Tonyn with his East Floridians matched the dissension that in the 1760s had marked relations between West Floridians and their governors. The British Floridas are usually, and rightly, described as loyalist. James Willing in West Florida had as little success in spreading enthusiasm for the revolution as had the Georgian invaders of East Florida in 1777. But Floridians had a practically based loyalty to the king that did not extend to royal governors. The king's troops protected them from the Indian majority in the Floridas which, rightly or

The former Spanish Governor's House on the plaza in St. Augustine served the British governors of East Florida from 1763 to 1784. This watercolor sketch, of British origin, is dated November 1764.

wrongly, they feared, and, in theory at least, from Spanish neighbors. The king's parliament supplied the annual subsidy without which the Floridas could not have survived economically.

Most new colonies in America suffered severe hardships and made major adjustments before their societies worked tolerably. The process often took decades. The British Floridas had less than twenty years to solve difficulties of provincial infancy like gubernatorial autocracy and recurrent tensions between civilians and soldiers. Although, through empiricism, both provinces found the road to viability, neither province became economically self-sufficient.

Britain did not lose a great opportunity by surrendering the Floridas to Spain in the peace treaty concluding the American Revolution. Nothing but Gibraltar, which the British public fiercely opposed surrendering, could have placated the Spaniards for ceding back the province that Gálvez had conquered. Even if the Spaniards had returned West Florida, the United States would have been as unwilling to let the British throttle their important Mississippi trade as, in the end, they were unwilling to let the Spaniards. As for East Florida, its trade with Britain, like West Florida's, was heavily unbalanced in Britain's favor, but its exports, again like West Florida's, were never large enough to make Britain dependent on them. Consequently, the British government considered both Floridas disposable, and, to achieve peace, it disposed of them in the Treaty of Paris, signed on 3 September 1783.

Bibliography
Manuscripts

British Library, London. Additional MSS 21661–21892 (Haldimand Papers). Colonial Williamsburg Inc., Williamsburg, Va. Carleton papers.

Great Britain, Public Record Office, Kew. Colonial Office 5 (vols. 540–73 for East Florida; vols. 574–635 for West Florida).

William L. Clements Library, Ann Arbor, Michigan. Gage Papers.

Printed Primary Materials

Bartram, William. *Travels through North and South Carolina, Georgia, East and West Florida*. Charlottesville: University Press of Virginia, 1980 (originally published London, 1790).

Dalrymple, Margaret Fisher, ed. *The Merchant of Manchac: The Letterbooks of John Fitzpatrick, 1768–1790*. Baton Rouge and London: Louisiana State University Press, 1978.

Romans, Bernard. *A Concise Natural History of East and West Florida*. Gainesville: University of Florida Press, 1962 (originally published New York, 1775).

Williams, Samuel Cole, ed., *Adair's History of the American Indians*. Johnson City, Tenn.: National Society of the Colonial Dames of America, 1930 (originally published London, 1775).

Secondary Works

Alden, John R. *John Stuart and the Southern Colonial Frontier.* New York: Gordian, 1966 (originally published Ann Arbor, 1944).

Braund, Kathryn E. Holland. *Deerskins and Duffels: Creek Indian Trade with Anglo-America, 1685–1815*. Lincoln and London: University of Nebraska Press, 1993.

Fabel, Robin F. A. *Bombast and Broadsides: The Lives of George Johnstone.* Tuscaloosa and London: University of Alabama Press, 1987.

———. *The Economy of British West Florida, 1763–1783.* Tuscaloosa and London: University of Alabama Press, 1988.

Johnson, Cecil. *British West Florida, 1763–1783.* New York: Archon Books, 1971 (originally published New Haven 1942).

Mowat, Charles Loch. *East Florida as a British Province, 1763–1784.* Gainesville: University of Florida Press, 1964 (originally published Berkeley, 1943).

Nelson, Paul D. *General James Grant.* Gainesville: University Press of Florida, 1993.

Rea, Robert R., and Milo B. Howard, Jr. *The Minutes, Journals, and Acts of the General Assembly of British West Florida.* University: University of Alabama Press, 1979.

Rojas, F. de Borja Medina. *José de Ezpeleta, Gobernador de la Mobila, 1780–1781.* Seville: Escuela de Estudios Hispano-Americanos de Sevilla, 1980.

Searcy, Martha Condray. *The Georgia-Florida Contest in the American Revolution, 1776–1778.* University: University of Alabama Press, 1985.

Starr, J. Barton. *Tories, Dons and Rebels.* Gainesville: University Presses of Florida, 1976.

Wright, J. Leitch, Jr. *Florida in the American Revolution.* Gainesville: University Presses of Florida, 1975.

9 The Second Spanish Period in the Two Floridas

William S. Coker
and
Susan R. Parker

The newly restored Spanish rule, which took effect after exchanges of flags in 1784, claimed sway over the same colonial boundaries in Florida established by the British: two separate colonies, West and East, divided at the Apalachicola, ranging west as far as the Mississippi, and governed from two capitals, Pensacola and St. Augustine.

Great Britain lost West Florida to the Spaniards in three military campaigns between August 1779 and May 1781: Baton Rouge, Mobile, and Pensacola. Although Spain occupied the colony for two years, 1781–83, it did not officially become Spanish again until the Treaty of Paris in 1783.

From the beginning, Spain faced to the north a young and aggressive new nation, the United States, intent upon expanding its horizons. As a result, Spanish West Florida became the first victim of what some historians would later call Manifest Destiny. The history of Spanish West Florida from 1783 to 1821 is really a history of defeats—some economic, some diplomatic, and a few military—that ultimately cost Spain her newly regained colony.

West Florida was the larger of the two Floridas. It extended from the Chattahoochee and Apalachicola rivers on the east to the Mississippi River and the Isle of Orleans on the west. The Gulf of Mexico and the Louisiana lakes Borgne, Ponchartrain, and Maurepas formed its southern boundary. Initially, the northern border had been set at latitude 31° north, but in 1764 it was moved up to 32° 28″ north in order to include more fertile lands and fur-trapping ranges.

Only four towns of any consequence contained the urban popula-tions of West Florida: Mobile, Baton Rouge, Natchez, and Pensacola, the capital. In addition to the military forts in each of those towns, there were two others in the interior, Fort Choiseul (York) and Fort Toulouse.

Without counting the native peoples, the population of West Florida was approximately 3,660 in 1785 and 8,390 in 1795. Between 1795 and 1814, the population grew significantly, but substantial territorial losses to the United States reduced the area and population of West Florida by 50 percent or more.

Spanish West Florida was under the jurisdiction of the civil and mili-tary commandant stationed at Pensacola. The title of his office was later changed to governor, but the duties remained essentially the same. All of West Florida's commandants/governors were military officers, nor-mally appointed to serve a term of five years. In practice, they stayed until they were formally relieved of duty. Thirteen officers served as commandant/governor of the colony between 1781 and 1821. Colonel Vicente Folch y Juan held office the longest, 1796–1811; Colonel Ar-turo O'Neill y Tyrone was second in length of service, 1781–94.

The duties of these officers included supervision of the military, Indian affairs, foreign relations directly affecting the colony, financial matters and the economy, land grants, and the church. These officers were under the supervision of the governor-general and the inten-dant of Louisiana and West Florida until 1806. After that date, the cap-tain-general of Cuba assumed direct command over West Florida's governors.

Although within the boundaries of Spanish West Florida, the Natchez District, whose principal officer was changed from a commandant to a governor in 1787, was under the direct command of the governor-general of Louisiana. Colonel Manual Gayoso de Lemos served there from 1789 to 1797, by which time the United States had acquired the area. Gayoso then became the governor-general of Louisiana and West Florida.

The Roman Catholic faith was the only religion officially permitted in the colony, although persons of other religious denominations could worship in private. The church in West Florida followed the same pat-tern of jurisdiction as did the civil and military government: It was under the governor of West Florida except for strictly religious matters. For those, after 1787, it was under the auxiliary bishop of Louisiana and West Florida.

Father James Coleman served as the priest of the parish of San Miguel in Pensacola from 1794 until 1822. In 1806, he was appointed

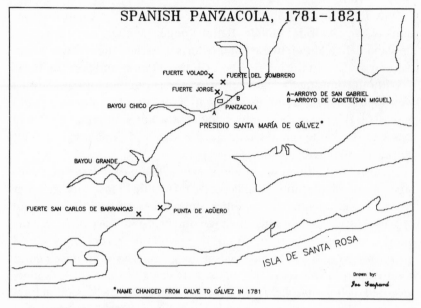

A plan of the Pensacola Bay region in the period 1781–1821. Pensacola (Panzacola) was the capital of Spanish West Florida. Other towns of consequence in the colony were Mobile, Baton Rouge, and Natchez. Drawn by Joe Gaspard.

the vicar-general and ecclesiastical judge of West Florida. He became perhaps the best known of all the priests in colonial West Florida. After 1806, confusion reigns about who had official jurisdiction over the church in West Florida, but Father Coleman looked to the bishop of Havana.

By 1795, it is estimated, about 15 percent of the population of West Florida was Protestant. Father Coleman's religious censuses of Pensacola in 1796–1801 indicated that about 25 percent of its population was Protestant; this strong showing resulted from the presence of British residents who decided to remain in West Florida, as well as from Protestant immigration after 1783. Mobile, with its large French population, remained predominantly Catholic.

West Florida had the potential of being an important colony economically. Early on, the area did reasonably well with tobacco, indigo, and lumber. Tobacco flourished but soon lost out from overproduction and competition from Mexico. Indigo also did well until pollution problems developed. Timber, especially ships' masts, yielded a good return, but the market was limited. And, unfortunately, a cotton boom came too late. Seafood and livestock production never reached their potential. The population was too small to support large-scale manufacturing and related industries. For Spain, West Florida was simply not a profit-making colony. Its importance lay in its strategic position on the Gulf Coast. There was one way to make a profit—the Indian trade—but the profit went to the British, not to the Spaniards.

The person who was to have an important economic impact on West Florida was a Scotsman, William Panton, one of the partners in the Indian trading firm of Panton, Leslie and Company. The company had already achieved considerable success in East Florida. Panton and his assistant, John Forbes, reached Pensacola in 1784, shortly after the Spaniards had reached an agreement with the Creeks to supply them with trade goods. Panton was a friend of Alexander McGillivray, an influential mixed-blood Upper Creek chief, and, with McGillivray's support, Panton, Leslie and Company eventually secured a large part of the Indian trade.

The company traded English-made goods, especially guns, powder, and shot, for deerskins and other furs. It extended credit to the Indians who were soon heavily in debt—$200,000 or more—to the firm. Panton and his partners spent years collecting these debts. One thing worked to their advantage: The Indians owned large tracts of land which they traded, not always willingly, to cancel their debts.

Since the United States eagerly wanted Indian lands, the company pressured the Indians in 1805 into trading 8 million acres to the United States. The land was actually in U.S. territory. With the cash that they received, the Indians paid off part of their debts to the company.

Later, the Indians and the Spanish government gave the company 2.7 million acres in West Florida as recompense for losses sustained by the company during the War of 1812. Eventually, and because of a technicality, the United States confirmed only 1.4 million acres of this grant, known as Forbes Grant I. At its peak, Panton, Leslie and its successor firm, John Forbes & Co., exercised significant control over the Indians of the Floridas and played an important role in the history of both East and West Florida during the years 1783 to 1821.

Even before it acquired the Indian lands in 1805, the United States had begun its acquisition of Spanish West Florida, a piece at a time. The area between the 31st parallel and 32°, 28" north was in dispute between Spain and the United States from 1783 until 1795. By 1795, Spain's problems in Europe, and the French Revolution and its consequences, pushed it to resolve its dispute with the United States. The result was Pinckney's Treaty, or the Treaty of 1795, which gave the disputed area, including the Natchez District, to the United States. The United States had then sovereignty over all of the lands north of 31° to the Great Lakes and from the Appalachian Mountains to the Mississippi River.

In 1803, the United States purchased Louisiana from France (to whom it had reverted in 1800), and although Spain protested the sale stood. The United States claimed, without any justification, that the Louisiana Purchase included all lands from the Mississippi River east to the Perdido River, an area that had been part of French Louisiana prior to 1763. Officially, those lands had been included in British West Florida from 1763 to 1783 and in Spanish West Florida after that.

In order to confirm its claim to the disputed area, Spain commissioned a number of persons to write the history of that region. Among those who contributed was John Forbes, Panton's successor, who now headed the Forbes company, but his paper was more concerned with the economic improvement of West Florida than with its history. He believed that it could be developed into one of the best agricultural and commercial colonies in the Spanish empire, but his recommendations were lost in the international intrigue of the time.

Unfortunately, conditions did not improve for West Florida, and plots to acquire the area west of the Perdido River continued until 1810. In September of that year, insurgents took the fort at Baton Rouge, quickly declared their independence, and created the Republic of West Florida. They adopted a constitution modeled after that of the United States and elected as their governor Fulwar Skipwith. Their flag had a white star on a blue field, thus making West Florida the first lone star republic. By 1812, the United States had annexed all of the territory between the Perdido and Mississippi rivers. The area between the Pearl and Perdido rivers was made a part of the Mississippi Territory, while the area west of the Pearl was incorporated into the State of Louisiana; to this day, the latter area is known as the Florida parishes of Louisiana.

By 1814, the United States had occupied Mobile and had built Fort Bowyer on Mobile Point and a lookout post on the Perdido River. The Spaniards at Pensacola continually protested such blatant aggression, but because of the Peninsular War then raging in Europe they could do little about it.

The War of 1812 reached the Gulf of Mexico in 1814. General Andrew Jackson, who had just led the U.S. forces to victory in the Creek War, commanded the military at Mobile.

The British decided to use Pensacola as their base of operations in the planned attack upon Fort Bowyer, Mobile, and New Orleans. Their justification was that Great Britain and Spain were allies in the Peninsular War. More important, if the British succeeded in their Gulf Coast cam-

This engraving of Andrew Jackson (1767–1845) was based on a painting for which Jackson sat in 1815. Leading Tennessee troops, Jackson made two invasions of the Spanish Floridas, first during the War of 1812 and again during the First Seminole War of 1818. In 1821, when Florida became a possession of the United States, he returned a third time to serve a brief stint as military governor. At Pensacola he clashed repeatedly with the outgoing Spanish governor, José Callava, over change-of-flag details, at one point clapping the Spaniard in jail. Jacksonville, a site he never visited, is named for him.

paign and captured Mobile and New Orleans, it was clear that they would return those places to Spain. Thus, a British victory would have serious consequences for the United States.

Jackson learned of the British plans from James Innerarity, a Scottish merchant in Mobile. He had received the warning from his brother, John, in Pensacola and from a Havana merchant, Vincent Gray. John Innerarity had also sent a rider to warn the Americans at Fort Bowyer of the anticipated British attack. Thus, the Americans were prepared when the attack began on 15 September 1814. But after the destruction of one of their warships, *Hermes,* by the fort's cannon, the British withdrew and returned to Pensacola. Two months later, Jackson commanded a U.S. force that attacked Pensacola to drive the British out.

Because the Spaniards were not at war with the United States, they refused to assist the British against the Americans. The British then abandoned Pensacola, but they took out their anger at the Spaniards by destroying their Fort San Carlos de Barrancas and the redoubt on Santa Rosa Island before leaving. The British actively recruited blacks and Indians to assist them in their efforts to capture New Orleans which, by December 1814, had become their main objective. The results of that battle are well known: Once again, the Americans were victorious.

After the Battle of New Orleans, the British occupied Dauphin Island near Mobile. Determined to win a victory over the Americans, the British attacked Fort Bowyer on Mobile Point on 9 February 1815. This time they succeeded, but two days after their victory they received word that the war was over. They quickly abandoned Fort Bowyer and left the Gulf Coast. This was the last battle of the War of 1812. Fortunately for the United States, the Stars and Stripes still flew over Fort Bowyer, Mobile, and New Orleans.

In the years after the Creek War and the War of 1812, some of the Indians who had fled to the Spanish Floridas, the so-called Red Sticks, and their black allies conducted raids into Alabama and Georgia. In retaliation, the United States in July of 1816 attacked and destroyed one of their strongholds, Negro Fort, on the Apalachicola River. But this did not end the problem, and in March 1818, General Jackson again invaded Spanish West Florida.

Jackson marched to the Suwannee River, where he engaged in a limited skirmish with the Indians before they slipped away. Although frustrated by this failure, he captured a British soldier of fortune, Robert Chrystie Ambrister, and learned that the Red Sticks had been forewarned. Jackson then took the Spanish fort, San Marcos de Apalache, which he suspected of supplying the Red Sticks. He also took prisoner a British merchant, Alexander Arbuthnot, who was in the fort, and two Red Stick chiefs. Jackson summarily had the two chiefs executed and court-martialed the two Englishmen for assisting the Red Sticks in their war against the United States. Both were found guilty. Ambrister was shot by a firing squad; Arbuthnot was hung from the yardarm of his own ship, *The Last Chance.* Thus, two British subjects had been tried and executed in Spanish territory by U.S. troops.

After San Marcos, Jackson marched west to Pensacola. He believed the Spaniards there were still supplying the Indians and encouraging them to raid nearby Alabama territory. The Spaniards put up a brief defense, but the main body of troops, led by Colonel José Masot, abandoned the city and took refuge in the reconstructed Fort San Carlos de Barrancas. Jackson engaged them, and after a short fight Masot surrendered. The Spanish officials and soldiers were put aboard ship and sent to Havana. Pensacola's Spanish archives went with them. En route, however, the ship was captured by corsairs and the records were thrown overboard. Thus, much of Pensacola's written history disappeared.

For the next nine months, 26 May 1818 to 4 February 1819, Colonel William King, a Jackson appointee, served as the civil and military governor of Pensacola and West Florida. The Spanish minister in Washington, Luis de Onís, voiced Spain's disapproval of this invasion of Spanish territory but accomplished little. Finally, the Spaniards returned to Pensacola in February 1819, and Colonel José Callava became the last Spanish governor of West Florida.

All these events occurred at a bad time for Spain. Ferdinand VII was again on the throne, and Spain's financial state was terrible. The Peninsular War had drained the country of much of its resources. On top of that, rebellion was rampant in the Americas, and Spain devoted much of its attention and money to problems there. Meanwhile, to no one's surprise, U.S. Secretary of State John Quincy Adams and Luis de Onís were negotiating for the transfer of the Floridas to the United States. To the inhabitants of West Florida it seemed clear that an exchange of flags was only a matter of time.

Spanish rule had returned to East Florida, too, in 1784. In St. Augustine troops from Cuba again walked the capital's streets gossiping in Spanish, former émigré residents moved in to reclaim old homes, and Mass was heard again in the parish church. In the countryside English-speaking settlers debated what their fate might be under the new regime while they planted their crops and felled timber.

Most histories of the Second Spanish Period of East Florida, which retained the same borders as the British colony of that name, reflect the Anglophile viewpoints of earlier historians. The era is generally portrayed as an interval of decline wedged between the British and American periods, merely awaiting an inevitable takeover by the United States and its institutions. That view arose largely from reliance upon English-language sources, which aggrandized conditions during those two periods while minimizing developments during the Spanish period. Historian David J. Weber has observed that Englishmen and

When Spaniards returned to occupy St. Augustine after the twenty-one-year British interregnum, they found the physical appearance of the city substantially unchanged. The gate of the walled city stood as stoutly as before, while wood plank balconies of the coquina houses still did arabesques over winding St. George Street.

Anglo-Americans writing at the time of the Second Spanish Period "uniformly condemned Spanish rule." They saw only Spanish misgovernment, which "seemed the inevitable result of the defective character of Spaniards themselves" (1992, 336). More recent attention to Spanish-language documents, including those written in East Florida, reverses that negative assessment. Meanwhile, new appraisals of the British period in East Florida have called into question previously accepted claims about the magnitude of British development of Florida, while re-examination of other pre–Revolutionary War colonies and of the contemporary Atlantic world have also placed East Florida within new contexts.

In 1784 there was widespread doubt that the republican government of the new United States could control even its own large land mass awarded in treaty negotiations, much less take over additional territory in the Floridas. Many British citizens remained in East Florida in hopes of taking advantage of failure of the United States. These former British subjects joined Spanish soldiers and returning families, their slaves, free blacks, white and black immigrants from the United States, refugees of both races from the Caribbean, especially Saint-Domingue (Haiti), sailors and opportunists of many nationalities, and Seminole Indians in the interior of the peninsula to make East Florida's Second Spanish Period the most culturally and racially heterogeneous era of its history until the second half of the twentieth century. The population of the countryside was more homogeneous than that of the towns and ports. In the first years of the Second Spanish Period rural residents beyond the immediate outskirts of St. Augustine were overwhelmingly Protestant; they were planters or farmers and natives of the southern British colonies, especially South Carolina, and about half owned slaves. The diversity among the province's populace contributed to the unsettled feelings of the era.

The presence of a heterogeneous population was just one of the ways in which the period differed from the province's earlier Spanish occupation. The role and power of the military and the Roman Catholic Church during the Second Spanish Period was diminished in comparison to the first two centuries, although both institutions remained strong presences. East Florida's raison d'être within the Spanish empire was still to protect the richer areas belonging to the Crown, particularly the mineral wealth of Mexico. Thus, Spain continued to subsidize a military presence in East Florida financially disproportionate to the colony's productivity. But the military budget no longer overwhelmingly supplied the financial base of the province, as in the First Spanish Period, and over the years it became an ever smaller part of the economy, reflecting the vicissitudes of the Spanish Crown and government. Spanish East Florida's governors complained about the irregular arrival of monies needed to maintain the troops and fortifications, but the accounting records reveal that the funds usually did arrive and were usually on time; the problem lay with the manner of distributing the funds in an annual lump sum. Over the years diminishing troop strength meant smaller budgets, which translated into the ever decreasing financial and social influence of the military. Between 1790 and 1800 East Florida lost 30 percent of its soldiery, and units continued to diminish in strength although at a slower rate.

The weakened role of the church in East Florida reflected its position throughout the Spanish empire, as the monarchy and its bureaucracy gained power by taking over functions once performed by the church, such as the approval of marriages. In East Florida the financial wellbeing of the church was tied to that of the provincial government through its inclusion in the defense budget. Although the Franciscans had wished to return, there was no revival of the missions in Florida to parallel the prosperity of the order's missions in California during the late eighteenth century. Catholic priests visited East Florida's largely Protestant rural population soon after the Spaniards returned and baptized many young children, but there was no subsequent establishment of parishes or church-sponsored schools outside of St. Augustine. Thus, the opportunity to incorporate the residents of the countryside into the province's society was lost, and they remained English-speaking, unchurched, and omitted from most official festivals and celebrations—events that revolved around religious feast days and commemorative rituals. For example, in 1789 when the residents of St. Augustine staged a three-day festival for the coronation of King Carlos IV, featuring Masses, an enthroning re-enactment, parades, and plays, no counterpart took place in the rural area to involve the settlers in that moment of national celebration.

Residents of East Florida participated in the Atlantic-wide economy that was fed by the mass production of the emerging Industrial Revolution. It was a period marked by the rise of the British navy and merchant marine and the lifting of Spanish trade restrictions. East Florida's reliance upon imports probably was in line with economic activity in surrounding areas of both the Caribbean and the United States. Foodstuffs from ports in the United States were the major imported item. Manufactured goods arrived in East Florida in vessels from England and the United States; wines, sugar, rum, coffee, and some tablewares were shipped via Cuba. In the early years of the second period, Florida planters saw planting rice as a way to riches. Others with fewer resources or less capital looked to timber and cattle raising for profit. As the nineteenth century arrived, cotton was replacing corn, rice, and other staples on East Florida's acreage. Planter Francis Fatio claimed that an acre of cotton would yield ten times the profit of an acre of corn. The departure of money from the province to the United States to purchase food for slaves in East Florida now engaged in raising inedible cotton so alarmed Spanish Governor Enrique White in 1800 that he officially prohibited the planting of cotton and ordered the immediate sowing of corn.

Despite the differences between the first and second Spanish regimes in East Florida the province's continued role as an adjunct of a European power meant a close connection with wars in Europe. Spain's enemies were East Florida's enemies, whatever the reality within the province. The border with the United States offered constant problems as neither the United States nor East Florida's colonial government was able to control border violations, and raids and rustling persisted.

Thirteen years after their return, Spanish residents of St. Augustine enjoyed use of a new Roman Catholic church, larger than any that had stood in the city before. Designed by royal engineer-architect Mariano de la Rocque, the coquina stone structure was erected on the north side of the central plaza during the years 1793–97. Its neoclassic facade was typical of parish and mission churches built elsewhere in the Spanish Americas during the period. This photograph was taken 100 years after its completion.

U.S. citizens found the availability of land to be encouragement enough to immigrate, particularly when, in 1790, the king of Spain invited foreigners to settle in East Florida by offering homestead grants. Settlers from the southern states especially began to move in. The Crown granted each head of a household 100 acres, and each additional family member or slave qualified for an additional 50. Title to the land passed to the homesteaders after ten years of occupancy, farming, erecting appropriate buildings, and maintaining livestock. Two events tied to the international conflicts, however, were devastating to the settlement and development of the province. Both were insurgent military activities fomented in the United States.

In 1793, some residents of Georgia, ostensibly acting on the precepts of the French Revolution, joined to take over East Florida militarily in order to free the Spanish province of what they considered monarchical tyranny. According to their plan, an expeditionary force would provide support for Florida residents who might wish to establish an independent republic in East Florida and subsequently request annexation into the United States. Doubtful of the loyalty of residents in the northern part of his province in the presence of such a force, Governor Juan Nepomuceno de Quesada and his council of war ordered the evacuation of the area between the St. Marys and St. Johns rivers during the first week of 1794. To deprive the invasion force of any assistance, the council also demanded that crops be harvested or destroyed, buildings in the area burned, and residents either removed to another part of the province or made to leave the colony. These decisions reflected East Florida's role as a military outpost, where strategic requirements superseded all other considerations in time of threat. Not until 9 July 1795, however, did the strike against Spanish sovereignty come, when Florida residents and compatriots from the United States seized the Spanish fortification of San Nicolás in present-day downtown Jacksonville. The rebels persisted in their affiliation with the French cause, identifying themselves as French forces and cheering for the Republic of France during the skirmish. But by mid-October, Spanish troops had routed the insurgents from the province, and settlers had relocated in the northern region to take advantage of newly available lands, abandoned by those who had fled.

In the War of 1812, Spain was allied with Great Britain against Napoleon while the United States readied for war against Great Britain. Known as the "Patriot War" in Florida, the conflict reflected expansionist desires on the part of the United States and the anger of slaveowners in the southern United States over the less controlled existence of blacks in Spanish East Florida. American slaveowners wanted especially to eliminate the frightening example of African Americans in Florida possessing firearms. Complicating matters, Amelia Island, the northeasternmost settlement site in East Florida, had developed since 1807 into an important "neutral" transshipping port for U.S. merchants who wished to bypass their own government's embargo. In 1812, James Madison's administration supported actions against Spain's colony of East Florida in order to expand the jurisdiction of the U.S. Non-Importation Act, to assert U.S. hegemony in the region, and to pre-empt any self-serving British activity in Florida.

Crossing into Spanish Florida on 10 March 1812, the Georgian expeditionary force, led by General George Mathews, did not find the anticipated cooperation from East Florida residents. The invaders took the town and port of Fernandina on Amelia Island, and by mid-April they were encamped at the site of Fort Mose, two miles north of St. Augustine, when President Madison withdrew official support for the venture in the face of public disapproval. But the filibusterers did not withdraw. That summer, the Seminole Indians and their African-American allies entered the conflict. The Patriots turned toward the interior and then occupied lands claimed by the Seminoles.

Die-hard adherents of the Patriot cause held on in East Florida until May 1814, causing widespread devastation. Various factions burned plantations and farmsteads on the Florida side of the St. Marys River, both sides of the St. Johns River, and the estuaries of today's intracoastal waterway as far south as present-day Daytona Beach and to within two miles of St. Augustine. Planters lost their 1812 crops and were unable to plant in 1813, meanwhile depleting their resources in order to maintain an idle slave force. Livestock strayed or were consumed by the invading troops. John Fraser of Greenfields Plantation at the mouth of the St. Johns River claimed that he lost $111,000 in property and potential profit from his unplanted cotton crop. Equally important to a smaller farmer was the destruction of his houses and barns, food crops, rifles, and miscellany such as a coffee mill, a fiddle and sheet music, and a fishing net. One rancher never recovered the 800 head of cattle he owned before the disruptions. Judge Isaac Bronson declared that by the time the invaders retired, "the whole inhabited part of the province was in a state of utter desolation and ruin" (Patrick, 1954, 302). The depredation discouraged a number of settlers who had opted to remain in East Florida after their losses in 1794, and they departed the province in disgust after the so-called Patriot War.

East Florida continued to be prey to the designs of invaders. Citizens of the U.S. southern states favored acquiring Florida as an American possession in order to eliminate the province as a destination for runaway slaves and to remove the Seminole presence from the northern region of the colony. The good harbor at the mouth of the St. Marys River at Fernandina attracted smugglers and adventurers. East Florida's last colonial governor, José María Coppinger, endeavored to maintain Spain's presence with dignity despite minimal support from his superiors in Cuba and troops who were inadequate both in number and in character. Coppinger even endured the experience of smugglers kidnapping his son and holding him ransom for food and other supplies from St. Augustine.

To encourage the loyalty of the residents in the northern area, Coppinger wisely instituted a form of local government that allowed some degree of representative decision-making through the election of militia officials and magistrates, although the practice violated Spanish law. The capture of Amelia Island in July 1817 by English-born Gregor MacGregor, a notorious insurgent, again disrupted peace in the region as well as Coppinger's successes with the citizenry. In December, U.S. soldiers, not Spanish troops, expelled MacGregor and occupied Amelia Island. In the second half of the following year, Coppinger readied for another invasion by MacGregor while residents lived also in fear of troops from the United States.

On 22 February 1819, the often-discussed treaty ceding East Florida to the United States was finally negotiated and signed in Washington by Adams and Onís. The Spanish crown vacillated on affirming the treaty, and the United States threatened instead to take East Florida forcibly in 1820. Among the items in dispute were new, large land grants to Spanish nobles, which would eliminate that acreage from the public domain under American rule and make the parcels either unavailable for settlement or unacceptably expensive.

On 22 February 1821, the treaty of cession was finally ratified by both countries. According to its terms, the United States assumed $5 million worth of Spanish debts to American citizens and surrendered any claims to Texas. Governor Coppinger urged East Florida residents to emigrate to Cuba, Texas, or Mexico. He received instructions to encourage the relocation of the Seminoles to the U.S.-Texas border, where they could serve as a valuable and strategic buffer to American penetration of Texas. On 10 July 1821, at 5:00 A.M., the Spanish flag was raised at St. Augustine for the last time. By 6:00 P.M. the last remaining Spanish soldier had departed from the city to the vessels waiting to take Spanish subjects to new posts and homes. A formal transfer of flags took place at Pensacola on 17 July.

More than three centuries of sunrises and sunsets lay between the first and final appearances of the Spanish flag in Florida. It will be the twenty-second century before the same can be said about the flag of the United States.

Bibliography

Bermúdez, Ligia. "The Situado: A Study in the Dynamics of East Florida's Economy During the Second Spanish Period, 1785–1820." Master's thesis, University of Florida, 1989.

Coker, William S. "Father James Coleman, Vicar and Ecclesiastical Judge,

Parish of San Miguel de Panzacola, 1794–1822." In *The Spanish Missionary Heritage of the United States,* edited by Howard Benoist and Sr. María Carolina Flories, C.P., pp. 29–45. San Antonio: U.S. Department of the Interior/National Park Service and Los Compadres de San Antonio Missions, National Historical Park, [1991].

————. "How General Andrew Jackson Learned of the British Plans Before the Battle of New Orleans." *Gulf Coast Historical Review* 3, no. 1 (1987):85–95.

————. "The Last Battle of the War of 1812: New Orleans. No Fort Bowyer!" *Alabama Historical Quarterly* 43, no. 1 (Spring 1981):42–63.

Coker, William S., and Douglas G. Inglis. *The Spanish Censuses of Pensacola, 1784–1820: A Genealogical Guide to Spanish Pensacola.* Pensacola: Perdido Bay Press, 1980.

Coker, William S., and Jerrell H. Shofner. *Florida: From the Beginning to 1992.* Houston, Tex.: Pioneer Publications, Inc., 1992.

Coker, William S., and Thomas D. Watson. *Indian Traders of the Southeastern Spanish Borderlands: Panton, Leslie & Company and John Forbes & Company, 1783–1847.* Gainesville: University Presses of Florida, 1986.

Coker, William S., et al. *John Forbes' Description of the Spanish Floridas, 1804.* Pensacola: Perdido Bay Press, 1979.

Cusick, James Gregory. "Ethnic Groups and Class in an Emerging Market Economy: Spaniards and Minorcans in Late Colonial St. Augustine." Ph.D. dissertation, University of Florida, 1993.

East Florida Papers Manuscript Collection, Library of Congress. On microfilm at the P. K. Yonge Library of Florida History, University of Florida, Gainesville.

Gannon, Michael V. *The Cross in the Sand: The Early Catholic Church in Florida, 1513–1870.* Gainesville: University of Florida Press, 1965.

Holmes, Jack D. L. "West Florida, 1779–1821." In *A Guide to the History of Florida,* edited by Paul S. George, pp. 63–76. New York: Greenwood Press, 1989.

Marchena Fernández, Juan. "The Defense Structure of East Florida, 1700–1820." *El Escribano* 21 (1984):37–52.

McAlister, L. N. "Pensacola During the Second Spanish Period." *Florida Historical Quarterly* 37, nos. 3, 4 (January–April 1959):281–327.

McGovern, James R., ed. *Colonial Pensacola.* Pensacola: Pensacola-Escambia County Development Commission, 1974.

Murdoch, Richard K. *The Georgia-Florida Frontier, 1793–1796: Spanish Reaction to French Intrigue and American Designs.* Berkeley: University of California Press, 1951.

Norris, L. David. "The Squeeze: Spain Cedes Florida to the United States." In *Clash Between Cultures: Spanish East Florida, 1784–1821,* edited by Jacqueline K. Fretwell and Susan R. Parker. St. Augustine: St. Augustine Historical Society, 1988.

Parker, Susan R. "Men Without God or King: Rural Settlers of East Florida, 1784–1790." Master's thesis, University of Florida, 1990.

Parks, Virginia. *Pensacola: Spaniards to Space Age.* Pensacola: Pensacola Historical Society, 1986.

Patrick, Rembert. *Florida Fiasco: Rampant Rebels on the Georgia-Florida Border, 1810–1815.* Athens: University of Georgia Press, 1954.

Patriot War Claims. Manuscript Collection, St. Augustine Historical Society.

Spanish Land Grant Claims. Manuscript Collection, Florida Division of Historical Resources, R. A. Gray Building, Tallahassee.

Tanner, Helen Hornbeck. *Zéspedes in East Florida, 1784–1790.* Coral Gables: University of Miami Press, 1963. Reprint, Gainesville: University Presses of Florida, 1989.

Ward, Christopher. "The Commerce of East Florida During the Embargo of 1806–1812: The Role of Amelia Island." *Florida Historical Quarterly* 68, no. 2 (October 1989):160–79.

Weber, David J. *The Spanish Frontier in North America.* New Haven: Yale University Press, 1992.

10 Free and Slave

Jane Landers

The African presence in the Americas and in Florida dates to the earliest days of Spanish exploration, yet persons of African descent remain largely "invisible" in the historical literature. This absence is due, in part, to the difficulty of the sources (their locations are scattered and their language is eighteenth-century Spanish) and in part to the lack of interest among earlier scholars. But the Spaniards were meticulous bureaucrats, and the exceptionally rich documentary evidence on Africans in Florida tells much about their long-neglected history.

Florida was part of the Spanish Caribbean world for over 300 years before it became an American territory in 1821, and the influence of Spanish legal traditions and race relations had a lasting impact on the African experience in the region.

Like other areas in the Spanish Caribbean, Florida suffered from early and dramatic Indian depopulation and a shortage of European manpower, and this demographic imperative created a demand for the labor, artisanal, and military skills of blacks. Once Africans entered Florida they interacted closely with the remaining Indian populations and, in effect, became culture brokers on the frontier, moving between the Spanish and Indian worlds.

Florida's first slaves came from southern Spain, where a significant African population filled a variety of important functions—laboring in mines and agriculture and in less onerous tasks as artisans, petty merchants, and domestics. Although most Africans in Spain were slaves, not all were. Spanish law and custom granted slaves a moral and legal personality, as well as certain rights and protections not found in other slave systems. They had the right to personal security and legal mechanisms by which to escape a cruel master. Further, slaves were permitted to hold and transfer property and to initiate legal suits—a significant right that in the Americas evolved into the right of self-purchase. Social and religious values in Spanish society promoted honor, charity, and paternalism toward "miserable classes," which often ameliorated the hardships slaves suffered and sometimes led owners to manumit them. This is not to suggest that Spain or its New World colonies were free of racial prejudice. Nevertheless, the emphasis on a slave's humanity and rights, and the lenient attitude toward manumission embodied in Spanish slave codes and social practice, made it possible for a significant free black class to exist, first in Spain, later in the Spanish Americas.

Africans, both free and enslaved, crossed the Atlantic on the early voyages and participated in the conquest and settlement of the new territories claimed by Spain. With the Europeans they formed a specialized pool of human resources circulating throughout the circum-Caribbean in many different expeditions. One member of this tightly knit group, a free African named Juan Gárrido, sailed from Seville to Hispaniola, where he befriended other blacks such as Juan González [Ponce] de León, an interpreter of the Taíno language. The two adventurers took part in Juan Ponce de León's "pacification" campaigns against the native populations of Hispaniola, his expedition to explore and conquer Puerto Rico (San Juan de Boriquén) in 1508, and in slaving raids against the Carib Indians on surrounding islands.

When Juan Ponce de León made his "discovery" in 1513 and initiated European exploration of the American Southeast, the free Africans Juan Gárrido and Juan González [Ponce] de León accompanied him. Although Juan Ponce de León's first contact with the Florida natives was hostile, it enabled Spain to claim exclusive sovereignty over the continent and led to further attempts to explore its interior.

After a second trip to Florida proved fatal to Juan Ponce de León, another Spanish adventurer (and slave raider), Lucas Vázquez de Ayllón, attempted a settlement on the Atlantic coast in 1526. The site, called San Miguel de Gualdape, is believed to be near present-day Sapelo Sound in Georgia (see chapter 2). Ayllón's expedition included 600 Spanish men, women, and children as well as the first known contingent of African slaves brought to the present-day United States. As historian Paul E. Hoffman has pointed out, these were probably skilled artisans and domestics from Spain rather than African-born field

The free African Juan Gárrido participated in the early Spanish exploration in the Caribbean, in Ponce de León's 1513 voyage to Florida and in the conquest of the Aztec empire of Mexico by Hernán Cortés. He is shown here as a spear carrier behind Cortés in an illustration from Fray Diego Durán, *Historia de las Indias de Nueva España y islas de Tierra Firme.*

hands. Ayllón's ambitious enterprise was undermined by disease, starvation, and his own death. Mutiny ensued, African slaves set fires to the compound, and the Guale Indians rebelled. The surviving Europeans straggled back to the Caribbean, but ethnohistorians maintain that the Africans took up residence among the Guales, becoming maroons, as many of their counterparts were doing in Hispaniola, Puerto Rico, Jamaica, Cuba, and Mexico.

Despite the slave arson at Gualdape, African slaves were included in the next expedition to La Florida—that of Pánfilo de Narváez, who landed somewhere near Tampa in 1528. Like Ayllón's, his was a major colonization effort involving approximately 600 persons and unknown numbers of Africans. This colony, too, proved a disastrous failure, undone by hurricanes, supply losses, and separation of the forces. Of the four survivors who "came back from the dead" after eight years of wandering along the Gulf Coast and westward to the Pacific Ocean, the most famous was the expedition's treasurer, Alvar Núñez Cabeza de Vaca, who left a written account of his trials. A less noted survivor was Estévan, the African slave of Andrés Dorantes, who quickly learned the language and belief systems of indigenous groups and whose skills helped sustain his party.

Hernando de Soto next took up the challenge of exploring the Southeast. Many of the men who accompanied de Soto to Florida in 1539 took with them their African slaves. De Soto's secretary wrote of Gómez, the slave of André de Vasconcelos, who helped the chieftainess of Cofitachequi to escape from the Spaniards and later became her husband. Other slaves and Spaniards from the de Soto expedition also "went over" to the Indians, further blending the Indian, African and European populations of the Southeast.

Other Africans remained with de Soto's force for the duration. Bernaldo, a free caulker from Vizcaya and formerly the slave of one of de Soto's captains, survived the many bloody Indian battles, severe hunger, killing marches, and finally a voyage down the Mississippi River in hastily constructed boats. After an epic voyage of over four years, during which the expeditionaries traversed 600 miles and ten of the present-day United States, Bernaldo was among those who limped back to Mexico City dressed only in animal skins.

Several more attempts failed before Pedro Menéndez de Avilés finally established the first permanent settlement at St. Augustine in 1565. By that time persons of African descent had already taken up residence in the peninsula. When Menéndez first explored his claim, he found a shipwrecked mulatto named Luis living among the fiercely resistant Ais nation to the south. Luis's knowledge of the Ais language had saved other shipwreck victims whose freedom Menéndez negotiated— among them an unnamed black woman. Luis became a translator for Menéndez and returned to live among the Spaniards, but other "captives" chose to stay with the Indians. Menéndez complained later that slaves from St. Augustine ran to and intermarried with the Ais. The possibility of an alternative life among the Indians would temper race relations in Florida well into the nineteenth century.

Although a royal charter permitted Menéndez to import 500 African slaves to do the difficult labor required in settling a new colony, he never filled that contract and probably fewer than fifty slaves may have accompanied the first settlers. The loss of those slaves who ran to the Ais was significant. White manpower was in short supply in Florida, as it was in other areas of the Caribbean, and Spaniards considered Indians to be too weak, lazy, and transient to be a dependable labor force. Moreover, the native populations were extremely vulnerable to European diseases which had already ravaged their counterparts in the Antilles. Thus, the slaves who remained performed many critical functions in Spanish Florida, first at St. Augustine and later at Santa Elena, Spain's northernmost settlement, in present-day South Carolina. Slaves logged and sawed the timber for fortifications and ships, built structures, and cleared and planted the fields, "with no other expense but their oil and salt."[1] The Crown considered black labor indispensable to the maintenance of Florida, noting that the entire government subsidy would not suffice if wages had to be paid for their labor. By the seventeenth century, the government was depending on royal slaves to quarry coquina from Anastasia Island, make lime, load and unload government ships, and row government galleys. Private owners of slaves employed them in domestic occupations, as cattlemen and overseers on Florida's vast cattle ranches, and in a myriad of plantation jobs.

In times of crisis slaves and free Africans were also expected to help defend the colony and provide military reserves for the badly understaffed military garrison. After the late sixteenth century, the "Spanish Lake" was infested with corsairs from England, France, and Holland who raided Spanish shipping and settlements with seeming impunity. Florida's long exposed coastline made it particularly vulnerable to attack. By 1683 free blacks in St. Augustine had formed themselves into a formal militia unit and were commanded by officers of their own election. Similar units served in Hispaniola, Cuba, Mexico, Puerto Rico, Cartagena, and throughout Central America.

The men who formed the black militias were usually free black artisans or skilled workers. They were Catholics who lived as Spaniards and were integrated into their communities through powerful social institutions such as godparentage and patron/client networks. Leading useful and orderly lives, they mirrored the early free African communities of Spain and enjoyed the protections promised by Spanish law and custom. Military service was an important way for free blacks to prove themselves to their community and also to advance themselves through occasional opportunities for plunder. Moreover, through the militias, free blacks acquired titles and status and eventually full military privileges. It is possible that the militia units also functioned to reinforce relationships within the African community, as "natural" leaders rose to command and assumed responsibility for their men. Parish registers from St. Augustine show that militia families commonly intermarried and served as godparents and marriage sponsors for one another. Church records also suggest that the double connection of family and military corporatism may have worked to move some men out of slavery. Although their slave past was certainly not forgotten, it was in a sense excused by appropriate behavior, valuable services, and the sponsorship of Africans of whom the community already approved.

Michael Mullin's recent study of slavery in the contemporary British Caribbean demonstrates how geographic context and the organization of labor shaped the institution of slavery. In Florida slavery exhibited a number of the features that Mullin contends mitigated its oppressive nature: it was generally organized by the task system, and slaves had free time to engage in their own social and economic activities; slaves were able to utilize the resources of both frontier and coast to their advantage; the trade in slaves was never massive; and the paternal model of plantation management prevailed, even on Florida's largest ranches and plantations. Moreover, the geopolitical pressures exerted by Spain's circum-Caribbean rivals meant additional leverage for slaves and more Spanish dependence upon free people of color.

In 1670 English planters from Barbados challenged Spain's claim to exclusive control of the Atlantic seaboard by establishing Charles Town. St. Augustine lacked sufficient force to mount a major attack against the usurpers, but Spanish governors initiated a campaign of harassment against the English colony that included slave raids by the Spaniards and their black and Indian allies. These contacts may have pointed the way to St. Augustine and suggested to English-owned black slaves the possibility of a refuge among the enemy, for in 1687, after a dramatic escape by canoe, eight men, two women, and a nursing child appeared in Florida. The fugitive slaves requested religious sanctuary in St. Augustine, and, despite an early ambiguity about their legal condition, only in one known example were the runaways returned to their English masters. The rest were sheltered in St. Augustine, instructed and baptized in the Catholic faith, married, and employed, ostensibly for wages. Royal policy regarding the fugitives was finally set in 1693 when Charles II granted the newcomers to Florida freedom on the basis of religious conversion, "the men as well as the women . . . so that by their example and by my liberality others will do the same."[2] In gratitude the freedmen vowed to shed their "last drop of blood in defense of the Great Crown of Spain and the Holy Faith, and to be the most cruel enemies of the English."[3] The runaways had considered their options and made their choices.

During the next decades more fugitives from Carolina flowed into St. Augustine, and in 1738 the Spanish governor established the freedmen and -women in the town of Gracia Real de Santa Teresa de Mose, about two miles north of St. Augustine. Florida's governor recognized the group's spokesman and the captain of their newly formed militia, Francisco Menéndez, as the "chief" of Mose and referred to the others living at the village as his "subjects." The residents of Mose established complex family and fictive kin networks over several generations and successfully incorporated into the founding group incoming fugitives, Indians from nearby villages, and slaves from St. Augustine. Community

MILICIAS de MORENOS LIBRES de VERACRUZ y de LA HABANA 1770-1776.
Segun Reglamentos y Modelos de la Epoca, Archivo Gral. de las Indias Sevilla.

Many former slaves and free African Americans served in Spanish militias in Florida and throughout the circum-Caribbean in the eighteenth century. The soldiers depicted here were posted at Havana, Cuba, and Vera Cruz, Mexico.

and familial ties were further reinforced by a tradition of militia service at Mose.

However, despite the best efforts of Menéndez and his men, the first town of Mose was destroyed when General James Oglethorpe commanded a joint naval and land assault against St. Augustine in 1740. Mose's inhabitants took up residence in St. Augustine until Governor Fulgencio García de Solís attempted to relocate the freedmen to Mose in 1752. The former residents feared further attacks and did not want to move back, but after the governor promised to fortify the settlement better and to post soldiers at the site, the freedmen rebuilt Mose, constructing a church and a house for the Franciscan priest within an enclosed fort as well as twenty-two shelters outside the fort for their own households.

Kathleen Deagan of the Florida Museum of Natural History directed an interdisciplinary investigation of Mose that has added to the documentary record archaeological, or material, evidence about daily life at this unique site. In two seasons of excavations her team uncovered the foundations and earthen walls of the fort, parts of the palisade, sections of the moat, and several of the interior structures. They also recovered military artifacts such as bullets, gunflints, and buttons and domestic items such as bone buttons, pins and thimbles, clay pipe bowls, beads, and a variety of eighteenth-century ceramics and bottles. One valuable find was a handmade pewter St. Christopher's medal, which may be a reference to the Africans' travels over water or suggest links to Havana, for which St. Christopher was the patron.

While conditions at Mose were rugged, the homesteaders were at least free to farm their own lands, build their own homes, and live in them with their families. A house-by-house census of Mose from 1759 identified thirty-seven men, fifteen women, seven boys, and eight girls living at the site. Included were members of the Mandinga, Congo, and Carabalí nations, as well as many others, but over time the diverse ethnic-linguistic groups formed a cohesive community that survived until 1763. Then, through the fortunes of war, Spain lost Florida to the British, and the Spanish Crown evacuated St. Augustine and its black and Indian allies to Cuba.

Under British rule (1763–84), black freedom in Florida became only a remote possibility. Anglo planters established vast indigo, rice, sugar, and sea island cotton plantations modeled after those in South Carolina and Georgia. Historian Daniel L. Schafer has found that wealthy planters, such as Richard Oswald and John Fraser, imported large numbers of African slaves from Sierra Leone for the back-breaking work involved in establishing new plantations. Soon Africans were the most

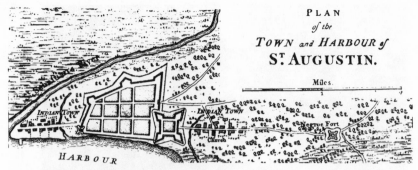

In 1738 slave runaways from Carolina and Georgia received civil and religious sanctuary in Spanish Florida. With support from Governor Manuel de Montiano, they established the legally sanctioned free community of Gracia Real de Santa Teresa de Mose. Two miles north of St. Augustine, Mose is shown as "Negroe Fort" (*right*) on this 1762 plan by English cartographer Thomas Jefferys (1699–1775).

numerous element of Florida's population. The American Revolution accelerated that trend, for after the Patriots took Charleston and Savannah, planters shifted whole work forces into East Florida, the last Loyalist haven in North America. The colony's population grew by about 12,000 persons, over half of whom were black, making the black-white ratio approximately three to one. Although a small number of these blacks were free—for example, those who had performed military service for George III—most were not. British Floridians restricted the movement of free blacks, adopted a slave code based on that of South Carolina, and often subjected slaves to brutal punishments.

At the conclusion of the North American revolution, Florida was retroceded to Spain, and many slaves took advantage of the chaos of war and the subsequent colonial transfer to escape British control. Untold numbers found sanctuary among the Seminole nation, which had established flourishing villages in the central plains of north Florida. Others, however, claimed a refuge among the incoming Spaniards on the grounds of religious conversion; although the Spanish governor doubted their religious motivation, the 1693 sanctuary policy was still in effect, and he was forced to honor it. After appearing before notaries to be documented and to show proof of work, at least 251 individuals were manumitted under the sanctuary provisions.

Prince Witten, his wife, Judy, and their children, Polly and Glasgow, were among those presenting themselves to be manumitted, and their lives demonstrate how ambitious persons were able to maximize the benefits of free status in Spanish Florida. Prince and Judy were

Some escaped slaves found refuge among the Seminole villages of Florida and later joined in three wars against U.S. forces bent on removing the Seminole from their lands (see chapter 11).

Guinea-born slaves who escaped from Georgia. Runaway notices reported that Prince had fled to Florida "to avoid a separation from his family to which he is much attached."[4] Once Witten and his family were granted sanctuary in Florida, they adapted to the civil, religious, and military expectations of successive Spanish governments and prospered. The family's freedom was dependent upon religious conversion, and the children were baptized within a year of entering the province. Adult baptism required religious instruction and usually took somewhat longer to accomplish, but in 1792 Prince and Judy were also baptized. Later they had their marriage of twenty-one years legitimized by the Catholic Church and became favored godparents for the black community, free and slave. Prince served as godfather to twenty-three children, and Judy was godmother to thirty-one children, including the child of her own slave. When Polly and Glasgow grew older, they, too, were popular godparents.

Witten was a skilled carpenter and hired himself out to a variety of employers. He also earned money working on government construction projects, and by 1793 he and his family were living between prominent white neighbors in the city. By the following year, Judy, a laundress and cook, owned a female slave. Prince joined the free black militia and defended St. Augustine on numerous occasions, including the French-inspired invasion of 1795, the State of Muskogee's war against Spain from 1800 to 1803, and the Patriot War of 1812, in which he earned heroic status and the rank of lieutenant.

While the free black population grew during the second Spanish rule of Florida (1784–1821), so did the enslaved African population. Englishmen who accepted Spanish dominion in Florida and Spaniards alike operated plantations and cattle ranches with sizable labor forces of 50 to 200 slaves. One large planter, Zephaniah Kingsley, credited his success to a moderate view of race relations, the task system, and the employment of highly skilled slaves in management positions on his diversified estates. Other successful operations such as the plantations of Francisco Xavier Sánchez were devoted to cattle, which required a mobile and fairly autonomous work force, as did Sánchez's timbering operations. A black overseer, Edimboro, managed Sánchez's enterprises when Sánchez was in Cuba. The corporate establishments of the Panton, Leslie trading company, which included trading stores, agricultural plantations, and cattle ranches, employed African work forces of up to 250 laborers, as well as black linguists and black Indian traders.

On both corporate and privately owned plantations, it was common for several generations of slave families to live and work together. The paternal model of slave management was reinforced by religion, law, and community norms. Slave masters were often linked to their slaves as godparents, which further underscored paternal obligations. Slaves used these intangible but real assets to improve their conditions, petitioning the courts when they were ill treated, were not materially provided for in the required manner, or wished to change owners. They also went to court to effect self-purchase arrangements. Even slaves on remote plantations were linked to urban institutions and networks through economic activities, the mobility of free blacks, and visits of the parish priest and other city dwellers.

Treasury accounts, census returns, notarized instruments, and civil petitions provide insights into the lives of St. Augustine's black community. Although censuses are inconsistent and must be used with caution, they show that the black population of the Second Spanish Period in Florida ranged from 27 percent of the total recorded population in 1786 to 57 percent in 1814. Whatever the limitations of the counts, it is obvious that Spanish Florida had a sizable and growing population of African descent. A variety of economic opportunities existed in this Atlantic port city, and as they had in the First Spanish Period, many black males worked for the government, on fortifications projects, in the royal armory, unloading ships at the wharf, delivering the mails, cutting timber, and as pilots and oarsmen on government boats. Although in some major cities of Spanish America blacks were forbidden to compete with whites in the marketplace, no such restrictions operated in St. Augustine. Free blacks were cartwrights, jewelers, shoemakers, tanners, butchers, and innkeepers, to name a few of their varied occupations. Antonio Coleman was a skilled tailor who also supported himself by playing the fiddle at dances. Manuel Alzendorf fished for turtles when he was not barbering. One black entrepreneur, Juan Bautista Collins, had mercantile links to South Carolina, Havana, New Orleans, Pensacola, and the Seminole nation in the heart of Florida. He bought and sold everything from butter to large herds of cattle, acquired property, and, like other ambitious free men of color in St. Augustine, observed the Catholic faith and joined the black militia.

Although the lives of women are more difficult to document, records show that free black women in St. Augustine were laundresses or cooks or had small businesses, selling crafts or foodstuffs. Others, like Nancy Wiggins and Anna Madgigaine Jai, advanced themselves through unions with, and sometimes marriages to, white men of property. They managed homesteads and even sizable plantations, bought and sold property, including slaves, and entered into business agreements with both black and white townspeople. Miscegenation was a common and accepted feature of life in St. Augustine, and although most white fathers did not marry black women, they routinely acknowledged their children at baptism and in their wills. Children of interracial unions in St. Augustine often received education, training, or property from their white fathers. Free black parents also left more modest properties to their children. They tried to arrange good marriages for their daughters and sought to advance their sons by enrolling them in St. Augustine's parochial school or by apprenticing them to tradesmen.

But while some of their former slaves went about creating new lives for themselves, Georgian slaveowners complained bitterly about the provocation inherent in Florida's sanctuary policy. Finally, in 1790, Spain bowed to the pressures of the new U.S. government delivered through its forceful secretary of state, Thomas Jefferson, and abrogated Florida's religious sanctuary policy. But all escaped slaves who had already claimed freedom in Florida remained free.

Enslaved people could no longer utilize Florida's religious sanctuary provision to achieve freedom, but they still had the possibility of purchased or granted freedom. Military service to the Crown was another avenue out of bondage. During the slave revolt in Saint Domingue, thousands of former slaves allied themselves to the Spanish Crown and were organized into a force known as the Black Auxiliaries of Carlos IV. Among its leaders was Jorge Biassou, who commanded an army of 40,000 men and outranked the famous Toussaint Louverture. When Spain concluded a peace treaty with the Directory of the French Republic, the Black Auxiliaries were disbanded and dispersed to various locations in the Caribbean and Spain. The decorated and well-pensioned Biassou, and his "family" of kin and dependent troops, chose relocation in St. Augustine, where they were absorbed into the polyglot black community.

Despite major language and cultural differences, Biassou's "family" quickly blended into the free black community. Within three months of their arrival in St. Augustine, Biassou's brother-in-law and heir apparent, Jorge Jacobo, married Prince Witten's daughter, María (Polly) Rafaela, effectively linking the leading families among the North American and Haitian refugee communities.

The Spanish governors were not pleased by the "proud and vain character" and "high temper" Biassou displayed and worried about the bad example he and his band might set. Still, they had no choice but to receive him. Biassou and his men were quick to remind Florida's governors and the captain general of Cuba of their service in various campaigns in Hispaniola, of the promises made them by the Spanish king, and of their status as his loyal and free vassals. Biassou retained the title of caudillo in St. Augustine, and Florida's governors employed him and his battle-hardened men in guerrilla operations against hostile Indians who terrorized Spanish Florida from 1800 to 1803.

The violence of the Saint Domingue slave revolt and the establishment of Haiti's free black government had hemispheric implications, and Florida's dependence upon black military forces was a continuing and grave concern to Anglo planters on its borders. Governor David Mitchell of Georgia warned President James Monroe that the Spaniards "have armed every able-bodied negro within their power. . . . Our southern country will soon be in a state of insurrection." In 1812, with the covert support of the U.S. government, John McIntosh led the so-called Patriot rebels to try to overthrow Spanish rule in Florida. He echoed Mitchell's sentiments in his own letter to Monroe complaining that Florida was a refuge for fugitive slaves and that its emissaries "will be detached to bring about the revolt of the black population of the United States."[5]

Violations of Spain's territorial sovereignty in Florida were a regular feature of U.S. foreign policy for the remainder of the decade: the Patriot War of 1812, a naval attack on the black and Indian fort and settlement at Prospect Bluff on the Apalachicola River in 1815, and Andrew Jackson's devastating raids against Seminole villages along the Suwannee in 1818. The same U.S. hostility toward free blacks living among the Seminole, and the Seminole refusal to return their allies and family members to slavery, contributed to the three Seminole wars from 1818 to 1858 (see chapter 11).

Florida's black troops were able to slow but not stem the tide of U.S. expansionism. When Spain finally turned Florida over to the officials of the U.S. territorial government in 1821, it did not abandon its free black citizens. As in Louisiana, cession treaties required that the legal status and property rights of free blacks be respected by the incoming government. Some free blacks, like Prince Witten and Edimboro Sánchez, who had won his freedom despite the protests of his former owner, had acquired property and invested years of hard work in improving it. They decided to stay in Florida and risk trusting the newcomers to honor their treaty promises. But Prince's daughter, María, and Edimboro's daughter, Nicolasa, joined their husbands and most of the free black community in a second exodus to Cuba. Like their predecessors in 1763, these exiles received government assistance as they remade their lives in Cuba.

Meanwhile, African Americans who had made their free lives among the Seminole rather than among the Spanish were still at risk from the incoming Americans, who brought with them chattel slavery and a firm conviction of their racial superiority. These new homesteaders had long objected to the free blacks living in Florida, fearing their militancy, their alliance with Native Americans, and the dangerous example they set for plantation slaves. Finding the racial climate in Florida increasingly restrictive, more free blacks from St. Augustine left for Cuba in the American territorial years, and in 1857 another community of free blacks living in Pensacola departed for Mexico.

These new migrations underscored the fact that Florida was an extension of the Caribbean, where Native Americans, Europeans, and Africans had interacted for centuries. Embroiled in the struggles of the European "superpowers" of their day, Africans in Florida and in the circum-Caribbean became adroit at reading the political tides. They were pragmatic diplomats, shifting allegiances when they saw the need. In some areas of the Southeast their strategic advantage lasted well into the eighteenth century, and in Florida it ended only when the region became part of the American South in the nineteenth century. Historians Daniel Schafer and Canter Brown, Jr., have shown that even then Spanish legal traditions and customs left an imprint in northeastern Florida that blunted some of the more restrictive and punitive aspects of territorial race legislation.

Free and enslaved Africans helped shape international geopolitics in the Southeast for over three centuries before slavery was finally abolished in Florida, yet their existence and their impact has been obscured by traditional historiography. As new historical and archaeological investigations are determining, African Americans exercised more important and varied roles in the colonial history of the Spanish frontiers of the United States than has previously been appreciated. These studies make it clear that no history of Florida, or the Southeast, is complete without considering this complex and multidimensional African experience.

Notes

1. Fernando Miranda to the King, 20 August 1583, cited in Verne E. Chatelain, *The Defenses of Spanish Florida, 1565–1763* (Washington: Carnegie Institution of Washington, 1941), p. 138.
2. Royal edict, 7 November 1693, Santo Domingo 58-1-26 in the John B. Stetson Collection, P. K. Yonge Library of Florida History, University of Florida, Gainesville (hereafter cited as PKY).
3. Fugitive Negroes of the English plantations to the King, 10 June 1738, SD 844, on microfilm reel 15, PKY.
4. Letter of Alexander Semple, 16 December 1786, "To and from the United States, 1784–1821," on microfilm reel 41, EFP, PKY. According to this letter, Prince had attempted twice before to escape.

5. J. H. Alexander, "The Ambush of Captain John Williams, U.S.M.C.: Failure of the East Florida Invasion," *Florida Historical Quarterly* 56, no. 3 (July 1977):286.

Bibliography

Colburn, David, and Jane Landers, eds. *The African American Heritage of Florida.* Gainesville: University Press of Florida, 1995.

Ferguson, Leland. *Uncommon Ground: Archaeology and Early African America, 1650–1800.* Washington: Smithsonian Press, 1992.

Hall, Gwendolyn Midlo. *Africans in Colonial Louisiana: The Development of Afro-Creole Culture in the Eighteenth Century.* Baton Rouge: Louisiana State University Press, 1992.

Landers, Jane. "Africans in the Land of Ayllón: The Exploration and Settlement of the Southeast." In *Columbus and the Land of Ayllón,* edited by Jeaninne Cook, pp. 105–230. Darien, Ga.: Lower Altamaha Historical Society, 1992.

———. "An Examination of Racial Conflict and Cooperation in Spanish St. Augustine: The Career of Jorge Biassou, Black Caudillo." *El Escribano* (December 1988):85–100.

———. "Gracia Real de Santa Teresa de Mose: A Free Black Town in Spanish Colonial Florida." *American Historical Review* 95, no. 1 (February 1990): 9–30.

Mullin, Michael. *Africa in America: Slave Acculturation and Resistance in the American South and the British Caribbean, 1736–1831.* Urbana: University of Illinois Press, 1992.

Mulroy, Kevin. *Freedom on the Border: The Seminole Maroons in Florida, the Indian Territory, Coahuila, and Texas.* Lubbock: Texas Tech University Press, 1993.

Patrick, Rembert W. *Florida Fiasco: Rampant Rebels on the Georgia-Florida Border.* Athens: University of Georgia Press, 1954.

Porter, Kenneth Wiggins. *The Negro on the American Frontier.* New York: Arno Press, 1971.

Thornton, John. *Africa and Africans in the Making of the Atlantic World, 1400–1680.* Cambridge: Cambridge University Press, 1992.

Usner, Daniel H., Jr. *Indians, Settlers, and Slaves in a Frontier Exchange Economy: The Lower Mississippi Valley Before 1783.* Chapel Hill: University of North Carolina Press, 1992.

Wood, Peter W. *Black Majority: Negroes in Colonial South Carolina from 1670 through the Stono Rebellion.* New York: Norton Press, 1974.

11 Florida's Seminole and Miccosukee Peoples

John K. Mahon
and
Brent R. Weisman

The Native Americans who today comprise Florida's Seminole and Miccosukee tribes have roots deep in the cultural prehistory of southeastern North America. The modern political division between the two tribes, dating formally only to the 1950s, belies their fundamental cultural similarity and shared historical origin in the lower piedmont of present-day Georgia and Alabama. Here dwelled the Creek, Yuchi, and other related groups, the immediate cultural ancestors of the Indians to be known in Florida as *cimmarones*. This word, Spanish for *wild ones* or *runaways*, became *Seminole* in the native Muskogean tongue, and it was in use in British Florida by 1765. The transformation of Creek into Seminole is the story of both cultural adaptation to environmental, political, and economic conditions and the cultural persistence of ancient customs and beliefs.

The foundations of both Creek and Seminole culture lie in the aboriginal mound-building chiefdoms of the lower Southeast. By the tenth century A.D., such societies were presided over by hereditary chiefs and a priestly elite who resided in formal towns consisting of temple and residential mounds arranged around a central plaza. Much of the populace lived in the surrounding countryside in small farming hamlets on the banks of streams or tributary creeks. Society was divided into matriarchal clans, that is, clan membership determined through the mother's line. In this system, a man's sons were not members of his clan, nor could they inherit from him. Instead, he had a set of responsibilities and obligations to his sister's sons and they to him. Thus, we see in Creek and early Seminole leadership the succession of chiefly power from a man to his nephew. It is likely also that the women and their families living together in the farming hamlets shared clan membership. In the historic Creek period, these small maternal clan groups were known as *huti,* while in Seminole society of the recent past such groups were known as *istihapo,* or clan camps.

Creek religion stressed purity of mind and body, which was achieved through the ritual use of tobacco, scratching or blood-letting, and imbibing the "black drink," a tea brewed from *Ilex* (holly) leaves and other herbs to induce vomiting. Annual or seasonal ceremonies held in the plaza or squareground emphasized community purity and solidarity. The most important and enduring of these ceremonies was the Green Corn Dance or busk (from the Creek *poskita,* to fast) still practiced by the Creeks and Seminoles today. This event, typically lasting four days, consisted of frenzied ball play, an airing of grievances, personal atonement, and the dance itself, in which the dancers circled a ritually prepared low mound of earth. Above all, the goal of aboriginal religion was to produce harmony for both the individual and the larger community.

The Creek cosmos, inherited from the Mississippian mound builders, was shaped by beliefs associated with the four cardinal directions. The east, for instance, associated with the rising sun, was thought to have beneficial power. Mythical serpents, horned monsters, and other creatures had their place in the Creek and Seminole cosmos. Colors also were given symbolic meaning, with red being the color of war and white that of peace.

In daily life, the principal occupation of men was to hunt and make war. Both activities usually required small groups of men to be absent from their households for extended periods of time, during which the women would tend garden plots, fish and gather plant foods available closer to home, take care of the children, make pottery and clothing, and engage in numerous other domestic tasks. Warfare was not the mass frontal assault familiar to Europeans but consisted rather of raids on the enemy. The rewards for personal bravery and stealth shown in such raids included increased prestige among the warrior's peers, the privilege of wearing a tattoo, and the opportunity for a young man to earn an adult, or warrior's, name.

The coming of the Europeans to the interior Southeast, beginning with the Spanish conquistadors in the mid-sixteenth century, had drastic and far-reaching consequences for the aboriginal populations of the region. The Creek, possibly owing to their interior, buffered loca-

Archaeological and historical sites and Indian reservations on a modern map of Florida.

tion, were spared immediate extinction, although the effects of depopulation, due to both introduced disease and direct conflict with the Europeans, and the movement of towns did much to unsettle the traditional social structure. However, with the arrival of British colonists, first on the Carolina coast and, by 1670, in Georgia, the Creek, by virtue of their location, assumed a pivotal position in the trade networks opening up on the emerging colonial frontier. Deerskins, in great demand in Europe for making clothing, saddles, and other items, passed from Indian hands to traders located at posts on the fall line or on the coasts, while the Indians reaped iron tools and utensils, beads, coarse "stroud" cloth, and guns and ammunition in the exchange. The Creeks were quickly and deeply enmeshed in an expanding commercial economy.

Meanwhile, in Florida, things had not gone well for the native tribes. The more populous groups—the Calusa of the southwest coast, the Timucua-speaking peoples of the central interior, and the Apalachee where the peninsula joined the Panhandle—had borne the brunt of the first encounters with the Spanish conquistadors beginning early in the sixteenth century. The Spanish colonial government in St. Augustine looked to the mission chain to provide a first line of defense should the British decide to expand southward. When the inevitable push did come, the small, isolated mission settlements, most of which were not garrisoned, could not hold. First in the 1680s, then, more seriously, between 1702 and 1704, the Florida missions were assaulted by well-armed, British-backed Yamasee, who swept 1,000 Florida Indians into plantation slavery on the rice coast of Carolina.

Despite the apparent good feeling between the British and the Creek, in 1715 "Emperor" Brim of the Coweta Creek attempted to organize a unified strike against the British, French, and Spanish colonists in former Indian territory. When the first attack of the so-called Yamasee War failed, some of the Creek towns moved to avoid retaliation, while these and other towns in the Lower Creek region of central Georgia began a cautious realignment toward the Spaniards in Florida. Taking advantage of this turn in allegiance, in 1716, 1717, and 1718 the Spaniards sent Diego Pena among the Lower Creek in an attempt to entice them to move to the largely vacant Florida peninsula. A number of towns—Oconee, Yuchi, Sawokli, Apalachicola—responded favorably to his offer, and the gradual native repopulation of Florida was begun. Slowly, in the middle decades of the eighteenth century, the old Apalachee area around present-day Tallahassee, the Apalachicola drainage, the central Florida region surrounding the great Alachua Savanna (Paynes Prairie; see map), and, to a lesser extent, the rolling uplands northeast of Tampa Bay witnessed the transformation of Creek into Seminole. With these peoples came languages new to the Florida peninsula. Hitchiti, ancestral to the Mikasuki language spoken by members of the contemporary Seminole and Miccosukee tribes, could be heard in the Alachua Savanna and the Apalachicola and Tallahassee areas. Muskogee, or Creek, today spoken on the Brighton Seminole reservation, was also to be heard in some of the Tallahassee towns and in the settlements above Tampa Bay.

Early Seminole history can be divided into two periods: colonization (1716–67), the initial migrations of the Creek towns into Florida, and enterprise (1767–1821), the era of prosperity under British and Spanish rule of Florida prior to the American presence.

The exact dates for the settlement of Florida by the Creek are not certain, nor are they likely to be given in the uneven documentation of the time. The period 1716–67 is as much as we can say. It appears that their first Florida towns virtually replicated in architecture and social structure the Creek settlements to the north. Squareground towns, notably at Latchua or Latchaway (on the rim of today's Paynes Prairie) and on the west bank of the Suwannee River in the vicinity of Old Town (Dixie County) continued to be the hub of social and political life and were presided over by chiefs or "kings," like Cowkeeper of Latchaway and White King of the Suwannee town. Red towns still battled white in the ball game, as they had in Creek country, the peace pipe or calumet ceremony still opened important proceedings, and the black drink (actually known to the Indians as the "white drink") still purified both mind and spirit.

Despite the basic continuity of the Creek culture pattern, there was an increasing and purposeful separation by the Florida Indians from the political affairs of their Creek counterparts to the north. In 1765, when Governor James Grant of the British colonial government called the Creek leaders together for the Picolata Congress, at which he hoped to gain from them boundary concessions to land east of the St. Johns River, the shrewd Cowkeeper was not in attendance, preferring to pay the governor a personal visit a month later. By Cowkeeper's own testimony, he had had little formal contact with the Creek leadership during the preceding decade. Cowkeeper's case also illustrates how difficult it is to characterize any aspect of Seminole history with simple generality, for while he led his band of Oconee to settle in Spanish Florida, he boasted of killing eighty-six Spaniards and hoped to do away with more. Yet he seemed to have little use for the British in Florida (although he was regarded as friendly) and little direct interest in Anglo-Creek politics. Perhaps his strongest inclination was in maintaining a degree of autonomy for his people.

At St. Marks in the former Apalachee territory, the Spaniards established a trading post in 1745, hoping to lure neighboring Lower Creek into permanent settlement. For a time they were successful, and the Creek founded towns in the area under the leadership of Secoffee, the son of Brim. However, the Spaniards had difficulty provisioning the post's store to meet demand as the quantity of deerskins brought in far surpassed their expectation, and Indian restlessness grew in this part of Spanish Florida.

The archaeological remains, what few there are that can be confidently dated to the colonization period, show a strong continuity of Creek material culture. Pottery vessels, the best collection of which is from the Suwannee River, are of the same form and function as similarly dated Creek vessels and bear the same "brushed" surface treatment and styles of rim decoration. Trade goods found, such as razors, knives, gun parts, glass beads, silver cones and earrings, buckles, and horse tack indicate full participation in the trade economy.

As the native involvement in trade intensified, and as tensions between Indian, Anglo, French, and Spanish on the colonial frontier continued to mount, the underpinnings of traditional Creek society began, slowly at first, to give way. The power of hereditary leadership began to diminish as traders plied the interior looking to make deals with anyone they could. As socially sanctioned warfare became an unacceptable means for young men to gain their manhood because of the turbulence and disruption it caused for the colonists, gangs of mounted warriors roamed the frontier looking for opportunities to test their bravery and courage. Such was the temper of Indian Florida when the British gained control in 1763 in accordance with the terms of the Treaty of Paris. By the end of British rule twenty years later, it could be said that there were no longer any Creek in Florida, only Seminole.

Despite their overall administrative prowess, the British in Florida seemed ill prepared to deal with increasingly complex questions of Indian trade and land rights. Through a series of conferences with the Creek set to clarify these concerns—at Augusta in 1763, St. Marks in 1764, and Picolata in 1765—John Stuart, Indian agent for the Southern District, became aware of increasing Indian dissatisfaction and demands relating to trade and of the emerging separateness of the Seminole from the Creek. Specific treaty negotiations also imply that there was a separateness, perhaps even antagonism, between the Alachua and St. Marks settlements. Although the beginning date for the period of enterprise could be set at 1763, when Great Britain took possession of Florida, Anglo-Indian relations were relatively stable by 1767, and the term *Seminole* or some derivative thereof was coming into common use. To the British the term meant *wild people,* possibly a reference to the remoteness of the Seminole from the affairs of the Creek Confederacy.

This was a time of tremendous radiation of the Seminole across the Florida landscape and, of course, a great increase in their numbers. In addition to Cowkeeper's Alachua Seminole, now settled at Cuscowilla, major towns were found at Talahasochte on the Suwannee River, on the St. Johns River near present-day Palatka, and at Chukochatty near present-day Brooksville. By 1774 nine substantial towns, most if not all with squaregrounds, were present in Florida; by 1821 this number had increased fourfold. In the old Apalachee area, major villages were located at Mickasuki (also called Newtown) and at Tallahassee.

The impetus for this Seminole expansion was trade. Using fire drives and firearms obtained by trade or direct gift, Indian hunters took large numbers of deer for the skin trade, ranging far south to the Everglades. For eighteen pounds of skins a hunter could obtain a new gun, for sixty pounds (a not unrealistic take in a good year) a new saddle. The British "one trader–one town" policy, designed to prevent competitive traders from unduly promoting village factionalism, had the unintended effect of stimulating the formation of new towns. Not everything the Seminole supplied to the traders came from the forest. Particularly in the fertile uplands east and northeast of Tampa Bay, plantation agriculture developed. Corn, rice, watermelons, peaches, potatoes, and pumpkins grown in large fields were taken to St. Augustine to provision the perpetually needy citizens of that city.

Using large, seaworthy canoes, Seminole from the Suwannee towns and from a town at the head of today's Charlotte Harbor traveled to Spanish Cuba to trade in the hope of getting better prices than those offered by the British. When Spain again took possession of Florida in 1783 following the American Revolution, trading houses established under British rule were encouraged to remain by Governor Vizente Manuel de Zéspedes to ensure continuity in trade relations. The leader of the Creek Confederacy, Alexander McGillivray, attempted to promote peaceful conditions between the Creek and Seminole and the Spaniards by nurturing the Indian trading company of Panton, Leslie while fending off increasing pressure from the encroaching Americans. But peace in Spanish Florida was not to be had. Tensions mounted between the Florida Seminoles and the new American residents of Georgia, and armed conflict erupted in the border regions. The tensions culminated in what amounted to the American invasion of Spanish Florida and the inevitable cession of Florida to the United States. For the Seminole, as shall be seen, this event would have cataclysmic results.

The prosperity of this enterprise period has left an archaeological landscape strewn with an abundance of trade goods. Glass beads, glass bottle shards, transfer-print and shell-edged pearlware ceramics, iron and brass kettles, kaolin smoking pipes, gun hardware, metal belt buckles, and silver earrings and brooches mark Seminole archaeological sites of this period. Brushed and decorated aboriginal pottery pieces found at these sites illustrate a basic continuity with the Creek tradition, yet prosperity brought a break with it as well. Inheritance may have passed less frequently along matrilineal lines than was customary, passing instead from father to son. By the first decades of the nineteenth century, major Seminole settlements may have resembled the typical southern plantation more than the traditional Creek square-ground. Certainly elements of both were combined at such places as Paynestown, the settlement of Payne, successor to Cowkeeper, where the archaeological concentrations of artifacts are thought to represent numerous outbuildings associated with the main house. A harbinger of things to come, Payne was wounded in an 1812 campaign against his town led by Colonel Daniel Newnan of the Georgia militia, and he died shortly thereafter.

Coming into history at this time are the bands of Seminole blacks, or Black Seminoles, descendants of those who had fought for the Spaniards at Fort Mose, established above St. Augustine in 1738, or more recent runaways from plantation slavery in Carolina and Georgia. Siting themselves in separate villages near Seminole towns, the blacks entered into a peculiar type of vassalage with the Seminoles, supplying them with agricultural produce and expecting some degree of protection in return. Having the blacks in Spanish Florida became a major point of antagonism between the Seminoles and the Georgians, while American attempts after 1821 to separate the blacks from their Seminole owners (as the Indians felt themselves to be) became a contributing factor in the Second Seminole War.

The next period of Seminole history, the time of the three Seminole wars, covered the years 1817–58. Without question, these were years of great trauma and upheaval for the Seminole people. From death in combat or deportation west to Indian territory, Seminole population decreased from about 5,000 persons just before the pre-American period to perhaps fewer than 200 by 1858. Yet this was the period that most strongly shaped the cultural identity of the modern Seminoles. Through adversity, maybe because of it, a revival of traditional Creek religion and customs took place. Archaeological and documentary evidence suggests the presence of a nativistic pulse during the early years of the Second Seminole War, driven, perhaps, by influences from militant Red Stick Creeks who had unsuccessfully resisted the increasing American presence in Alabama. Because there has not been any significant in-migration to swell Seminole ranks in the twentieth century, the cultural repertoire of Florida's contemporary Seminole Indians—including the Green Corn Dance—must have been passed down by those few Seminole who remained in 1858.

It is hard to isolate the so-called First Seminole War from the constant violence that characterized Florida during the opening decades of the nineteenth century. Incursions by the militia of Georgia and Tennessee at the start of the War of 1812, besides resulting in the death of Payne, scattered the Alachua Seminoles widely throughout the peninsula, some as far as present-day Miami. The weakness of Spain coupled with pressure by the United States to acquire Florida contributed to the turmoil. White men and non-Florida Indians raided the peninsula to capture slaves, red and black. Slaves from Georgia and Alabama escaped to mingle with the Seminole, as mentioned, in a form of servitude less onerous than the chattel slavery they ran from. The institution of slavery determined much that went on in troubled Spanish Florida. It was clear, too, that the races, red and white, could not live in proximity without friction, often violent.

In 1816, the United States established Fort Scott in the southwestern corner of Georgia just a few miles from the Spanish boundary. The administration decided to supply the fort by boats sent up the Apalachicola River through Spanish territory. Spain's government protested, but not militarily. The major military obstacle was the so-called Negro Fort sixty miles south of Fort Scott, overlooking the river and garrisoned by 334 blacks armed with ample military supplies left by the British after the War of 1812. If these blacks opposed the advance, they would give the United States the chance it sought to eliminate them. They did attempt to block the passage upstream but then were blown sky-high on 27 July 1816 when a lucky hotshot exploded the open powder magazines. The blast killed 270 blacks and injured more, depriving the Seminoles of efficient black warriors and tons of military stores.

Across the Flint River from Fort Scott was the Mikasuki village of Fowltown. The chief there, Neamathla, warned Colonel Edmund P. Gaines not to cross the river. Irritated by so blunt a threat, Gaines moved with 250 men to attack the town on 21 November 1817, killing five Indians and later burning the place. In retaliation the Indians opened fire on a boat coming up the river and killed thirty-seven of the forty soldiers aboard plus six women and four children. This, with other retaliatory acts, caused Secretary of War John C. Calhoun to order Major General Andrew Jackson to Fort Scott with power to wage war as he judged best. Jackson reached the fort on 9 March 1818. His force of 4,800, of which 1,500 were Creek Indians, facing 1,000 Seminoles and 300 blacks, easily advanced southwestward, destroying Indian settlements and crops. Late in March he obliterated Kenache's (or Kinhajo) town (close to Lake Miccosukee), the largest in Florida. His next conquest was not an Indian town but the Spanish town of St. Marks. Then in April 1818, he wiped out the town of Bowlegs, brother of Payne, on the Suwannee River. Bowlegs's band, displaced from the Alachua area by the Georgians in 1813, this time moved far south to the vicinity of Lake Harris (Lake County). Jackson had eliminated the fighting power of the Indians west of the Suwannee River and had dispersed the bands there. He had cleared the Indians from the Georgia border and closed one route used by slaves escaping into Florida.

Jackson wrote to the secretary of war, "Let it be signified to me through any channel that the possession of Florida would be desirable . . . and in sixty days it will be accomplished." Convinced that he had government approval, he turned back westward to capture Pensacola. Late in May 1818 he retook the city which he had occupied in 1814. Only St. Augustine remained under effective Spanish control, but the general looked beyond that: Given permission, some shipping, and a few more troops, he wrote, "I will assure you that Cuba will be ours in a few days."

President James Monroe, in justifying the First Seminole War to Congress, said that the Seminoles had provoked the United States into punitive action that had been purely defensive. According to Jackson his campaign had been "to chastise a savage foe, combined with a lawless band of negro brigands" carrying on a "cruel and unprovoked war against the citizens of the United States." One result of the American invasions of Florida was the transfer in 1821 of the peninsula and Panhandle east of the Perdido River to the United States.

For half a century before this transfer, the Florida Seminoles had prospered and increased their numbers tenfold. They carried on a profitable trade with British suppliers even during the Second Spanish Period. The trading system in those fifty years had the effect, as we saw, of diminishing the power of chiefs and increasing the power of autonomous bands. When the United States acquired Florida, there was no longer any strong central leadership among the Seminoles.

The prosperity of the Seminoles, described in the discussion of the enterprise period, was their undoing. Florida had become economically desirable. Therefore, the policy of the United States was first to restrict the Seminoles within a limited area, then remove them altogether to the west. Removal would end their threat to the institution of slavery. In a series of treaties the U.S. government undertook to carry out its policy, but it was hampered by the lack of a central Indian command with which to deal. It could always find Indians to sign treaties, but the signers were usually not acknowledged by the bands to have the authority to commit them to crowd onto a reservation or to leave Florida.

During the 1820s and early 1830s white encroachments drove the Florida Indians toward what would be called the Second Seminole War (1835–42). Slave raiders harassed the Indians and their black associates. The United States, by the Treaty of Moultrie Creek (1823), confined them to a reservation. They depended on the government for food but were usually hungry or actually starving. In 1835 there were between 800 and 1400 warriors fragmented into numerous bands. These warriors had 400 black men as allies, rated by whites as better fighters than the Indians. Each band had a hereditary chief, but there was still no principal chief over them all. Closest to a head chief was Micanopy, a descendant of Cowkeeper (possibly nephew to Payne and Bowlegs), but he did not take the initiative against white encroachment.

The man who did was Osceola, son of a white father, William Powell, and a Creek mother. White men often referred to him as Powell. He came to Florida with the Red Stick Creek as a boy of ten. Lacking any claim to hereditary leadership, he nevertheless personified the determination of the Seminoles to keep their homeland. It was he who planned the destruction of Major Francis Dade's detachment of 108 soldiers and the murder of agent Wiley Thompson with four other men on 28 December 1835. Three days later, he led the Indian force that prevented a small army under brevet Brigadier General Duncan L. Clinch from penetrating the Seminole refuge, about 100 square miles, known as the Cove of the Withlacoochee (Citrus County). Simultaneously with Osceola's offensive, Philip, a hereditary chief, perhaps in coordination with Osceola, ravaged plantations along the St. Johns River.

The U.S. force in Florida had one commander, but the position was rotated until seven had served. Clinch gave way to Brevet Major General Winfield Scott. Like all of his successors, Scott had to mix disparate types—regular army, volunteers, militia, and Indians hostile to the Seminole—to make an uneasy fighting force for seven years of war. In March 1836 Scott conducted his campaign in the European tactical tradition. He, too, aimed at the Cove, but by the time his three heavy columns converged on it, the Indians had already split into their basic bands and left.

Brevet Major General Edmund Pendleton Gaines, in New Orleans, hearing of the fighting, assembled 1,000 men and landed them in

"Osceola, Chief of the Seminole." Painting by George Catlin, 1838.

Florida without orders. After some marching and countermarching he was entrapped and besieged from 26 February to 5 March 1836, until relieved by troops sent by General Clinch. Gaines departed from Florida to the border of Texas. Scott charged him with spoiling his campaign, necessitating a court of inquiry held late in November 1836. The two generals vilified each other, but the court found both blameless.

When President Andrew Jackson relieved Scott on 21 June 1836, he made a political rather than a military appointment. His selection to command in Florida was a civilian, Richard Keith Call, governor of Florida Territory. Call assembled 2,500 men, a mixture of Tennessee volunteers, Florida militiamen, regulars, and Creek Indians, once again to penetrate the Cove. On 13 November he found it abandoned. Desperate to make a creditable showing, he received evidence that a substantial body of warriors was in Wahoo Swamp at the southern tip of the Cove. He attacked on 21 November but after several hours of fighting drew back without overcoming the foe. Jackson did not forgive him for this and dispatched Brevet Major General Thomas S. Jesup, quartermaster general of the army, to take command in Florida.

A year of conflict had borne hard on the Indians. Several chiefs, including Micanopy, entered into an agreement on 6 March 1837 to migrate. They stalled, enjoying the provisions and liquor provided by the government. At length, though, 700 encamped near Fort Brooke, waiting to be shipped west. Jesup thought the war was over. Then, during the night of 2 June, the 700 slipped away. Although Osceola's power had diminished, he, with the medicine man of the Mikasuki, Arpeika (Sam Jones to the white men), somehow coerced the Indians to decamp.

This exodus so disillusioned Jesup that he determined to subdue the Seminole by any means. The Indians, hungry and impoverished, were willing to come to the military camps to talk, eat well, and drink whiskey. At such a meeting on 9 September 1837, the general seized Coacoochee (Wildcat), who had arrived under a flag of truce. Wildcat's father was Philip, his mother a sister of Micanopy. He had a chief's lineage but was not yet a chief. Like Osceola he lacked formal authority and had to lead by force of personality.

More notorious was Jesup's seizing of Osceola on 27 October under a white flag. These two vital leaders were imprisoned in the old Spanish coquina fortress of the Castillo San Marcos at St. Augustine, known to the Americans as Fort Marion. Wildcat, with nineteen followers, made a miraculous escape on 29 November, then slipped southward to join the intransigents under Arpeika and Otulke Thlocco, called the Prophet. Arpeika, after hearing Wildcat's story, would never again risk attending a white council. Osceola, now too unwell to influence the war, died at Fort Moultrie, South Carolina, on 31 January 1838.

General Jesup held to this strategy. On 14 December 1837 he seized Micanopy, three other chiefs, and seventy-eight followers who had come to his camp to talk. He had by that time seriously cut into Seminole leadership. Still to come, though, were frequent skirmishes and the major pitched battle of the war. Colonel Zachary Taylor attacked a prepared position near Lake Okeechobee on Christmas Day of 1837. Halpatter Tustenuggee (known to the whites as Alligator), a close associate of Micanopy, commanded the center of the Indian line; Wildcat held the left with about eighty men; Sam Jones and the Prophet directed half the force on the right. Soldiers numbering 1,032, most of them regulars, assailed 480 Seminoles from diverse bands with no overall commander. Taylor's army drove the warriors out of their prepared position at a cost of 26 killed and 112 wounded. Because it was closer to a pitched battle than any other action during the conflict, it focused public attention on Taylor. He was commissioned a brigadier general for it and in the end became the only white commander to emerge from the war with an enhanced reputation.

In May 1838, General Jesup requested relief from the Florida command. He had crippled Indian fighting power, shipping 1,978 west and killing perhaps 400. He had created a rift between blacks and Seminoles so that more blacks were willing to serve as guides and interpreters for the U.S. forces. Although he vacillated on what to do with the Seminole blacks, finally he sent most of them west with their masters. Jesup continued as quartermaster general until his death in 1860, but he never lived down the stigma attached to his seizing the Indian leaders, particularly Osceola, under white flags.

Brigadier General Zachary Taylor assumed command on 15 May 1838. One thousand Indians remained in the territory: a cluster of bands in Middle Florida (between the Apalachicola and Suwannee rivers), another in the central part of Florida, and a third in the southwest region of the Big Cypress. They had little contact with each other, but the leaders in the southwest—Holata Micco (known as Billy Bowlegs), Arpeika, and Otulke Thlocco (Prophet)—sometimes met together. The Prophet was a renegade Creek who had escaped from Georgia following the Creek War of 1816. He became the messiah figure of the Second Seminole War. Because the other leaders feared his occult powers, he controlled much of the action in southwest Florida. In the end, though, he could not prevent an army detachment from destroying his own camp.

Zachary Taylor initiated a new strategy. He divided the territory north of the Withlacoochee River into squares twenty miles on each side, with a fort in the middle garrisoned by soldiers who built roads and regularly patrolled their squares. He intended to enlarge the area covered by squares when the commanding general of the army, Major General Alexander Macomb, arrived in Florida. Macomb met with such chiefs as he could assemble and in mid-May 1839 arranged with them to end the conflict. His peace document permitted the Seminole to remain in 6,700 square miles of southwestern Florida, about half of the Big Cypress Swamp. Floridians detested the settlement, but they were not the instruments terminating the peace. Certain Indian leaders who had not signed Macomb's pact struck at the new trading post on the Caloosahatchee River on 23 July 1839, totally destroying it and killing several soldiers. That move ended the peace. Taylor's strategy of squares was not continued. During his command, 800 Indians and 400 blacks had been shipped west.

At his request, Taylor was relieved by Brigadier General Walker K. Armistead in May 1840. The new commander established detachments of 100 men and sent them to explore little-known parts of Florida and to ferret out Indian hideaways. But when it seemed that all the Indians had been pushed into south Florida, destructive raids occurred in northeast and central Florida, where there had been none for months. Armistead did what he could to suppress them, and to corral more Seminoles to ship west. At the end of the year of his command, 700 hostiles, red and black, left Florida for the west.

Under a new policy of relying fully on regular troops, militia generals left the federal service. Once they were no longer present to outrank U.S. officers, it was possible for the first time to place a colonel, William Jenkins Worth, in command.

At a council in April 1841, Billy Bowlegs, Arpeika, and the Prophet reaffirmed their determination not to leave Florida and pronounced death for any Indian who carried messages from the whites. Far north in the Long Swamp east of Fort King, two months later, one Mikasuki chief, two Seminole chiefs, and Octiarche, a Creek fugitive from Georgia, took the same intransigent stand. No peace terms involving removal were acceptable.

When Colonel Worth took command in June 1841, he began to change his strategy. First, he rid north Florida of hostiles who held positions in proximity to new white settlements. The Indians had returned to the Cove of the Withlacoochee, and he divided his force into detachments of twenty men to clean them out. Second, using partisan tactics, he kept his troops campaigning right on through the sickly season in the swamps of south Florida. White Floridians approved of his strategy but howled when he sharply reduced the number of civilians and militiamen employed by the United States.

In June 1841, Major Thomas Childs seized Cooacoochee when he came into Fort Pierce. An officer shipped him west, but Worth ordered him returned to be used to induce other bands to surrender. Not even

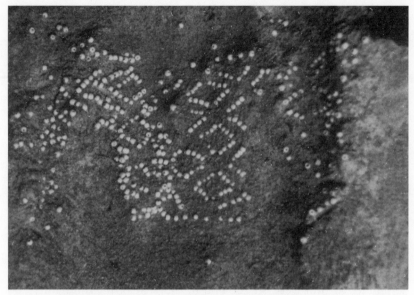

Remains of a beaded garter in a diamond pattern found with a Seminole burial at the Fort Brooke cemetery, dating from the Second Seminole War, ca. 1837.

Wildcat could persuade Arpeika to place himself in white hands. All in all, though, Worth's system was so successful that by April 1842 only 300 Indians remained in Florida, 112 of them warriors. They were hungry and miserable, especially the women and children. Worth, from his base of operations near Cedar Key, proposed to the War Department that this remnant be allowed to remain in Florida in the same 6,700-square-mile reservation proposed by General Macomb in 1839. White Floridians cried that it was shameful to tolerate any Indians in the peninsula, but in August 1842 the administration accepted the plan and the war ended.

Shipment of some of the 300 continued until 3,824 were gone by the end of 1843. It is not known how many of their number died during the war, but the Seminole had shown a rare ability to adapt to new circumstances and to survive as a culture. Their resilience would serve them well in the years ahead. Their fight to stay in their homeland is as gallant as any in history. That they held out for seven years is all the more remarkable because of the diversity of bands among them and their lack of continuous central leadership. It had been total war for them.

Not so for the United States, where the war required only a limited commitment from American citizenry at large. It did require a full commitment from the army, however. Every regiment served in Florida, straining the logistical and personnel staffs more than at any time since the War of 1812. There were 1,466 deaths in the regular army, 328 of them combat-related, 74 of them officers. The officer corps was further reduced sharply due to resignations of officers who saw no glory or honor for their service in Florida. Fifty-five citizen-soldiers were killed, and unknown hundreds died of disease. On the positive side, the war amounted to field training for officers who served later in the Mexican War and Civil War.

The army had to change its strategy and tactics more than once during the seven years of conflict. General Scott's heavy columns supported by logistical trains gave way gradually to small units that carried their supplies on their backs. These detachments had to penetrate nearly inaccessible hideaways, live partly off the land, recruit Indians and blacks as guides and interpreters, destroy the food sources of the Seminoles, endure extreme hardship, and, throughout, protect white settlements. The partisan style was not carried into the Mexican War or the Civil War, but the Union did finally employ a strategy against a people, not just against their military portion.

Following the end of the Second Seminole War in August 1842, Billy Bowlegs became principal chief over the 300 to 400 Indians remaining in Florida. Twenty warriors refused to acknowledge his authority. He and Sam Jones, head of the Mikasuki (one of several named tribal entities included generally within the Seminole nation), strove to abide by the terms of the peace settlement. Thus, when, in July 1849, after seven quiet years, five defiant young warriors killed and pillaged outside the reservation, Billy Bowlegs and Jones undertook to deliver the miscreants to the whites for justice. They did deliver three, and the hand of one killed, but the fifth had escaped. The next year they handed over three other rovers who had killed a white boy. Floridians were little affected by the conscientious effort that the chiefs had made. They simply wanted to be rid of the Seminole altogether. An editorial in a St. Augustine newspaper on 10 August 1850 asked that the natives be outlawed and a bounty of $1,000 placed on every male delivered dead or alive and $500 for every woman or child delivered alive. Senator Stephen Mallory said that they must get out or be exterminated.

For a time the U.S. government sought to achieve removal without war. Powerful chiefs were brought from among the Seminole in Indian Territory to persuade the Florida remnant to come west. In 1850, Major General David Twiggs, in command, offered Billy Bowlegs $10,000 to remove the entire group with a fee to each migrating Indian. In 1852, the government put the matter in the private sector. It designated Luther Blake to achieve the removal peacefully. Blake took Billy Bowlegs to Washington with three subchiefs to show them the power of the United States.

When Jefferson Davis was secretary of war, he heeded the cries of the Floridians and inaugurated a policy calculated to make the Seminole either leave or fight. It included an embargo on trade with them and survey of land within the reservation, followed by some sales. Efforts were made to rebuild some of the abandoned roads made during the Second Seminole War and to patrol them. Boats, too, appeared for use in the swamps. These white invasions of the reserved land did indeed push the Seminoles into war. Some accounts say that it was the vandalizing of one of Billy Bowlegs's camps "to see how Billy would cut up" that started the conflict. But it is more likely that the chiefs had decided earlier that they must fight. In any case, thirty warriors opened fire on Lieutenant George Hartsuff's detachment (the vandalizers) at 5:00 A.M. on 18 December 1855, wounding four of the ten and killing four. Thus began the Third Seminole War.

The U.S. commander, Colonel John Monroe, had at his disposal 800 regulars, 260 Florida militia in federal service, and 400 not in federal service. Since there were about 100 warriors left, the odds were fourteen to one. White organization, however, was faulty; there was poor communication between federal and state commanders.

Without a planned strategy, the Seminole attacked isolated habitations and small detachments at random. For six months they held the initiative. During 1856 they made fifteen raids and killed twenty-eight people. In September 1856, Brevet Brigadier General William S. Harney took command in Florida. He commenced a system of patrols that reduced the raiding but never found the retreats of Billy Bowlegs and Sam Jones. Harney left Florida in April 1857, followed in the command by Colonel Gustavus Loomis.

Governor James Broome insisted that citizen soldiers would be required to defeat the Indians. He ordered militia companies into service, appealing in all cases to the federal government to muster them into U.S. service. In July 1857 he called for ten companies. Not all of the companies that he ordered into service were acceptable to the War Department, and some of them, never officially mustered by regular officers, waited decades before receiving any pay. Nevertheless, as the conflict lengthened, the number of citizen-soldiers in the field increased, while the number of regulars declined. In the fall of 1857 only four companies of regulars remained in Florida.

Since the volunteers and militia from south Florida were mainly ranchers, they insisted on serving as horse troops. But they could not enter the swamps and lakes to find the last refuges of the Indians. In the summer of 1857 the state organized three boat companies of shallow-draft vessels carrying sixteen men each. Manned by a motley, unmilitary assortment, this flotilla forced its way through the swamps and sawgrass into Billy Bowlegs's refuge on 19 November 1857, ending a two-year hunt. The boat troops burned down more than fifty dwellings, took large quantities of corn and rice and some oxen, and destroyed several hundred acres of crops.

Captain John Casey worked before and during the conflict to limit the violence. Because of his influence, the chiefs knew that they were safe from seizure when they entered white camps for talks. Sam Jones never came in. He was by this time more than one hundred years old, senile, and represented in meetings by Assinwah, Bowlegs's son-in-law. To induce migration, Congress in August 1856 created an area of 2 million acres in Indian Territory for Florida Indians, separating them from the Creek toward whom they were hostile. Congress also made substantial funds available to pay the Seminoles who were removed.

Billy Bowlegs, beaten down by the destruction of his refuge, finally accepted money to go west: $6,500 for himself, $1,000 each for four subchiefs, $500 each for all other warriors, and $100 for women and children. Under these terms 164 persons shipped out on 4 May 1858: all of Billy Bowlegs's band, all of Assinwah's, and ten from Sam Jones's band. They received a total of $44,600. Sam Jones, with perhaps seventeen warriors, remained hidden on an island deep in the Everglades. He died in Florida at an estimated age of one hundred and eleven.

Colonel Loomis, who succeeded Harney, received official permission to declare the war ended on 8 May 1858. In this third conflict there had been no action classifiable as a battle, but forty warriors and the same number of white fighters had lost their lives in combat. Whereas in the Second Seminole War the regular soldiers had done the final mopping up, in this one the citizen-soldiers performed that task.

No more than 200 Indians remained in the state after 1858, but they preserved the Seminole culture and were the basis for a slowly increasing number of inheritors.

Following the Third Seminole War the remaining Seminole understandably withdrew from any but the most fleeting contacts with the few non-Indian Floridians who inhabited the lower portion of the peninsula. Settlement for the most part was in small, remote, matrilocal camps located on tree islands in the Everglades and Big Cypress regions.

Seminole chickee in the Big Cypress Swamp; drawn by Clay MacCauley in 1881.

The familiar open-air pole and thatch Seminole chickee (from the Mikasuki word meaning "house") typified such settlements, which also had outdoor cooking and work areas and garden plots. Gradually a coalescence of settlements occurred, as Seminole regularly inhabited locations on the north side of Lake Okeechobee, the northern edge of the Big Cypress, and the Pine Island Ridge area west of Fort Lauderdale. The Okeechobee settlements would give rise to the Muskogee-speaking Cow Creek Seminole, ancestors of today's Brighton group occupying a reservation in the same area. The Mikasuki-speaking Big Cypress and Pine Island groups were generally ancestral to the present populations of the Big Cypress and Hollywood reservations, respectively, and contributed to the Trail Miccosukee as well.

Travel between islands was accomplished by dugout canoe. Trade contacts were established with stores on both coasts, where skins and pelts were exchanged for cloth, corn, beads, pots and pans, rifles and ammunition. Ceremonial life centered on the Green Corn Dance, when scattered camps would come together to a shared dance or busk ground. Each busk group also shared in common a medicine bundle, a gathering of sacred objects bundled in a deerskin pouch under the exclusive care of the medicine man. Major busk grounds were located at Pine Island, although the Cow Creek and Big Cypress groups also possessed medicine bundles and held separate busks.

After 1880 Seminole contact with whites became more frequent and, inevitably, with this increased interaction there came the makings of more "Indian trouble." The government again developed a plan of removal to Indian Territory. A succession of federal agents from the Bureau of Indian Affairs and government-sponsored investigators came to assess the current Seminole situation and to determine the feasibility of removal. During this time various plans were put forth by groups of sympathizers to purchase reservation lands in Florida for the Indians, and private funds were raised for this purpose. However, the problem of getting the Seminole to move to such lands was more complex than had been thought, and these plans came to naught. By 1891 the State of Florida agreed to set aside a 5,000-acre tract for an Indian reservation, to include lands then currently inhabited by the Seminole, but no allocation was made for proper boundary survey. By 1917, largely through the efforts of Minnie Moore-Willson, the state designated nearly 100,000 acres for reservation use in the swamps of Monroe County, although few if any Indians actually ever resided there. With the creation of Everglades National Park in 1935, the Monroe County lands were exchanged for acreage in Broward and Palm Beach counties.

Through the diligence of Lucien Spencer, U.S. government special commissioner to the Seminole, and a few others, the Seminole gradually began moving to federal reservation lands during the 1920s, particularly to a small tract at Dania where the current Hollywood reservation is located. The opening of the Tamiami Trail highway (U.S. 41) across the Everglades in 1928 attracted far-flung northern and southern bands to establish tourist camps along the road. Here motorists could find colorful patchwork, palmetto dolls, palmetto baskets, skins, live baby alligators, and other items for sale. These groups and others still living in remote camps showed little interest in the reservation policy of the federal administration. Through the early 1930s less than 10 percent of the Seminole population lived on reservation lands. Exhibition villages, primarily in and around Miami, also housed a number of Seminole families in the early to middle decades of the twentieth century.

A burst of success by Christian missionaries in the 1940s, led by the Creek Baptist preacher Stanley Smith, created a schism between the new converts and those adhering to traditional religion, with the result that the Christian Seminoles began to move to reservations where they could establish churches. As the reservations at Dania, Big Cypress, and Brighton became true population centers, the Bureau of Indian Affairs had less difficulty in developing formal governing bodies through

which new policies and programs could be introduced and administered. The Seminoles living along the trail continued to have little interest in formal relationships with the federal government and resented
efforts to lump them with the reservation Seminoles for administrative
purposes.

Antagonism between the Trail Indians and the reservation Seminoles
was accelerated in 1950 when a small group of reservation Seminoles
with legal representation filed a land claims lawsuit before the Indian
Claims Commission. The suit, filed under terms specified in the Indian
Claims Commission Act of 1946, sought financial compensation for
land taken from the Seminoles in treaties before and during the Second
Seminole War and for the land lost to Everglades National Park in 1935.
The Trail Indians wanted nothing to do with the Seminole suit, fearing
the government would accept no future claims once this case was settled. In fact, fully one-third of the adult reservation Seminoles did not
back the case. Partly due to the impetus of the land claims case, a central
tribal government was formed in which the Big Cypress, Brighton, and
Dania reservations were politically linked. In 1957, the Seminole Tribe
of Florida was officially recognized by the U.S. government. The Trail
Indians also found it necessary to organize, and in 1962 they were
granted federal recognition as the Miccosukee Tribe of Florida.

In 1970, after years of expensive legal maneuvers by both sides and
the entry and exit of numerous third parties, the commission determined that the Seminoles should be awarded a little over $12 million,
at less than market value, for lands taken in the 1820s and 1830s. Unfortunately, the commission failed to specify how the money was to be
divided among the Seminole, Miccosukee, and Oklahoma Seminole
tribes. After an appeal by the Seminoles, the commission awarded the
tribes $16 million in 1976 but did not resolve the distribution problem.
In 1990, twenty years after the initial award, Congress mandated a
75/25 split of the $50 million settlement (the 1976 award plus interest)
between the Oklahoma and Florida Seminoles. The Florida share,
amounting to some $12.3 million, was divided among the Seminole
tribe (77.2 percent), the Miccosukees (18.6 percent), and independent
Seminoles, legally recognized full-blooded Indians who are not tribal
members (4.6 percent).

The Seminole Tribe—divided in its population of less than 1,500
among the Brighton, Hollywood, Big Cypress, Immokalee, and Tampa
reservations—is governed by an elected tribal council and, through its
corporate branch, engages in many sophisticated and complex business
ventures. The smaller Miccosukee Tribe, similarly organized, conducts
tribal business from its headquarters on the Tamiami Trail reservation.

One of its newest ventures is a large bingo operation overlooking the Everglades on the outskirts of Miami.

All too often, the relationship between the tribes and local, state, and federal governments continues to be defined by legal battles over land and water-use rights and issues of tribal sovereignty. Sales of tax-free cigarettes and bingo revenues have been financially beneficial for the Seminole Tribe and have resulted in surprising political clout. In 1982 it was reported that the tribe contributed $48,300 to the campaigns of candidates seeking statewide political office, making it the largest corporate campaign contributor of the year. In 1984, a total of $55,350 was contributed, again the largest from any single corporate source. The recent push for casino gambling has generated a great deal of controversy and antagonism and is certain to test the political friendships developed over the last decade. In another effort to garner tourist revenue, perhaps recalling the days of the exhibition villages, the Seminoles recently opened a "safari" camp on the Big Cypress reservation, where the visitor can spend the day touring the swamp aboard a swamp buggy and at night find lodging in a traditional Seminole chickee. Adding to the diversified economic portfolio are more conventional pursuits including cattle ranching, particularly on the Brighton reservation (where it has become a multimillion-dollar enterprise), and growing lemons, grapefruits, and oranges.

Although the concrete block house has virtually replaced the chickee on the modern reservation, polyester has replaced patchwork, and Christianity has long since been accepted, much remains of traditional Seminole culture. In early summer, dance grounds are prepared for the annual Green Corn Dance, directed by a tribal medicine man much as was done in the nineteenth century and before. The desire for ritual purity through traditional religious rites is a concern for a growing number of Seminole youth. These same youths are attending college in record numbers, financed by bingo and cigarette proceeds. The future for this generation is anything but certain, a statement that equally could have applied to previous generations back at least to 1812. That there in fact has been a modern history of the Florida Seminoles is in itself remarkable and perhaps bodes well for the future.

Bibliography

Blackard, David M. *Patchwork and Palmettos: Seminole-Miccosukee Folk Art Since 1820*. Fort Lauderdale: Fort Lauderdale Historical Society, 1990.

Covington, James W. *The Seminoles of Florida*. Gainesville: University Press of Florida, 1993.

Fairbanks, Charles H. "The Ethno-Archaeology of the Florida Seminole." In *Tacachale: Essays on the Indians of Florida and Southeast Georgia During the Historic Period,* edited by Jerald T. Milanich and Samuel Proctor, pp. 163–93. Gainesville: University Presses of Florida, 1978.

———. *Ethnohistorical Report of the Florida Indians.* New York: Garland Publishing, Inc., 1974.

Garbarino, Merwyn S. *Big Cypress: A Changing Seminole Community.* New York: Holt, Rinehart and Winston, 1972.

Kersey, Harry A., Jr. *Pelts, Plumes, and Hides: White Traders among the Seminole Indians 1870–1930.* Gainesville: University Presses of Florida, 1975.

———. "The Florida Seminole Lands Claims Case, 1950–1990." *Florida Historical Quarterly* 72, no. 1 (July 1993):35–55.

MacCauley, Clay. "The Seminole Indians of Florida." In *Fifth Annual Report of the Bureau of Ethnology,* pp. 469–531. Washington, 1887.

Mahon, John K. *History of the Second Seminole War.* Gainesville: University of Florida Press, 1967.

The Seminole Tribune. Published biweekly by Seminole Communications for the Tribal Council of the Seminole Tribe of Florida, 6333 Forrest Street, Hollywood, Florida 33024.

Sprague, John T. *The Origin, Progress, and Conclusion of the Florida War.* Introduction by John K. Mahon. Floridiana Facsimile and Reprint Series. Gainesville: University of Florida Press, 1964; originally published 1848.

Sturtevant, William C. "Creek into Seminole." In *North American Indians in Historical Perspective,* edited by Eleanor Burke Leacock and Nancy Oestrich Lurie, pp. 92–128. New York: Random House, 1971.

———. "The Medicine Bundles and Busks of the Florida Seminole." *Florida Anthropologist* 7, no. 2 (June 1954):31–70.

———. *A Seminole Source Book.* New York: Garland Publishing, Inc., 1987.

Weisman, Brent R. *Like Beads on a String: A Culture History of the Seminole Indians in North Peninsular Florida.* Tuscaloosa: University of Alabama Press, 1989.

Wickman, Patricia R. *Osceola's Legacy.* Tuscaloosa: University of Alabama Press, 1991.

Wright, J. Leitch, Jr. *Creeks and Seminoles: The Destruction and Regeneration of the Muscogulge People.* Lincoln: University of Nebraska Press, 1987.

12 U.S. Territory and State

Daniel L. Schafer

On 17 July 1821, as the Stars and Stripes replaced the Spanish flag in the public square outside Government House in Pensacola, America's greatest living military hero supervised the ceremony. General Andrew Jackson, the hero of New Orleans, had accepted President James Monroe's offer to become the first American governor of Florida.

The transfer of sovereignty marked a moment of triumph for Jackson, who had led American armies on punishing invasions of the Spanish Floridas in 1814 and 1818. It had been the latter campaign, the destructive raid commonly known as the First Seminole War, that, more than any other factor, persuaded Spain to cede East and West Florida to the United States in the Adams-Onís Treaty of 1819.

Jackson had expected praise from Washington, but instead his political opponents impugned his Florida victory as an outrageous usurpation of military power and a threat to the supremacy of constitutional government. Understandably, therefore, he took satisfaction from presiding over the ceremonies in which Spain relinquished all claims to territories east of the Mississippi River. Certainly he felt vindicated.

There had been frustrating delays and vexations in the months of negotiations that preceded the exchange of flags. Jackson waited from late April until 17 July for Spanish governor José Callava to transfer command. Negotiations with Spanish governor José Coppinger for the transfer of East Florida also proceeded slowly. The exchange of flags in St. Augustine finally occurred on 10 July 1821.

One week later, similar ceremonies were held in Pensacola, but Jackson had not forgotten the indignities suffered during the waiting period. Before Callava left Pensacola in mid-August, Jackson had him jailed briefly for obstructing delivery of documents pertinent to a lawsuit. Jackson's explosive temper led to this diplomatic blunder, but the order was given, he said, to protect the rights of a free quadroon woman, who, for fifteen years, had been cheated of her inheritance. His motive, he explained later, had been to prevent "men of high standing" from "trampl[ing] upon the rights of the weak."[1]

More troubling to Jackson was President Monroe's refusal to appoint the governor's nominees to the principal posts in the Florida administration. Jackson had expected wide powers of patronage to reward his loyal associates. Instead, Monroe appointed the higher-ranking secretaries, judges, and attorneys. Jackson was allowed to choose office-holders for Escambia and St. Johns counties, two vast administrative units he created, nearly coterminous with the old West and East Floridas, which faced each other at the Suwannee River. He also selected judges for the county courts and mayors and aldermen for St. Augustine and Pensacola.

Richard Keith Call would turn out to be the most important of Jackson's appointees for the next four decades. He had joined a volunteer unit under Jackson's command in 1813 and had followed him on both Florida campaigns and in the Battle of New Orleans. Call handled the early negotiations with Governor Callava and later was named to the Town Council. He established a thriving law practice; he served on the Florida Legislative Council in 1822 and 1823, as territorial delegate to Congress in 1824, and as brigadier general of the militia; and he was twice named governor of the territory. Call became the leader of the first governing elite in American Florida.

Jackson established an effective governing structure in a few weeks, working long hours though troubled by sickness and by the heat and humidity of a Pensacola summer. As soon as the provisional government was functioning, he resigned as governor effective 5 October 1821 and returned to Tennessee. William P. DuVal, a U.S. judge at Pensacola, succeeded him as governor.

In March 1822, Congress replaced the provisional structure with a single territorial government, after disregarding requests from both Georgia and Alabama for incorporation of West Florida and from residents of St. Augustine for two separate territories. Executive and legislative leadership would come from a governor, a secretary, and a legislative council—all appointed by the president. Federal courts were

William P. DuVal, first civil governor of the U.S. Territory of Florida, served four consecutive terms, from 1822 to 1834. Born in Richmond, Virginia, in 1784 of Huguenot descent, he grew up in Kentucky and became a member of Congress from that state. His appointment to office in Florida was owed to his friendship with Andrew Jackson. Never popular, he showed favoritism in his decisions and complained constantly about his salary, the weather, and the inhospitable nature of the people.

established at Pensacola and St. Augustine, their judges appointed by the president. Only the delegate to Congress would be elected.

Governor DuVal called the first Legislative Council into session on 10 June 1822 at Pensacola, but the ship carrying the St. Johns delegates that departed St. Augustine on 30 May experienced storms and shipwreck and did not arrive until 22 July. Another shipwreck claimed the life of a council member. A yellow fever outbreak necessitated moving to temporary quarters north of Pensacola and claimed the life of the council's chairman, Dr. James C. Bronaugh. Despite these adversities the first council created civil offices, courts, a militia, and revenue measures and carved two new counties, Duval and Jackson, from the unmanageably large counties of St. Johns and Escambia. Congress had ordered that annual sessions of the council should alternate between St. Augustine and Pensacola, but when the delegates from Escambia to the 1823 session in St. Augustine also experienced dangers and delays, DuVal commissioned Dr. William H. Simmons and John Lee Williams to select a compromise site for a permanent capital between the Ocklockonee and Suwannee rivers, midway between St. Augustine and Pensacola.

Simmons and Williams selected Tallahassee, where the old fields and council houses of the Apalachees once stood. Hernando De Soto camped there in the winter of 1539–40; Franciscans built Spanish missions there a century later; and in the eighteenth century Creek migrants established Tallahassee Taloofa and Mikasuki, towns that were burned by Jackson's army in 1818. Simmons and Williams met Seminole chiefs Neamathla and Chefixico there while conducting surveys. Neither chief seemed anxious to leave the region, yet Governor DuVal named Tallahassee the permanent capital in March 1824.

Settlers began arriving at the site in the following month, living in tents while they acquired land and built houses. By the time the council met in November 1824, a hotel had been constructed for legislators. Governor DuVal lived briefly in a log cabin adjacent to the site of the temporary log and board structure that became the capitol in 1824. A two-story brick building replaced the wood building in 1826, and it was followed by a more permanent structure in 1839.

Congress made the legislative council elective in 1826 and bicameral in 1838. Members of the House of Representatives were elected at the county level based roughly on population, and senators were chosen from judicial districts: three each from the eastern and western, four from the middle, and one from the southern districts.

The most important elected official in the territory was the delegate to Congress. Joseph M. Hernández, a sugar planter of Spanish and Mi-

The first meeting of Florida's territorial legislature at the compromise capital of Talla-hassee took place in 1824 inside a rude log hut. Two years later, the cornerstone was laid for a permanent brick statehouse, shown here after its completion. The legislature, called the Legislative Council, occupied the upper story, the executive and judicial branches the lower. Governor DuVal kept a log cabin nearby. A new and larger capitol was completed in 1839.

norcan ancestry, was appointed by the first legislative council in 1823. All subsequent delegates were elected by the voters of the territory, with suffrage open to white males twenty-one years old who had been residents for at least three months. Richard Call succeeded Hernández in 1824. Neither man could vote in Congress, but both lobbied for the interests of Florida residents, which included naval construction, roads, bridges, and other internal improvements. Joseph M. White served as delegate from 1825 to 1838. By the time his successor was elected in May 1837, candidates were pledged to political parties. Charles Down-ing was elected as a Whig Party candidate advocating opposition to statehood. His opponents were a State Rights Whig, a Jacksonian Dem-ocrat, and a Democrat opposed to the territory's banking laws. By the late 1830s, political parties and heated partisan issues enlivened elec-tion debates. A Democrat from St. Augustine, David Levy, was elected in 1841 and 1843, running on an antibank and prostatehood platform.

Until Florida became a state in 1845, its governors were presidential appointees. William DuVal served until 1834, when President Andrew Jackson appointed John H. Eaton to succeed him. Call, still a Jackson favorite despite his opposition to Democratic Party policies in Florida, became governor in 1836, but President Martin Van Buren replaced him with Democrat Robert R. Reid in 1839. Call supported Whig Party candidate William Henry Harrison's successful presidential campaign in 1840 and was rewarded with a return to the governor's office for the 1841–44 term. Democrat John Branch served as governor for the one remaining year that Florida was a territory.

During the early territorial years most Florida residents were too busy acquiring land or cultivating it to pay close attention to political affairs in Tallahassee. They had not waited for legislation or deeds before settling on tracts of open land. More than 450 settlers from the United States were living near Pensacola prior to final approval of the Adams-Onís Treaty. Two thousand Americans had marched with Jackson from the Suwannee River to Pensacola in 1818; some remained, others returned to their homes with news of fertile and unclaimed land in Florida. Land-hungry Americans, pioneers on the southern frontier, began moving into Florida seeking a fresh start.

Journalist and historian Clifton Paisley has written of the 300 persons living in log cabins and planting crops at the Spring Creek settlement in northwestern Jackson County months before the Stars and Stripes were raised at Pensacola. By 1825, Jackson County had 2,156 residents; some were already cotton planters, and about one-third were black slaves. In 1819, Henry Yonge was living on the Apalachicola River in what was to become Gadsden County. He brought twenty slaves from Georgia and began clearing and building, waiting for the American flag to catch up.

It was Middle Florida, lying between the Apalachicola and the Suwannee rivers, that attracted the majority of settlers in the territorial years. Tallahassee grew to 1,500 residents by 1835, a combination government town and merchant center. In the rural areas outside Tallahassee growth was immediate and continuous. Men from aristocratic families in Virginia and Maryland brought large numbers of slaves to cultivate sugar and cotton in the fertile Red Hills of Florida. Thomas E. Randolph and his son-in-law Francis Eppes, a grandson of Thomas Jefferson, settled in Leon County. John G. and Robert Gamble migrated from Richmond, Virginia. Thomas Randall, William B. Nutall, and Hector Braden also came from Virginia.

Thomas Brown arrived in Middle Florida during the winter of 1826–27 with an advance party of slaves to clear land and plant crops.

During the territorial and early statehood periods, the Middle Florida cotton counties between the Apalachicola and Suwannee Rivers accounted for Florida's largest population, wealth, and number of black slaves.

In 1828, he led a wagon caravan of twenty-one planters, their families and slaves, from Virginia to the Red Hills. Brown himself brought 140 slaves to Florida. Following statehood he was elected governor, serving from 1849 to 1853.

Dr. John A. Craig migrated from Maryland. Benjamin Chaires, the wealthiest of the Middle Florida planters, moved there from North Carolina. James Gadsden came from South Carolina, Richard K. Call from Virginia via Kentucky, and Joseph White from Kentucky. Prince Achille Murat, son of the exiled king of Naples and the sister of Napoleon Bonaparte, created Lipona, an estate in Jefferson County which became famous for elegant entertainment. With such personages Middle Florida became the center of an aristocratic social life and the dominant region of Florida from 1821 to 1861.

Census takers counted fewer than 2,400 persons living in Middle Florida in 1825 and 11,000 in the rest of the territory. By 1830, Middle Florida had grown to nearly 16,000, approximately 45 percent of the territory's total population. Ten years later, it had 34,000 residents, West Florida only 5,500, and East Florida 15,000. The counties centered around Tallahassee harvested 80 percent of the territory's cotton crop produced that year; black slaves formed the majorities of their populations.

Migrants came to East Florida as well, by land and sea. Many forded the St. Marys River and followed the King's Road to homesteads in what became Nassau and Duval counties. Others continued southward, crossing the St. Johns River at a narrow bend known as Cowford. There they found the best land already under cultivation, owned by families who had lived in the area for decades. One family, that of Francisco Xavier Sánchez, had witnessed three changes of flags at St. Augustine. Descendants of Sánchez owned cattle ranches and plantations, some begun as early as the First Spanish Period. Francis Phillip Fatio's family lived on St. Johns River properties acquired from the British in the 1770s. Francis Richard arrived in 1791, fleeing the slave rebellion in Haiti, and by 1821 his sons had acquired a sawmill and thousands of acres of prime woodlands and plantations. There were also Browards, Williamses, Christophers, Houstons, Flemings, McIntoshes, Clarks, Perpalls, Solanos, Ugartes, Bethunes, and Hartleys among the hundreds of families with long tenure in northeast Florida.

Zephaniah Kingsley, an African slave trader, maritime merchant, shipbuilder, and planter, had arrived in the region in 1803. Kingsley's wife was from Senegal, a victim of the slave trade he had profitably engaged in. Anna Madgigaine Jai Kingsley became a free woman, a planter, and a slave owner herself. In 1821, Kingsley lived with his wife and his free African-American family at Fort George Island, a cotton plantation located where St. Johns River meets the Atlantic Ocean. He eventually owned plantations in what became five northeast Florida counties, cultivated by more than 300 slaves.

Isaiah D. Hart, another long-time resident of northeast Florida, saw the exchange of flags and the arriving settlers as opportunity. One of the Patriot rebels in 1812–14, Hart was living on the St. Marys River at the time the treaty of cession was signed, one of the *banditti* raiding for cattle and slaves. In 1820, he traded cattle for acreage near the ferry crossing at Cowford on the St. Johns River and built a boardinghouse and store. His acreage became the heart of the town of Jacksonville when it was founded in 1822, and he soon became a wealthy merchant and planter.

St. Augustine was the only town of significant size in East Florida. The Ancient City had a diverse mix of Spanish and American residents by 1830. Minorcan and Greek descendants of the New Smyrna colonists occupied one-quarter of the town and Anglo-Americans, Europeans, free blacks, and slaves the rest. Seminoles often came to town to sell cattle and horses. After 1842, the growth and the pace of the city slowed as Jacksonville, Fernandina, and other new towns eclipsed it in commercial importance. In the decade before 1861, tourism became a staple of the city's economy.

South of St. Augustine along the Matanzas, Tomoka, and Halifax rivers were large plantations carved from the Florida wilderness by British entrepreneurs. Initially indigo, rice, and cotton producers, many were converted to sugar cultivation after the Spaniards returned. Many of these sugar estates were worked by more than 100 slaves.

Beyond the St. Johns River, travelers heading west toward Talla- hassee encountered several Seminole villages, where long-established inhabitants understandably resisted Anglo-American intrusion. General Duncan Clinch and John H. McIntosh had sugar plantations in the inte- rior district of Alachua, however, as did Moses Elias Levy, a Sephardic Jew who had lived in Morocco, Spain, St. Thomas (Virgin Islands), and Cuba before arriving in East Florida in 1818 with title to 60,000 acres purchased from a Spanish Florida merchant, Fernando de la Maza Arredondo. Levy planned to establish a colony of Jewish settlers from Europe. When recruiting efforts failed, he purchased African slaves. His son, David Levy, became one of Florida's leading politicians.

Throughout the territory, two issues were of fundamental impor- tance: access to land (or validation of existing deeds) and removal of the Seminole Indians. Spain ceded nearly 40 million acres of land, much of it uninhabited and a potential bonanza to speculators and settlers. The absence of land records for West Florida complicated transmittal of deeds. For East Florida, where the bulk of Spanish and British land grants had been made, records were acquired by U.S. marshal James Grant Forbes during a mission to Havana in 1821. But even with these documents, claims dragged through the courts for decades. Particularly vexing were legal problems associated with the Arredondo grant of 300,000 acres in Alachua and the Forbes Purchase, a grant to John Forbes and Company by the Spanish crown of one million acres on both sides of the Apalachicola River.

Under terms of the Adams-Onís Treaty, the United States agreed to recognize valid Spanish titles, and Congress created a board of commis- sioners for Pensacola and St. Augustine to adjudicate the claims. In 1826, unsettled Spanish land grant claims were assigned to the receiver of the Land Office and later to the federal courts. Congress also passed a Donation Act in 1824 to permit squatters to acquire valid titles to a maximum of 640 acres. In 1828, it became possible to "pre-empt" pre- viously settled land from public sale for a fee of $1.25 an acre.

Land offices for sales of surveyed public land were established in Tallahassee and St. Augustine in 1825 and 1826 and in Newnansville after 1842. During the territorial years most public land sold was located in Middle Florida and went for an average price of $1.29 per acre. Land speculators made fortunes.

The appointment of Andrew Jackson as first governor sent a warning to the Seminole that their days in Florida were numbered. Removal of the Indians of the Southeast from their traditional lands to reservations beyond the Mississippi River was national policy, and no one would administer it with more efficiency than the man the Creek called "Sharp Knife." His election to the presidency in 1828 and 1832 and passage of the Indian Removal Law of 1830 only hastened the inevitable.

Governor DuVal insisted that the 5,000 Seminole living in villages along the Apalachicola and Suwannee rivers, in Alachua, and near Tallahassee, evacuate the territory, but their leaders refused to leave. Violent conflicts with settlers prompted volumes of angry letters and petitions to the governor and the president. Plantation owners charged that the Seminole killed cattle and enticed slaves to escape, and newspaper editors called for speedy removal of the "murderous savages." Seminole leaders also solicited the governor's protection, accusing the settlers of stealing cattle and capturing free blacks and slaves from Indian villages.

A commission headed by James Gadsden met with Seminole leaders in 1823 to pressure them to move to a reservation in south Florida. Two weeks of negotiations at a site five miles south of St. Augustine led to the Treaty of Moultrie Creek in September 1823. Reluctantly, thirty-two chiefs agreed to terminate their rights of occupancy in north Florida in exchange for a reserve of 4 million acres located between the Peace and Withlacoochee Rivers, compensation for lost improvements, and twenty years of financial subsidies. The government thus added 24 million acres in north Florida to the public domain, much of it prime planting land, in exchange for what even Governor DuVal thought to be worthless land located "in the most miserable region I ever beheld." DuVal feared that "white men will crowd near . . . and steal their horses and cattle" and felt some shame that he "had not the power to obtain for them their own rights and property held by our citizens."[2] In Gadsden's mind, moving the Seminoles to the reserve would concentrate them for eventual removal to the west.

After further pressures, the Seminoles reluctantly began trekking south. They found poor land, drought, crop failure, and suffering, prompting one sympathetic army officer to predict they would either starve or be forced to leave the reserve and steal from settlers. Colonel George F. Brooke distributed rations rather than watch them die of starvation.

The Seminoles soon began returning to their former homes in north Florida, renewing conflicts with settlers and pressures for removal. In 1832, President Jackson sent Gadsden to persuade the Indians to leave Florida for the west. The Treaty of Payne's Landing, which emerged from that meeting, has been embroiled in controversy since it was marked (in lieu of signatures) by fifteen Seminole leaders on 9 May. Gadsden insisted that the Seminoles agree to a mass evacuation within three years. They vehemently refused, claiming that they intended to send a delegation of chiefs to inspect the lands in the west and report back to their people. Departure was contingent on a favorable vote of the Seminole nation.

The delegation of seven that visited the western lands signed another pact on 28 March 1833, often referred to as the Treaty of Fort Gibson. John Phagan, the Indian agent representing the government, interpreted it as an agreement that the land was acceptable even though it was controlled by the Creek nation. Seminole leaders rejected this interpretation, insisting that they would never agree to merge with their bitter enemies despite their mutual origins. They also accused Phagan of refusing to transport them back to Florida unless they signed the pact.

Historian John K. Mahon, the leading authority on the subject, has concluded that coercion, bribery, and deceit produced the signatures at Payne's Landing and Fort Gibson. But coercion mattered little to Jackson; he gave orders to expedite removal. The outraged Seminoles refused to cooperate and began planning to attack the Americans. The attacks soon escalated to major and lengthy armed conflict, called in history the Second Seminole War (1835–42) and the Third Seminole War (1855–58). (The military history of those wars is given in chapter 11.) At their end, battle casualties and forced removal to the trans–Mississippi West had reduced the number of Seminoles in Florida to no more than 200. They lived in small, scattered bands in the most remote regions of south Florida, where they would seldom be seen for the remainder of the century.

At the conclusion of the Second Seminole War, Congress passed the Armed Occupation Act (AOA) of 1842 to encourage white population growth in south Florida and to add to pressure for the remaining Seminoles to emigrate. The act permitted a head of family or a single man capable of armed defense to claim 160 acres of land south of Gainesville and north of the Peace River. In this way nearly 1,200 individuals received title to 200,000 acres of land and 6,000 persons moved to south Florida. Claimants rushed to formerly remote regions such as Indian River on the Atlantic Coast and Hillsborough County in southwest Florida.

Near the deactivated military outpost at Fort Pierce on Indian River a colony of migrants from Augusta, Georgia, created a thriving settlement. Caleb Lyndon Brayton, one of the Augusta migrants, had moved from Massachusetts to Augusta in the 1830s and prospered as a merchant. When he heard of the AOA he headed for the south Florida frontier. Despite periodic bouts with tuberculosis, Brayton threw himself into pioneer life with remarkable energy, clearing land and building a cabin on high ground overlooking the Indian River. By spring 1845 he had planted over 140 acres of arrowroot, pumpkins, and other produce and had begun to market poultry, dried fish, and green turtles in Key West. He acquired a schooner to facilitate his trade and dreamed of the wealth he would gain from pineapples and other fruits and vegetables planted on an additional 160-acre tract he purchased. Filled with unbridled enthusiasm, Brayton's letters to his wife in Augusta are an enduring testimonial to the rigors as well as to the exhilarations of pioneer life. They also document the profound loneliness of solitary life on the south Florida frontier.

Across the peninsula from Fort Pierce, the AOA stimulated development of Hillsborough County, where only ninety-six permanent residents had been counted in 1840. Over 6,000 acres were claimed on the rich virgin soils of Manatee River and Sarasota Bay. Some families who had moved from Virginia and Maryland to Middle Florida in 1820s, and had prospered until acquiring huge debts during the national depression of 1837, moved in 1842 to their second Florida frontier. Distinguished families like the Bradens, Gambles, and Craigs transplanted large slave forces to begin sugar plantations along the Manatee River, where a longer growing season protected canefields against the early frosts common in north Florida. Northeast Florida men like Jacob Summerlin drove herds of cattle south to graze free on the vast open range of Hillsborough County. By 1860 there were 30,000 head of cattle roaming the inland grasslands. More than 900 people lived among the prosperous Manatee River plantations. Historian Janet Snyder Mathews has characterized the Hillsborough settlements as "the edge of wilderness" and an important part "of a new American frontier."[3]

The Gambles and Bradens were frontier aristocrats, not the "plain folk" who pioneered in Florida from adjacent southern states after 1842. James M. Denham has written with understanding of the culture of the Florida "crackers" who brought their families and farm animals to Florida seeking better soils. Highly individualistic and mobile, fiercely dedicated to popular democracy, generally possessing antipathy toward Indians and African Americans, and quick to anger, the crackers would become the majority of the population in farming regions of the state. Denham suggests three possible origins of the term used to describe these frontiersmen: their skill at cracking a whip while driving cattle; the jokes (cracks) they bantered about; or their practice of grinding (cracking) corn for bread flour.[4]

Peace following the Seminole wars also contributed to the growth and development of northeast Florida. The rural plantations had been periodically disrupted by Indian attacks between 1835 and 1842, but the stimulus of a military garrison and supply post at Jacksonville led to the doubling of Duval County's population between 1830 and 1840. After 1842, wagon caravans of settlers and their slaves, crowded with tools and supplies, rolled through Jacksonville headed for new homes in the backcountry that became Clay County and beyond to the Alachua Prairie. The wagons soon rolled farther south and west, carrying Georgians and South Carolinians to cotton plantations in Marion and Columbia counties. A record 530 vessels carried exports from Jacksonville in 1855. Reports of streets jammed with wagons and carts loaded with cotton and other plantation produce prompted the editor of the *Jacksonville News* to boast on 18 December 1856 that Florida's "crop is greater in quantity of cotton, and aggregate value, than any State in proportion to its population."

In 1842 there were three steam-powered sawmills on the St. Johns River, supported by commerce with the military; in 1854 there were twenty, making Jacksonville, one newsman said, "the largest lumber market in the South."[5] Mills on the Nassau and St. Marys rivers and Black Creek also cut yellow pine and shipped Florida lumber to ports throughout the world. Late in the 1850s railroads tapped new timberlands, sustaining a boom of major proportions.

As the loggers cut the pine, new homesteads were cleared for settlement. Clay County, already a land of white yeoman farmers, was separated from Duval County in 1858. In 1860, Clay was 73 percent white, and 93 percent of the whites had been born in slave states. Only 19 percent of the heads of Clay households owned slaves, and more than half of all bondsmen were held at only six estates.

Whites were 57 percent of Duval County's 5,074 residents in 1860.

Slaves numbered 2,046 (40 percent), and 164 (3 percent) of the residents were free black persons. Approximately 41 percent of all Duval residents lived in Jacksonville in 1860, working at diverse occupations that reflected the expansion of the region's economy. There were slightly more whites than blacks among the 2,128 residents of the town, and 44 percent of the household heads were born in the North or in foreign countries. Outside the town, however, four of every five white household heads were from slave-holding states. The growing town of Fernandina, just north of Jacksonville, with a population of 1,360 residents in 1860, showed similar patterns.

By the 1840s and 1850s, governmental affairs in Florida were characterized by the same fierce partisan battles between Democratic and Whig politicians that raged throughout the nation. In Florida, a coalition of elites led by Richard K. Call and known as the "Nucleus" dominated government. A combination of early Monroe and Jackson appointees and wealthy migrants from Virginia who had settled in Middle Florida, they had gained control of the Florida Land Office as well as executive and judicial posts throughout the territory. Often land speculators, slaveowners, and cotton planters, they advocated government-assisted internal improvements and liberal bank charters. Their banking policies evolved into the most controversial political issue during the territorial years.

Between 1831 and 1835 the Legislative Council approved bank charters for groups in Pensacola, Tallahassee, and St. Augustine. Directors of the banks, stockholders, and loan recipients were all members of the ruling elite. With inflated evaluations of their property from bank officers who were their friends and relatives, planters traded mortgages for stock in the Union Bank of Tallahassee and then received generous loans to finance additional purchases of land and slaves. Capital came from bond sales to investors in New York City, Boston, Amsterdam, and London, sales made possible largely by the "good faith" promise of the Legislative Council to back the bonds. Call and his associates had been followers of Old Hickory in earlier years, but in Florida they evolved into a conservative ruling class opposed to the policies advocated in the 1830s by the Jacksonian Democrats.

In less troubled times the banks may have prospered, but the bitterly cold winter of 1835 that destroyed the citrus industry in East Florida, the Panic of 1837 that led to bank failures throughout the nation, and the economic dislocations during the Second Seminole War threw them into insolvency. The council fulfilled demands for interest payments on the "faith bonds" by taxing Florida residents, an act many Floridians condemned as corrupt and narrowly conceived to protect the elite.

Men outside this circle of influence, outraged by the banking policies and anxious to acquire properties and business, became resentful of the antidemocratic politics of the Florida elite. Denouncing inherited privilege and monopolies that denied opportunities to the common man, leaders like Robert R. Reid, David Levy, and James D. Westcott formed the Jacksonian Democratic Party as a vehicle to unseat the entrenched aristocracy.

The Florida "Bank War" opened on an unlikely front, as the unexpected featured issue in the drive for statehood that Richard Call and the nucleus spearheaded in the mid-thirties. Statehood was heatedly opposed in East Florida, strongly supported in the Red Hills region, and approved by a slight majority in the Pensacola area. Wealth, population growth, and economic development were certain to come to Florida with statehood, its adherents claimed. Call pointed to the millions of acres of land in the territory controlled by Congress that could be granted to Florida and used by state officials as inducements for internal improvements.

When a referendum in May 1838 produced a majority of voters in favor of statehood, Governor Call authorized elections of delegates to a Constitutional Convention to be held in December at St. Joseph, the new Gulf Coast port near Apalachicola. During the elections of delegates to the convention, candidates pledged to antibank positions denounced speculators and aristocrats who profited from the banks and excluded the laboring classes. The antibank delegates won the majority of the seats.

The leading men of the territory assembled at St. Joseph on 3 December. Future governors Robert R. Reid, Thomas Brown, and William Marvin were there, as were future senators James D. Westcott, David Levy Yulee (who had adopted his family's honorary Moorish title), and Jackson Morton. Also elected as delegates were future state supreme court justices, legislators, and county and municipal leaders. Former governor DuVal presided over opening ceremonies but lost the vote for permanent chairman to antibank leader Judge Robert R. Reid.

Delegates debated until 11 January 1839, when a constitution was approved, with only one delegate, Richard Fitzpatrick of Dade County, voting against it. Written into the document were provisions that severely restricted banking policies—a clear repudiation of the conservative elite. In a referendum conducted in May, voters of the territory approved the constitution, but the ratification campaign was again controversial and closely contested.

It was the leadership of congressional delegate David Levy Yulee that most directly led to admission of Florida to the Union. Although some voters would have preferred to see the territory divided into two states, Levy was able to build consensus for statehood as a single entity. He wrote numerous letters, gave countless speeches, and published an influential pamphlet in support of statehood, arguing that internal improvement lands would become available to support railroad projects throughout the territory and that Florida's national prominence would grow.

In Washington, Yulee worked through southern congressmen, reminding them that admitting Florida would correct the free state–slave state imbalance in the senate that was expected to occur with the admission of Iowa in 1846. His hard work was rewarded. In January 1845, the House of Representatives reported out a bill calling for admission of Iowa and Florida. Both houses of Congress approved the bill by 1 March 1845, and President John Tyler signed it into law only two days later. On 3 March 1845, Florida became the twenty-seventh state of the United States of America.

Governor John Branch set 26 May 1845 as the date for election of officers for the new State of Florida. Democrats met at a state convention in Madison on 14 April and nominated Jefferson County planter William D. Moseley for governor and Levy for congressman. The Whigs held a series of county-level meetings and chose Richard Call and Benjamin A. Putnam for those same posts. Economic crises, banking policies, and events of the Second Seminole War were the leading topics debated during the campaign. Moseley and Levy were victorious, and the Democrats won majorities in both houses of the General Assembly.

The inauguration of Governor Moseley took place on 26 May 1845 on the eastern portico of the new capitol building. Following his address, the Stars and Stripes were raised, with a twenty-seventh star added for the occasion. Also raised was the new state flag, blue, orange, red, white, and green horizontal stripes inscribed with the words "Let us alone." In subsequent weeks, newspapers attacked the design as having inflammatory overtones of secession, and it had an early retirement.

The first General Assembly met on 23 June 1845, only to adjourn immediately to mourn the death of Andrew Jackson. When reassembled,

The name David Levy Yulee (1810–86) is memorialized in today's Levy County and the city of Yulee. One of Florida's most prominent developers in the territorial and early statehood periods, he constructed the first cross-state railroad, from Cedar Keys to Fernandina, in 1861. As territorial delegate to the Congress in 1841–45, he adroitly lobbied for statehood. When it came in 1845, he was elected one of the state's first two U.S. senators—the first Jew in the country's history to hold that office. Despite his strong Unionist activities, he supported secession in 1861 and served as a member of the Confederate Congress during the Civil War.

Democrats David Levy Yulee and James D. Westcott were chosen to represent Florida in the U.S. Senate. By the time the first session adjourned on 26 July, the assembly had created the executive and judicial structure of the new state and passed tax and revenue bills to support it.

Democrats, insistent on states' rights and with increasingly radical demands for secession from the Union they had just joined, would control politics statewide until after the Civil War. While some twentieth-century Floridians have raised doubts that secession and the Civil War were in any way related to the institution of slavery, political leaders in Florida during the late antebellum years saw the defense of states' rights and of slavery as inseparable. "Southern rights" meant the implicit and unrestricted right to own slave property and to move slaves into western U.S. territories. Defense of property rights had come to mean protection of slave property from abolitionists.

From Florida's inception as a territory, slave labor was considered essential to economic development. The policy began during the British period and continued after 1784, when the Spanish also encouraged large-scale importation of Africans. Most Spanish-era planters kept their estates and slaves after 1821. In 1830, slaves comprised 47 percent and free blacks another 5 percent of the total population of three northeast Florida counties, St. Johns, Duval, and Nassau. Nearly every owner of six or more slaves had been a Spanish colonial. By 1860, the Spanish holdovers were deceased and the ratio of slaves to total population had dropped to 30 percent, but slaves were still considered vital to the economy.

In Middle Florida there were no holdover planters. Land was generally unclaimed and inexpensive, and migration boomed. Slaves were brought in immediately and increased over time in both total numbers and percentage of population. Gadsden County had 2,501 slaves among its 4,894 residents in 1830, or 41 percent. By 1860 the total population had nearly doubled, but the slave ratio increased to 58 percent. Jefferson County's slave ratios increased from 48 to 65 percent in the same period, and Leon County's were even higher in 1860, at 74 percent of its 12,243 residents. Free blacks were only rarely seen in Leon and the surrounding counties; migrant planters brought with them the slave codes and the two-caste racial system, with its anti–free black bias, that prevailed in their home states.

Slaves in the populous Middle Florida counties produced and transported cotton crops, ran sawmills, made brick, and were masons, carpenters, blacksmiths, and even overseers. The Jefferson County cotton crop of 11,000 bales ranked second in Florida in 1860, its value estimated at $1.3 million. As historian Larry Rivers has shown, slaves were the most valuable property in Florida, and slaveowning was the preferred route to status and power. In Middle Florida, judges, legislators, attorneys, preachers, merchants, and medical doctors all owned slaves.

In East Florida the Spanish three-caste system of race relations (white owners, free blacks, and black slaves) was operative when the United States took possession in 1821. The new government moved quickly to implement a two-caste system. Blaming free blacks for creating discontent among slaves, the Legislative Council passed restrictive laws aimed at eliminating their status. A near ban on future manumissions, discriminatory laws against free blacks, and harsh punishments for those found guilty of minor infractions prompted an exodus of over 150 blacks from Pensacola to Mexico in the 1850s. Free blacks from St. Augustine and Pensacola emigrated to Cuba and the free black Republic of Haiti. In 1837, Zephaniah Kingsley moved his free black family from Duval County to a colony he established in Haiti, along with fifty slaves he liberated and hired as wage laborers.

On 12 July 1851, the editor of St. Augustine's *Ancient City* castigated free blacks as "useless" troublemakers and "hopeless, degraded, wretched, and forbidden outcasts." This instance would not be the last deliberate misreading of the historical record. St. Augustine had long been home to educated free blacks who owned property, held responsible jobs, and led productive lives. With a single exception during the Second Seminole War, free blacks had not acted to overthrow slavery. In fact, many had been slaveowners. The newspaper editor was reacting to the racial hysteria and heightened attachment to white supremacy that escalated during the 1850s. His castigations were symbolic of underlying tensions throughout Florida.

Cotton prices were at record highs in the 1850s. Slave prices doubled, leading some politicians to suggest reopening the African slave trade. Lumbermills boomed from Pensacola to Jacksonville, and subsidiary industries were being established. At the end of the decade, the Florida Railroad, under the direction of David Levy Yulee, spurred on by generous grants of land by the federal and state governments, was under construction between Fernandina and Cedar Keys. South Florida cattlemen were furious that the western terminus would not be at nearby Tampa Bay, but Yulee proceeded to link the two towns where he had quietly acquired title to a majority of the property. The Florida, Atlantic and Gulf Central Railroad was being built between Jacksonville and Lake City, and from there the Pensacola and Georgia Railroad was to extend to Tallahassee. It was an era of unparalleled expansion, with population growing from 87,000 to 140,000 during the decade. Florida's towns were growing as well, drawing white workmen from northern and southern states. And yet there were serious shortages of laborers that prompted employers to place continuing newspaper advertisements for black or white wage laborers. By mid-decade, Irish immigrants could be found in local work crews.

Newspapers throughout the state carried notices of slave runaways and, in several instances, chilling accounts of slaves arrested for murdering their owners. Fear of slave rebellions became common after the shock that spread through the South following the Nat Turner rebellion in Virginia in 1831 and was intensified in Florida by the black warriors who fought alongside the Seminole Indians from 1835 to 1842. News of runaway attempts in 1852 led angry citizens of Jacksonville to meet and denounce "abolitionists and their tools" who were allegedly "attempting to entice our slave population to abscond."[6] New laws were called for to restrict the town's slaves and free blacks further. White working men supported hefty license fees for free black laborers, as well as prohibitions on slaves arranging their own employment and living apart from their owners. Despite a rapid influx of northern and foreign-born workers, the flourishing urban labor force was still mostly black, prompting fears of insurrections unless blacks could be properly restrained.

National political passions of the 1850s added to racial tensions in Florida. At town meetings in 1850, speakers angry about debates in Congress over the admission of California to the Union and the resultant Compromise of 1850 denounced northern-born residents of Florida as abolitionists and called on fellow citizens to defend southern rights and secede from the Union rather than compromise away the rights of slaveholders to carry human property into the western territories. Firebrand speakers warned that further compromises would encourage northern abolitionists to place chains of slavery around the necks of white Floridians. Democrats in Florida overwhelmingly opposed the Compromise of 1850, calling it abolitionist inspired.

In the presidential elections of 1860, southern Democrats refused to support candidate Stephen Douglas, backing John C. Breckenridge of Kentucky instead. The Republican party chose Abraham Lincoln, and the remnants of the southern Whigs hoped for a miracle behind John Bell of Tennessee, the candidate for the Constitutional Union party.

Lincoln was not on the ballot in the 7 November elections in Florida. Douglas received only 367 votes. In a surprise showing, John Bell polled 5,437 votes, running strong in east coast cities. Representing the southern Democrats, Breckenridge tallied 8,543 votes to lead the field. He had been supported by eighteen of the states's twenty-four newspapers. In the race for governor, Democrat John Milton tallied 6,994 votes to Constitutional Union candidate Edward Hopkins's surprising 5,248. Although Democrats swept the statewide races and controlled both legislative and congressional delegations, it was clear from the election returns that many Floridians were still anxious to find a compromise and remain in the Union.

Lincoln's victory, however, triggered mob rallies, newspaper denunciations, and calls for immediate secession. The *Tallahassee Floridian and Journal* said on 10 November: "Lincoln is elected. There is a beginning of the end. Sectionalism has triumphed. What is to be done? We say resist." Regulators and other vigilantes increased their activities, and the ranks of militia companies swelled. Newspapers throughout the state called for resolutions to the General Assembly to hold a convention to consider secession as frequently as they denounced Lincoln and the Black Republicans as abolitionists intent on forcing racial equality for slaves.

On 26 November, Governor Perry told the General Assembly to consider secession. The alternative he foresaw was slave insurrection. He called for a reorganization of the militia and set 22 December as the date for elections of delegates to a 3 January 1861 convention.

While candidates campaigned, a South Carolina convention voted on 20 December to sever ties with the Union. Fire-eaters in Florida became increasingly vocal. Still, in some counties, Duval and Clay in particular, delegates were elected on public platforms embracing moderation and Union. Others were intent on delaying secession and planned to require that the final document be submitted to the voters for approval. Calvin Robinson, a Jacksonville merchant and a strong Unionist born in the North, recorded in his diary that many of the delegates elected had been supporters of the Union but that they had been overwhelmed by the prosecession pressures.

The convention opened in an atmosphere of secessionist euphoria. Fire-eater John C. McGehee of Madison County was elected president.

With leading secessionists from South Carolina and Alabama in the galleries, the delegates had finished their committee work and prepared an ordinance of secession by 9 January. Efforts by old Whigs Jackson Morton and George T. Ward to delay and submit the ordinance to the voters in a referendum were defeated. Secession fever had spread too rapidly, and turning back was no longer possible.

The final vote taken on 10 January 1861 was sixty-two to seven in favor of secession. By 4 February, Florida representatives would be in Montgomery to participate in the formation of the Confederate States of America. It was time to change the flags again, write another constitution, and hold new elections, all under the shadow of looming war.

The parades and gun salutes, speeches and toasts, and pure jubilation that greeted the news of secession was evident in every hamlet in Florida. Crowds filled the hotels in Pensacola, Tallahassee, and Jacksonville and danced in the streets amidst torchlight parades and fireworks. Bonfires and the sounds of church bells and cannon-firings were common. Militia units paraded jubilantly. Unionists became cautious and soft-spoken.

John Darling of Tampa would later claim that his advocacy of secession had not been motivated by thoughts of war but rather by the "conviction that it was a rightful and proper remedy to break down the policy of Negro emancipation believed to be intended by the Republican Administration then about to come into office." Confederate Congressman John P. Sanderson, a Vermont-born attorney and planter in Duval County, said that he had not voted for secession with the expectation that war would follow. Rather, Sanderson said, he had acted on behalf of those "states interested in the institution of slavery" expecting to "secure permanent guarantees for the interests and institutions of the South."[7]

Whig Unionist Richard Call had no such illusions as the galleries erupted in applause when the secession vote was counted on 10 January. His immediate reaction was to condemn the delegates and shout, "You have opened the gates of Hell, from which shall flow the curses of the damned which shall sink you to perdition."[8] Strong words, but, by late 1863 many Florida secessionists would come to agree with him.

Notes

1. Remini, *The Life of Andrew Jackson*, p. 134.
2. Dovell, *Florida: Historic, Dramatic, Contemporary*, p. 241.

3. Mathews, *Edge of Wilderness: A Settlement History of Manatee River and Sarasota Bay, 1528–1885,* p. 137.
4. James M. Denham, "The Florida Cracker Before the Civil War as Seen Through Travelers' Accounts," *Florida Historical Quarterly* 72, no. 4 (April 1994):453–62.
5. *The Florida Republican,* 11 October 1851.
6. *Jacksonville News,* 15, 22, 29 May, 5 June 1852.
7. Both quoted in Brown, "Ossian Bingley Hart."
8. Quoted in Doherty, *Richard Keith Call: Southern Unionist,* p. 158.

Bibliography

Brown, Canter, Jr. *Florida's Peace River Frontier.* Gainesville: University Presses of Florida, 1991.

———. "Ossian Bingley Hart, Florida's Loyalist Reconstruction Governor." Ph.D. dissertation, Florida State University, 1994.

Covington, James W. *The Seminoles of Florida.* Gainesville: University Press of Florida, 1993.

Dodd, Dorothy. *Florida Becomes a State.* Tallahassee: Florida Centennial Commission, 1945.

Doherty, Herbert J., Jr. *Richard Keith Call, Southern Unionist.* Gainesville: University of Florida Press, 1961.

———. *The Whigs of Florida, 1845–1854.* Gainesville: University of Florida Press, 1959.

Dovell, Junius E. *Florida: Historic, Dramatic, Contemporary.* Vol. 1. New York: Lewis Historical Publishing Co., 1952.

Ellsworth, Linda, and Lucius Ellsworth. *Pensacola: The Deep Water City.* Tulsa: Continental Heritage Press, 1982.

Mahon, John K. *History of the Second Seminole War, 1835–1842.* Gainesville: University of Florida Press, 1967.

Mathews, Janet Snyder. *Edge of Wilderness: A Settlement History of Manatee River and Sarasota Bay, 1528–1885.* Tulsa, Okla.: Caprine Press, 1983.

Paisley, Clifton. *The Red Hills of Florida, 1528–1865.* Tuscaloosa: University of Alabama Press, 1989.

Reiger, John F. "Secession of Florida from the Union––A Minority Decision?" *Florida Historical Quarterly* 46, no. 4 (April 1968):358–68.

Remini, Robert V. *The Life of Andrew Jackson.* New York: Harper and Row, 1988.

Rivers, Larry. "Dignity and Importance: Slavery in Jefferson County, Florida, 1827–1860." *Florida Historical Quarterly* 61, no. 4 (April 1983):404–30.

———. "Slavery in Microcosm: Leon County, Florida, 1824–1860." *Journal of Negro History* 66, no. 46, (Fall 1981):244–45.

Schafer, Daniel L. "'A class of people neither free men nor slaves': From Spanish to American Race Relations in Florida, 1821–1861." *Journal of Social History* 26, no. 3 (Spring 1993):587–609.

Smith, Julia Floyd. *Slavery and Plantation Growth in Antebellum Florida*. Gaines-ville: University of Florida Press, 1973.

Thompson, Arthur W. "David Yulee: A Study of Nineteenth Century American Thought and Enterprise." Ph.D. dissertation, Columbia University, 1954.

———. *Jacksonian Democracy on the Florida Frontier*. Gainesville: University of Florida Press, 1961.

13 The Civil War, 1861–1865

Canter Brown, Jr.

"The smallest tadpole in the dirty pool of secession!" For many Americans these words summarized Florida's role in the Civil War, and in some respects the assertion hit close to the mark.[1] The state contained 54,000 square miles of land and its coastline stretched for nearly 1,200 miles, but its population was only 140,000, making it by far the least populous of the Confederate states. Of that number, almost 63,000 individuals were either free blacks or, far more likely, slaves. In the population category most vital to military needs—white males between the ages of eighteen and forty-five—a mere 16,000 lived within Florida's borders.

Compounding the state's problems, many of the free inhabitants were poor and lived in frontier conditions far removed from those associated with the Old South plantation belt. For these men and women subsistence farming and cowhunting provided their livelihood. Further reflecting the state's underdeveloped condition, it had few cities and few sizable towns. The ten largest communities served as home for only 13 percent of the population. Pensacola and Key West vied for honors as the largest city, but each had fewer than 2,900 residents. Jacksonville, Tallahassee, St. Augustine, Apalachicola, Milton, Monticello, and Fernandina followed in size. Tiny Lake City, with about 650 inhabitants, came tenth.

Judging a town's importance solely by its population could be misleading, however. Rural residents and the agricultural economy increasingly had come to depend upon them. Fernandina and Cedar

Keys, for instance, contained good harbors and served as termini for the state's only transpeninsular rail link, the Florida Railroad. Jacksonville, on the navigable St. Johns River, was developing as a hub for the lumber industry and a shipping point for cotton. Apalachicola even more than Jacksonville serviced the cotton trade, particularly in the Chattahoochee, Flint, and Apalachicola river system. Pensacola and Key West were military and shipping centers with extensive fortifications and naval supply and repair facilities, and the village of Tampa and the frontier outpost at Fort Meade were focal points for the emerging cattle industry.

Frontier traditions, a small population, and a paucity of urban centers masked Florida's regional diversity, a circumstance that was to have important implications during the war. East of the Suwannee River lay East Florida, characterized by more tolerant patterns of race relations and the northern origins of some of its noteworthy citizens. Opponents of secession lived in every part of the state, but they were most numerous in the east. West Florida stretched from the Perdido River to the Apalachicola. Exclusive of Jackson County, the territory was remote from much of the rest of the state. Over half of its inhabitants resided in Santa Rosa and Escambia counties, where Pensacola's less rigid racial patterns were influential. The area held fewer than 15 percent of Florida's population and 8 percent of its slaves.

Juxtaposed with the frontier conditions and subsistence economies of East and West Florida was the Middle Florida plantation belt of Jackson, Gadsden, Leon, Jefferson, and Madison counties, which had expanded by 1861 to include Columbia, Alachua, and Marion. Possessing only a little more than one-third of the state's white residents, the belt contained two-thirds of Florida's slaves and 65 percent of its wealth. It also had most of the state's 5,152 slaveowners. It was in Middle Florida, despite the Unionist sentiments of many of its prominent men, that one found the principal support for secession.

Florida's regional diversity had been matched prior to 10 January 1861 by a bitter division between Unionists and secessionists. Once the step of secession was taken, though, most white inhabitants accepted the situation, at least temporarily, while prosecession advocates celebrated what they believed would be easily won independence. "That night prominent men predicted that the war would not last sixty days," recalled a Madison resident, "and some men offered to drink all the blood that was spilt." She continued, "The young men were eager to enlist and go forward at once, for fear the fighting would be over before they arrived."[2]

Expectations of a short war were common during the weeks and months following secession as volunteer infantry, artillery, and cavalry companies formed throughout the state. Already, the Federal arsenal at Chattahoochee, Fort Clinch at Fernandina, and Fort Marion (as the Castillo de San Marcos was now known) at St. Augustine had been occupied without the firing of a shot. Far more formidable were the key fortifications at the state's two largest towns, and there the optimism of secession's initial hours first was blunted. Thanks to Captain James M. Brannan's determination, Federal forces remained in control at Key West. Similarly, and with a complement of fewer than 100 men, Lieutenant Adam J. Slemmer complied with orders to prevent seizure of Pensacola's forts and facilities.

The Civil War almost began, in fact, at Pensacola rather than at Fort Sumter, South Carolina. Forces from Alabama and Florida had been gathering near the town since the secession vote, but a promise by Federal authorities not to reinforce the Union presence had resulted in an informal truce. Nonetheless, the Confederate forces slowly were augmented, and by early February 1861 over 1,000 men were manning positions opposite Fort Pickens on Santa Rosa Island. One month later the new Confederate government designated General Braxton Bragg to command them, and by 1 April the general possessed a force of 5,000, with 2,000 more on the way.

President Abraham Lincoln, who was inaugurated on 4 March, at first considered abandoning Fort Sumter while holding on to Fort Pickens. Eight days after his inauguration, orders were dispatched to Captain Israel Vogdes to land reinforcements from Union warships. Because of the reluctance of a naval officer to comply with the captain's request for boats, the effort was delayed until the night of 11 April. In the meantime Lincoln had decided to resupply Fort Sumter, as a result of which Confederate artillery opened fire on the Union position in Charleston harbor the next morning. Two days later, violence erupted at Pensacola as Union naval vessels easily repulsed a Confederate force.

After this first incident an uneasy peace emerged as both forces faced supply and health problems. In May the Confederates sank several vessels to block the channel between the Gulf of Mexico and Pensacola Bay. Union men countered in September by destroying the town's huge dry dock and other naval repair facilities as well as an armed Confederate blockade runner, the *Judah*. The following month the Confederates attacked a New York infantry regiment camp on Santa Rosa Island. Substantial quantities of supplies and equipment were destroyed, although Confederate casualties—eighteen killed, thirty-nine wounded, and thirty taken prisoner—outweighed Union losses. An artillery duel in late November saw 5,000 shells expended with little effect, and on New Year's Day 1862 the same scene was replayed on a smaller scale. Faced with a stalemate and pressed for troops elsewhere, Bragg announced on 27 February his intention to abandon the siege. The desolate and virtually deserted town was taken by Union forces on 12 May.

As Confederate forces faced frustration at Pensacola, the Union counterattacked elsewhere in the state. In early January 1862, Cedar Keys briefly was occupied and the town's wharf and railroad facilities destroyed. Apalachicola likewise became a target in early April. Fernandina, St. Augustine, and Jacksonville also were seized. The first two remained in Union hands for the remainder of the war, but Jacksonville was evacuated on 9 April, forcing many area Unionists to depart on Federal warships. Union vessels also commenced raiding at isolated locations on the coast and conducted occasional patrols up the St. Johns River as far as Enterprise, destroying property of secessionists and compelling slaveowners to withdraw with their bondsmen into the interior.

Confederate setbacks in Florida were mirrored by reverses in other theaters of operation, particularly the loss of strategic portions of the Tennessee River valley and of the South's largest city, New Orleans. The Confederacy's growing need for fighting men soon prompted withdrawal of all but about 2,500 soldiers from Florida. "The effect of the order," declared an alarmed Governor John Milton, "is to abandon Middle, East and South Florida to the mercy of the Lincoln Government."[3] The manpower shortage also prompted the Congress at Richmond to enact in April 1862 a conscription law that subjected most white males between the ages of eighteen and thirty-five to involuntary service. By late September the age limit had been increased to forty-five.

Passage of the conscription law loosed upon Floridians patrols of conscription agents intent upon filling the state's manpower quotas. Increasing opposition to Confederate service away from home and revived Unionist sentiment provoked numerous individuals to "lay out" in swamps, forests, and other remote locations. In turn the conscription patrols intensified their efforts. "Union men they threaten to hang, and do shoot" reported a Federal officer, "as we have lamentable proof."[4] Added another account, "Every man between the ages of 18 and 45 . . . is being remorselessly pressed into the rebel army, and if any objections are made they are handcuffed and tied, and then marched off, no matter what the condition of their families."[5] The problem was particularly severe in East Florida's cattle-ranging areas, a situation relieved

Laurie M. Anderson, of Tallahassee, served in the Bradford Light Infantry, Company A, Florida Battalion. He fell in the Battle of Shiloh, 7 April 1862. Of approximately 16,000 Floridians who went off to war, at least 5,000 died. Colonel William Scott Dilworth, commander of the Third Florida Regiment, wrote at war's end, "One by one they fell by the wayside. Some lie buried by Georgia streams, some on the hillsides of Alabama, some in the valley of Tennessee, some on the bloody fields of Kentucky, some under the blue skies of Mississippi; some survived and struggled on until they reached the Carolinas; while a few came back to the old homestead and died in the arms of their loved ones."

only in October 1862 when one draft exemption for every 500 head of cattle was authorized.

The conscription efforts alienated from the Confederate cause many Floridians who lived outside the plantation belt, but they proved successful in other ways. Coupled with continued support for independence in Middle Florida and elsewhere, they permitted the state to furnish the Confederate military with almost 16,000 soldiers and sailors. Given the available manpower pool, the figure is phenomenal.

The departure of so many adult males for out-of-state military service had serious ramifications. One such result was the burden imposed on the women who were left responsible for their families, for protecting their property, and, in some cases, for overseeing the work of potentially rebellious slaves. "When [my husband John] enlisted in the army," remembered Amanda Comerford, "he left me on a farm with a year's provisions for myself and four small children, the eldest being but eleven years of age, and these responsibilities were afterwards added to by the birth of twins." She continued, "It is difficult to describe my struggles to provide food and clothing for this large family. . . . But somehow I managed to struggle through as did many other women during those trying times."[6]

Amanda Comerford was fortunate that she began her wartime experience with a supply of provisions. Many women, especially conscripts' wives, were not so lucky. Even for those who had money or items to barter, necessary commodities often were unavailable. Most country stores had closed after selling out their inventories in the war's early months, and in towns those that remained open were dependent upon the few daring mariners able to run an increasingly tight Union naval blockade. A Lake City resident recorded the reaction to news that a blockade runner had brought supplies to a nearby town. "You can imagine the excitement this report created among the ladies," she wrote. "A great crowd of us hurried to Providence, some in buggies, some in wagons and others horseback, hoping we might be able to purchase at least a calico dress, but after all the anticipations and our long ride we were doomed to disappointment, and had to be content with our homespun dresses."[7]

With commodities scarce, women learned to make do. The coontee plant offered starch, and the sweet potato and "hayti" potato filled many stomachs. Thread was colored from natural dyes, cotton was spun, and homespun clothing sewn. Hats evolved from plaited palmetto fronds, myrtle berries perfumed candles made of tallow and beeswax, and orangeade and blackberry wine slaked thirst. Perhaps the rarest commodity was salt. Works were established at many points on the coast, but inefficiency, distance, profiteering, and Union raiders kept prices high. In the circumstances many a mother "boiled her smokehouse," utilizing "the dirt rich with twenty years' dripping of smoked bacon, to get the salt."[8]

The creativity and innovation necessary for supplying such commodities was only the beginning of wartime responsibilities. Hard, physical labor also was demanded. "Every where women did man's work, as well as women's," a survivor noted. "They curried leather, did blacksmithing, plowing, cobbling. They made fence, drove ox-carts, went to mill, repaired the furniture, drenched sick horses, butchered hogs, set traps for the thieving larks and crows, pulled the corn and hauled it to the barn." She concluded, "It would be much easier task to tell what they did not do."[9] A Gainesville resident later expressed the resentment felt by many women at the failure of men to recognize their sacrifices and accomplishments. "No historian has ever dipped his pen in ink," she wrote, "to tell of the grand and glorious deeds of this or that *woman*—eulogizing and giving in detail how she watched over her sick child, alone all through the midnight hours, with no husband within hearing of her voice to speak to for advice or comfort, while her heart was breaking with anxiety for the safety of *that* husband; or how she spent her days at hard labor to provide for her fatherless children and then half of the night spinning and weaving cloth wherewith to clothe them, and even making shoes for their tiny feet." She added, "It is beyond the power of the Historian or his pen to picture her patriotic devotion, her self sacrifice, her mental sufferings and anguish."[10]

Despite the sacrifices and struggles many Floridians slowly sank into the mire of privation and poverty. By 1864 the governor estimated that over 13,000 white residents within the area under Confederate control required relief. The dilemma was particularly critical for thousands of refugees on both sides of the political divide. One officer described the lot of Unionist families encamped at Cedar Keys. "The houses of these families have been pillaged and burned, their fields laid waste, and their stock driven off to feed the armies of our foe," he commented. "They are houseless, homeless, wandering refugees in their own State."[11] At Fernandina a teacher observed of others similarly situated, "They, as a general thing, are *miserably poor,* many have been unable, for the past year or two, to purchase a single article of clothing, it requiring their united earnings to procure food for their families."[12]

The refugees coming within Union lines also included runaway and captured slaves, and their circumstances were, if anything, more

Mary Martha (Smith) Reid (1812–94), widow of Territorial Governor Robert Raymond Reid (1839–41), established the Florida Hospital at Richmond, Virginia, in 1862 for sick and wounded Florida soldiers. Upon her death at Fernandina in 1894, the magazine *Confederate Veteran* eulogized her at length: "By her exhaustless mental resources and tireless energy, success crowned her efforts, and thousands of hearts were solaced, and suffering bodies comforted through her personal ministrations." Her only son, Lieutenant Raymond Jenks Reid (another had died in childhood), adjutant of the Second Florida Infantry Regiment, was killed in the Battle of the Wilderness.

desperate than those of whites. "[They] are the most pitiable-looking objects I ever beheld," explained one Northerner, "having been driven about in the Rebel woods, many of them for weeks, half naked and half starved."[13] Future African Methodist Episcopal Bishop Abram Grant's experience, though extreme, offers an example. His torturous road to freedom began at Lake City, required hundreds of miles of travel, and encompassed his temporary seizure by deserters, swimming rivers, theft of a small blockade runner, recapture by his owner, sale at Columbus, Georgia, and a second escape attempt. He finally entered Union lines near Montgomery, Alabama.

Although Union troops seized as many "contrabands" as they could and others fled into Federal lines when an opportunity presented itself, most of Florida's slaves spent the war confined to plantations and farms. Confederate military policy was designed to protect the Middle Florida plantation belt and adjacent areas, and there the majority of slaves remained. Owners, fearful of departure by stealth or outright rebellion, attempted to deprive the bondsmen of any news. Starvation was not a problem, but the privation and hard work experienced by their owners were magnified in slaves' lives. Squire Jackson recalled, for instance, that, while a white mistress wore homespun, slave women might possess only "grass skirts woven very closely with hoops around on the inside to keep from contacting the body."[14] Some slaves were commandeered to support the war effort directly. Acie Thomas hauled food and ammunition between Tallahassee and Virginia; many others were expected to perform all manner of services for the Confederacy.

A substantial portion of Florida's white population continued to support the Confederacy throughout the war, but resentments of conscription, news of deaths at the front, and deteriorating economic conditions took a toll on morale. The impact of the War Tax Act of 19 August 1861, the Impressment Act of 26 March 1863, and the General Tax Act (Confederate tithe) of 24 April 1863 further exacerbated the situation. The Impressment Act permitted the government to take goods and commodities at prices set by impressment boards and to pay for them in depreciated paper money. Floridians reserved their particular ire, though, for the Confederate tithe which imposed a tax in kind of 10 percent on all agricultural goods. "The citizens . . . in many parts of the State are indignant at the unnecessary abuse of their rights," Governor Milton informed Confederate authorities, "and the lawless and wicked conduct of Government agents in this State has produced serious dissatisfaction." Milton believed that the tax was the last straw for many residents. "The effect of the impressment made in West Florida," he explained, "was the desertion of a large number of the troops in that part of the State, a portion of whom have joined the enemy."[15]

As suggested, desertion had become frequent by 1864. Already in August 1862, Milton had asserted, "There is not within my knowledge a portion of the State free of skulking traitors."[16] Some soldiers naturally resented the circumstances under which their families were required to exist, and their own lives increasingly were subject to appalling conditions. Eventually, at least 2,000 and probably more men left the Confederate lines. Back in Florida they often joined with draft evaders, runaway slaves, and others in bands that preyed upon those more sympathetic to the war. The Apalachicola River area and Taylor, Lafayette, and Levy counties especially attracted them. William W. Strickland's "Independent Union Rangers" of Taylor County may have been the most famous of the bands. In an unsuccessful attempt to counter the depredations of Strickland's men, Confederate authorities ordered the burning of every house along the Econfina and Fenholloway rivers.

Some deserters chose to join Union army regiments raised within the state, and they were not alone. At Pensacola the First Florida Cavalry, headed by Eugen von Kielmensegge, had been authorized in September 1863, and subsequently a small artillery battery, the Florida Artillery, also was established. In September 1864 the First Florida and other Union forces penetrated inland as far as Governor Milton's hometown of Marianna, which they plundered. The Second Florida Cavalry was raised in the south Florida cattle country and operated out of Fort Myers and Cedar Keys under the leadership of Henry A. Crane, James Dopson Green, and Edmund P. Weeks. The February 1864 repeal of many draft exemptions, especially those for the cattle industry, spurred enlistments in these units, and eventually about 1,300 men served in them.

The state government under Governor John Milton, who succeeded Madison Starke Perry in October 1861, labored to meet the challenges it faced and to cooperate with Confederate leaders. Chronically short of funds and faced with opposition from what Milton called "a very large minority [who] were opposed to secession," its attempts at efficiency and exertion of control rarely were successful.[17] Milton particularly failed to convince cotton planters to grow food crops to feed hungry citizens and soldiers. Problems arose even within the legislature, where in 1862 several senators suspected of lack of enthusiasm had to be purged by legal sleight-of-hand.

Milton's greatest opportunity for service to the Confederacy, the supply of beef to Southern armies, also went unmet. When the strong-hold at Vicksburg, Mississippi, fell to General Ulysses S. Grant on 4 July 1863, western cattle no longer could be supplied to forces fighting in the East. Confederate supply officers demanded that Florida herds be dis-patched immediately to satisfy urgent needs. Milton quickly organized a commissary service under Quincy lawyer Pleasant A. White. He, in turn, named Tampa sea captain James McKay, Sr., to supervise collec-tions on the south Florida ranges where most herds were concentrated.

Unfortunately for Milton and White many south Florida cattlemen felt little loyalty to the Confederacy, concerned rather to safeguard the bulk of the herds until peace permitted their sale in Cuba. Complicating the situation, McKay apparently enjoyed a confidential relationship with Union authorities. As a result, the supply efforts were organized slowly. Within a few months of the first cattle drive northward from Fort Meade, elements of the Union Second Florida Cavalry operating out of Fort Myers began to disrupt the trade, whereupon the drives were suspended.

As cattle operations were abandoned early in 1864, the few Confed-erate soldiers in south Florida were withdrawn to meet a new danger to the north. On 7 February, Jacksonville had been occupied for a fourth time by Union troops. The following day the blue-clad soldiers marched westward in an apparent attempt to help cut the flow of cattle to the Con-federate army, seize supplies, and encourage slave enlistments in the army. Likely, the foray also was designed to bolster an eventually unsuc-cessful attempt to establish a Unionist state government to support Pres-ident Lincoln's reelection bid. Within three days General Truman Sey-mour had extended his lines thirty-three miles to Sanderson.

Alarmed at Seymour's threat to the Middle Florida plantation belt and to the state's cattle supply lines, Confederate leaders hurriedly con-centrated forces in the path of the Union advance. General Joseph Finegan eventually commanded about 5,000 men from a headquarters at Olustee, ten miles east of Lake City. There, from noon until after six o'clock on 20 February, just to the south of Ocean Pond, Finegan's men clashed with 5,500 Union troops, one-third of whom were black vol-unteers. In that largest battle to take place in Florida during the war, the result was a clear-cut Confederate victory. Seymour's force was com-pelled to retreat to Jacksonville, which the Union held for the re-mainder of the war.

The Confederate triumph at Olustee, while serving as a balm for morale, did little to secure the state. Its major towns remained in Union hands, substantial portions of its territory either were occupied or could

BATTLE OF OLUSTEE, FLA.

Though there were numerous skirmishes, only one major Civil War battle took place on Florida soil. Fought on 20 February 1864 at Olustee, ten miles east of Lake City, the battle was occasioned by a Federal push west out of occupied Jacksonville into the interior, in order, if possible, to cut off Florida beef and salt exports to the rest of the Confederacy, to round up black recruits for the Union army, and to take Florida out of the war. The Federal force of 5,500, commanded by Brigadier General Truman Seymour, was met at Olustee by a near-equal Rebel force commanded by Brigadier General Joseph Finegan. Drawn into a hunter's funnel between a lake and a cypress swamp, Seymour's dense blue columns were mauled by Confederate fire. The Battle of Olustee lasted from noon to shortly after six o'clock, when the Federals were forced to retreat, leaving much of their weapons and ammunition behind. Losses in Seymour's force numbered 203 killed, 1,152 wounded; in Finegan's, 93 killed, 847 wounded. This rendering of the battle by artist Louis Kerz shows in the foreground the 8th U.S. Colored Infantry Regiment, one of three black regiments that fought on the Union side.

be occupied virtually at will, its coastline was blockaded, many of its residents were in want, the value of its currency had plummeted, and most of the few troops within its borders were bled away to fight elsewhere. About the only truly effective presence remaining in East Florida was the small light cavalry force commanded by John J. Dickison, "the Swamp Fox of Florida." Utilizing guerrilla tactics, Dickison's men guarded interior Middle and East Florida while harrying Union positions and Unionists along and to the east of the St. Johns River. When called for service at Olustee, they had been on their way to Fort Meade to confront the Union Second Florida Cavalry. Later, in August 1864 at Gainesville, the cavalrymen particularly distinguished themselves by dispersing a large Union raiding party intent on pillaging the community.

The withdrawal of so many Confederate troops left the south Florida cattle ranges defenseless. Compounding the situation, the conscription exemption for the cattle industry had been repealed three days before the Battle of Olustee, forcing most adult men not yet in service to choose to join either the Union or the Confederate army. In the circumstances, commissary officer McKay urged creation of armed commissary units for south Florida. When approved, the companies were known collectively as the Cow Cavalry. The largest of them was headquartered near Fort Meade and was headed by cattleman Francis Asbury Hendry.

Florida beef still was needed desperately by Confederate armies and that fact, coupled with bureaucratic delays in approving Cow Cavalry units, encouraged Union aggression. The Second Florida Cavalry and companies of the Second and Ninety-ninth United States Colored Infantry temporarily occupied Tampa, destroyed Fort Meade, marched on Brooksville, raided out of Cedar Keys, and otherwise extended their influence in the peninsula. By fall 1864, however, that influence had been contained: yellow fever, conflicts between the Florida men and their northern and black counterparts, and assertive actions by Cow Cavalry units had confined the Union efforts to the vicinities of Fort Myers and Cedar Keys. In February 1865 emboldened Cow Cavalry units attacked the Union men at Fort Myers but were forced to retreat after losing the element of surprise.

The presence of Confederate men before the walls of Fort Myers provoked the final major military initiative in Florida during the war. Union General John Newton believed that enemy troops had been moved away from the Tallahassee area into south Florida for the Fort Myers assault. Sensing a strategic opening, he ordered 1,000 men to St. Marks, near which they landed on 4 March. Local militia, a cadet company from the West Florida Seminary (a predecessor of Florida State University), and some regulars met them at Natural Bridge two days later. With only three killed and twenty-two wounded, the Confederates emerged victorious. Florida's capital remained uncaptured to war's end.

The Union defeat at Natural Bridge briefly lifted the spirits of die-hard Confederates, but by early March 1865 most Floridians had accepted the fact that the South ultimately would lose the war. A few months earlier, Confederate soldier Albert Chalker had voiced the feelings of many in a letter to his sweetheart Mattie Barden. "I long to see the dawning of peace," he wrote. "I hope there ere next April we will have what is wished a thousand times every moment. That is Peace !! when we can all return to our home and once more live in peace and contentment."[18]

Many state residents despaired in the opening months of 1865 that the end was not yet at hand. "Sometimes I am led to think God has fore-saken us," Tampa's Catharine Hart lamented in January, "and intends to let us destroy each other."[19] Countless residents appealed ever more intensely to religion for comfort and protection in a world gone mad. "I expect to go to church Sunday," Mattie Barden matter-of-factly in-formed Albert Chalker on January 31, "and may get converted."[20]

Some secessionists despaired over the loss of the war rather than the delay of the peace. Governor Milton, for one, was unable to bear the de-feat. In late March he journeyed to his Marianna home, and there on 1 April he killed himself with a shotgun. The suicide offered some Con-federates a focus for their frustrations and bitterness. "I thought him one of the best speakers I ever listened to, and a very smart man," one soldier recorded, "but when the Confederacy was overthrown a short time after this and he ended his existence . . . I changed my opinion of him."[21] Milton was succeeded by state senate president Abraham K. Al-lison of Gadsden County who, ironically, had fought four years earlier to delay secession.

Robert E. Lee surrendered his Confederate army to Ulysses S. Grant at Appomattox Courthouse, Virginia, on 9 April 1865, but word did not reach Florida for one week. At Union-held Jacksonville its reception re-sulted in a gala celebration, declaration of a holiday, and the booming of a 250-gun salute. Other occupied towns followed suit, although the spirit was dampened not long thereafter with news of President Lin-coln's assassination. With flags lowered to half mast, blockade vessels fired their guns every half hour in tribute. Already, though, word of the war's-end celebratory cannon fire at Jacksonville had passed into the interior and offered most individuals within Confederate lines the first hint of the peace. Some refused to believe it, but in the weeks that fol-lowed the truth became plain. A few soldiers murmured of fighting on as guerrillas, but nothing resulted from their plans.

Florida's official surrender came with General Joseph E. Johnston's

From 1861 until the last days of the war, Jackson County planter John Milton was governor of the Confederate State of Florida. Believing that "death would be preferable to reunion," he took his life on 1 April 1865, one month before Union troops occupied Tallahassee without opposition.

capitulation of the Army of Tennessee to William Tecumseh Sherman on 26 April. Sam Jones, commander of the District of Florida, followed his superior's lead several days later. Tallahassee was occupied on 10 May. A few days afterward black soldiers of the Third United States Colored Infantry paraded their colors in its streets to the accompaniment of "John Brown's Body," signifying for Middle Florida planters the revolution that had been brought to fruition. Thereafter, Federal troops slowly fanned out through the state to alert slaves to their freedom and to parole the vanquished.

Floridians held varied opinions about the war and its outcome.

Future governor Francis P. Fleming was distraught. "I don't believe that I can live under Yankee rule," he informed his aunt.[22] Another young soldier, along with his comrades, was gleeful. "The majority of this Com[man]d," he related, "and nearly all in our Comp[an]y seem rejoiced and do not hesitate to express themselves to that effect."[23] Most, though, probably agreed with Cow Cavalry Captain Francis A. Hendry. When informed of the result he sighed, "Thank God it is over with one way or the other."[24]

Notes

1. Joe M. Richardson, *The Negro in the Reconstruction of Florida, 1865–1877* (Tallahassee: Florida State University Press, 1965; reprint ed., Tampa, 1973), p. 1.
2. Caroline Mays Brevard, *A History of Florida from the Treaty of 1763 to Our Own Times*, 2 vols. (DeLand: Florida State Historical Society, 1925), 2:51.
3. U.S. War Department, *War of the Rebellion: A Compilation of the Official Records of the Union and Confederate Armies*, 128 vols. (Washington, 1880–1901), ser. 1, vol. 6, pp. 402–4 (hereafter *ORA*).
4. U.S. War Department, *Official Records of the Union and Confederate Navies in the War of the Rebellion*, 30 vols. (Washington, 1894–1927), ser. 1, vol. 17, p. 309.
5. *Boston Daily Journal*, 31 October 1862.
6. Amanda Comerford, "Experiences of Amanda Comerford," in Florida Division, United Daughters of the Confederacy Scrapbooks, vol. 1, Florida Collection, State Library of Florida, R. A. Gray Building, Tallahassee.
7. Mrs. M. M. Scarborough, "Suffering of Southern Women," ibid.
8. Mrs. John M. Taylor, Mrs. R. L. Harper, and Miss B. Kelley, "The Burdens the Women Bore," ibid., vol. 5.
9. Ibid.
10. Mrs. L. W. Jackson, "The Heroines of the Southern Confederacy," ibid., vol. 4.
11. *Oswego* (N.Y.) *Daily Palladium*, 5 September 1864.
12. New York *Freedman's Advocate*, May 1864.
13. Ibid.
14. George P. Rawick, ed., *The American Slave: A Composite Autobiography*, 19 vols. (Westport, Conn.: Greenwood Publishing Co., 1972; originally published 1941), vol. 17, *Florida Narratives*, p. 181.
15. Quoted in John F. Reiger, "Deprivation, Disaffection, and Desertion in Confederate Florida," *Florida Historical Quarterly* 48, no. 3 (January 1970):285–86.
16. *ORA*, ser. 1, vol. 52, pt. 2, supp., p. 336.
17. Ibid., ser. 4, vol. 2, p. 92.

18. Albert S. Chalker to Martha S. Barden, 12 October 1864, Albert S. Chalker Papers, Florida State Archives, R. A. Gray Building, Tallahassee.
19. Catharine S. Hart to "My dear Mother, Sisters & Brothers," Tampa, 5 January 1865, Dena E. Snodgrass Collection, P. K. Yonge Library of Florida History, University of Florida, Gainesville.
20. Martha S. Barden to Albert S. Chalker, 31 January 1865, Chalker Papers.
21. Joshua Hoyet Frier memoir, M76-134, Florida State Archives.
22. Francis P. Fleming to "Aunt Tilly," 3 May 1865, Francis P. Fleming Papers, Florida Historical Society, University of South Florida Library, Tampa.
23. Davis Bryant to Willie Bryant, 4 May 1865, Stephens-Bryant Papers, P. K. Yonge Library.
24. Francis C. M. Boggess, *A Veteran of Four Wars* (Arcadia, 1900), p. 74.

Bibliography

Brown, Canter, Jr. "Tampa's James McKay and the Frustration of Confederate Cattle-Supply Operations in South Florida." *Florida Historical Quarterly* 70, no. 4 (April 1992):409–33.

Buker, George E. *Blockaders, Refugees, and Contrabands.* Tuscaloosa: University of Alabama Press, 1993.

Coles, David James. "'A Fight, a Licking, and a Footrace': The 1864 Florida Campaign and the Battle of Olustee." Master's thesis, Florida State University, 1985.

———. "'A Terrible and Sad Result': The End of the Civil War in Florida, March–June 1865." In *Proceedings of the 90th Annual Meeting of the Florida Historical Society at St. Augustine May 1992.* Tampa: Florida Historical Society, 1992.

Curenton, Mark. *Tories and Deserters: The First Florida Federal Cavalry.* Laurel Hill: privately printed, 1988.

Davis, William Watson. *The Civil War and Reconstruction in Florida.* New York: Columbia University, 1913; reprint ed., Gainesville: University of Florida Press, 1964.

Dickison, John J. "Military History of Florida." In *Confederate Military History,* edited by Clement Anselm Evans, 12 vols., vol. 11, pt. 2, pp. 1–198. Atlanta: Confederate Publishing Company, 1898.

Dickison, Mary Elizabeth. *Dickison and His Men, Reminiscences of the War in Florida, 1890.* Edited by Samuel Proctor. Gainesville: University of Florida Press, 1962.

Dillon, Rodney E., Jr. "The Civil War in South Florida." Master's thesis, University of Florida, 1980.

Gannon, Michael V. *Rebel Bishop: The Life and Era of Augustin Verot.* Milwaukee: The Bruce Publishing Company, 1964.

Johns, John E. *Florida During the Civil War.* Gainesville: University of Florida Press, 1963; reprint ed., Macclenny: Richard J. Ferry, 1989.

Martin, Richard A., and Daniel L. Schafer. *Jacksonville's Ordeal by Fire, A Civil War History.* Jacksonville: Florida Publishing Company, 1984.

Nulty, William H. *Confederate Florida: The Road to Olustee.* Tuscaloosa: University of Alabama Press, 1990.

Reiger, John F. "Anti-War and Pro-Union Sentiment in Confederate Florida." Master's thesis, University of Florida, 1966.

Taylor, Robert A. *Rebel Storehouse: Florida in the Confederate Economy.* Tuscaloosa: University of Alabama Press, 1995.

14 Reconstruction and Renewal, 1865–1877

Jerrell H. Shofner

The fighting was over in the spring of 1865, but there was much to be done. Everything was at a standstill. There was no government. After Governor John Milton killed himself, Union General Edward McCook had suppressed efforts to reorganize a civil government. There was no inkling of how or when Florida would resume relations with the United States. Abraham Lincoln's assassination had removed the only person who had plans to bring the seceded states back into the Union. Newly inaugurated President Andrew Johnson was still formulating his ideas. There was no economy. Money and credit had disappeared with the fall of the Confederacy. The means of production had ended with the abolition of slavery. There were no markets and little transportation. It was planting time and, while the new president pondered the situation, something had to be done if crops were to be put in so that people could eat the following winter.

In the existing political vacuum, military officials took the initiative. General John Newton instructed Florida planters to assemble their former slaves, explain that they were now free, and ask them to remain on the plantations and work for wages. Compensation was to be paid in shares of the harvest. When the Freedmen's Bureau agents reached the field, the freedmen were already at work. The agents subsequently supervised the contracts between freedmen and their former owners, but they did so in accordance with the system implemented by the U.S. Army as an emergency measure. The Florida Legislature legitimized the system with appropriate legislation. There would be years of controversy over the legal status of freedmen, but the labor system that replaced the institution of slavery came by military order.

Sharecropping, crop liens, and tenant farming extended across the old plantation belt and affected both black and white farmers for decades after the Civil War. Cotton was produced by this inefficient system at a time when demand for it was constantly declining. The result was that the economy of old Middle Florida languished at the same time that East Florida and the peninsula began to grow.

Florida's readmission to the Union and the status of freedmen as citizens were matters that consumed much time and left a bitter legacy. Lincoln had anticipated the anger and bitterness that eventually engulfed the nation over these matters. Wishing to avoid as much conflict as possible, he had tried to rebuild loyal governments in Union-occupied territories such as northeastern Florida while the war was still being fought. Eager Florida Unionists such as Lyman Stickney, Calvin Robinson, and John Sammis seized upon the president's "ten-percent plan," but their efforts were thwarted by the Union military defeat at Olustee in early 1864. Little more was heard of Lincoln's plan, but the Direct Tax Commission, of which Stickney and Sammis were original members, carried out its duties to foreclose upon and sell Confederate property within Union lines. The ensuing "direct tax sales" transferred hundreds of pieces of property from Confederate owners to Unionists, many of whom were freedmen, and caused tremendous difficulties when President Andrew Johnson subsequently restored ownership to the former Confederates. The problem that arose is illustrated by the case of Confederate General Joseph Finegan's home in Fernandina. It was auctioned to Chloe Merrick of Syracuse, New York, for twenty-five dollars. Miss Merrick, who later married Republican Governor Harrison Reed, made the house into an orphanage for black children. When General Finegan marched home with President Johnson's amnesty proclamation in hand and found little black children playing on his veranda and the U.S. Army guarding them, the tenuous peace of Fernandina was sorely tested. Much of the tax-sale land was eventually returned to its former Confederate owners, but the matter exacerbated the struggle over Reconstruction in Florida and remained an issue until the 1890s.

With Freedmen's Bureau agents encountering increasing resistance from planters unaccustomed to limits on their autonomy, and confrontations between contesting owners of tax-sale property, President Johnson's Reconstruction plan was implemented. Following Lincoln's nonpunitive ideas, Johnson permitted most former Confederates to participate in forming a new government. He appointed William Marvin, a former federal judge from Key West, as provisional governor. Working closely with Major General John Foster, the military commander, Marvin registered those adult white males who took the requisite oath and called an election for delegates to a constitutional convention. The convention wrote a new constitution to conform with recent developments. Slavery was repudiated, as was the right of a state to secede from the Union. All debts incurred in support of the Confederacy were also repudiated. Laws enacted by Congress since 1861 were recognized, and a committee was appointed to review the state statutes and make recommendations for necessary changes when the first legislature met. In the ensuing election David Walker became the new governor, and Ferdinand McLeod was elected to the national House of Representatives.

The legislature was composed of many prominent former Confederates. There were, of course, no black members, and James Dopson Green of Manatee County was the only former Unionist named to the body. Former governor William Marvin and former Confederate Wilkinson Call were elected by the legislature to the U.S. Senate. There was some grumbling among Congressmen in Washington about the predominance of Confederates in Florida's restored government, but the major portent of future difficulties came with the report of the three-member committee on statutory changes. Speaking for the committee, Anderson J. Peeler recommended that the legislature preserve, insofar as possible, the beneficial features of the "benign, but much abused and greatly misunderstood institution of slavery."[1] The legislature complied. Freedmen were given customary civil rights except that they were not permitted to give testimony in cases involving white people. Since most of their difficulties were with their employers, this was a major shortcoming. Beyond that, a lengthy series of laws clearly discriminated between white and black citizens, even to the extent of substituting corporal punishment for fines and imprisonment for blacks convicted of crimes.

Already angered by President Johnson's decision to proceed with "presidential Reconstruction" without calling them into session, some congressmen watched with growing alarm as Florida and most other southern states enacted legislation denying equal citizenship to the freedmen. When it convened in December 1865, Congress refused to recognize Johnson's efforts. Marvin, Call, and McLeod were denied seats in their respective houses along with everyone elected from the other former Confederate states. A joint committee was named to investigate the conditions in the South and recommend an alternative course of action.

An acrimonious deadlock developed between President Johnson and Congress. It became increasingly clear that Johnson's program would not be approved without significant modifications. It was equally clear that the president was unwilling to compromise. The standoff became ugly. Congress enacted a Civil Rights law in April which expanded the rights of national citizens and gave enforcement authority to the U.S. Army. President Johnson vetoed the legislation and proclaimed an end to the "insurrection" in the South, with the apparent intention of removing martial law. Floridians applauded the president, but their elation was premature. Angered by the president's arbitrary actions and unwilling to readmit the seceded states without some guarantees of fair treatment of the freedmen, Congress voted to override the president's veto of the Civil Rights Act and another measure extending the life of the Freedmen's Bureau.

The continuing controversy between president and Congress gradually eroded the effectiveness of both the army and the bureau in protecting freedmen and Unionists in Florida. As chief of staff of the U.S. Army, General Ulysses S. Grant had at first instructed his field commanders to protect all freedmen and Unionists from abuses of their civil and property rights. But he was acting under the laws of Congress while his commander-in-chief was at odds with those laws.

In Florida, General John Foster tried to follow General Grant's instructions. Governor David Walker understandably agreed with the proclamations of the president. Both were reasonable men, and they tried to keep order in a situation that was becoming increasingly unclear. When the U.S. Army and a Nassau County sheriff's posse faced each other in the street in front of General Finegan's house, the two men went on the same train to Fernandina and prevented a violent confrontation. But they could not give personal attention to the hundreds of incidents arising throughout the northern Florida counties. Freedmen were treated atrociously by the county criminal courts. When Freedmen's Bureau agents attempted to intercede, they often confronted county sheriffs with large armed posses. General Foster felt compelled to declare martial law in nine counties in the summer of 1866. His action angered Governor Walker and did little to improve the plight of the freedmen.

The deteriorating situation in Florida was accompanied by increasing acrimony between President Johnson and Congress in Washington. In

August 1866, Johnson issued an even stronger proclamation restoring civil law in Florida. Still sympathetic with congressional efforts to protect freedmen in their civil rights, General Grant was, after all, accountable to the president who was commander-in-chief of all armed forces. The general accordingly issued new instructions to the field commanders which left their authority unclear. Increasingly frustrated at his inability to protect freedman from mistreatment, General Foster resigned in November 1866. He told his superiors that he would happily return to Florida but only if the laws were made adequate for him to execute his duties to protect all citizens in their civil rights.

The failure of President Johnson's Reconstruction plan in Florida coincided with the eclipse of his authority in Washington. Congress wrested control from him and implemented its own plan. Under congressional Reconstruction, martial law was reinstated with Major General John Pope in command. He appointed Ossian B. Hart of Jacksonville as supervisor of registration for a new electorate, which this time included all adult black males. New elections were held for delegates to yet another constitutional convention. The new document was to include a guarantee of black suffrage. When a suitable constitution was ratified by Florida voters and the legislature ratified the Fourteenth Amendment to the U.S. Constitution, military occupation would be ended and the state would be able to resume its normal place in the Union.

At the end of the war many native white Floridians had time only "to worship the Confederate dead and hate the Yankee living," but they had "gradually learned to manage" under the Johnson plan of Reconstruction.[2] Now, nearly two years after the war, Congress was forcing black suffrage upon them. There was talk of white immigration to Latin America or the unsettled American West, and a few Floridians did resettle in Brazil. A larger number simply abandoned Middle Florida and moved southward to Brevard, Orange, Hillsborough, and other sparsely populated central Florida counties. Most of them remained where they were, but they were badly divided over what course to follow. Some chose not to participate in elections involving blacks, but Hart's registration teams administered the oath of loyalty to several thousand who decided to make the best of the situation.

The demoralization and division of the white population left an open field for the evolving Republican Party, but it was also badly divided. At a convention called by Hart in the summer of 1867, vigorous disagreements emerged. A group led by Daniel Richards, a former tax commissioner, Liberty Billings, a former commander of a black regiment, and

A Florida family photographed in the 1870s. Despite the fact that a few African Americans won election to government offices, Reconstruction did not result in securing for blacks an equal part in Florida society. In his book on Florida during that period, *Nor Is It Over Yet,* Jerrell Shofner wrote, "The moderate Republicans who implemented the 1867 Reconstruction acts in Florida had never given Negro rights more than secondary consideration. Black voters contributed more to the Republican party than they received from it. Even their basic right to vote was diluted by provisions for disproportionate legislative representation. Yet their situation between 1868 and 1877 was infinitely better than it was to be for the next seventy-five years."

William U. Saunders, a representative of the Union League, joined by Charles H. Pearce, a Canadian minister of the African Methodist Episcopal Church, wanted to emphasize rights for blacks at the expense of native whites. Another faction headed by Harrison Reed, William H. Gleason, and Thomas W. Osborn, among others, took a more moderate position. They realized that congressional requirements would have to be met, but they were more interested in developing the vast vacant lands of the state. They were willing to include blacks in the new electorate, but they also wanted the native whites to participate in the new government.

The Republicans elected nearly all of the forty-three delegates to the convention, which met in January 1868, but they were varying kinds of Republicans. The Radical Republican Billings-Richards faction was able to control the organization of the convention and seemingly would be able to write a constitution suitable to them. White delegates sympathetic to Reed and Gleason bolted the convention and wrote a contesting document with the cooperation of Charles E. Dyke and McQueen McIntosh, both of whom represented the native white leadership of the state. They then returned to Tallahassee in the middle of the night, took possession of the assembly hall, and reorganized the convention while the Billings-Richards delegates slept. The Radical delegates were dumbfounded that following morning to find themselves locked out of the assembly hall by a cordon of U.S. soldiers. After several stormy days and some amazing decisions by Congress, the moderate version of the constitution—despite its unorthodox origin—was sent to the polls and approved by Florida voters. Harrison Reed was elected governor and William H. Gleason lieutenant governor. At a Fourth of July ceremony, Colonel John T. Sprague, commander of the occupation force, relinquished authority to Governor Reed. Radical Reconstruction had led to a constitution which, according to the new governor, would "prevent a Negro legislature."[3]

Reed's was a stormy administration. In his continuing effort to retain the support of native whites for the new government, he appointed Robert Gamble and James Westcott to cabinet positions, but that move backfired when Gamble openly opposed Reed's deficit financing plans. Having supported him against the Billings-Richard faction, Charles E. Dyke now leveled the powerful guns of his *Tallahassee Floridian* against the governor in particular and all Republicans in general. A sizable minority of native white legislators calling themselves Conservatives used their votes in the legislature to thwart Reed and embarrass the new Republican Party. Attempting to tread the narrow path between Conservatives on one hand and black legislators on the other, the governor angered both. His ambitious lieutenant governor was not much help either: Gleason supported a move to impeach Reed and remove him from office. The wily governor bested him, retained his office, and strengthened his position by appointing Jonathan C. Gibbs, a capable and influential black, as secretary of state. Gleason subsequently turned his considerable abilities to developing vacant lands in peninsular Florida and founding the town of Eau Gallie on the Indian River.

Born a slave in Virginia, Josiah T. Walls served in the Union army and settled in Florida after Appomattox. Aided by Republican reconstruction politics, he entered public life as a state representative and senator. Then, in 1870, he became Florida's first African-American member of the U.S. House of Representatives, to which he was elected twice more. Following politics he turned to truck farming. Other black politicians in Florida during the 1870s were John Wallace, Henry Harmon, Charles Pearce, Robert Meacham, and the Dartmouth-educated Jonathan Gibbs, who became secretary of state under Governor Harrison Reed (1868–73).

While Conservative editors and legislators fought Reed in Talla-hassee, others took more direct action in the outlying areas. Controlling most of the land and credit, Conservative planters and merchants de-nied credit and land rentals to freedmen who continued to vote the Re-publican ticket. Vigilantes such as the Ku Klux Klan and the Young Men's Democratic Clubs used violence and intimidation to discourage or prevent newly enfranchised blacks from exercising their voting priv-ileges. Leaders were threatened, beaten, and killed. Polling places were disrupted by gunfire and threats. Former Confederate cavalry com-mander J. J. Dickison even led bands of mounted men in cavalry charges through crowds of potential voters. Without financial and per-sonnel resources, Reed was obliged to rely on the U.S. Army garrison to maintain order. But its numbers were small, it was far removed from the many scenes of violence, human life was lightly regarded, the stakes were high, and the violence continued.

Congress ultimately responded with legislation empowering the president to restore martial law, but violence and disorder remained se-rious problems during most of Reed's four and a half years in office. In-traparty factionalism and repeated impeachments of the governor, some of which were inspired and encouraged by U.S. Senator Thomas W. Osborn, kept the state in turmoil and discredited both the Reed ad-ministration and the Republican Party.

While Reconstruction brought unwelcome changes and political and racial strife to the Middle Florida plantation belt, it concomitantly helped to open up peninsular Florida to settlement. Until the 1860s the Florida peninsula had been a sparsely populated cattle range where drovers grazed their herds over miles and miles of open range. When William Gleason accompanied Freedmen's Bureau agent George F. Thompson on a tour of southern Florida in 1865–66, they reported vast open lands and a balmy climate—only the first of many touting the Florida peninsula to receptive audiences across the nation. Northerners were attracted by available open land where the winters were mild. Southerners liked the idea of an unsettled region where they could es-cape the conditions of Reconstruction.

Soon magazines, newspapers, and railroad companies were sending reporters to observe and report on this paradise. By 1870 Floridians were publishing the *Florida New Yorker* to attract settlers and investors. Jacksonville, which had been almost destroyed by the frequent inva-sions of the war years, bounced back to become the center of winter tourism, the gateway to southern Florida via the St. Johns River, and a budding financial center where northern capital was increasingly

President and former Union general Ulysses S. Grant (*seated, left front*) and a party of northern friends journey down Florida's most picturesque river, the Ocklawaha, on the paddle steamer *Osceola*. Similar steamboats plied the St. Johns, Suwannee, and Apalachicola rivers. One nervous passenger on the Ocklawaha recorded, "The hull of the steamer went bumping against one cypress-butt, then another, suggesting to the tyro in this kind of aquatic adventure that possibly he might be wrecked, and subjected, even if he escaped a watery grave, to a miserable death, through the agency of mosquitoes, buzzards, and huge alligators."

available for investment. Hubbard Hart's line of steamers was one of several which carried passengers and freight up the St. Johns. He and others made a tourist attraction of Harriet Beecher Stowe's winter home at Mandarin, easily visible to passengers eager to catch a glimpse of the lady who Abraham Lincoln had once credited with starting the Civil War. But Hart also added a popular tourist attraction by opening up the Ocklawaha River to Silver Springs which by 1873 was being visited by 50,000 tourists annually.

Frederick DeBary, a Belgian wine merchant, also transported visitors up the St. Johns as far as Lake Monroe, where he built a hotel at the new community named for him. The Brock Line operated between Jacksonville and Enterprise on the northern shore of Lake Monroe. Small shallow-draft steamers plied the tortuous channels of the upper St. Johns with passengers and cargo bound for the Indian River settlements of Titusville, Rockledge, and Eau Gallie. With three large hotels, Rockledge soon became known as the southernmost winter resort in the nation.

One of the Yankees who invested largely in peninsular Florida was Henry S. Sanford, a former Union general and powerful member of the national Republican Party. He founded the town of Sanford about 1870 on Lake Monroe's south shore. Using both Swedish immigrant and native black labor, he developed two large orange groves. He also sold numerous tracts to other northerners, among whom were William Tecumseh Sherman, Senator Henry Anthony of Rhode Island, and Orville Babcock, personal secretary to President Grant. With Sanford's vigorous support, several Boston investors started the South Florida Railroad to run southward through Orlando to Kissimmee, thus opening more of the peninsula to settlers. President Grant was induced to turn the first shovel of earth in 1879.

In the absence of suitable transportation, settlement of the western part of the peninsula lagged behind the St. Johns River valley, but Tampa boasted a few hundred inhabitants near the old Fort Brooke army reservation in the early 1870s. A colony of "Downeasters" settled at Sarasota in 1868, and tourists were able to find lodging at several locations in Manatee County by the early 1870s. Jacob Summerlin, Zibe King, Francis A. Hendry, the Curry family, and others continued grazing their herds uninterrupted on the south Florida range, but the citrus and tourist industries were already on their way during the Reconstruction years.

The missing link was suitable railroad transportation, but the state's Internal Improvement Fund was unable to use its millions of acres of public lands as incentive to potential builders because of a complicated lawsuit that prevented it from conveying clear titles. Efforts in 1866 to revive the war-damaged Florida Railroad from Fernandina to Cedar Keys had resulted in a federal court injunction prohibiting sale of state lands except for cash. Unable to effect such a sale the state could not clear the so-called Vose injunction until 1881. The Reed administration assisted Milton Littlefield and George W. Swepson with their Jacksonville, Pensacola, and Mobile Railroad venture, but that firm also became embroiled in litigation which was not settled until 1879. Railroad construction in Florida had to wait until the 1880s.

Events surrounding the Jacksonville, Pensacola, and Mobile Company were catalysts for one of the four attempts to remove Governor Reed from office by impeachment. These internecine squabbles added to the confusion that brought Reed's administration to an end in 1873. A fractious Republican convention bypassed him in 1872 and nominated for governor Ossian B. Hart, the native Florida Unionist who had good relations with black leaders. His running mate was Marcellus L. Stearns, a former bureau agent and prominent legislator who was aligned with white party leaders.

The Hart-Stearns ticket defeated a straightout Conservative-Democratic slate headed by former Confederate William D. Bloxham. Hart guided several progressive measures through the 1873 legislature, most important of which was a funding law that helped improve the state's financial condition. It seemed for a time that some political harmony had been achieved by the bickering Republican Party, but Hart became ill and remained hospitalized for months before he died. In the meantime, Stearns first acted in Hart's absence and then became governor in fact. His elevation to the governorship did little to nurture harmony in the party. Blacks felt increasingly alienated as Stearns tried to build his strength with the white, office-holding faction of the party. His actions led to new feuds. Congressman William J. Purman and Senator Simon B. Conover both broke with him, and the newspapers were filled with their acrimonious assaults on each other.

The Conservative-Democrats had not been idle. Despite Bloxham's poor showing in 1872, they were steadily gaining seats in both legislative branches. After the 1874 election, they claimed a small majority in the assembly and a 12–12 tie in the senate. The assassination of Republican Senator Elisha Johnson broke the tie, but reminded everyone of the fragility of relations between native white Conservatives and their Republican opponents. Although they denied involvement in the murder, many Conservatives noted the political result. One of them wrote privately that "in losing Johnson we gain a county. Who could not afford to make this sacrifice?"[4] The 1876 election was approaching, and "bloody shirt politics" was back in the headlines.

Lingering memories of the war and Confederate defeat, abolition of slavery and enfranchisement of the freedmen, military occupation, and a disorderly and fractious government allegedly controlled by "carpetbaggers" and "scalawags" had a left a heavy burden on native white Floridians by the mid-1870s. Ellen Call Long was reminded of this when she sought assistance from her friends to place a Florida exhibit at the Philadelphia centennial celebration to be held in 1876. Old acquaintances from all over the state found myriad reasons why they could not help, but the problem was summed up when a friend wrote, "I'm sorry your effort in behalf of our oppressed state has been abortive . . . fifteen years bitter struggle has crushed nearly every spark of patriotism from the Southern breast . . . and it will be hard to bury the past."[5]

Despite such sentiments, which were widely held, Conservative-Democratic leaders were much more pragmatic in 1876 than they had been four years earlier. They had noticed that many newcomers to peninsular Florida, while still favoring the national Republican Party, were tired of the disruptiveness in the state capital for which they blamed Florida Republicans. Henry Sanford, for example, expressed willingness to support a Conservative-Democrat for governor while voting for a Republican presidential candidate. Determined to take advantage of such a split ticket opportunity, the Conservative-Democrats named George F. Drew, a prominent lumberman and former Unionist, for governor.

Still fighting among themselves, the Republicans renominated Marcellus Stearns for the position he held. In an election that was overshadowed by the national presidential contest between Democrat Samuel Tilden and Republican Rutherford Hayes, about 48,000 Floridians voted in an election that was so close that fewer than a hundred votes would decide the outcome. With the presidential election depending on the outcome of the elections in Florida, Louisiana, and South Carolina, "visiting statesmen" from both parties rushed to the three state capitals to do what they could for their respective candidates. They joined numerous curious observers and several companies of U.S. soldiers and literally overran Florida's small capital city.

The newcomers in the peninsular counties who had split their tickets had created a dilemma for the state canvassing board, composed of two Republicans and one Democrat. Since the presidential election depended on fewer than 100 votes, it appeared that Republican Hayes deserved Florida's four electoral votes, but split tickets had left Stearns and the Florida Republicans several hundred votes behind Hayes. Governor Stearns told some of the "visiting statesmen" that he would not be pleased with a Hayes victory in which he did not share. The majority of the canvassing board voted to throw out several hundred votes on grounds that they were improper. Those excluded votes tended to come from counties which returned Conservative-Democratic majorities. The result was majorities for Republicans at both presidential and state levels. The "visiting statesmen" left Tallahassee believing that Florida would be counted in the Republican column.

Local Conservative-Democrats had said nothing until the visitors were gone. They then induced the state supreme court to order a recount of the votes as they had been received from the counties, that is, to restore those votes which had been thrown out for various reasons. The recount showed that Hayes still had a small majority, but that Democrat George F. Drew had defeated Stearns for governor. Drew was inaugurated without incident on 2 January 1877.

The dispute over the presidency caused a near deadlock in Washington. After nearly three months, an electoral commission declared Hayes victorious, and he was sworn in as president in March 1877. In April, he removed the remaining U.S. troops from Louisiana and South Carolina. There were none in Florida after 23 January 1877. This disputed election and the so-called Compromise of 1877, which involved the withdrawal of the troops, came to symbolize the end of Reconstruction.

An immediate result of the events of late 1876 and early 1877 was consolidation of their control of the state by the newly empowered Conservative-Democrats. Drew used the extensive powers of his office in the same way that his Republican predecessors had. Soon his party controlled most state and county offices, including the all-important election machinery. Blacks continued to hold some local offices but in diminished numbers. Many of the defeated Republican officials left the state, but a number made Florida their home. Harrison Reed, for example, remained in Jacksonville and died in his adopted state in 1899. Senator Simon Conover and Secretary of State Samuel B. McLin joined several others who lived out their lives in the developing citrus country of peninsular Florida. Horatio Bisbee was elected to Congress from east Florida in 1882. But the Republicans' political strength was waning. In 1884 they attempted to fuse with a dissident wing of the Democratic Party, but the fusion ticket was easily defeated by the regular Democratic candidate, former Confederate General Edward A. Perry.

Florida's capitol at Tallahassee as it appeared in the 1870s. A cupola would be added in 1891, and the building would serve until a new capitol was built nearby in 1978.

By 1884, Democrats, who had by then dropped the "Conservative" from their party name, were confident that they had solidified their majority status in Florida. In an attempt to rid themselves of one more reminder of Reconstruction days, a majority of them voted in 1884 for a constitutional convention to write still another fundamental law for the state. It would replace the onerous 1868 document which they still regarded as an imposition on the state from outsiders. Dominated by Democrats, the convention wrote a new constitution that weakened the powers of the governor, made most offices at state and local levels elective, and strengthened the powers of local officials. It also provided for a poll tax, which was enacted by the 1889 legislature. That law effectively kept most black voters away from the polls. The Republican party ceased to be a serious challenge to Democratic control of the state, and Florida would be a one-party state for many decades.

The years of Reconstruction had been turbulent and traumatic for many Floridians, and the Democrats successfully used recollections of those years to cement political control, but there were other important results. There was a definite shift of the population southward and a corresponding diminution of the hegemony of Middle Florida planters. The plantation belt remained comparatively static until well into the twentieth century while the peninsula, all the way from Jacksonville southward, was settled by both permanent inhabitants and winter residents. Many of both groups engaged in citrus culture and tourism. Others turned to railroad construction to bind the new section to the rest of the nation. These changes were set in motion during the Reconstruction era, but their development is a matter for later chapters.

Notes

1. Florida, *House Journal,* 1865–66.
2. Helen Moore Edwards, *Memoirs* (privately printed, n.d.).
3. H. Reed to D. L. Yulee, 16 February 1868, David L. Yulee Papers, P. K. Yonge Library of Florida History, University of Florida, Gainesville.
4. Henry L'Engle to E. M. L'Engle, 23 July 1875, Edward M. L'Engle Papers, Southern Historical Collection, University of North Carolina, Chapel Hill.
5. Ida Wood to Mrs. Long, 8 April 1872, Richard Keith Call Papers, Southern Historical Collection, University of North Carolina, Chapel Hill.

Bibliography

Brown, Canter, Jr. "'Where Are Now the Hopes I Cherished?' The Life and Times of Robert Meacham." *Florida Historical Quarterly* 69, no. 1 (July 1990):1–36.

Clark, James C. "John Wallace and the Writing of Reconstruction History." *Florida Historical Quarterly* 67, no. 4 (April 1989):409–27.

Cox, Merlin G. "Military Reconstruction in Florida." *Florida Historical Quarterly* 46, no. 3 (January 1968):219–33.

Cresse, Lewis H., Jr. "A Study of William Henry Gleason: Carpetbagger, Politician, Land Developer." Ph.D. dissertation, University of South Carolina, 1977.

Davis, William Watson. *The Civil War and Reconstruction in Florida.* New York: Columbia University, 1913.

Reid, Whitelaw. *After the War: A Southern Tour.* Cincinnati, New York: Moore, Wilstach & Baldwin, 1866.

Richardson, Joe M. "The Florida Black Codes." *Florida Historical Quarterly* 47 (1969).

———. *The Negro in the Reconstruction of Florida, 1865–1877* Tallahassee: Florida State University, 1965.

Shofner, Jerrell H. "Andrew Johnson and the Fernandina Unionists." *Prologue, The Journal of the National Archives* (Winter 1978):211–24.

———. "The Constitution of 1868." *Florida Historical Quarterly* 41, no. 2 (April 1963):356–74.

———. "A Merchant Planter in the Reconstruction South." *Agricultural History* 46, no. 2 (April 1972):291–96.

———. "Militant Negro Laborers in Reconstruction Florida." *Journal of Southern History* 39 (1973).

———. *Nor Is It Over Yet: Florida in the Era of Reconstruction 1865–1877.* Gainesville: University of Florida Press, 1974.

———. "Political Reconstruction in Florida." *Florida Historical Quarterly* 45, no. 2 (October 1966):145–70.

Wallace, John. *Carpetbag Rule in Florida: The Inside Workings of the Reconstruction of Civil Government in Florida After the Close of the Civil War.* Gainesville: University of Florida Press, 1964; originally published in 1888.

15 Prelude to the New Florida, 1877–1919

Samuel Proctor

The remaining contingent of Federal troops began departing from Florida on 18 January 1877. There was no special ceremony anywhere, and most Floridians were happy that home rule could now be proclaimed. Governor George F. Drew in his inaugural address on 2 January 1877 pledged a middle-of-the-road program and promised to rebuff all extremists and restore the state to peace and tranquillity, "We are a law abiding people," he proclaimed, "resolved to perpetuate free institutions."[1] These statements, he hoped, would reassure not only white Floridians but also black citizens who had gained much during Reconstruction and who now wondered how they would fare under the new regime and without northern soldiers to protect them. They had reason to be fearful of the future.

In stating his program, Drew had the support of a legislature that was solidly Democratic: in the senate fourteen to nine, in the house thirty-two to eighteen. Although there were no blacks appointed, Drew's cabinet was balanced, with William D. Bloxham, perhaps the most popular Bourbon in Florida, serving as secretary of state. The Drew-Bloxham tie was short lived. By 1880 the two men were bitter political enemies, and the ill feeling would continue throughout their lives. While the most important offices were filled by men from north Florida counties, Drew recognized the growing economic and political importance of peninsular Florida, and he appointed William P. Haisley of Hillsborough County as superintendent of public instruction and Walter Gwynn of Orange County as treasurer. The absence of any Radicals in the cabinet further confirmed that Drew would serve as a conciliator.

An immediate problem was the precarious financial condition of the state. The Internal Improvement Fund was in receivership. The trustees who administered state lands and controlled payments on railroad bonds guaranteed by the state could not offer land for railroads or for economic expansion. The cost of operating government had skyrocketed since the war, and taxation had almost tripled. Drew noted in his first address to the legislature that "government will be the most highly esteemed, that gives the greatest protection to the tax payer." Florida, he cautioned, would "spend nothing unless absolutely necessary."[2]

Fiscal conservatism has been an overriding objective of Florida's political leaders—state and local—from 1876 to the present. "Cut back," "retrenchment," and "hold the line" were the state's goals. To reduce taxes and to balance the budget, there were cutbacks, particularly in social programs. Notwithstanding the commitment to support public schools, education was hard hit. At one time Governor Drew and the superintendent of public instruction advocated limiting free public instruction only to grammar (primary) schools, but that plan was dropped. At one point in his administration, Drew also advocated the elimination of public high schools.[3] The legislature slashed the county school tax by one-half, and both small and large counties found it increasingly difficult to keep schools open, maintain buildings, pay teachers' salaries, and buy supplies. Secondary and higher education were badly neglected. Until the Florida Agricultural College was established in Lake City in 1884, the state did not have an institution of higher learning.

If the educational system in Florida was poor, even by comparison with other states in the South, it was far more deplorable for the black population. The legislation enacted in 1869 had authorized a uniform system of common schools whose instruction would be free. In some counties there were no schools at all for black students. Even in the urban areas, white and black schools were poorly equipped and teachers were inadequately trained and poorly paid. The literacy rate in Florida was one of the lowest in the South.

Convict leasing was the state's remedy for the cost of housing and caring for criminals. Convicts, usually those who were sentenced for more than a year, were leased out to private contractors who paid the state a minimal amount for their services. The convicts worked, usually under brutal conditions, constructing railroads, digging canals and drainage ditches, in turpentine and lumber camps, and on farms and plantations. Little or no effort was made to supervise the treatment of the convicts, and the mortality rate was extremely high.

The state arsenal in Chattahoochee was converted from a prison into an insane asylum. The motivation was not humanitarian but economic. The insane would no longer need to be boarded in other states' institutions, and Florida would save $25,000 a year.

Florida was very much a frontier state in 1876, isolated from the rest of the South, and it would remain so for many decades. Agriculture was the dominant industry. The same crops that had been grown in antebellum Florida—cotton, corn, vegetables, and some sugarcane and tobacco—continued to be harvested in the post–Civil War period. Land was perhaps more widely distributed. Many large plantations had changed owners and had been divided up. Some white yeoman farmers, and even a few blacks, owned small plots, but the majority of the acreage was held by a relatively small percentage of the population. Without slaves to work the land, sharecropping and tenant farming developed in Florida and throughout the South. This was basically the system of landownership and land use in the South until the 1930s.

Throughout the South, there was a growing need for transportation, and in a state as large as Florida the need for railroads was critical. If Florida was to become prosperous and productive it would have to develop its economic resources, but the impoverished state did not have the necessary capital. Encouraging northern investment was an important objective. The Internal Improvement Commission needed the freedom to grant public land for railroad and canal construction and for general economic development. In 1881, William D. Bloxham, who had succeeded Drew as governor, negotiated a land sale with Hamilton Disston, the thirty-six-year-old head of a large Philadelphia saw and tool manufacturing company. For $1 million Disston would receive 4 million acres of swamp and overflowed land. Actually, little of the land was underwater, and the part that was would be drained. Much of it was in south Florida, around Lake Okeechobee.[4] Although there was criticism from Bloxham's political opponents, who labeled the sale as a "giveaway" (land was valued at $1.25 an acre), it accomplished its main goal: the Internal Improvement Commission could resume its work. With public lands and grants now available, a dozen or more railroad companies revealed plans for new lines to cover the state. Henry B. Plant, a Connecticut Yankee, developed the Plant System—railroads, hotels, and steamship lines—along the Gulf Coast and into central Florida. The system connected Florida by rail with the North for first time. After Plant's death, the system became the Atlantic Coast Line Railroad, one of the country's largest. Plant's Tampa Bay Hotel (now the University of Tampa), with its Moorish architecture and its ornate furnishings, became world famous for its accommodations and excellent service. During the Spanish-American War it was headquarters for newspaper correspondents, writers, and military officers, including Theodore Roosevelt.

The Louisville and Nashville Railroad Company extended its line east from Pensacola, giving the Panhandle a long-needed route. Directing its operations was William D. Chipley, who also controlled West Florida politics and became one of the great nineteenth-century power brokers in the state.

The best known and perhaps the most glamorous of the developers was Henry Morrison Flagler, who, as a partner of John D. Rockefeller, had made an enormous fortune in Standard Oil. Described as a "dreamer and a visionary," Flagler spent the last thirty years of his life developing a multimillion-dollar railroad, shipping, hotel, and land development empire that would forever change the economic face of Florida. When he arrived in St. Augustine in 1883 on his honeymoon, he was dismayed at the inadequate facilities he found. Florida needed a grand hotel, and to design one he hired the same architects who later would design the New York Public Library. When the Ponce de Leon Hotel was completed in 1888, it was one of the most palatial in the world. But it was just the beginning: His hotel chain eventually would include the luxurious Royal Poinciana and The Breakers in Palm Beach, as well as the Royal Palm in Miami.

In 1888, Flagler bought the thirty-six-mile Jacksonville, St. Augustine, and Halifax River Railroad, the first leg of what would become the Florida East Coast System. By 1894, the road reached West Palm Beach, and Flagler planned that to be its terminus. The road would carry freight and passengers but also wealthy visitors to Palm Beach, the fashionable resort that Flagler was developing.

Florida was devastated by two record-breaking freezes during the winter 1894–95. Losses to citrus and vegetable growers ran into the millions of dollars. When Flagler saw that the freeze had not extended to the Miami area, he was persuaded by the offer of Julia D. Tuttle of a townsite and additional land from William B. Brickell to extend his railroad to Miami. When it reached there in 1896, there were only 502 registered voters in the newly incorporated city. Once it was certain that the United States would build the Panama Canal and open up the

Henry M. Flagler (1830–1913), whose Florida East Coast Railroad and resort hotels provided the foundation of modern Florida development.

A passenger train pulled by a steam locomotive passes along the overseas rail line that Henry Flagler built on bridges from the mainland to Key West. Completed in 1912, the Key West Extension united the long-isolated island city with the rest of Florida. Flagler rightly regarded it as the crowning achievement of his life. The line would be badly damaged in a 1935 hurricane and replaced by the overseas automobile highway still in use.

Caribbean for expanded commercial activity, Flagler decided to extend his railroad to Key West. It reached there in 1912, just a year before his death.[5]

While Flagler, Plant, and Disston never held political office, they and other corporate and railroad interests helped determine the course of Florida politics. They were land-hungry investors, and Tallahassee was more than willing to satisfy their voracious appetites. Flagler was the recipient of a huge amount of land, 8,000 acres per mile, plus rights of way, for rail construction south of Daytona. The *Jacksonville Florida Weekly Times* reported in 1884 that the past Democratic legislature had granted railroads 22,360,000 acres although only 14,831,739 acres were in the public domain. Patronage-oriented Republicans from the North were horse-trading with Bourbon Democrats to get what they wanted from the State of Florida, but the demand for reform and change was growing.

By 1884, an anti-Bourbon coalition, consisting of reform-minded white Republicans, Negro Republicans, and Independent Democrats, became the state's second party. Frank W. Pope, an able orator but without much political clout, ran for governor as a reform candidate.

The Independents charged the Republicans with corruption, racial prejudice, and fraud. The Democratic Bourbons came in for similar bitter accusations. The Disston land sale was only one example of what was wrong with government. "A free ballot, a full vote, and a fair count" were the themes of the Independent platform. Not unpredictably, Pope lost the election, although he received 46 percent of the vote and carried nine counties. General Edward A. Perry of Pensacola, a Confederate war hero, was elected governor. The reformers and dissenters had lost this battle, but their day would come. For the moment, however, Florida was a one-party state with the Democrats in charge.[6]

Florida's political and business leaders enthusiastically endorsed Henry W. Grady's New South philosophy. The state could offer a favorable climate, good transportation facilities, cheap labor, low taxes, and cooperative government in exchange for fresh capital and settlers. There was lots of public land to be given away.

Florida continued to be a rural and agrarian state. The population in 1880 was 269,500, of whom 127,000 were black. Leon was the largest county (19,662), and Key West was the largest city (9,890), followed by Jacksonville and Pensacola. The state organized efforts to attract settlers and tourists. Railroad companies and other promoters and developers tried to lure settlers to buy their lands and to utilize their rail facilities. Brochures and travel books were published and distributed, all extolling the virtues and beauty of Florida and the great economic opportunities the state offered.

The 1884 Florida Independent movement and the controversy over calling a constitutional convention in 1885 were indications of some of the political problems plaguing the state. The political constituency that had succeeded in winning the election for the Democrats in 1876 was becoming factionalized in the 1880s. Farmers, laborers, and small businessmen questioned whether the Bourbon Democrats were showing enough concern for their interests and needs. For all practical purposes the new Constitution of 1885 had eliminated the blacks as a factor in Florida government and the Republican party as a political threat.

Everyone, particularly farmers, citrus growers, and cattlemen, knew that Florida needed more railroads, but they wanted protection from arbitrary charges and discriminatory treatment. Responding to pressure, the legislature, somewhat reluctantly, authorized in 1887 a three-member railroad regulatory commission. It was purposely created as a weak and ineffectual agency.[7]

Transportation was not the only problem facing farmers and businessmen. A restricted currency, a scarcity of lending agencies, high interest rates, and the inability to determine either buying or selling prices added to the plight and discouragement of the debtor classes. Farmers continued to grow cotton—nearly 55,000 bales in 1880—even though cotton prices were declining toward a low of four cents a pound by the end of the century. A lack of capital and an absence of knowledge of how to convert to other crops locked the farmer into a seemingly unending life of poverty.

Agrarian discontent was not isolated in Florida. Throughout the country after the Civil War, political and economic organizations emerged promising to help farmers. The Florida State Grange was organized in 1873, and within two years it counted 5,000 members. It did not survive as a major organization in this state, losing members rapidly after 1877. Encouraging female participation and the involvement in some instances of blacks made the grange too radical an organization for white conservatives.[8]

The Farmers Alliance first appeared in Texas in 1876. Organization began in Florida in Marianna in 1887, and it spread rapidly through the northern counties. There was a need for an organization that looked to farmers' concerns and possessed the ability to bring about needed change. At first it concerned itself only with remedying bad economic conditions, but this noninvolvement in politics was temporary. By 1890, the Alliance was actively involved in the election. Its members controlled the Florida Democratic state convention, and candidates won because they had the organization's endorsement. Alliance men were in the majority in the legislature after the November elections.

The high point of the movement in Florida was the national Alliance convention held in Ocala in December 1890. The Ocala Demands drafted there became the basis for the platform of the Populist Party when it organized in Cincinnati in 1891. The Ocala convention gave Florida a great opportunity to advertise the state and to encourage settlers and investors.[9]

The Farmers Alliance was not as powerful in Florida as it was in other southern states. The fruit and vegetable growers and the cattlemen in central Florida did not face the same problems as the cotton and tobacco farmers elsewhere in the South. An effort to elect an alliance man for governor failed in 1892; the prize went to Judge Henry L. Mitchell of Tampa, who ran on the Democratic Party ticket. The legislature abolished the railroad commission over strong Alliance opposition.[10] The

The high-wheel ox-drawn wagon was common transportation at the turn of the century.

fact that the Democratic Party became concerned about some of the farmers' needs was a strong reason for declining Alliance enthusiasm in Florida.

The Populist Party borrowed freely from the Alliance platform. It called for fair elections, an end to convict leasing, prohibition of child labor, stronger railroad commissions, good roads, revision of the tax structure, interest rates limited to 6 percent, expansion of the currency, and a ten-hour day for laborers. The program was designed to appeal to farmers, laborers, and small businessmen, but it was not a successful or enduring party in Florida.

With the Republican Party no longer a force in Florida, the Democratic Party did not feel the need to speak with one voice as it had earlier during Reconstruction or in the election campaign of 1876. Throughout the eighties, dissatisfaction with Bourbonism continued to grow. It was obvious again in 1891 in the bitterly contested legislative battle for appointment to the U.S. Senate. Wilkinson Call, the more liberal and more moderate incumbent, won out over William D. Chipley, the conservative "Mr. Railroad of West Florida."[11]

In 1896, the Democratic Party selected as their gubernatorial candidate William D. Bloxham, who had identified with the Bourbon philosophy throughout his political career. Now somewhat more moderate, he was chosen as the candidate best able to unite the party and to bring the dissidents back into the fold.[12] The Populist-Progressives scored some victories during the Bloxham era. A stronger railroad commission was created in 1897, and the inauguration of a direct primary to nominate local officials was a major triumph.[13] By 1904, all state candidates would be nominated under the primary system.

If the closing years of the nineteenth century had brought many changes—political, economic, social—that were advantageous for white Floridians, it was a disastrous time for blacks. Whatever dubious gains they had achieved during the Reconstruction Era had been taken by the white man's government. The assurances that blacks would be guaranteed their rights turned out to be empty promises. A declining number of blacks continued to vote and even to hold public office in the 1890s, but their influence in Florida politics was insignificant. Black leaders like Joseph E. Lee, deputy port collector of Jacksonville, and former Congressman Josiah T. Walls of Gainesville were no longer able to protect black rights.

There only were eight blacks out of a total of 108 delegates attending the 1885 Constitutional Convention in Tallahassee, and the new constitution that was drafted was neither liberal nor fair to their interests. The most damaging article authorized a poll tax as a prerequisite to voting.[14] The fact that it would mean the disfranchisement of poor whites as well as the bulk of the black population did not deter overwhelming white support for the tax. The convention endorsed the segregated schools that were already in place in Florida, and voted against establishing a state normal school for blacks.[15]

The further erosion of black rights was an expected consequence. The legislature in 1889 borrowed a practice from South Carolina and instituted the system of using separate ballot boxes for each office to confuse the black voters.[16] The poll tax, as authorized by the constitution, was also enacted in 1889.[17]

Florida experienced a series of disasters in the closing years of the century that impacted its economy. In 1886, record-low temperatures caused major crop damage. The freeze of February 1895 caused even more havoc, with damages estimated as high as $100 million. After that freeze the major citrus groves were concentrated south of Orlando.[18] The freeze of January 1899 brought snow to Florida, almost two inches in Jacksonville, and some subfreezing temperatures. One result of these freezes was the shift in south Florida from citrus to truck farming. Refrigerated cars carried Florida vegetables and tropical fruits to northern markets.

Yellow fever was a dreaded scourge that periodically appeared in Florida. In 1887 there were reported cases in Key West, Manatee, and Tampa. The following summer, the epidemic spread to Jacksonville, with 4,656 cases of fever and 427 deaths. Many people fled the city in terror, and most businesses closed down except for the hospitals and undertakers. To maintain better control of epidemics and health conditions, the legislature in 1889 created the State Board of Public Health with headquarters in Jacksonville. Dr. Joseph Y. Porter of Key West became the first state health officer.

Because of its proximity to Cuba, its substantial Hispanic population, and its long historical association with the island, Florida was early involved in the events leading up to the Spanish-American War. Tampa became the major port of embarkation for American troops en route to Cuba. General Staff officers were lodged at the Tampa Bay Hotel, along with a large number of newspaper correspondents, including some from Europe. There were training camps in Jacksonville, Fernandina, Miami, and Lakeland. William Jennings Bryan was stationed for a short while at Camp Cuba Libre in Jacksonville. Key West was a bustling port. This "short and splendid war" profited Florida greatly, particularly the towns where military personnel were stationed. The war advertised Florida and provided another opportunity to attract settlers and tourists, something that the state needed to pull it out of the economic depression that began in 1893.

By the beginning of the twentieth century, Florida's economy was stronger and more diversified than at any time since the Civil War. Citrus growers, recouping from the calamitous freezes, were shipping oranges and grapefruit to markets all over the United States and even to

Europe. Cattle raising in the area north of Lake Okeechobee and south of Orlando had long been an important Florida business. There were no fence laws in Florida, and cattle were free to graze on the open range of public lands. While Florida beef was not prize, there was a ready market for both meat and hides. Florida was one of the largest cattle-producing states east of the Mississippi.

Although tobacco had been grown in Florida since the territorial period, it was shade tobacco grown in north Florida that was the most lucrative. Cigar manufacturing was a staple of Key West's economy until the 1880s when it transferred to Tampa, where the workers were Cuban, Italian, and Greek, a diversified population unusual in the South. By 1900, Florida was among the world's largest cigar producers. Lumber, turpentine, and the manufacture of fertilizer were also major Florida industries.

River pebble phosphate was discovered by accident in 1888 along the Peace River, launching an important industry for the state. More discoveries in the Dunnellon area caused a phosphate boom not unlike California's gold rush. Florida became the major world supplier of phosphate, with much of it being shipped out of the port of Jacksonville.

Tourism had been a thriving industry also since before the Civil War. As early as the 1840s, Florida was advertising its advantages and noted that no one needed to "visit Italy or the south of France for the improvement of their health as our climate is equally salubrious." After the war a number of celebrities visited Florida and advertised its wonders. Whitelaw Reid described the state as a "grand national sanitarium." There were well-publicized visits by General Robert E. Lee, the poet William Cullen Bryant, former president Ulysses S. Grant, president-to-be Chester Arthur, and President and Mrs. Grover Cleveland. Henry Flagler's and Henry Plant's railroads and steamship lines provided visitors with the means of traveling to Florida, and their luxurious hotels provided comfortable places to stay. Tourism in those years was geared to the affluent visitors who arrived for the winter season— January, February, and March. Flagler's own magnificent Palm Beach mansion, Whitehall, which he built as a wedding present for his third wife, provided a setting for great balls and receptions.

The Progressive Era, the period after 1896, impacted Florida as it did the rest of the South and country. State and local governments were responding to the demands for change in matters relating to public health, child labor, school attendance laws, and the creation of more ameliorative institutions. These things were accomplished in Florida through a government that was dominated by Democratic Party whites.

The white primary had finally eliminated black voters, and Jim Crow legislation had sealed blacks into a segregated world. A Republican Party would continue to function, but it was mainly for the purpose of dispensing federal patronage.

Florida's population in 1900 (421,511 persons) was still predominantly rural; 80 percent of these people lived outside the towns and cities. The state was divided into two political factions. One group— the Progressive-Populists—included farmers and small businessmen, known as the "wool hats." The "silk hats" included the more conservative corporate-railroad interests, land developers and speculators, bankers, and professionals such as lawyers and accountants.

William Sherman Jennings, who served as governor from 1901 to 1905, greatly accelerated the Progressive movement in Florida. Through the courts he successfully recouped some of the public lands that Florida had so generously granted to railroad builders and other corporate interests. The state railroad commission after 1900 quickly gained more regulatory power. By 1911 all consolidation, leasing, or purchasing of railway lines had to have commission approval.

With the beginning of the twentieth century women began to play a more active and visible role in public life. This was certainly the case with Jennings's spouse, May Mann, a woman of intelligence, vision, and energy, who for over half of the century encouraged her gender to come out of the kitchen and the schoolroom, to which in large measure women had been relegated since colonial times, and to make a difference in the quality of Florida's political and social development. By 1914, when she became president of the Florida Federation of Women's Clubs, she was without question the most influential woman in the state. From her home in Jacksonville she directed an "old-girl" network that struggled in the public arena on behalf of women's suffrage, the Democratic Party, conservation of the natural environment, and reservations for the Seminoles, as well as for the establishment of compulsory education, stock fence laws, the Florida State Library in Tallahassee, and a State Park Service. When in 1947 President Harry S. Truman dedicated the new Everglades National Park, it was the culmination of a thirty-three-year-long fight that May Mann Jennings had waged to preserve the beauty and uniqueness of the glades. Her biographer concluded that, by the date of her death in 1963, she stood forth as "Florida's most impressive and successful female citizen."[19]

Many fundamental changes were taking place in Florida education. Under the leadership of State School Superintendent William N. Sheats, strides were made in building more schools, in demanding that teachers

May Mann Jennings, Florida's most prominent woman citizen in the first half of the twentieth century. Photograph taken on 8 January 1901, the day of her husband's inauguration as the state's first twentieth-century governor.

be more proficient, and in forcing more students to attend schools for longer periods of time. By the beginning of the century, more than 71 percent of Florida's children of school age were attending school.

In 1905, the state was supporting a number of so-called institutions of higher learning scattered around Florida. They were not being adequately funded, and they did not rank with colleges elsewhere in the South. The legislature in 1905 passed the Buckman Act which created three new institutions: the University of Florida for white male students in Gainesville; the Florida Female College in Tallahassee (after 1909 the Florida State College for Women); and the Colored Normal School in Tallahassee (later Florida Agricultural and Mechanical College). A school for deaf, speech-impaired, and blind children in St. Augustine was also authorized.

Several religious denominations supported private educational institutions in Florida. The Methodists funded Florida Southern College, which moved from Leesburg to a site near Clearwater in 1906, then later relocated in Lakeland. Rollins College, named for Alonzo W. Rollins of Chicago, opened in Winter Park in 1885 with support from the Florida Congregational Association. Stetson University began in 1883 with thirteen students and help from the Florida Baptist Convention. John B. Stetson was its benefactor, and the school took his name in 1899. The following year, it opened the first law school in Florida. The renowned black educator Mary McLeod Bethune started the Daytona Literary and Industrial Training School for Negro Girls in 1904. In 1923, it would become Bethune-Cookman College. Edward Waters College, with roots going back into the 1860s, operated as a school for blacks in Jacksonville.

More than any other political leader, Governor Napoleon Bonaparte Broward was the leading spokesman for the Progressive movement in Florida. A native of Duval County, he became famous as a filibusterer supplying guns to the Cuban rebels before the Spanish-American War. In 1904, he launched his gubernatorial campaign as the liberal, anti-railroad, anticorporation candidate and was elected with strong wool hat support. During his administration both the railroad commission and the primary system were strengthened. Broward began the Everglades drainage program which was aimed at making thousands of acres of rich muckland available for agricultural development. The concept was to dig drainage canals that would allow surplus water to drain off into the Atlantic Ocean and the Gulf of Mexico.[20] While it helped to open the south Florida area for development, this ill-advised program greatly damaged the environment and eventually threatened the water

Napoleon Bonaparte Broward, a native of Duval County, was governor of Florida from 1905 to 1909, a time when the state had a population of about 530,000 people, smallest of any of the southern states. By his energetic leadership and charisma, Broward became the leader of the Populist-Progressive movement in the South, speaking with effectiveness to the needs and aspirations of the laborer and farmer. In his own state he pushed through farm-to-market road construction, social services, tax reform, child labor laws, railroad regulations, increased pay for teachers, a unified system of higher education, and drainage in the Everglades for the development of muckland agriculture.

supply for a vast region of the state. By 1913, over $2 million had been spent to complete 142 miles of canals and construct two locks.

Broward served only one term as governor (1905–9), but his political philosophy and program were so dominant that the Progressive Era in Florida is often called the Broward Era. While neither of the two governors who followed him, Albert W. Gilchrist or Park Trammell, was as liberally oriented as Broward, the state did not abandon its progressive program. Business continued to expand, although organized labor faced many obstacles, particularly after the panic of 1907 and the economic recession that followed. Opposition came from both the business community and the general public. City newspapers like the *Florida Times-Union* in Jacksonville and the *Tallahassee Democrat* were strongly opposed to unions.

A new Florida emerged in the twentieth century. Population grew steadily, about equal to the national average. The federal census in 1900 listed a population of 528,542 persons. Peninsular Florida grew actively: Hillsborough County by 141 percent between 1890 and 1900 and, the most spectacular growth in that decade, Dade County by almost 500 percent. In 1910 the state's population was 752,619 persons. Jacksonville was the largest city with 28,249 persons, followed by Pensacola, Key West, and Tampa. In May 1901, a fire in Jacksonville devastated almost the entire city; 146 blocks and all but one public building were destroyed. Rebuilding started immediately, and by 1913 most of the scars had been erased. Many of the new structures—business buildings, apartment houses, and private residences—were designed by the renowned Prairie School architect Henry J. Klutho.

Most of Florida's growth came in the white population. The black population declined steadily from nearly 50 percent of the total at the beginning of the Civil War.

Florida had long been known as a place for settlement by retirees. The salubrious climate and low cost of living made a move to Florida attractive. The state accelerated its efforts to attract new settlers of all ages by instituting a liberal taxation system. This effort was supported by private land developers like the United Land Company, which had purchased the Disston land, and the Model Land Company, which was selling the acreage granted to Flagler. Swamplands were drained and forests cleared to be replaced by scores of new communities.

In addition to expanded railroad mileage, the automobile made its advent. Every car owner had to register his vehicle with the secretary of state and pay a $2.00 annual tax. Beginning in 1911, cars had to display a license tag. Agitation for the establishment of a good road system grew

The most devastating fire ever to engulf a southern city struck Jacksonville shortly after noon on 3 May 1901. Fiber laid outside a factory caught fire, and wind-blown sparks ignited nearby combustible wooden roofs. The flames spread through the drought-dry city as rapidly, it was said, as a man could walk. By 7:30 P.M., when the wind died, most of the city's downtown area was destroyed and 10,000 residents were left homeless. This view after the fire looks down Forsyth Street from the top of the Federal Building.

as the automobile became more popular. The first road department was established during the Trammell administration, and license fees helped pay for city and county road construction and paving. Both automobiles and Florida enjoyed national publicity when racing began on the hardpacked sand at Daytona Beach in 1903.

Prohibition, resisted by the liquor distributors and saloon keepers, had been widely debated in Florida for decades. It was the major issue in the Democratic gubernatorial campaign in 1908. Many counties were already dry at the time, but the new governor, Albert Gilchrist, saw the need for a statewide referendum. As a result, by the time the Eighteenth Amendment was added to the federal Constitution in 1919, Florida was totally dry. During the campaign and throughout his administration, Gilchrist proved to be a middle-of-the-road politician. Early in his public career he had adopted the motto "Hear no evil, speak no evil, see no evil." Pursuing a policy of fiscal conservatism, he was able to bequeath a cash balance of over $373,000 to his successor.

Former attorney-general Park Trammell was elected governor in 1912. In the presidential election that year Democratic voters supported Woodrow Wilson, although only the *Miami Metropolis* among the Florida dailies had endorsed him when he was first nominated. Trammell bolstered the Progressive programs that had been instituted earlier and initiated legislation that would make government more responsive to voters. A primary law enacted in 1913 imposed a ceiling of $4,000 on campaign expenditures and eliminated runoff primaries by substituting second-choice votes. It resulted in a confusing situation for voters in 1916 when Sidney J. Catts waged a fierce gubernatorial battle against William V. Knott of Tallahassee, a former state treasurer and now state comptroller, who had the backing of the Democratic Party.

Catts, a Baptist preacher and part-time insurance salesman from De-Funiak Springs, was one of the most colorful and controversial politicians ever to be elected governor of Florida. Without a strong political organization and lacking financial support, he represented himself as the champion of the poor people in perhaps the wildest campaign in Florida's history. He strongly supported prohibition, but his greatest enemy was the Roman Catholic Church. He played upon the fears and suspicions of Protestant fundamentalists who believed that Catholics were inherently evil and a threat to society. Knott defeated Catts in the Democratic primary by a slim twenty-one-vote margin. Catts then ran in the general election as the underdog, and, with the support of the Prohibition Party, he won the governorship.

Throughout his four years in office, Catts was criticized for using the spoils system and for placing relatives on the state's payroll. He appointed his son state adjutant general. But his legislative record included many constructive features, including an effort to eliminate the convict lease system. Prohibition of the manufacture, sale, or use of alcoholic beverages in Florida was enacted in 1917, but most of the state was already dry. The Nineteenth Amendment was added to the U.S. Constitution in 1920, but Florida ratification did not come until 1969. Florida women, however, began to vote in 1920 and to play an active role in politics.

The United States declared war against Germany on 6 April 1917, and two days later the Florida Naval Militia was ordered to duty. A total of 42,030 Floridians served during the conflict. Five of the thirty-five flying schools in the country were in the state, the most important at Pensacola. Key West was the site of a submarine base and naval training station, where Thomas A. Edison worked on the development of depth bombs. There were large shipyards in Jacksonville and Tampa, and lumber and allied products were in great demand. There was also a demand for Florida-grown fruits and vegetables. Florida came out of World War I as a growing, prospering state.

Notes

1. *Tallahassee Floridian,* 2 January 1877; *Jacksonville Daily Florida Union,* 3 January 1877.
2. *Florida Senate Journal,* 1877, pp. 37–49; *Florida Assembly Journal,* 1877, pp. 27–28.
3. Edward C. Williamson, "George F. Drew, Florida's Redemption Governor," *Florida Historical Quarterly* 38, no. 3 (January 1960):206–15.
4. Edward C. Williamson, *Florida Politics in the Gilded Age, 1877–1893* (Gainesville: University Presses of Florida, 1976), pp. 72–78.
5. Of two recently published biographies of Flagler, the more comprehensive is Edward N. Akin's *Flagler: Rockefeller Partner and Florida Baron* (Kent, Ohio: Kent State University Press, 1988). The other is David Leon Chandler, *Henry Flagler: The Astonishing Life and Time of the Visionary Robber Baron Who Founded Florida* (New York: Macmillan, 1986).
6. Williamson, *Florida Politics,* pp. 104–5, 124–27.
7. *Florida Laws,* 1887, chap. 3746.
8. Charlton W. Tebeau, *A History of Florida* (Coral Gables: University of Miami Press, 1971), pp. 297–98; Peter D. Klingman, *Neither Dies Nor Surrenders: A History of the Republican Party in Florida, 1867–1970* (Gainesville: University Presses of Florida, 1984), pp. 86–87.
9. Samuel Proctor, "The National Farmers' Alliance Convention of 1890 and Its 'Ocala Demands,'" *Florida Historical Quarterly* 28, no. 3 (January 1950):161–81.
10. Williamson, *Florida Politics,* p. 174.
11. Williamson, "William D. Chipley, West Florida's Mr. Railroad," *Florida Historical Quarterly* 25, no. 4 (April 1947):341–45; *Tallahassee Daily Florida,* 14, 16, 23 April, 12, 20, 26 May 1891.
12. Tebeau, *History of Florida,* p. 302.
13. Ibid., pp. 302–4.
14. *Journal of the Proceedings of the Constitutional Convention of the State of Florida,* 1885, p. 612.
15. Ibid., pp. 616, 216–17.
16. Williamson, *Florida Politics,* pp. 159–60.
17. *Florida Senate Journal 1889,* pp. 766–67; *Florida House Journal,* 1889, pp. 591, 995–1000; *Florida Laws,* 1889, chaps. 3850, 3879.
18. Jerry Woods Weeks, "Florida Gold: The Emergence of the Florida Citrus Industry, 1865–1895 (Ph.D. diss., University of North Carolina, 1977), pp. 216–18.
19. Linda D. Vance, *May Mann Jennings: Florida's Genteel Activist* (Gainesville: University Presses of Florida, 1985), p. 140.
20. Samuel Proctor, *Napoleon Bonaparte Broward, Florida's Fighting Democrat* (Gainesville: University of Florida Press, 1950), pp. 240–50.

Bibliography

Abbey, Kathryn T. "Florida Versus the Principles of Populism, 1896–1911." *Journal of Southern History* 4, no. 4 (November 1938):462–75.

Adams, Charles S. *Report of the Jacksonville Auxiliary Sanitary Association of Jacksonville, Florida.* Jacksonville: Times Union, 1889.

Carson, Ruby Leach. "William Dunnington Bloxham: Florida's First Two-Term Governor." Master's thesis, University of Florida, 1945.

Cash, William T. *A History of the Democratic Party in Florida.* Tallahassee: Florida Democratic Historical Foundation, 1936.

Church, George B., Jr. "Henry Laurens Mitchell." Master's thesis, University of Florida, 1969.

Dovell, Junius E. "A History of the Everglades of Florida." Ph.D. dissertation, University of North Carolina, 1947.

Flynt, Wayne. *Cracker Messiah: Governor Sidney J. Catts of Florida.* Baton Rouge: Louisiana State University Press, 1977.

———. "William V. Knott and the Gubernatorial Campaign of 1916." *Florida Historical Quarterly* 51, no. 4 (April 1973):423–30.

Graham, Thomas. "Flagler's Magnificent Hotel Ponce de Leon," *Florida Historical Quarterly* 54, no. 1 (July 1975):1–17.

Kerber, Stephen. "Park Trammell: A Political Biography." Ph.D. dissertation, University of Florida, 1979.

Lanier, Sidney. *Florida: Its Scenery, Climate and History.* Philadelphia, 1875; reprint ed., Gainesville: University of Florida Press, 1973.

Parker, Oswald L. "William N. Sheats, Florida Educator." Master's thesis, University of Florida, 1948.

Pettengill, George W. *The Story of Florida Railroads, 1834–1903.* Boston: Railway & Locomotive Historical Society, 1952.

Proctor, Samuel. *Napoleon Bonaparte Broward, Florida's Fighting Democrat.* Gainesville: University of Florida Press, 1950.

Schellings, William J. "The Role of Florida in the Spanish-American War 1898." Ph.D. dissertation, University of Florida, 1958.

Shofner, Jerrell H. "Florida in the Balance: The Electoral Count of 1876." *Florida Historical Quarterly* 47, no. 2 (October 1968):122–50.

Staid, Sister Mary Elizabeth. "Albert Walker Gilchrist, Florida's Middle of the Road Governor." Master's thesis, University of Florida, 1950.

Vance, Linda D. *May Mann Jennings, Florida's Genteel Activist.* Gainesville: University Presses of Florida, 1980.

Williamson, Edward C. "Independentism: A Challenge to the Florida Democracy of 1884." *Florida Historical Quarterly* 27, no. 2 (October 1948):131–56.

Ziegler, Louis W., and Herbert S. Wolfe. *Citrus Growing in Florida.* Gainesville: University of Florida Press, 1961.

16 Fortune and Misfortune: The Paradoxical Twenties

William W. Rogers

Florida's social matrix in the 1920s combined reality and fantasy. Its parts included people, land, automobiles and highways, banks, hurricanes, insects (Mediterranean fruit flies, mosquitoes, and ticks), and the intangible—but no less real—emotions of greed, optimism, faith, and despair. Politics was less prominent than usual, but there was no lack of strong candidates and hard-fought campaigns. The biggest race of 1920, a year in which women gained the right to vote with the adoption of the Nineteenth Amendment, was for the U.S. Senate. It was decided by the Democratic primary victory of incumbent conservative-progressive Duncan U. Fletcher over the populist and flamboyant governor Sydney J. Catts. In the general election Fletcher easily defeated his Socialist and Republican opponents.

The state's one-party system had been dominated since the end of Reconstruction by the Democrats, whose shibboleths were honesty, frugality, efficiency in government, and white supremacy. Tainted by the alleged and real corruption of Reconstruction, the Republicans offered only token opposition. Nomination in the Democratic primary guaranteed victory in the general election. Black voters had been disfranchised, first by extralegal means and since the 1890s by legal means, especially by laws that permitted Democratic officials to exclude them from participating in the primaries. Beyond that, the poll tax eliminated many black voters (and poor whites as well). By the 1920s black citizens were not a viable part of the political process.

In the 1920 gubernatorial primary Cary A. Hardee, a Live Oak banker and lawyer, won over two rivals before vanquishing his Republican and Socialist adversaries in the general election. In the primary for that office in 1924, John W. Martin, a lawyer and long-time mayor of Jacksonville, ran as the businessman's candidate. Emphasizing a road-building program, he was nominated over three opponents. Two years later, Senator Fletcher won another term with his primary victory over Florida's colorful hotel commissioner, Jerry W. Carter, a Catts appointee. In 1920 and 1924, Republicans won the White House, but Florida routinely awarded its electoral votes to Democrats James M. Cox and John W. Davis.

Vote tallies in 1928 produced no surprises at the state level, but Florida joined four other states in deviating from the South's solid Democratic norm in the national presidential contest, which pitted Republican Herbert Hoover against New York's Democratic governor Alfred E. Smith. Wauchula's Doyle E. Carlton, descendant of a pioneer family, defeated four primary opponents, including perennial candidate Catts, in the gubernatorial race. Catts supported the victorious Hoover, but Carlton went on to win the general election. U.S. Senator Park Trammell defeated former governor John Martin in the primary and easily bested Republican Barclay H. Warburton.

Al Smith had won the Democratic presidential nomination without any delegate support from Florida. Senator Joseph T. Robinson of Arkansas had received the vice-presidential nomination to placate southern voters, most of them Protestants who opposed electing a Catholic president. Smith's liabilities in Florida and the South included his "shanty Irish" immigrant background, ties with Tammany Hall and eastern big city politics, and opposition to Prohibition. His East Side accent and wardrobe of spats, bowler derby, and striped suits further repelled southern voters. Many Florida politicians gave only tepid support to the national ticket. Local and statewide church groups, antiliquor organizations, and civic leaders endorsed Hoover. Many women voters also approved of the Republican candidate's support of prohibition. Besides, Hoover promised to continue Republican prosperity begun under Calvin Coolidge, and by 1928, still reeling from a real estate bust, Floridians had good cause to want prosperity.

Hoover received 144,168 votes to Al Smith's 101,764, and carried Florida with 56.8 percent of the popular vote. Socialist Norman Thomas got 4,036 votes and Communist William Z. Foster 3,704. Large victory margins by other Democratic candidates in the state suggested no massive shift by white voters to the Republican party. Their voting patterns in the 1930s would remain solidly Democratic. Hoover owed his victory to special circumstances: Democratic overconfidence, the Prohibition issue, and strong religious feelings of Florida's voters.

Too much was going on in Florida during the 1920s for citizens to concentrate solely on politics. Prohibition, for example, went into effect in 1919. Subsequently, enforcement became a major problem. With 3,800 miles of tidal shoreline containing an extensive system of bays and inlets, Florida became a major port of entry for alcoholic beverages. Airplanes, speedboats, and other vessels came in under cover of darkness from the Bahamas and Caribbean islands. While smugglers operated with near impunity, native Floridians set up moonshine stills and put their imaginations to full use devising innovative marketing techniques. One Duval County bootlegger was caught dispensing "white lightning" from the back of a truck where he kept it hidden beneath sacks of pecans and sweet potatoes.

As one British traveler put it, "Florida, from my personal experience in it, was the wettest country I have ever known."[1] Noted gangster Al Capone, no novice to liquor trafficking, came to Miami in the 1920s, presumably to escape the stress of Chicago and Cicero, Illinois. However law-abiding he may have tried to be, the mobster's presence set off official but unsuccessful efforts to bar him from the state.

Religion, especially the modernist-fundamentalist controversy over teaching evolution in the public schools, also diverted attention from politics. Florida remained a Protestant stronghold, although it had substantial numbers of Catholics and Jews. Many whites and blacks were devout church members, and ministers, especially black ministers, exercised great influence in their communities. An eclectic theological domain, Florida sheltered groups ranging from evangelical preachers thundering hellfire and damnation to tent audiences to Episcopalian ministers intoning scriptures to upper-class congregations.

The Great Commoner, William Jennings Bryan, three-time Democratic presidential candidate who had made Florida his residence, was a devout fundamentalist, as were many educational, civic, and political leaders. Despite pressure from such persons, and numerous heated debates on the subject, the state—unlike Tennessee, Arkansas, and Mississippi—did not statutorily forbid the teaching of evolution in the public schools. Such acts were known popularly as Monkey Laws. Even so, in 1923 the legislature did pass a joint resolution opposing the teaching of Darwinian thought. There was on-going controversy over bills banning textbooks that denied spontaneous creation as described in the book of *Genesis*, and certain scientific books were placed on restricted use or were taken from university and college library shelves, but no anti-evolution law passed as such. The controversy did not end until well after the Scopes trial in 1925 at Dayton, Tennessee.

Fundamentalists also frowned on gambling. They and a majority of citizens did not approve of efforts to establish thoroughbred racing in Florida. Despite antibetting laws, sporadic meets were held in the 1920s at sportsman Frank A. Kenney's track between Jacksonville and St. Augustine. In 1925 Joseph M. Smoot's Miami Jockey Club (renamed Hialeah in 1931) opened. But public outcry curtailed racing until the 1931 legislature, desperate to raise revenue, legalized pari-mutuel wagering.

Politics and popular distractions aside, the state's spectacular land boom became the main object of attention. It remained so until supplanted by an equally spectacular bust. In economic decline at the turn of the decade, Florida was on the road to prosperity by 1923. The rapid recovery was based largely on a dramatic rise in real estate transactions and land development. The phenomenon began at Miami Beach, spread through Dade County, moved up the east and west coasts, and infused central Florida before finding its way north to Tallahassee and west to the Panhandle. To many Florida seemed a lotus land, and there was no shortage of individuals anxious to exploit its potential.

Near-legendary figures of Florida's development included John Collins, who created Miami Beach from mangrove swamps and salt marshes in the 1910s. His efforts were furthered by Carl G. Fisher, an Indiana native. Nearby to the south, George E. Merrick promoted Coral Gables, a planned community featuring Mediterranean architecture and distinguished by an artful blending of exotic landscaping and canals. Northward lay Hollywood, another designed community founded in 1921 by Joseph W. Young and his California associates. Even farther north, Addison Mizner, an extraordinary promoter-architect, designed homes for the wealthy at Palm Beach. His Mediterranean style was enhanced by the use of pastel colors—utilitarian in combatting the sun's rays and aesthetic in their soft-hued variety. Backed by eastern millionaires, Mizner's most ambitious project was Boca Raton. Unfortunately, he fell victim to the collapse of the land boom, and his corporation failed in 1926.

Elsewhere, other projects transformed the state. The distance between Tampa and St. Petersburg was more than halved by George S. Gandy's toll bridge, erected with financial assistance from St. Petersburg promoter Eugene M. Elliott. In Tampa, D. P. "Doc" Davis converted three land spits into the lucrative Davis Islands network, but another Davis effort failed at St. Augustine with the end of the land boom. Orlando's growth resulted from the early work of H. Carl Dann. William Lee Popham of Kentucky, a Baptist minister who combined oyster production with real estate deals, raised hopes in the Apalachicola area. His ventures on St. George Island ultimately failed but not before his fame spread far and wide. Pensacola, Panama City, and Jacksonville also expanded, and supposedly staid Tallahassee opened numerous subdivisions.

Chambers of Commerce advertised their cities and initiated beautification projects, as the state touted its advantages and strengthened its transportation network. Public auctions of lots attracted large crowds and combined economics with entertainment. Private business groups trumpeted the message that one did not have to be rich to own a winter home in Florida. No less an authority than the Bible was utilized to lure settlers. One promoter quoted chapter and verse: "Arise, and go toward the south" (*Acts*, 8:26); "I have bought a piece of ground and I must needs go and see it" (*Luke*, 14:18); and "Search you out a place to pitch your tents in" (*Deuteronomy*, 1:33).

Railroad construction increased, and trains traveling on the rival Seaboard Air Line and Atlantic Coast Line roads were packed with passengers. Thousand of Americans still had savings accumulated from wartime prosperity. Florida was easily accessible to most states east of the Mississippi River, and countless northerners longed to exchange cold winters for the semitropical paradise. So much of the state was still undeveloped that land was supposedly inexpensive. Urged on by controversial state comptroller Ernest Amos, state senator John P. Stokes of Pensacola, and others with eyes toward improving the money crop, the legislature amended the state constitution to prohibit income taxes and inheritance taxes. One newspaper commented perceptively that the move was "a very unique way of encouraging capitalists and investors to bring their money to this state."[2]

Real estate promoters and developers swarmed into Florida, and an estimated 300,000 people settled there between 1923 and 1925. Thirteen new counties were created, nine of them in south Florida. One result of the boom was a permanent population increase. Florida started the 1920s with 968,470 people, and by 1930 had 1,468,211. The white population rose from 638,153 to 1,035,205, blacks from 329,487 to 431,828. The number of men and women in both races was almost equally divided. Jacksonville remained the largest city (129,549), but Miami had moved from fourth place to second by 1930. Florida's urban population in 1930 was 72.3 percent white and 27.7 percent black.

An awed northern journalist asked, "Was there ever anything like

Land auctions were conducted everywhere in Florida during the 1920s land boom. Often what was offered was just-filled mangrove swamps or just-cleared pinelands, with rough-scraped dirt roads to outline subdivisions. But in the land delirium of mid-decade, even that sold quickly to northern "snowbirds" who wanted a piece of paradise. Bused to these rude sites by spellbinding promoters, their phantasmagoria was such that, having alighted, the visitors beheld not a barren landscape but a mirage of finished pleasure domes waiting for occupancy.

the migration to Florida? From the time the Hebrews went into Egypt, or since the hegira of Mohammed the prophet, what can compare to this evacuation? The Forty-Niners did not go out in such great numbers, nor can the gold rush to the Klondike be put in the same class with this flight to Florida. Entire populations are moving away bodily. The personal columns of our local press are unable to chronicle the daily departures."[3]

In 1925 alone, 2.5 million tourists visited Florida. The majority arrived by automobile on an expanding road system. Jacksonville and Lake City were the main entry points. Floridians, like other Americans, loved automobiles and by 1916 owned ninety different models. Besides those familiar today, they favored such cars as the Aurora, Metz, Kritt, Regal, Peerless, and Empire. By the 1920s assembly line production and installment buying made Model T Fords and similar cars inexpensive and available to the masses so that less affluent citizens could afford transportation to Florida. Cars arrived packed with people and supplies. Their occupants camped out, thus creating tourist camps. In 1919, at

Tampa's DeSoto Park, a number of them happily adopted an egalitarian nickname, the "Tin Can Tourists of the World." Annual meetings were held among parked vehicles and pitched tents, as visitors engaged in socializing, dancing, eating, and sports. Privately owned tourist courts opened, and Florida was on the threshold of achieving what became its mammoth motel industry.

The creation of a state road department in 1915 enabled Florida to take advantage of the Federal Road Aid Act of 1916 and the Federal Highway Act of 1921. The section of U.S. 90 between Jacksonville and Lake City opened in 1923 as the state's first concrete highway. Later, it was extended to Pensacola. Not far behind were north-south connectors U.S. 1, 41, and 27. Earlier plans for the Tamiami Trail connecting Fort Myers and Miami were resurrected, and the highway across the Everglades was officially opened on 25 April 1928. Florida entered the decade with fewer than 1,000 miles of roadway, but by 1930 had 3,800 miles surfaced with everything from clay to grouted brick, Macadam, concrete, and asphalt.

Airplanes, as well as automobiles, revolutionized transportation, and by the end of the twenties commercial airlines were carrying passengers to and within Florida. The first airplane flight in Florida was at Orlando in 1910, and the state's first airport opened at Miami Beach in 1912. By 1926 nine Florida cities had airports, and early mail flights had added passengers. Eastern Air Transport (later Eastern Airlines) and Pan American were among the burgeoning and increasingly important corporations offering passenger service.

To accommodate newcomers eager to invest in Miami real estate, a large freelance sales force emerged. Called "Binder Boys," these fast-talking hucksters, in golf knickers and two-toned shoes, purchased lots for 10 percent down (a binder that held a property for thirty days), then sold the binders for a profit to other speculators. A binder could be sold and resold many times before payment became due. Paper profits rose to dizzying heights. At one time Miami had 25,000 such street brokers, many of them men who had quit jobs in the North as butchers, taxi drivers, or railroad conductors, to take advantage of the Florida bonanza. Promoting real estate, not necessarily selling it, became another industry, with such luminaries as William Jennings Bryan, who informed outlanders about the attractions of Merrick's Coral Gables.

By 1925 the *Miami Herald* was the world's largest newspaper in terms of advertising lineage. One issue of the *Miami News* set a record by publishing 22 sections containing a total of 504 pages. Clearly ignored, one critic observed, were certain biblical admonitions: "If riches increase, set not your heart upon them" (*Psalms*, 62:10) and "Thou shall neither vex a stranger nor oppress him" (*Exodus*, 22:21).

Property prices soared with inflated land values and affected the entire economy: transportation, construction, and banking. Some worried that if all of Florida basked in the sunshine of prosperity, a collapse would be equally widespread, but it seemed folly to engage in such gloomy musings when there was so much profit to be made. One movie of 1923 that attracted Floridians to theaters (also growing in number) was appropriately titled "Money, Money, Money."

The expansion of banking was a concrete indication of economic growth. State and national bank deposits peaked in 1925 at $900 million. The number of national banks increased but lagged behind new state banks that benefitted from lower capital requirements and less strict regulations for loans and investments. When 1923 ended, Florida had 194 banks. The state comptroller and his increased staff moved into more commodious quarters. The legislature failed to enact any major banking laws, and the comptroller boasted that in the typical Florida bank "deposits exceed loans by a very material and substantial margin."[4] No national banks failed from 1920 until 1925, but, ominously, in the same period eighty state banks failed.

The years 1925 and 1926 were pivotal for Florida. Problems began in 1925 with a national backlash of hostility against the excesses of the real estate boom. Promoters and "Binder Boys" were lacerated by the northern press. Governor Martin and a group of leading Floridians met with editors and publishers at the Waldorf Astoria Hotel in New York City. Their mollifying efforts to "tell the truth about Florida" were not completely successful.

The problems were compounded when, in October 1925, a strike on the Atlantic Coast Line Railroad swamped competing lines with freight. The Interstate Commerce Commission called an embargo so that railyards and freight houses could be cleared of the backlog. In the meantime, Florida builders were left without materials, retailers could not obtain merchandise, and travelers—frustrated by cancellations and long delays—raised an angry chorus. In January 1926, a ship sank in Miami harbor and further disrupted the flow of supplies. The embargo was short lived, but trains ran irregularly as late as February and thousands of vacationers spurned Florida. Their boycott dealt the economy a stinging jolt.

The most dramatic blow was just that: a violent hurricane that ripped across south Florida in September 1926, killing 400 people, injuring 6,300, and leaving 50,000 homeless. Many newcomers abruptly left the

A languorous day, 7 May 1926, at Boca Grande Beach near Charlotte Harbor. The Florida real estate boom had collapsed, but the sun still shone and the water was fine.

state but not before withdrawing their money from banks. Realtors and developers began leaving also, and, adding to the problems, the cost of living soared. The boom was over, and worse conditions lay ahead. Few Floridians who had basked in prosperity just one year before would have predicted such an abrupt reversal.

The banking situation remained volatile. Sheer volume of activity forced an increase in the number of state bank examiners to eight. A new law required state banks to be examined annually and "more often if necessary."[5] Comptroller Amos, who had easily been reelected in 1924, was full of confidence and exhibited impressive statistics about 1925. As illustrated by his example, there was an absence of prudence and cautious skepticism in Florida. H. R. Doughy, sales manager and lecturer for Daytona Shores, said, "The sunshine state is now entering upon the most extraordinary era of substantial growth and business activity ever known in the history of the world." The January 1926 issue of a national financial journal featured several articles on Florida's economic stability. Governor Martin and the mayor of Miami were among its contributors. Speculating on the future the publication's editor declared, "The bubble will not burst for the very good reason that there is no bubble."[6]

The truth was that in 1925 and 1926 numerous Floridians went from

On the night of 18 September 1926, a hurricane packing winds of 130 to 150 miles an hour caught the boomtime population of Dade County unaware. Ninety-two coastal residents were killed by the storm, the first in the region since 1910; another 300 were drowned at Moore Haven in the interior. Over 600 persons were injured and 18,000 made homeless. From Miami (see downtown damage, *above*) to Fort Lauderdale, 5,000 homes were destroyed and 9,000 were damaged. Boomtime tent cities and tourist camps were leveled. Two years later, almost to the day (16 September), a hurricane of equal strength hit the Florida shoreline at Palm Beach and caused Lake Okeechobee to overflow, deluging surrounding communities. Nearly 2,000 persons drowned, three-quarters of them black farm workers.

riches to rags, and sometimes not even rags were left. As 1925 ended, even Comptroller Amos grew glum and admonished state banks to maintain strong cash positions. He wanted "plenty leeway" between deposits and loans.[7] The directive was academic. It was already too late. Inflation was at its peak. Although the average state bank had a comfortable cash reserve in 1925, the new year was a different story. Money flowed out and deposits dropped as previously stable banks had difficulty obtaining call money. Emergency meetings produced some funds but not enough to meet needs, and banks saw their cash reserves melt away.

Bank heads and state officials met to discuss a crisis they could not solve. Unable to maintain cash reserves, more banks failed in the last months of 1926. A stoical Amos appealed for calm. One newspaper warned against rumors and innuendoes: "The whisperer who talks about banks is a good deal like the purveyor of backstairs gossip about a good woman. They are equally dangerous members of society."[8] An additional serious problem resulted from various Florida cities floating large bond issues, which caused a slump in the bond market.

Despite a reeling economy, Floridians partly regained their optimism in 1927 and 1928 as tourism rebounded and real estate made a comeback. The two years proved only a prelude, though, to the stock market crash of 1929. During the period even national banks were hard pressed to hold their own. It was probably just as well that Florida's citizens could not foresee coming afflictions.

With some exceptions, state banks suffered crippling declines in deposits, loans, and cash reserves. In 1927 many were unable to meet depositors' demands, and failures became daily headlines. Amos was indicted in 1927 on charges of permitting two insolvent banks to remain open, but the state supreme court ruled in his favor. Unchastened and undaunted, he was reelected in 1928, carrying every county and receiving more votes than any candidate for state office. Other questionable activities earned the comptroller additional charges in 1930, but again the court dismissed the case. One cynical observer was prompted to declare that Florida needed "more bankers in Raiford [prison], and more leadership in Tallahassee."[9]

The state's malaise would soon be repeated nationally. A restoration of public confidence in Florida's banking institutions was needed, but conferences of state leaders failed to restore morale. Few doubted that the boom was over. Walter Fuller, a candid land developer in St. Petersburg, wrote, "We just ran out of suckers. That's all. We got all their money, then started trading with ourselves. . . . That isn't quite correct. We became the suckers."[10] A requiem from *The Nation* declared, "Like a mad, bad dream the real-estate delirium passed." The phenomenon "vanished like a soap bubble."[11]

If hope sprang eternal, it was blown away by a series of tropical disturbances followed by a devastating hurricane in the fall of 1928. Floridians had learned something from their 1926 experience, but they could do nothing about a storm that contained wind gusts of 130 miles per hour. Striking first at Palm Beach, the hurricane caused Lake Okeechobee to flood nearby communities. An estimated 2,000 lives were lost. Even that figure may have been low because emergency burials in mass graves proved necessary to avoid the possibility of epidemics. Most of the casualties were black seasonal workers, some of them from the Bahamas.

For some Floridians, Doyle Carlton's election as governor in 1928 signaled better times, but no one realistically expected a return to the halcyon days of the first half of the twenties. Others expected national leadership to revive the state, but President Hoover's administration was crippled by the beginning of the Great Depression. An accumulation of events and circumstances caused the nation's economic collapse: high tariff walls and an insistence on debt repayment in gold effected a drastic decline in the export market; a worldwide glut of raw materials and agricultural products sent prices plummeting; the cost of consumer goods exceeded the range of most Americans' buying power, causing overproduction and rising inventories; and there was a serious maldistribution of the nation's wealth—a few people had too much money, and too many people had too little.

Historians and economists usually date the Great Depression from the panic that hit the Wall Street stock market in late October 1929. Frenzied liquidation ended an unprecedented bull market that had lasted for six years. The collapse in values halted the optimistic and speculative enthusiasm that had permeated American society. Making money had seemed simple and automatic. Now, in October 1929, the country had a bear market, and things were dismally different.

Hoover moved to offset the panic by obtaining promises from management to sustain production and wages and from organized labor not to strike or seek pay increases. Even so, matters grew increasingly worse, while distress of Old Testament proportions continued in much of Florida. In April 1929 the Mediterranean fruit fly was found at a grapefruit grove in Orlando. From there it spread across the state, requiring quarantines and embargoes on the shipment of fruit and agricultural products. The destruction wrought by the insect (the "Medfly" resembled an ordinary house fly but was slightly smaller and had yellow and black wings) forced the destruction of citrus groves and temporarily devastated the industry.

Economic and fruit fly problems notwithstanding, agriculture remained Florida's predominant source of wealth. The number of farms had increased from 54,005 in 1920 to 58,906 in 1930; 5,244 farmers had traded in their mules and horses for tractors; 3,525 farm families had telephones and 7,559 had water piped into their homes. In 1930 the state's 300,000 acres of fruit and truck products represented 10 percent of the total value of such crops in the country. By contrast, Florida's traditional field crops, such as corn and cotton, had declined in value from well over $27 million to about $10.2 million.

The number and worth of livestock increased during the decade. The costly presence of ticks had hampered the cattle industry, but in 1923 a compulsory statewide eradication plan was enacted. The difficulty of rounding up free-ranging livestock caused opposition from some cattlemen, but a tick quarantine was put in place. Some ranchers sold their herds rather than comply, but corrals and dipping vats became commonplace and the program succeeded. Significant and permanent upgrading occurred but was hampered by the lack of a fence law—an acrimonious economic and political issue involving public safety that was not resolved until 1949.

As the twenties came to a close, the large number of bank failures was attributed to an excess of localities dependent on a single industry or crop, too few restrictions on banks, and "too many unknown rascals and bad management."[12] Banking scholar Raymond B. Vickers contends that many banks failed through the machinations of grasping men who were outright crooks. In 1929 the wily Amos told a state bankers' convention that Florida had "new blood and new money" and was "on the road to a safe and sound banking system."[13] With strong public backing, Governor Carlton demanded banking legislation. The legislature responded with a major statute that changed capitalization requirements, tightened loan limitations, limited dividends, raised requirements, and increased bank directors' and stockholders' obligations. Failure continued, but in the fall of 1929 some banks reopened and a few new ones were established.

Many prominent officials, including Senator Fletcher and Governor Carlton, attempted to quiet fears by treating the depression as if it could be talked away or written off with positive thinking. In January 1930 one paper noted, "The state is enjoying its best tourist season. . . . Almost every city and county has pledged itself to its greatest effort this year in construction work. The outlook is indeed bright."[14] Those were hollow words to the person whose property had been lost or whose savings had disappeared. In 1930, Florida's bank failures were still as ubiquitous as mosquitoes.

Looking back over the era, objective Floridians saw a mixed record of accomplishments. Women began entering the work force in greater numbers, but their entrance and acceptance in the professions was slow. In the field of penal reform, Florida abolished the inhuman convict lease system with its lash and sweatbox that had been in place since 1877. Convict leasing by the state was prohibited in 1919 and at the county level in 1923. The latter action resulted from a scandal involving the beating death at a lumber camp of Martin Tabert, a young white man from South Dakota, who had been arrested for vagrancy.

Although public education remained rigidly segregated, the state could claim "progress." In 1920, Florida's school-age population (six to twenty-one years) was 292,199; there were 193,302 whites and 98,898 blacks. Of those, 64 percent of the eligible whites attended school and 47 percent of the blacks. Teaching was one of the few professions in which women were dominant: 5,077 white female teachers as opposed to 902 white males and 1,444 black women teachers contrasted to 196 black men. The doctrine of "separate but equal" as enunciated by the U.S. Supreme Court in 1896 was only half-fulfilled in Florida: separate, yes; equal, no. The average monthly wage in 1920 for a white male teacher was $143.06; his black male counterpart received $71.51. The monthly salaries for white and black women teachers were $99.96 and $51.08, respectively. Total school expenditures for white schools was $8,262,903, for black schools $643,701. Whites were more numerous than blacks, but the lopsided funding indicates a pronounced bias for whites.

Yet there were persons of good faith, such as State Superintendent of Public Instruction W. S. Cawthon, who reported, "While our progress has been slow [in funding education for blacks], still we are getting more definite and tangible results accomplished and under way."[15] No major educational changes were implemented by 1930, although improvements had been made. The number of white and black teachers, their salaries, and the physical plants where they taught reflected the existing Jim Crow society. The average length of the school year for blacks was 132 days, for whites 160 days. In higher education the state provided three public institutions: Florida Agricultural and Mechanical College for Negroes and Florida State College for Women, both at Tallahassee, and the University of Florida, for white males, at Gainesville. A number of private institutions existed, including the University of Miami, which opened its doors in 1926.

In race relations Florida's record was bad, although lynchings declined from eight in 1920 to one in 1930. The revived Ku Klux Klan had a large membership, influenced politics, and used extralegal violence to perpetuate white superiority and black inferiority. The Klan declined toward the decade's end but kept its organization into the 1930s. The twenties had witnessed some frightful racial episodes. On election day in 1920, a pitched battle at Ocoee in Orange County resulted in the deaths of whites and blacks. A combination lynching and race riot occurred at the small Levy County community of Rosewood during the first week of January 1923. Before it ended at least eight people, two of them whites, were killed, and the homes and churches owned by blacks were burned.

In many ways black and white cultures, though separate, ran parallel and often overlapped. The mass of Florida's blacks remained second-class citizens and victims of prejudice throughout the 1920s. Still, there was more progress than retrogression, as some blacks—in the professions and in business—gained economic independence and became a part of the middle class.

Several black Floridians were beginning or continuing distinguished careers. Zora Neale Hurston, born at Eatonville in 1907, would soon establish an enduring literary reputation. Crescent City was the birthplace of A. Philip Randolph, who organized the Brotherhood of Sleeping Car Porters in 1925 and became one of the nation's leaders in both the trade union movement and the civil rights crusade. James Weldon Johnson, born in Jacksonville, achieved national prominence as a poet, editor, teacher, and leader in the National Association for the Advancement of Colored People (NAACP).

The 1920s were a significant period in Florida's modern history. The state gained an international reputation as a vacation spot for tourists and as a desirable place in which to live. Increasingly, retirees selected the peninsula and Panhandle as the domicile of their senior years. Although southern in many ways, Florida had moved into the mainstream of American life. Florida's rate of urbanization was greater than that experienced by its neighboring states. Its image became one of vitality and excitement, of shining cities, of "skyscraper" hotels and banks, of business opportunity, and of the good life. Floridians knew that, despite the prevailing economic crisis, the sun would still shine brightly, the Atlantic and the Gulf would continue to bathe paradise with their warm waters, the fish would bite, and the soil would provide.

Notes

1. See James A. Carter III, "Florida and Rumrunning During National Prohibition." Patricia Buchanan, in "Miami's Bootleg Boom" (1960), quotes Congressman (later mayor of New York City) Fiorello LaGuardia, from the notoriously wet state of New York, as saying, "There are more prohibition lawbreakers in Florida than in my state."
2. *Tallahassee Democrat,* 8 June 1923.
3. Ibid., 16 October 1925, quoting unnamed northern publication.
4. *Annual Report Banking Department [Florida]* 1924, 9, hereafter cited as *ARBD.*
5. *Florida Laws 1925,* 1:64–66, 58.
6. *Annual Report Florida Comptroller 1925 and First Six Months 1926,* pp. xiii–xxiv.

7. *ARBD*, 20 June 1926, n.p.

8. *Tallahassee Democrat*, 29 July 1926.

9. Quoted ibid., 14 July 1930.

10. Walter P. Fuller, *This Was Florida's Boom* (St. Petersburg, n.p., n.d.), p. 8.

11. Henry S. Villard, "Florida Aftermath," *The Nation*, 6 June 1928, p. 635.

12. H. E. Bierly, in "Open Forum," a column in the *Tallahassee Democrat*, 24 April 1929.

13. The remarks were made at the Florida Bankers Association meeting at Pensacola. See *Tallahassee Democrat*, 22 April 1929.

14. *Tallahassee Democrat*, 16 February 1930.

15. For Cawthon's quote see *Biennial Report of the Superintendent of Public Instruction of the State of Florida, 1920–1922*, p. 131. For other educational statistics see ibid., pp. 36, 38–39, 44–45, 76–77.

Bibliography

Buchanan, Patricia. "Miami's Bootleg Boom." *Tequesta* 30 (1970):13–31.

Carper, N. Gordon. "Martin Tabert, Martyr of an Era." *Florida Historical Quarterly* 52, no. 2 (October 1973):115–31.

Carter, James A. III. "Florida Rumrunning During National Prohibition." *Florida Historical Quarterly* 48, no. 1 (July 1969):47–56.

Chalmers, David. "The Ku Klux Klan in the Sunshine State: The 1920s." *Florida Historical Quarterly* 42, no. 3 (January 1964):209–15.

Colburn, David R., and Richard K. Scher. *Florida's Gubernatorial Politics in the Twentieth Century*. Tallahassee: University Presses of Florida, 1980.

Doherty, Herbert J., Jr. "Florida and the Presidential Election of 1928." *Florida Historical Quarterly* 26, no. 2 (October 1947):174–86.

Dovell, Junius E. *History of Banking in Florida, 1828–1954*. Orlando, 1955.

Flynt, Wayne. *Cracker Messiah: Governor Sidney J. Catts of Florida*. Baton Rouge: Louisiana State University Press, 1977.

———. *Duncan Upshaw Fletcher: Dixie's Reluctant Progressive*. Tallahassee: Florida State University Press, 1971.

France, Mary Duncan. "'A Year of Monkey War': The Anti-Evolution Campaign and the Florida Legislature." *Florida Historical Quarterly* 44, no. 2 (October 1975):156–77.

Fuller, Walter P. *This Was Florida's Boom*. St. Petersburg, n.d.

George, Paul S. "Passage to the New Eden: Tourism in Miami from Flagler through Everest G. Sewell." *Florida Historical Quarterly* 59, no. 4 (April 1981):440–63.

Gross, Eric L. "'Somebody Got Drowned, Lord': The Great Okeechobee Hurricane Disaster of 1928." Master's thesis, Florida State University, 1991.

Hughes, M. Edward. "Florida Preachers and the Election of 1928." *Florida Historical Quarterly* 67, no. 2 (October 1988):131–46.

McDonnell, Victoria H. "The Businessman's Politician: A Study of the Administration of John Wellborn Martin, 1925–1929." Master's thesis, University of Florida, 1968.

Nolan, David. *Fifty Feet in Paradise: The Booming of Florida*. New York: Harcourt Brace Jovanovich, 1984.

Rogers, William Warren. *Outposts on the Gulf: Saint George Island and Apalachicola from Early Exploration to World War II*. Pensacola: University Presses of Florida, 1986.

Sessa, Frank B. "Anti-Florida Propaganda and Counter Measures During the 1920s." *Tequesta* 21 (1961):41–51.

———. "Miami in 1926." *Tequesta* 16 (1956):15–36.

———. "Miami on the Eve of the Boom, 1923." *Tequesta* 21 (1961):41–51.

———. "The Real Estate Boom in Miami and Its Environs [1923–1926]." Ph.D. dissertation, University of Pittsburgh, 1950.

Shofner, Jerrell H. "Florida and Black Migration." *Florida Historical Quarterly* 57, no. 3 (January 1979):267–88.

Vickers, Raymond B. *Panic in Paradise: Florida's Banking Crash of 1926*. Tuscaloosa: University of Alabama Press, 1994.

17 The Great Depression

William W. Rogers

Governor Doyle Carlton and state legislators faced hard times in 1931. Old problems had persisted, and new ones demanded attention. Economic news was dismal—both the Florida East Coast and the Seaboard Air Line railroads sank into receivership that year—and the state's financial structure appeared ready to collapse. As Carlton told the legislature, "In the minds of many banking presents the major issue."[1] No one challenged his analysis. The legislature responded with the Banking Act of 1931 which limited depositor withdrawals and directed some banks to call loans in to meet existing obligations. Comptroller Ernest Amos anticipated New Deal legislation to protect deposits. "I know the mere mention of 'guaranteeing deposits' is 'arsenic to banks' but some effective plan could be designed," he asserted.[2]

Florida banks, like those in other states, continued to fail in 1931. Whether large (the Central National Bank of St. Petersburg) or small (the Bank of Chipley), failures did not respect age or prestige. The situation prompted a bit of doggerel: Lawyers are red/ Business is blue/ If you were a banker/ You'd be white-headed too.[3]

The governor and the legislature also grappled with the overall economic crisis. The presidential election would determine the state's and the nation's direction but not until November 1932. Florida's constitution, which forbade bonded indebtedness, prevented bankruptcy, but it also prohibited emergency borrowing. Cities, counties, political subdivisions, and special tax districts were not so limited. Here Florida's debt liability led the nation and was largely in default. The state's lack of funds effectively barred borrowing money on a matching basis from the federal government. Even so, governors Dave Sholtz (1932–36) and Fred P. Cone (1936–40) adroitly obtained money from Washington that did not require matching.

Carlton trimmed services, recommended governmental streamlining, suggested paving roads on a pay-as-you-go basis, and argued for restricting local government bonding. He backed a sales tax to increase revenue while insisting that an income tax would cause the affluent to avoid Florida. His veto of an inheritance tax bill was sustained. The governor opposed another potential revenue source, legalized gambling, on moral grounds, but in 1931 the legislature created a State Racing Commission, legalized pari-mutuel betting, and taxed the proceeds. Joseph E. Widener of Miami's Hialeah racetrack lobbied the measure to enactment. When Carlton vetoed it, the solons overrode him and thus began the state's important involvement with horse and dog tracks and jai alai frontons. In 1934, income from admission taxes, commissions on pari-mutuel sales, occupational licenses, and other related receipts totaled $1,072,364; six years later it was $2,348,348.

Cities cut budgets and reduced tax millages. Chambers of commerce urged merchants to offer bargains for citizen home-improvement projects. "Buy Now" campaigns were launched. Typically, in Jacksonville, the Community Chest opened a soup kitchen for the hungry, and the city hired the unemployed on public works. Millionaire Alfred DuPont donated money to employ workers for its public parks. A Lee County commissioner remarked, "We've spent a pile of money but we haven't spent a cent that shouldn't have been spent."[4] Other cities and counties had similar programs, but none could cope with escalating unemployment problems. The state Board of Public Welfare, created in 1927, lacked resources to undertake large-scale relief. Accordingly, municipal and county relief efforts, however inadequate, were much more important before 1935 than was state aid. Pride and insufficient knowledge prompted one state committee on the unemployed to oppose federal assistance and strongly reject the dole system of relief.

Floridians who believed a depression could not occur in their vacationland deluded themselves. They fantasized that at worst—and always excluding affluent Palm Beach—a few thousand tourists would cancel or abbreviate their annual visits. Lacking smokestack urban centers, Florida presented no stark image of closed factories with padlocked gates. A balmy climate made it difficult to conjure long lines of out-of-work men wearing threadbare overcoats. Yet the Great Depression engulfed Florida and left many of its citizens in misery and out of work, just as elsewhere in the nation.

Of necessity, Florida soon abandoned its philosophy of self-sufficiency; fewer than twenty counties operated public welfare programs. Turning to Washington, Floridians suffered disappointment. President Herbert Hoover, while sympathetic, declined to order direct governmental economic intervention. By 1930 a political stalemate had developed between the White House and the Democratic Congress. Hoover's private relief policy had foundered. A discontented "Bonus Army" of veterans marched on Washington; their hovels and tents at Anacostia Flats were burned and the marchers were dispelled by force; a food strike was threatened by midwestern farmers; violence flared intermittently; and communist agitators stirred discontent. Across America the homeless huddled in their "Hoovervilles"—hastily constructed clusters of shacks. Many young men and women joined adult transients to ride the rails and camp in hobo jungles. Florida drew them like a magnet, and relief rolls swelled. Immigration was discouraged, and for three winter seasons state policemen blocked roads and refused to let indigent transients cross into Florida. Indecision, resentment, despair, and fear were evident everywhere—the United States had lost its confidence.

The impasse was broken partially in July 1932, when Hoover approved a law that extended Reconstruction Finance Corporation powers, but it was too little, too late. Governor Carlton asked for $500,000, and Florida got its first relief funds in September. The number of families that went on relief represented 36 percent of the black and 22 percent of the white population. Per capita income had reached a low of $289. The presidential elections of 1932 promised new directions in the government's attack on the depression. Hoover became the scapegoat for what had gone wrong, and, as the election approached, the nation demanded change. Florida Democrats, who controlled state politics, supported New York's governor Franklin D. Roosevelt against Hoover. Promising relief, recovery, and reform through a New Deal for the American people, Roosevelt won the White House and easily carried Florida, where he received 74.9 percent of the popular vote.

Significant contests in state elections, including the race for state comptroller, also occurred in 1932. Besides running against two strong candidates, John M. Lee and Van C. Swearinger, Ernest Amos had an extra burden. J. Tom Watson, his nemesis from a previous impeachment attempt, based a gubernatorial campaign on removing the comptroller from office. Prosperity would never return, Watson declared, until the political power of Amos and the state banking interests was broken. Lee won the run-off primary comfortably and ended the career of Florida's most controversial comptroller. In the general election Lee had no difficulty defeating Republican Armonis F. Knotts.

The gubernatorial primary bulged with eight candidates, among them former governors Cary A. Hardee and John W. Martin. Brooklyn-born David Sholtz, a Jewish lawyer from Daytona Beach, placed second to Martin in the first primary. Known for his state Chamber of Commerce work, Sholtz advocated improved education. Despite traces of anti-Semitism, he carried the runoff to win by over 71,000 votes. Sholtz then defeated Republican William J. Howey, winning as a strong Roosevelt supporter. The prohibition issue prompted some cynics to say that Sholtz won because people confused him with Schlitz and thought they were voting to bring back beer. Repeal came with ratification of the Twenty-first Amendment on 5 December 1933.

Unlike the hotly contested governor's race, U.S. Senator Duncan U. Fletcher faced no opposition in 1932. Two years later, the senate election pitted incumbent Park Trammell against former Alabamian Claude Pepper and three other candidates, one of them Hortense E. Wells, a World War I ambulance driver and Democratic National Committeewoman. Trammell won easily.

Politics remained important to Floridians throughout the decade. In 1936 they reaffirmed their support of Roosevelt by giving him 76.1 percent of the vote over Republican Alfred M. Landon. The deaths of Senators Trammell and Fletcher in 1936 forced the calling of a special primary to fill their seats. Pepper was elected to one seat without opposition. Charles O. Andrews beat former governor Carlton in a close primary, then defeated Republican H. C. Babcock. After serving an uncompleted two-year senate term, Pepper ran for reelection in 1938 and did so as a strong New Dealer. Facing four opponents, including former governor Sholtz, he won the primary without a runoff. Pepper's 82.4 percent of the vote in the general election was a stinging defeat for Republican Thomas E. Swanson.

Even by Florida standards the fourteen opponents who sought the Democratic nomination for governor in 1936 were a large number. The field included former governor Martin, as well as Raleigh W. Petteway, who finished first, and Fred P. Cone, who trailed by 5,000 votes. Although voters gave Roosevelt a landslide, Cone's performance demonstrated their independence. The Lake City banker's conservative campaign called for "lowering the budget to balance taxes instead of raising taxes to balance the budget." The voters agreed, and Cone handily defeated Petteway in the runoff primary. He then swamped Elvey E. Callaway, his Republican adversary.

The 1940 contests likewise commanded state attention. Roosevelt won an unprecedented third term over Republican Wendell L. Willkie, taking Florida by 359,334 to 126,158 votes. Seeking reelection to his senate seat, Charles O. Andrews faced five opponents, among them Jerry W. Carter, former governor Cone, and Bernarr McFadden, a political novice better known as a physical culturalist and publisher of true romance magazines. Andrews led runner-up Carter by 100,000 votes and increased his margin in the runoff primary. Republican Miles H. Draper withdrew, leaving the incumbent unopposed. The Democratic gubernatorial nomination was sought by eleven candidates. Future governor Fuller Warren was one of them, but the leading aspirants were Polk County's Spessard L. Holland and Volusia's County's Francis P. Whitehair. Holland finished first, but Whitehair forced a runoff in which Holland repeated his primary victory. Republicans declined to oppose him in the general election.

Florida's politics were highly partisan and individualistic during the Great Depression, which resulted in a string of one-term governors and the absence of political machines. Within the framework of a one-party system, the politics were deceptively complex. Roosevelt's personality and federal government activities overshadowed state politicians and their accomplishments. No sweeping political changes occurred, although in 1937 the poll tax, a means of disfranchising blacks, was repealed. Repeal meant the addition of more poor white voters but had no significant impact on blacks. Women did not vote as a bloc, but they became important in the overall political process. Increasingly they sought political office, especially at the local level. At the decade's end the state was still solidly Democratic, and, with few exceptions, Roosevelt was a folk hero. Many named their children after him.

Early in the decade, though, Floridians had been too caught up in the present to worry about future politics. Even before the new president took office in March 1933, the national experience became an action movie with the film speeded up. Sometimes in the frantic whir of the reels, images blurred. An air of unreality loomed, for instance, around an event in Florida that occurred on 15 February. President-elect Roosevelt had begun to speak at Miami's Bayfront Park when pistol shots rang out. An assassin's bullets missed him but wounded five others. Unemployed bricklayer Guiseppe Zangara was arrested as the assailant. After wounded Chicago mayor Anton Cermak died, Zangara was retried for murder, convicted, and electrocuted.

Roosevelt's election as such accomplished little toward calming fears. Before he took office the banking crisis became so serious that numerous governors began calling "banking holidays," and the index of industrial production continued to drop. Runs on banks and hoarding of currency were rampant. On 4 March, Governor Sholtz, in Washington for the inauguration, declared a five-day banking holiday for Florida (later extended to 15 March). Roosevelt then decreed a four-day national banking holiday effective 6 March. The use of scrip was briefly allowed, and an embargo was put on the export of gold, silver, and currency. The public responded well, and within two weeks stock prices rose, some hoarded currency was reinvested, and gold and gold certificates were returned to the treasury and reserve banks. With the prompt passage of a banking act and a reassuring fireside chat from Roosevelt, confidence rose and the banking crisis was checked.

Sholtz soon permitted state banks to resume business under certain conditions. He promised "banking laws with teeth," and the legislature responded by increasing the powers of liquidators and receivers, regulating how banks issued preferred stock, and toughening penalties. Floridians took the crisis calmly. Instead of hoarding money, they used their cash for local purchases. Many stores took personal checks even though they could not be deposited, and credit was extended. Businesses advertised that they would accept checks and held "New Deal Sales." In a statewide radio address, Sholtz proclaimed that he wanted each citizen to "keep your chin where you have it now—up. If you have confidence in God and man, maintain that confidence."[5] Many state banks and a number of national banks were operating by 14 March, and Comptroller Lee remarked in June, "I believe that we are soon to be on the threshold of a new era in banking."[6] He was correct. The decade's remaining legislative sessions did not have to deal with either the deflation of the twenties or the severe depression of the early thirties.

During the special congressional session of 1933, known as the "Hundred Days," a record number of acts permanently changed Florida and the nation. They spawned a bewildering array of bureaus and agencies. A bemused public called the mixture "alphabet soup." Confusion and conflict inevitably arose. Some of the programs succeeded, others did not. Even so, the American people got the action Roosevelt had promised: the Emergency Banking Act; the Glass-Stegall Act, which divorced investment banking from deposit banking and created the Federal Deposit Insurance Corporation (FDIC); the Securities and Exchange Act; and many others. Rural and urban citizens were helped by the Emergency Farm Mortgage Act and the Home Owners Loan

Corporation Act (HOLC). To aid in distributing relief funds, the Federal Emergency Relief Administration (FERA) was created. Interior Secretary Harold L. Ickes directed a massive building program known as the Public Works Administration (PWA). To offer relief even faster and more directly the short-lived Civil Works Administration (CWA) was established. It gave the word "boondoggle" to the country and was criticized in Florida by some turpentine operators and citrus growers who objected to "high" CWA payment levels.

Southern states such as Florida benefitted from a myriad of other programs. The most popular New Deal agency was the Civilian Conservation Corps (CCC). Known as the "tree army," the CCC engaged in various reforestation and conservation projects. Nationally it provided work for over two million young men between the ages of eighteen and twenty-five. Most were from economically impoverished families, and no state benefitted more than did Florida. Agricultural problems were addressed through allotment and crop reduction programs established under the Agricultural Adjustment Act. The AAA affected all of Florida's farmers. Because industry and organized labor were no less devastated than agriculture, Congress created the National Recovery Administration (NRA). With its symbolic Blue Eagle, the NRA attempted to put into effect industrial codes of fair competition and prices among the nation's industries. Its other aim was to secure collective bargaining for organized labor.

The popular New Deal measures resulted in a great Democratic victory in the 1934 off-year elections, and set in motion the Second New Deal. What followed was a policy of deficit financing—the idea that direct government intervention or "pump priming" was sometimes necessary in a capitalist economy. While continuing some relief and recovery programs, the administration concentrated on long-range reform. One many-faceted program was the Works Progress Administration (WPA), which aimed to provide work for the employable in positions they were able to handle. Between 1935 and 1941 the WPA completed almost 1.5 million projects, although critics claimed that the initials meant "We Poke Along." Many WPA projects benefitted Florida, including the work of its subdivisions such as the National Youth Administration (NYA), Federal Theatre Project, Federal Writers' Project, and Federal Art Project. By 1935 the WPA was primarily responsible for most of the able-bodied workers on Florida's relief rolls. Opposition to the National Social Security Act of 1935 yielded eventually to acceptance, and Social Security became a permanent part of American life. Also in 1935, the National Labor Relations Act (NLRA) reflected the

New Deal's sympathy toward organized labor, and its provisions spurred the growth of the AFL (American Federation of Labor) and especially the CIO (Congress of Industrial Organizations).

In the late 1930s, leftist radicals attacked the New Deal for not going far enough, while extreme conservatives believed that it had gone too far. After 1938, conservative southern politicians often allied with Republicans to defeat or emasculate New Deal measures, and popular support also declined. Roosevelt had cause to be grateful to Florida's Senator Pepper whose campaign included support of a stalled wages and hours bill. Pepper's reelection assured congressional passage. Roosevelt's attempted "purge" of conservative Democratic senators and representatives in 1938 failed. As New Deal support waned, gathering threats to world peace by Germany, Italy, and Japan resulted in war in Asia and Europe. Roosevelt, by shifting his emphasis to a program of domestic preparedness and support for the Allied powers, held the Democratic coalition of liberals, southerners, blacks, ethnic groups, and organized labor together and won a third term.

The experiences of Apalachicola and Franklin County were a microcosm of the New Deal. People there were reassured on seeing evidence of FDIC membership posted in the local bank's window and the Blue Eagle posters in various stores. The WPA took over local public works projects and employed hundreds of people. FERA funds financed a Carrabelle mattress factory and an airport at Apalachicola. Other WPA and PWA allocations further stimulated the economy. A new courthouse was built and opened with federal monies. In 1937, forty-six county men were enrolled in the CCC. By 1938, the county had 125 citizens working on federal projects and another 281 engaged in part-time work. The most visible achievement was the opening of the John Gorrie bridge. Contact with east Florida had been restricted for over 100 years by Apalachicola Bay; the townspeople now had a convenient modern bridge and causeway, which stood as a symbol of hope.

State and local politics and programs also had their influence. The state's most valuable possession was its people. The state grew more slowly than during the twenties, but it did not stagnate. Total population increased between 1930 and 1940 by 409,203. There were 1,897,414 Floridians in 1940; blacks numbered 433,714 and whites 1,037,198. Black and white women slightly outnumbered their male counterparts.

Few jobs in urban centers, reduced living expenses, and greater availability of food caused many people to remain in rural areas. Between 1930 and 1940 Florida's urban white population increased only slightly, from 72.3 to 72.5 percent. Its black urban population actually declined from 27.7 to 27.4 percent. The number of farms grew by 3,500, and the average acreage rose from 85.2 to 133.0. With 173,065 residents, Jacksonville was only marginally larger than Miami, which had 171,172. Tampa was the state's third city with over 100,000. Florida was urban, but St. Petersburg was the only other city with over 50,000. Otherwise, only Orlando and West Palm Beach had more than 30,000 people.

Changes during the depression also affected the state's Native Americans. In 1930 Florida had approximately 500 Indians. Known collectively as Seminoles, they were dispersed through much of south Florida. Poverty, lack of organization, and the presence of at least two distinct groups threatened their tribal integrity. In 1934, the federal government offered a program that encouraged tribal government, land purchases to permit concentration of population, and education. This Indian New Deal fostered a sense of viability. Aid was channeled through CCC–Indian Division work programs to help fight persistent social problems.

Since its people were Florida's greatest asset, their overall health was fundamentally important. In the 1930s significant progress was made in this area. The Florida constitution of 1885 had mandated a State Board of Public Health, but the agency remained underfunded and neglected until 1931 when the legislature provided for county health departments. Counties were allowed to levy special taxes to support them, and Taylor County was the first to establish a health unit. Ultimately the activities of these units included communicable disease control, hygienic programs, protection of food and milk, and extensive laboratory work. After the Social Security Act of 1935, more health funds became available. By 1940 the state board operated a mobile X-ray unit and had many clinics (segregated by race). Because Florida led the nation in deaths from syphilis, sixty-seven clinics were set up and they proved effective. Important work was accomplished in combatting hookworm, malaria, and pneumonia. In 1939, state officials drafted a school health plan and coordinated it with community health programs. WPA funds also were expended for sanitation and various medical projects.

For Floridians to achieve their potential the state had to have an efficient public school system. The depression dealt a crippling blow to that ambition. Funding for public education dropped, and in 1931 Florida ranked forty-third in average teacher pay and thirty-ninth in money spent annually per student. A wrenching austerity program eliminated small high schools, enlarged elementary classes, retained old textbooks,

Seminole family members gather outside Miami in 1929.

pooled library books countrywide, and reduced purchases of equipment. Tallahassee and Leon County were among Florida's more stable areas, yet in 1933 many schools, most of them black, were closed, and the academic year was reduced to six months. In 1934 Florida had 446 school buses with factory-made bodies and 752 with homemade ones. Salary reductions meant that by 1934 the state owed teachers $312,408 in back pay. The average salary in 1936 was $1,039 for a white and $495 for a black teacher. In the mid-thirties the state department of education estimated that only 10 to 15 percent of school children would attend college. Based on that projection, the department opposed making the achievement of college entrance requirements a goal of a high school education.

With returning prosperity in the late 1930s, the public school system improved. The educational budget was increased under Governor Cone, although teachers' salaries remained low and tied to race, with blacks always at a disadvantage. On the plus side, the average length of school terms in grades one through twelve achieved near equality: for blacks 165 and for whites 175 days. State laws required compulsory school attendance. By the end of the 1930s, while much remained to be done, progress had been made, especially by blacks. Of the 663,547 young white people of school age, 54.7 percent attended in 1940. There were 195,274 blacks eligible to attend school, and 49.2 percent of them did so.

Federal funds greatly helped Florida education. More than 500 schools, in addition to playgrounds and athletic fields, were built or refurbished by the WPA. Its funds were also used to provide school lunches. The state's colleges received WPA appropriations for capital improvements programs, and the WPA's education division employed more than 1,600 teachers. Vocational courses were encouraged, including home economics, agriculture, trade and industrial education, distributive education, and rehabilitation. Beginning in 1935 the National Youth Administration (NYA) administered a work-relief and employment program for school-age persons and provided part-time employment for needy secondary, college, and graduate students.

The state's school program, including higher education, remained segregated by race. Florida Agricultural and Mechanical College for Negroes at Tallahassee continued as one of two land grant institutions. It offered a variety of courses other than engineering and agriculture. A much larger choice of fields was possible at Gainesville's all-white, all-male University of Florida. It boasted a College of Law and a broad liberal arts program, while no state law school was available for blacks. The Florida State College for Women at Tallahassee had programs in teacher education but built its strongest reputation in the liberal arts.

Private colleges and universities, such as the University of Miami, begun in 1926, struggled to survive. Despite the times, the University of Tampa opened as Tampa Junior College in 1931 and in 1933 became a four-year institution. Palm Beach Junior College was established in 1933, and the next year Jacksonville Junior College began classes (it became Jacksonville University in 1956). St. Petersburg Junior College, Stetson University, Florida Southern College, and Rollins College all weathered the storm. Black private institutions such as Edward Waters College and Bethune-Cookman College continued to serve their students.

Because of Florida's climate, geographical location, and soil, agriculture was of paramount importance. In 1940 Florida had 4,500 more white farm owners or operators than in 1930; black owners and operators decreased by 2,700. Only slight increases in farm mechanization were registered. The greatest change came in the number of farm dwellings lighted by electricity. Federal programs helped reduce regional utility rates of private corporations, and Floridians benefitted directly from the Rural Electrification Administration, which, after its

Picking and crating celery in April 1930 at Sanford, where one-third of the nation's celery supply was grown.

creation in 1935, generated and distributed electricity in isolated rural areas. The 11 percent of Florida farm homes lighted by electricity in 1930 increased to 26.5 percent in 1940.

From the decade's beginning to its end, the state's production of beef cattle and chickens increased. Income from milk ($15,859,946) grew fivefold. Florida established itself as a permanent major producer of winter vegetables. Plant pathologist Herman Hamilton Wedgworth developed viable fertilizers for the rich muck soil of the Everglades and grew disease-resistant vegetables, and by 1934 his Belle Glade plant was shipping vegetables in refrigerated railroad cars to northern markets. The Duda family and others soon transferred the new techniques to the muckland north of Lake Apopka. By 1940 tomatoes, watermelons, string beans, lima beans, green peas, cucumbers, peppers, and celery offered significant sources of income. The Everglades's persistent flooding problems were eliminated when FERA and WPA funds were used to build a dike around Lake Okeechobee and improve the adjacent drainage canals. This work, plus the establishment of a federal sugarcane experiment station at Canal, made possible the development of a lucrative private sugar industry. Corn brought in $4 million in 1940; it remained an important money crop, as did Irish potatoes, peanuts, velvet beans, and tobacco. The cotton crop of 1940 generated less cash ($1,225,000) than did cabbage ($2,620,533).

Timber was considered a crop, and from it emerged a large pulp paper industry. The Florida Forest Service (created in 1935), the CCC, and private individuals launched reforestation programs. At the same time, Charles H. Henry developed an inexpensive way to manufacture paper from southern slash pine. Cutover land was replanted, and existing forests offered the possibility of cheap paper products. The decision of the nation's newspaper owners to convert to pulp paper newsprint was especially important to Florida. In 1931 the International Paper Company's operation at Panama City became Florida's first mill. Other companies followed, and by the late 1930s pulp mills also were operating at Pensacola, Port St. Joe, Jacksonville, Fernandina, and Palatka. Alfred I. DuPont purchased 70,000 acres of land in the Gulf counties of Walton, Bay, and Franklin. His Port St. Joe mill, opened in 1938 at a cost of $7 million, was the largest in Florida.

The citrus industry expanded. Dating from the establishment in 1909 of the Florida Citrus Exchange, growers had attempted to formulate industry-wide policy. The advantages of volume buying and selling were advocated by local exchanges, but many growers preferred independent marketing. Such practices prevented uniformity of product, and grove owners who shipped green fruit injured the industry. Improvements came in 1935 when the state legislature created the Florida Citrus Commission. The agency, which was financed by a tax on citrus, encouraged growers to ship quality fruit and engaged in an effective advertising campaign. The state's share of the 1940 citrus market was impressive: tangerines brought in $1,671,656, grapefruit $7,637,836, and oranges $25,342,079.

Federal land banks aided Florida's farmers by providing long-term loans, and federal involvement in the broad area of agrarian life was profound: government subsidy payments in 1935 amounted to $1,129,878. AAA agents, county agents, and various agricultural specialists were funded in part from Washington. Nathan Mayo, Florida's commissioner of agriculture, established farmers' markets with New Deal financing. The WPA attempted to aid Florida's commercial fishing industry, which rewarded its participants mostly with hard work and meager incomes. The agency worked out a cooperative program of replanting and renewing the geographically limited industry. The main profits came from oyster beds located along the upper Florida Coast from Cedar Key in Levy County to Panama City in Bay County. The shrimp industry soon became an additional means of income.

Changes in farming operations that had long-run benefits were sometimes painful in the short run. As large-scale agriculture became necessary for economic survival, increased use of machinery diminished the number of tenant farmers. Although the transition for tenants was difficult, the curse of sharecropping was ending. Unskilled fruit and vegetable pickers received low pay for their seasonal work. The migrant laborers followed the harvest seasons, working the Florida vegetable farms and fruit groves in the fall and winter and moving north for the spring and summer berries and vegetables. No labor was more difficult than the relentless leaning over required of cutters in Florida's sugarcane fields, where charges of peonage occasionally were raised.

New Deal legislation favored union activity resulting in tense confrontation between some owners and workers. A Polk County citrus workers' union, for instance, met physical opposition. In 1938 the United Cannery, Agriculture, Packing and Allied Workers of America, a CIO union, struck over wage reductions. Governor Cone helped to mediate the dispute, which ended in compromise.

The natural environment, as well as the work environment, was fostered by governmental action. The national government bought land in north Florida for the St. Marks Wildlife Refuge and elsewhere added many acres to the Ocala, Apalachicola, Osceola, and other national forests. The CCC's work also had environmental and aesthetic consequences. By the 1930s naval stores and logging firms had practically depleted longleaf yellow pine forests, and the timber industry had declined. Profits were low, and operators kept their black workers in virtual peonage, especially in the turpentine camps. The turnaround came through reseeding programs led by the CCC. Many of the twenty-six agency camps were in national forests. In its nine years in Florida the agency enrolled over 50,000 young men in segregated camps and about $30 million was expended. The CCC planted 13,605,000 trees, cut 14,554 miles of firebreaks, and improved thousands of acres of forest land. It cooperated with the Florida Parks Service and the National Park Service to build Torreya State Park and similar projects that became models for the nation.

In these and other ways the New Deal left an indelible mark on Florida. The WPA's public works projects continued into the early forties. Florida led the nation in WPA airport construction. Tampa benefitted, for example, by expansion of its airport and construction of a large dry dock. Statewide, the WPA built 800 public buildings and constructed bridges, roads (more than 6,000 miles), culverts, parks, playgrounds, athletic fields, public housing, and hospitals. It conserved

The Civilian Conservation Corps (CCC), the first New Deal agency to operate in Florida, began at Eastport in Duval County in 1933. Before its termination in 1942 the CCC gave work to more than 50,000 Floridians between the ages of eighteen and twenty-five. Though best known for planting millions of trees and clearing thousands of miles of fire-breaks, the agency also helped to establish wildlife preserves and numerous state parks, including Hillsborough near Tampa and O'Lena near High Springs. In the photograph, a CCC official is shown in September 1936 inspecting a bridge and road fill constructed at O'Lena State Park.

beaches against erosion, built seawalls, and helped complete the intra-coastal waterway. Artists, writers, sculptors, musicians, and teachers were funded in their work. The Federal Writers' Project employed historians and others to collect public records, and an excellent guide to Florida was compiled. The Federal Theatre's productions at Miami, Jacksonville, and Tampa, plus its statewide touring company, employed out-of-work actors, playwrights, and stage personnel.

In 1935, Key West became a monument to federal-state-local cooperation. Bankrupt, and with 80 percent of their citizens on relief, local officials asked the governor to declare a state of emergency. His decree authorized the FERA to take over the city. By those means Key West was revitalized, as citizens contributed long hours to cleaning streets, developing beaches, renovating houses and hotels, and improving sanitation facilities. New Deal funds enabled the town to become a bustling resort city, aided by construction of a highway to the mainland, 100 miles away. The project was threatened when disaster struck on Labor

Day, 2 September 1935. A hurricane slashed the keys, where about 400 lives were lost. Henry Flagler's overseas railroad, completed in 1912, was so badly damaged that it was sold to the state. With federal and state assistance, the Monroe County Toll Bridge Commission took it over, and U.S. Highway 1 was completed to Key West in 1938.

At the state level the State Board of Public Welfare, backed by Governor Sholtz, concerned itself with a broad range of social problems, including child welfare. After 1935, when state participation in relief programs increased, the board enlarged its operations and in 1937 became the Department of Social Welfare. Sholtz pushed the state toward a greater role but was restrained when the state supreme court declared unconstitutional his attempt to pledge Florida's credit on a loan. Sholtz persisted, and in 1935 the state allocated $2 million toward its responsibility for the welfare program. Tax revenues were to be applied to relief payments (this required the successful passage of a constitutional amendment), for schools, for the State Welfare Board, and for a State Planning Board.

After 1935, Florida evolved past its traditional status as a small government state. The forces of change were inexorable, and the result was inevitable: complex, complicated government on a scale necessary to meet the needs of a growing state. The trend took on momentum as the economic situation improved toward the end of the Sholtz administration and throughout that of Governor Cone. Setbacks occurred, but the line on the prosperity graph was upward. Floridians welcomed a constitutional change that authorized a homestead tax exemption. State government action and recovery were further aided by the Murphy Act. The collapse of the twenties' land boom had left much real estate abandoned and subject to delinquent taxes. Cone wanted taxes collected and homesteads settled on the lands. In 1937, the Murphy Act allowed the sale of tax-delinquent land for tax certificates, whereby shrewd buyers obtained deeds at a fraction of land value. The public gained by having the land restored to the tax rolls.

Tourism and its economic benefits experienced renewed vigor. The number of tourists had dropped to half a million in 1932, but a comeback was evident by 1934. The two million who came in 1935 created the largest tourist season in state history, and Floridians welcomed the $625 million they left behind. In 1936, the *Tampa Tribune* boasted that tourism "is our richest crop. . . . It rides in and rides out, leaving its money as it goes."[7] Building permits for hotel and residential construction had dropped to less than $400,000 in 1932—one real estate developer was reduced to advertising five-acre farms for $60 each—but in

Marjorie Kinnan Rawlings came to Florida from Rochester, New York, in 1928. Living in the sparsely settled scrub at Cross Creek south of Gainesville, she divided her time between growing oranges and writing fiction. In several notable books, which included *South Moon Under* (1933), *The Yearling* (1938), which won a Pulitzer Prize, and the autobiographical *Cross Creek* (1942), she took as her subjects the proud taciturn Crackers who eked out a bare subsistence from the fields, woods, and lakes of Florida's half-wild interior. In a fitting tribute, her friend and attorney, Philip S. May, of Jacksonville, wrote her in 1947, "Ponce de León discovered Florida in 1513, but he had found only the physical and material Florida. Then, more than 400 years later, you came to discover the heart and spirit of Florida and revealed them to the world in writings of rare beauty and sensitiveness."

1936 building permits exceeded $9 million, and on Miami Beach's Collins Avenue a line of Art Deco hotels rose from the sand.

Commercial aviation, begun in the 1920s, expanded. By 1939 Florida had three scheduled airlines: Pan American, Eastern, and National. Adding to the growing private freight and passenger service was the decision of the Army Air Corps to train many of its pilots in Florida. By 1940 Army and Navy airfields were established at Miami, Tampa, Orlando, Jacksonville, Pensacola, Valparaiso, and Arcadia. Others followed as military aviation became a major industry.

New Deal programs did not solve unemployment in Florida, nor did

The Miami Beach Lions Club exhibits its optimism in the midst of the Great Depression.

they end the Great Depression. World War II did that. Yet they galvanized Floridians and reversed the slide of economic decline. Without question the New Deal supplied desperately needed funds, and Roosevelt's leadership gave Florida citizens a powerful psychological boost. The 1930s were a massive lesson in overcoming adversity. During the decade the state's physical contours, urban and rural, changed. A new concept of state government responsibilities emerged, and the necessary agencies to fulfill the obligations became fact.

Floridians sought ways to lift themselves out of their misery (hence the popularity of Margaret Mitchell's novel *Gone With the Wind* and the movie that followed). Unable to afford membership in a country club, they seized on miniature golf as a leisure-time substitute. In numerous inspiring ways they discovered that they possessed reservoirs of fortitude, strength, and good humor. As one writer noted, the title song of Walt Disney's cartoon, "Who's Afraid of the Big Bad Wolf," became a metaphor for their struggle against the Great Depression.

Notes

1. *Tallahassee Daily Democrat,* 18 April 1931.
2. *Annual Report Banking Department [Florida],* 30 June 1931, p. 5, hereafter cited as *ARBD.*
3. *Tallahassee Daily Democrat,* 2 February 1933.
4. Lyn Rainard, "Ready Cash on Easy Terms: Local Responses to the Depression in Lee County," p. 297.

5. *Jacksonville Florida Times Union,* 10 March 1933.
6. *ARBD,* 30 June 1933, p. 6.
7. *Tampa Tribune,* 6 April 1936.

Bibliography

Buchanan, Patricia. "Miami's Bootleg Boom." *Tequesta* 30 (1970):13–31.

Cox, Merlin G. "David Sholtz: New Deal Governor of Florida." *Florida Historical Quarterly* 43, no. 2 (October 1964):142–52.

Dunn, James William. "The New Deal and Florida Politics." Ph.D. dissertation, Florida State University, 1971.

Ginzl, David J. "The Politics of Patronage Florida Republicans During the Hoover Administration." *Florida Historical Quarterly* 61, no. 1 (July 1982): 1–19.

Hughes, Melvin Edward, Jr. "William J. Howey and His Florida Dreams." *Florida Historical Quarterly* 66, no. 3 (January 1988):243–64.

Kersey, Harry A., Jr. *The Florida Seminoles and the New Deal, 1933–1942.* Boca Raton: Florida Atlantic University Press, 1989.

La Godna, Martin M. "Greens, Grist and Guernseys: Development of the Florida State Agricultural Marketing System." *Florida Historical Quarterly* 53, no. 2 (October 1974):146–63.

Loftin, Bernadette K. "A Woman Liberated: Lillian C. West, Editor." *Florida Historical Quarterly* 52, no. 4 (April 1974):396–403.

Long, Durward. "Key West and the New Deal, 1934–1936." *Florida Historical Quarterly* 46, no. 3 (January 1968):209–18.

Lowry, Charles B. "The PWA in Tampa: A Case Study." *Florida Historical Quarterly* 52, no. 4 (April 1974):363–80.

Mardis, John. "Federal Theatre in Florida." Ph.D. dissertation, University of Florida, 1972.

Rainard, R. Lyn. "Ready Cash on Easy Terms: Local Responses to the Depression in Lee County." *Florida Historical Quarterly* 64, no. 3 (January 1986): 284–300.

Sewell, J. Richard. "Cross-Florida Barge Canal, 1927–1968." *Florida Historical Quarterly* 46, no. 4 (April 1968):369–83.

Shofner, Jerrell H. "Roosevelt's 'Tree Army': The Civilian Conservation Corps in Florida." *Florida Historical Quarterly* 65, no. 4 (April 1987):433–56.

Snyder, Robert E. "Marion Post and the Farm Security Administration in Florida." *Florida Historical Quarterly* 65, no. 4 (April 1987):457–79.

Stoesen, Alexander R. "The Senatorial Career of Claude D. Pepper." Ph.D. dissertation, University of North Carolina, 1965.

18   World War II

Gary R. Mormino

For a state that trafficked in optimism and imagination, Florida had good reason to welcome the first Sunday in December 1941. Not since the giddy years of the early 1920s had Floridians seen signs of recovery and growth. Symbolically and socially, the first Sunday in December marked the official beginning of Florida's tourist season. By Sunday afternoon, December 7, news of Pearl Harbor shattered the dream of Florida beaches filled with tourists in swimsuits; yet, ironically, out of the maelstrom of war came a huge new stream of visitors, wearing khaki, olive drab, and navy blue.

"Japan has done one thing for us," proclaimed the *Tallahassee Democrat*. "The cowardly attack . . . has united the nation as nothing else could have done."[1] On the eve of Pearl Harbor, Floridians seemed deeply divided over the question of intervention or isolation. Now a surge of patriotism swept the state. In Pensacola, a civic club pledged fifty dollars to the first aviator to drop a bomb on Tokyo. News of Lieutenant Colonel Jimmy Doolittle's raid on Tokyo on 18 April 1942 thrilled Floridians—even more so when it was revealed that the crew had trained at Eglin Field in the Panhandle near Valparaiso.

The most tangible evidence of war in Florida was the explosive growth of military establishments. Florida laid claim to 172 military installations, ranging from megacomplexes at Camp Blanding and the Jacksonville Naval Air Station, to fledgling facilities such as the Sopchoppy Bombing Range and Immokalee Army Air Field.

Pork-barrel politics, ample sunshine, and jungle-like terrain made Florida especially attractive for military training. The evolution of Eglin Field and Camp Blanding provides dramatic examples of military growth. In the early 1930s, the Works Progress Administration installed a runway in Okaloosa County, and the Eglin Bombing and Gunnery Range opened in 1935. Okaloosa County supported a population of only 10,000 residents in 1930, but the county garnered the largesse of Congressman Robert "He Coon" Sikes. Before his retirement in the 1970s, Sikes had obtained nine bases and three shipyards for his district. The war's imperatives allowed Sikes to lobby for the expansion of Eglin Field, which eventually became a 724-square-mile base.

Camp Blanding, conceived in 1939 as a $700,000 summer camp for the Florida National Guard, expanded dramatically with the coming of war. Officials selected a 27,000-acre preserve in rural Clay County, not far from Starke and thirty miles southwest of Jacksonville. Clay and Bradford counties, historically poor entities, suddenly brimmed with carpenters and contractors. Construction companies, in need of 21,000 laborers, pulled unemployed workers from throughout the Southeast. Obtaining housing became nearly impossible; many workers slept in cars and tents. So many migrants flocked to the area that the Florida Welfare Board distributed food to the needy. Transportation demands created a traffic gridlock. To relieve the congested roads, a special train carried over 1,000 workers between Jacksonville and Starke, the latter an instant boomtown.

Camp Blanding became Florida's fourth largest city during the war. The complex, which featured no building over two stories high, grew to 180,000 acres and provided housing to 55,000 army personnel. It included a 2,051-bed hospital and 125 miles of paved road. Construction costs spiraled to $60 million.

The urgency of mobilization imposed severe limits on America's military training facilities. An expedient solution was found in an unlikely setting: Florida's resort beaches. Critics initially attacked the prospect of raw recruits sweating in the splendorous Don Ce-Sar or Ponce de Leon Hotel, but Undersecretary of War Robert Patterson answered adroitly, "The best hotel room is none too good for the American soldier."

Florida's hotel operators, expecting a banner 1942 season, initially balked at the conversion proposal, but traveling restrictions, the presence of German U-boats off the Gold Coast, and appeals to patriotism and pocketbook persuaded the industry to turn over the keys to the military. By February 1942, the first wave of ninety-day wonders arrived in Miami. By the fall of 1942, almost 300 hotels in Miami and

Army Air Forces trainees march to their classroom in Miami Beach. The Air Forces occupied 70,000 hotel rooms on the beach, where one-fourth of all air officers and one-
fifth of all air enlisted men received basic training. The largest ground army basic
training center in the state was Camp Blanding, near Starke. At its peak, Blanding was
Florida's fourth largest city (after Jacksonville, Miami, and Tampa) during World War II.

Miami Beach hosted 78,000 military "guests." The government purchased some of the more elegant hotels, including the Biltmore in Coral
Gables. The Hollywood Beach Hotel became a naval training school
while The Breakers at Palm Beach saw service as an army hospital.
Even the rustic and isolated Rod and Gun Club in Everglades City
hosted the Coast Guard during the war. Dan Moody's experience must
have been repeated many times. The young Virginian arrived at Miami
Beach on 29 January 1944, and he wrote to his parents from the Hotel
Blackstone, "Mother, this is the most beautiful place that I have ever
seen. . . . I really think when the war is over, I'll move down here."[2]

Florida became a garrison state, armed and trained for every conceiv-
able military function. In Fort Pierce, 150,000 men passed through the
Naval Amphibious Training Base, which graduated frogmen and un-
derwater demolition experts. Along the Big Bend, at Camp Gordon
Johnston in Carrabelle, thousands of soldiers perfected future invasion
tactics that would be employed on beaches in North Africa, Normandy,
and Okinawa.

Wings over Florida became a familiar sight. In 1939, Florida boasted six aviation schools; by the end of the war in August 1945 the state claimed forty aviation installations. Residents became accustomed to the distinctive sounds and formations of Navy Hellcats, B-17 Flying Fortresses, and TBM Avengers. Airfields offered specialized training. Pilots at the Lake City and Sanford naval air stations flew fighters, while their counterparts at DeLand and Vero Beach perfected dive bombing. A young pilot named George Herbert Walker Bush learned to fly torpedo bombers at Fort Lauderdale's Naval Air Station.

The state also served as a backdrop for the South Pacific as filmmakers took advantage of Florida's good weather and impenetrable swamps in movies such as *Air Force* (1942) and *A Guy Named Joe* (1943). A not-yet-fashionable Key Biscayne doubled as Sisiman Cove, the Philippines, in John Ford's memorable *They Were Expendable* (1944).

To see the war Floridians did not need to attend the Bijou or Rialto; rather, the war came to them. German submarines, taking advantage of U.S. intelligence blunders and the strategic importance of the Gulf Stream, launched "Operation Drumbeat" in January 1942. German U-boats sank twenty-four ships off Florida's east and Gulf coasts. Residents and tourists at Jacksonville Beach and Cocoa Beach watched with horror as tankers burned and thick oil coated the white sand. Hundreds of lives and millions of dollars in cargo were lost until the Allies deployed an effective convoy system. Volunteers softened the human tragedy. Helen Muir wrote the story of a young nurse wiping tar off a traumatized merchant mariner, asking him, "Is this your first visit to Florida?"[3]

Floridians normally welcomed the sight of soldiers in uniform. German prisoners of war, however, met with suspicion and fear. Of the 372,000 German POWs incarcerated in the United States, 4,000 spent time in Florida, most of them imprisoned at Camp Blanding. They picked oranges at Dade City, Leesburg, and Winter Haven, cut sugarcane at Clewiston, and swept the streets of Miami Beach. When POWs assigned to the kitchen at MacDill Air Field in Tampa complained of the presence of African Americans, authorities appeased the Germans. In one of the war's more ironic moments, a contingent of German POWs picked cotton at El Destino, once one of Jefferson County's great antebellum plantations.

World War II unleashed the greatest economic boom in American history. From 1940 to 1945, federal expenditures soared from $9 billion to $98.4 billion. Nationally, per capita income doubled during the war, personal savings increased tenfold, and the labor force expanded by 9 million workers—all during a two-front war that absorbed 16 million

Twenty-four U.S. and Allied freighters and tankers were sunk in Florida coastal waters by German submarines (U-boats) during World War II, particularly during the period February–July 1942. Many torpedoed merchant vessels could be seen burning from the front porches of beach houses and from the balconies of tourist hotels. Here a stricken tanker burns off Hobe Sound.

soldiers. The American South, once a subject of pity, once the "Nation's No. 1 economic problem," was swept into the vortex of prosperity. *Fortune Magazine* translated the heady events into understandable terms: "For the first time since the War between the States, almost any native of the Deep South who wants a job can get one."[4]

The war poured huge sums of money into Florida's underdeveloped, narrowly based economy. In 1933 Floridians earned $424 million in income; by 1943 they earned $2 billion. War contracts revived the state's agricultural and manufacturing sectors, while tourism thrived (perhaps shockingly so). The war rejuvenated Florida's moribund ship-building industry, and Pensacola, Panama City, Jacksonville, and Tampa shared in the bonanza.

Panama City provides a vivid example of the war's galvanic effect. In 1940, Bay County languished in poverty, an isolated wedge supporting 20,000 residents along Florida's Big Bend. The county's population more than doubled by 1945. The Wainwright Company there constructed 108 vessels during the war. At its peak, the shipyards employed 15,000 workers, earning unheard-of wages. The general contractor, J. A. Jones, assumed the role of urban planner and city boss, building homes for workers and delivering milk and ice to families.

Defense contracts breathed life into Tampa, a city reeling because the Great Depression devastated the once-vaunted cigar industry. The construction of MacDill Air Field in 1939 and the reconstruction of a ship-building industry spelled a new prosperity. The Tampa Shipbuilding Company employed 9,000 workers by the end of 1942 and desperately advertised for more laborers, a problem exacerbated with the establishment of a second major shipbuilder in Tampa at Hooker's Point. The shipyards paid premium wages; by 1943 defense workers averaged $1.08 an hour, with unlimited overtime. The companies sponsored athletic teams, published a newspaper, *Tascozette*, and even provided alarm clocks for workers.

The war's cornucopia also enriched the economies of Pensacola, Jacksonville, Miami, and Orlando. The Pensacola Shipyard and Engineering Company employed 7,000 workers by early 1942. In addition, the government spent $55 million expanding and constructing the Pensacola Naval Air Station and auxiliary fields. Jacksonville's docks bustled with trade and defense. Local firms constructed 82 liberty ships and scores of wooden minesweepers and PT (patrol torpedo) boats. Jacksonville also served as headquarters for the Naval Overhaul and Repair facility. In Miami, vessels from the Caribbean and South America thronged the Miami River docks. Miami's economy surged from the syncretic stream of military recruits, defense contracts, and tourist spending. Orlando, not endowed with a deep-water port, nonetheless manufactured 9,000 assault boats. Local firms, such as Florida Aircraft Corporation, won $20 million in wartime contracts.

The parade of industrial statistics might lead one to believe that the Sunshine State had become the Steel State. For all the new and rejuvenated industries, Florida's economic standing changed little during the war; indeed, one can argue that the state actually slipped in areas critical to long-term growth. In 1939, Florida's manufacturing accounted for one-half of 1 percent of the national total, but the state's proportion declined by 1943 to two-fifths of 1 percent. Of nineteen manufacturing categories, Florida improved its relative position in only two sectors during the period 1939–43. Shipbuilding accounted for two-thirds of the industrial gains achieved in wartime Florida, but at war's end the lucrative shipbuilding contracts went to other states. Moreover, in industries critical to sustained growth—chemicals, oil refining, iron and steel foundries, aircraft manufacturing, electronics, automobiles—Florida cities fared poorly, even when compared with southern rivals such as Atlanta, Mobile-Pascagoula, Norfolk, Wilmington, Galveston, and Houston.

Agriculture achieved dramatic gains during the war, realizing new profits and incorporating new technologies. Southern farms in general, and Florida in particular, had experienced two lean decades since the flush times of World War I. But World War II brought the good times back. Cotton prices, for instance, rose from 10 cents to 22 cents a pound between 1939 and 1945.

Grove owners harvested orange gold during the war. Notable milestones in the marketing and processing of citrus occurred. Florida's citrus harvest surpassed California's for the first time in 1942–43, producing 80 million boxes of oranges and grapefruit. The 1942–43 yield also marked Florida's first $100 million citrus crop. Scientists helped solve a problem historically plaguing the industry: waste and spoilage resulting from blemishes, market conditions, and transportation. Chemists perfected a dehydrated citrus concentrate, an awful-tasting but welcome beverage in embattled England. In 1942, Florida plants produced 28 million cans of concentrate. More significantly in its implications, chemists at the Florida Citrus Commission patented a process to make frozen concentrated orange juice, a much better tasting product than the dehydrated beverage.

The war wrought a green revolution. While researchers at the Bureau of Entomology in Orlando worked to advance the frontiers of jungle warfare, they discovered an insecticide with revolutionary implications. By 1945, DDT was available for commercial use, promising an end to a south Florida teeming with palmetto bugs, cattle ticks, and saltwater mosquitos. A Sanford farmer exclaimed, "The product . . . kills insects like crazy." *Time* magazine cautioned against careless optimism: "Not much is known as yet about the full effect of DDT on large areas."[5] Undeterred, Floridians rushed to apply the new witches brew on swamps and backlots. Not until 1962 and the publication of Rachel Carson's *Silent Spring* would they learn how damaging pesticides were, particularly DDT, to the natural environment.

The war's new technologies augured a bright future for grove owners and planters, but one serious problem confronting farmers beginning in 1942 was a drastic labor shortage. The Draconian tactics used by some to recruit and coerce workers for the sugar plantations and truck farms resulted in what a CBS-TV special report called in 1960 a *Harvest of Shame.*

"Food will win the war and write the peace," promised a poster in Clewiston. Yet, beneath the veneer of patriotism rested a labor system more in practice with nineteenth-century peonage than twentieth-century egalitarianism. The roots of the labor crisis reflected the legacy of the Black Codes but also revealed a willingness to seek new solutions and alternatives.

State, county, and municipal officers worked to bolster the supply of agricultural workers. Experts predicted a shortage of 10,000 workers for the 1943–44 Florida citrus crop. Across Florida, cities passed new or enforced existing vagrancy laws, determined to punish slackers and recruit seasonal workers. In Clearwater, the *Tampa Morning Tribune* reported, "The city has put more than fifty chronic loafers, including some gigolos to work. . . . Many were Negroes and borrowed money from their girlfriends to aid their loafing."[6] Pinellas County officials announced a "Work or Jail" edict. Apopka strengthened its vagrancy law and arrested scores of African Americans, assigning them to the celery fields. Miami's police chief, Jimmy Sullivan, announced, "Able-bodied men in Dade County must find essential employment or face a charge of vagrancy."[7]

In 1945, Governor Millard Caldwell asked Florida sheriffs to eliminate indolence. The sheriff of Martin County stated with candor that it would be the policy of his office to cooperate with farmers, saw-mill men, and others doing essential work in seeing that they got all the help they needed. Few officials acted with the vigilance of Broward Sheriff Walter Clark. His deputies rounded up men from the area's slums and, without trial, impressed them to work on a farm owned by the Oakland Park mayor. The sheriff of Glades County was indicted on six counts of peonage for using Negro prisoners on his farm.

Nowhere was the line between freedom and bondage more blurred than on the vast sugar plantations of south Florida. Historically, the cane fields attracted the most desperate or oppressed workers. When the war began, the United States Sugar Company dominated Florida, controlling 86 percent of the state market. With the fall of the Philippines in 1942, U.S. Sugar successfully lobbied the government to lift the domestic quotas on sugar production, resulting in a scramble for laborers. Court testimonials and FBI records paint a dismal portrait of life inside the Clewiston camps. Florida's antiquated laws—declared unconstitutional by the U.S. Supreme Court in 1944 in *Pollock v. Williams*— prohibited debt-ridden workers from quitting a job, further reinforcing the prison-camp setting, serving the interests of Big Sugar but not those of the workers.

The short- and long-term solution to Florida's shortage of agricultural laborers came from afar. The U.S. Department of Agriculture (USDA) signed agreements with the governments of the Bahamas and Jamaica to allow the temporary immigration of 75,000 workers, and to pay for their transportation. Planters and corporations won what they had long sought: absolute control of a compliant labor force. L.L. Chandler, chair of the Dade County USDA War Board, openly observed, "The vast difference between the Bahama Islands labor and the domestic . . . is that the labor transported from the Bahama Islands can be deported and sent home if it does not work."[8]

What happened in Florida may well have been a harvest of shame, but it was also a harvest of plenty. The war provided Floridians, accustomed to decades of depression and scarcity, a taste of prosperity and abundance. City dwellers also came to terms with the dizzying changes brought by the war.

In September 1940, the *National Municipal Review* prophesied that American cities were threatened less by Stuka dive bombers than by mounting crises in public health. Had the editor visited Miami, Jacksonville, or Pensacola, he might have added alarming crises in public education, urban services, and affordable housing.

World War II accelerated Americans' mobile tendencies. Fifteen million Americans, in search of new opportunities, moved their residences and workplaces between 1940 and 1945. Another sixteen million men and women served in the armed forces. For most Americans, the war was more *Odyssey* than *Iliad*. Florida cities functioned as dynamic hives of activity as millions of Americans encountered Florida for the first time, trying to establish moorings in the quicksand of wartime. Never static, the cities shuffled constant streams of defense workers, rural migrants, tourists, and servicemen and -women, who all competed for scarce housing and transportation.

Jacksonville and Pensacola shared a symbiotic relationship with the Georgia and Alabama hinterlands. Jacksonville drew large numbers of rural residents from south Georgia. "Jacksonville came up in conversations like the weather," reminisced novelist Harry Crews, whose family left Bacon County for opportunities in Florida.[9] Pensacola's "official" population increased modestly from 37,000 in 1940 to 43,000 in 1945, but, according to James McGovern, these statistics ignore at least 100,000 temporary residents who spent time in Pensacola. Trailers and tents became commonplace as the city groaned under the burden of accommodating newcomers, many of whom spilled into unincorporated areas.

Unlike Pensacola, Key West enjoyed neither the luxury of new land nor the latitude of old land. The federal government had saved Key West from insolvency in the 1930s; now it would reshape the once isolated island. In the 1940s, the federal government not only primed the pump but built the pump, in this case the long-sought water pipeline from the Everglades to the Keys. Water began flowing in September 1942.

In 1940, Key West was a quaint community of 13,000 residents. Five years later, 45,000 persons crammed the city. "War has brought about many changes in Key West," lamented the *Miami Herald* in 1943. The reporter noted, "One of the last of the picturesque island's customs to disappear was the closing of doors to stores while a funeral procession passed. All business along the line of a funeral procession must be suspended as a final tribute to the dead. But the war ended that."[10]

Miami hummed with the surging currents of war, as tourists returned to the "Magic City" in 1943. Officially, Miami's population increased modestly from 173,065 residents in 1940 to 192,122 in 1945. Unofficially, the city's population fluctuated wildly. In January 1944, the *Miami Herald* estimated the city was "home" to 325,000 people, including winter residents, soldiers, and visitors. "Except for the land boom of 1925," observed journalist Nixon Smiley, "no other event in Miami's history had done so much to change the city as World War II. At the war's beginnings Miami still had many of the qualities of a small town. As you walked down Miami Avenue or Flagler Avenue you met person after person you called by their first name. . . . The war changed all that."[11]

What is now called the Gold Coast exploded. The collective population of Dade, Broward, and Palm Beach counties grew from 387,000 persons in 1940 to 692,000 in 1950, accentuating the increasing importance of southeast Florida.

Small-town Florida was not immune to wartime drama. The *New York Times's* Dora Byron toured Panama City, Starke, and Homestead in the fall of 1942. "Dime stores are thronged on Saturday nights and churches filled on Sundays," Byron wrote. Pointing out the inevitable loss of community that came with rapid growth, she stated, "Everywhere there is noise and hurry and crowds. All three quickly are strangers to small Florida towns." In Stuart, older residents criticized the improper wearing apparel, the "very short shorts and halter tops" of the new female residents shopping downtown.[12]

Tallahassee, a quaint community of 16,000 residents in 1940, also felt the war's tremors. Over one-third of the city's lawyers enlisted in the service. "On every street, in each store, and in the homes there is some reminder of the war," observed the *Tallahassee Daily Democrat.*[13] By 1944, the Florida State College for Women reached its largest enrollment ever, registering 2,227 women, in marked contrast to the 682 male university students at war-impacted Gainesville. On weekends, male soldiers and students, desperate for female companionship, descended upon the capital, many of them forced to sleep in hotel lobbies or on park benches.

In the big cities and small towns, residents expressed in words and deeds an outpouring of patriotic gestures and voluntary activities. On the home front, Floridians recycled scrap metal, planted victory gardens, and rolled bandages. In Lakeland, the Florida Citrus Bomber Fleet Committee raised funds to purchase fifteen Flying Fortresses. During one 1942 rally, Pine Island residents rescued ten tons of metal, including a steel dredge. In Zellwood, local children collected tons of paper and scrap metal during assorted drives. One official estimated that in 1943 Tampans tended 10,000 victory gardens. Floridians everywhere endured dimouts and ration coupons. In every community, a window flag bearing a blue star meant a son in the military. A gold star carried the somber news of a family's supreme sacrifice.

During World War I, a sardonic commentator had insisted, "War is the health of the State." During World War II, national leaders asked Americans to sacrifice, since, it was argued, the collective struggle to vanquish totalitarianism would bind society together. While that

President Doak Campbell (*foreground*) and student members of the "Victory Club" at Florida State College for Women form a V for victory on the Tallahassee campus. The students tilled "victory gardens" as part of the war effort.

proved out in part, the war's dynamism also created new fears and widened old fissures. The war revealed how fragile unity and patriotism were and how crises challenged democratic institutions. The wartime struggle for racial justice, in particular, is illustrative.

Deeply moved by the idealism of the war, inspired by President Franklin Roosevelt's call for "The Four Freedoms" and committed to defeating the evil empires of Japan and Germany, African Americans joined in fighting for what was to them an undemocratic nation. The war gave them new hopes for change, however. It was a period of transition and transformation, as the old painful elements of lynchings and Jim Crow collided with landmark civil rights cases and a new generation of leaders.

African-American leaders championed a "Double V" campaign, supporting the war against totalitarianism while continuing the fight against racism at home. On the eve of Pearl Harbor, over 500,000 African Americans resided in Florida and 605,000 in 1950. While other southern states were losing black residents to the "Second Great Mi-

USO clubs throughout the state entertained the 2,122,100 servicemen and -women who trained at Florida bases and camps. These GIs enjoyed a USO banquet at Tampa in April 1943.

gration" north, Florida cities attracted increasing numbers of black migrants.

World War II was the last American conflict fought with segregated units. In spite of the Jim Crow military, African-American servicemen performed wartime tasks both at home and overseas. A total of 51,467 Florida blacks were inducted into the armed forces, constituting one-fifth of the state's soldiers. While the U.S. Navy allowed blacks to serve only as messmen and the Marines refused black volunteers altogether, black units in the Army and Army Air Forces received high marks during the war. Daniel "Chappie" James, born in Pensacola in 1920, entered the Air Corps and in 1975 became a four-star general. The famed 99th Fighter Squadron, comprised of black fighter pilots in the Air Forces, trained at Tallahassee's Dale Mabry Field.

At the same time that Americans followed the military campaigns in the Pacific and Europe, another conflict was unfolding on the home front at hundreds of southern military bases and towns. Race relations became tense as Americans from all regions, ethnic groups, and races competed for services and respect. Floridians saw no reason to adjust the established color line for the visitors. But uniformed African Americans, soldiers fighting for democracy, expected to be treated with respect.

A series of incidents flared up in the strained wartime atmosphere. In Tallahassee, black soldiers stationed at Dale Mabry Field and black soldiers from nearby Camp Gordon Johnston frequented the capital's "Colored Recreation Center." Almost one-half of Tallahassee's population was African American, many of whom lived in the impoverished Frenchtown section. Two hundred black soldiers protested in August 1944 the arrest of five black servicemen in Frenchtown on charges of disorderly conduct. The *Pittsburgh Courier* and *Atlanta Daily World* asserted that overzealous local police aggravated the situation when they attempted to arrest the soldiers with drawn guns and tear gas. Black troops surrounded the police and insisted the accused men surrender to "colored military police." In the ensuing investigation, black troops from Camp Gordon Johnston were banned from visiting Tallahassee. The army subsequently required the base intelligence officer to file a "Weekly Report Concerning the Racial Situation." The officer noted in November 1944 that, while no racial incidents had occurred during the month, "there is of course still an occasional gripe from Negroes who are compelled to occupy rear seats in the city buses."[14]

In August 1942, the Fort Myers City Council unanimously enacted an "emergency ordinance to define the customs which promote and preserve the inter-racial disorders." The ordinance made it unlawful for blacks and whites to "loiter upon the streets" or to "patronize establishments serving food and intoxicating beverages . . . [without respect to] the divisional areas set apart by long established customs for colored and white occupancy and patronage."[15]

Elsewhere in the country a number of violent race riots erupted in Beaumont, Harlem, Detroit, and Los Angeles. In the aftermath of a June 1943 Detroit riot in which twenty-five people died, a *Miami Herald* editor wrote, "The Eleanor Roosevelt School of thought has been feeding the Negro a steady mixture of social equality that provokes such tragic incidents as Detroit's bloody battle."[16]

Florida prepared for the worst. The State Defense Council and Army Service Forces prepared a top secret plan in the event of race riots at Tallahassee, Jacksonville, Orlando, St. Petersburg, Tampa, or Miami. "In the City of Orlando," the report sketched out, "there is an undercurrent of tension, activated by union organizers and the presence of Northern Negro soldiers in the community."[17] Officials planned to impose military law in these cities in the event of riots. Detailed maps indicated key neighborhoods and institutions such as radio stations and newspapers.

The war forced some Floridians to reconsider the dilemma of race. In 1943, Herbert Krensky was traveling by train from Miami to Jacksonville. When the train stopped at Ocala, a platoon of German POWs, dressed in their Afrika Corps uniforms, boarded the train. The prisoners had been picking citrus. "When our train stopped at Waldo," remembered Krensky, "we stopped for a moment. . . . On the platform were these colored servicemen, one of them wounded and hobbling on crutches. They tried to board with their tickets in hand. The conductor refused to let them board. . . . He told them that since there were no colored coaches that they would have to ride in the baggage car."[18]

The most sensational and distressing racial episode occurred in Madison County. Jesse Payne, a black sharecropper, was lynched following a dispute with a white farmer. The spectacle brought ignominious attention to Florida since it was America's only lynching in 1945. A black army corporal wrote to Governor Millard Caldwell: "I had no idea that I would hear of similar acts of Fascism upon return to our great arsenal of democracy, America."[19]

But the war also offered hope. Across the South, the NAACP launched an attack upon the doctrine of separate but equal. Thurgood Marshall, representing the NAACP and black teachers, won several court cases in Florida, awarding African-American teachers salaries equal to their white counterparts. By war's end, blacks served on juries in Escambia and Pinellas counties, and cities such as Miami and Tampa hired black policemen. On 3 April 1944 the U.S. Supreme Court struck down the white primary. By 1946, African Americans in Florida broke the political color line, registered as Democrats, and voted in primaries. The seeds of the modern civil rights movement had been sown.

World War II served as a great watershed for American women. The most visible and powerful symbol of the war's impact on the home front was the presence of women in the workplace. The *Daytona Evening News* wrote, "Womenpower is available everywhere. Women are eager to give it whenever and wherever they can. Why does not the government take steps to organize, recognize, and use this valuable asset?"[20] The *Tampa Tribune* saw the war as a harbinger. "It may hurt the masculine pride a little to think that a woman can handle a man's job, but pretty soon a lot of Tampa women may be working at the benches and docks where men used to be."[21] The *Tribune* might have expanded the list to include orchards, welding shops, shipyards, and military bases.

Across America the number of working women rose from 14.6

million in 1941 to nearly 20 million in 1944. By war's end, married women outnumbered single women in the workplace, a landmark event. In Florida, newspapers noted the changes. One expert estimated that at least one-quarter of the state's farm workers were women. By March 1943, in Hillsborough County, 700 of 1,100 farm workers were females. "Women are doing virtually all of the cultivating and harvesting," noted the *Tampa Tribune*.[22] In Miami, milkmaids replaced milkmen at Southern Dairy, and women took jobs as pole painters at Florida Power and Light and as clerks and elevator operators at area hotels. Tallahassee hired Elizabeth McLean as the city's first policewoman. Women replaced men as transit workers in St. Petersburg. "Lumberjills [have] invaded Florida," claimed the *Miami Herald*.[23] "They are doing practically every job in the saw mill today, and they are even felling trees in the woods with probably a soprano 'Timber!'"

The Tampa Shipbuilding Company eagerly recruited "Rosie the Riveter" and "Joan of Arc." A bard of unspecified gender wrote a poem for the shipyard's newspaper, *Tascozette* in August 1942: "No more girdles these dark days,/No more brassieres, no more stays/Let your stout heads be resigned/ To breast and buttocks unconfined."

The Embry Riddle Aviation School in Miami and Arcadia employed large numbers of women in skilled positions, including twenty-five technical and flight instructors. Similar patterns occurred in Pensacola and Jacksonville.

The war effort relied heavily upon civic voluntarism, a field historically dominated by women. The day after Pearl Harbor, the *Tampa Morning Tribune* pleaded for "Tampa girls . . . to attend dances for soldiers."[24] In Miami Beach, 18,000 volunteers refurbished and staffed the Minsky Pier, a favorite recreation spot for soldiers. In St. Petersburg, teenagers volunteered as "Bomb-a-Dears," a recreational group, while the local chapter of the Grey Ladies distributed cigars and postcards at the Bay Pines Veterans' Hospital.

In a Rogers and Hammerstein musical, a lonely sailor stationed on an archipelago in the South Pacific summed up the feeling of countless American GIs: "What ain't we got? We ain't got dames!" Such was not a problem in Florida, if one believes newspaper accounts of alarming rates of VD and prostitution. The influence of sexually active men and women upon wartime manners and morals, a subject of scrutiny since the beginning of time, received tremendous attention from U.S. and Florida officials.

The war with its supercharged atmosphere of patriotism and sacrifice, strained the always confused world of gender and sexual relationships.

Newspapers conveniently blamed the problem on "Victory Girls," "VD Girls," and "Khacky-Wackies." Dorothy Parker suggested that it was time women "lost their amateur standing." Certainly it is difficult to stereotype wartime conduct or to assign labels of "victim" and "villain."

The fact is that prostitution posed a major problem around military bases and in major cities. In 1944, Pensacola's "VD Control Officer" estimated that Escambia County's population included 11,000 syphilitics. In Miami and Tampa, the military pressured city officials to eliminate red light districts. But while the police seemed to crack down on traditional houses of prostitution, the demands for illicit sex spawned new opportunities in new places. Helen Muir remarked, "Miami teenagers turned prostitute in Bayfront Park. . . . Early park closings and extra policing failed to stop this mass prostitution until all shrubbery was ordered trimmed."[25] The shrubbery at Tampa's Plant Park also inspired mutual affections, although one judge blamed local girls as much as prostitutes for the problem. Some military commanders, such as Colonel Edmund Gaines at Tallahassee's Dale Mabry Field, threatened to declare infected cities "off limits" to soldiers. The 1943 Florida legislature passed a State Quarantine Bill, converting four CCC camps at Miami, Ocala, Wakulla, and Jacksonville into VD hospitals. The bill empowered police to enroll for compulsory treatment any person testing positive for venereal disease.

Hundreds of thousands of wives, sweethearts, and children followed servicemen to Florida, hoping to reconstitute war-torn families or simply to be closer to loved ones. Florida, they learned, could be a cold place. Finding a home or apartment in crowded cities proved to be frustrating and often heartbreaking. Many called it a disgrace that servicemen with small children were turned away from homes and apartments. An "irate Navy wife" complained to a Florida newspaper in 1944 that, while there were houses and apartments galore in Florida, they seemed to be for tourists only. Philip Wylie, a trenchant critic of the hypocrisy of Florida's lavish life-style during the war, expressed outrage over the juxtaposition of the idle rich and the deserving poor in 1944 Miami. "Women and children walk the street," he complained in *Time*. "The men who have sacrificed most meet in Miami those who have sacrificed the least."[26]

Historians debate how women's lives and their roles in American history were affected by the war. One school of thought argues that for all their individual acts of employment outside the home, and for all their wartime service as Waves and Wacs, even as pilots, America's women willingly returned to the "traditional" home roles of mother-housewife when the war ended. Other scholars contend that World War II sowed the seeds for the modern women's movement, that the conflict profoundly changed the participants *and* the home front, and that, while many women did return to the homes, their expectations and experiences were incorporated into a changing American culture.

Largely overlooked during the war, a bill introduced and passed in the 1943 legislative session deserves mention. Representative Mary Lou Baker of St. Petersburg, the legislature's only female member at the time, introduced a bill known as the "Women's Emancipation Bill." Passed after a spirited debate, the law strengthened the rights of married women to manage their separate estates and to sue and be sued independently of their husbands. A bill to ensure the right of women to serve on juries failed.

News of the Japanese surrender ending the war swept across the peninsula and Panhandle on 14 August 1945. Collectively, in perhaps the most joyous celebration in state history, Floridians erupted in planned and spontaneous parades and demonstrations. In Miami, crowds of 30,000 filled Flagler Street with a parade of beeping automobiles and fluttering flags. In West Palm Beach, "Victory came . . . with a clattering din that served to release long-pent-up emotions with a flurry of miniature snowfalls of tattered paper."[27] Festive celebrants in Fort Lauderdale hanged an effigy of the Mikado on a rope. In Orlando, crowds gathered downtown, singing "Glory! Glory! Hallelujah!" In Jacksonville, the *Florida Times-Union* observed, "Sirens screamed, locomotives whistled, and automobile horns set up a deafening noise barrage."[28] In 1945 courthouse squares and downtowns figured prominently in the social lives of Floridians, and every one of them was filled with celebrants on what became known in history as V-J Day.

The war left lasting imprints on Florida, not the least of which was a list of war-tested political candidates. Within days after his enlistment in the Navy in 1942, Fuller Warren had launched a newspaper campaign to keep the home folks informed of his heroics and theatrics. The navy had also attracted other future governors, LeRoy Collins, Farris Bryant, and Haydon Burns. Daniel McCarty volunteered for the army and saw distinguished service with the field artillery. Claude Kirk enlisted in the marines at age seventeen and Reubin Askew served as a paratrooper. George Smathers's candidacy for the U.S. Senate was certainly enhanced by his reputation as a "Fighting Leatherneck."

Postwar politicians confronted a Florida government attempting to reconcile unprecedented demands for services with an antiquated tax structure. Educationally, Florida fared poorly, even by southern standards. In 1947, Florida still had no medical school, no community college system, and no public university south of Gainesville. The 1947 legislature passed a budget twice as large as ever approved but struggled to pay for the appropriations. In 1949 the legislature crossed a fiscal Rubicon when it approved, albeit reluctantly, a regressive three-cent sales tax.

World War II ushered in a dynamic new era in Florida history. The war years accelerated the pace of change and wrought significant developments in the social and economic lives of all Floridians.

Notes

1. *Tallahassee Democrat,* 9 December 1941.
2. Hemphill, *Aerial Gunner from Virginia,* p. 9.
3. Helen Muir, *Miami, U.S.A.* (New York: Henry Holt and Co., 1953), p. 2260.
4. *Fortune,* July 1943.
5. *Time,* 22 October 1954.
6. *Tampa Morning Tribune,* 27 November 1942.
7. *Miami Herald,* February 1945; clipping in the Agnew-Welsh Scrapbook, Miami-Dade Public Library.
8. *Miami Herald,* 19 March 1943.
9. Harry Crews, *A Childhood* (New York: Harper & Row, 1978), p. 128.
10. *Miami Herald,* 26 July 1943.
11. Nixon Smiley, *Knights of the Fourth Estate: The Story of the Miami Herald* (Miami: E. A. Seemann Publishing Co., 1974), p. 209.
12. *New York Times,* 15 November 1942.
13. *Tallahassee Daily Democrat,* 7 May 1944.
14. Frank J. Sasker, "Historical Report of Dale Mabry Field, Tallahassee," November 1944.
15. *Fort Myers New-Press,* 18 August 1942.
16. *Miami Herald,* 22 June 1943.
17. State Defense Council, Florida State Archives, Tallahassee, Record Group 191, Series 419, Box 57.
18. *Miami Herald,* 7 May 1985.
19. Millard F. Caldwell papers, Florida State Archives, Tallahassee.
20. *Daytona Evening News,* 5 October 1942.
21. *Tampa Tribune,* 28 December 1941.
22. Ibid., 14 March 1943.
23. *Miami Herald,* 22 August 1943.
24. *Tampa Morning Tribune,* 8 December 1941.
25. Muir, *Miami, U.S.A.,* p. 233.
26. *The New Republic,* 21 February 1944.
27. *Palm Beach Post,* 15 August 1945.
28. *Florida Times-Union,* 15 August 1945.

Bibliography

Primary Materials

Newspapers constitute an invaluable source for studying the war on the home front. The *Pensacola News Democrat, Panama City News Herald, Tallahassee Daily Democrat,* Jacksonville *Florida Times-Union, Fort Lauderdale Daily News, Miami Herald, Palm Beach Post, Fort Myers News Press, St. Petersburg Times, Tampa Morning Tribune, Gainesville Sun,* and *Orlando Sentinel* provide special insight into domestic events during the 1940s. Two out-of-state newspapers offer insights into race relations during the war, the *Pittsburgh Courier* (Florida edition) and *Atlanta Daily World.*

The P.K. Yonge Library of Florida History, University of Florida, Gainesville, and the State Historical Library and the State Archives in Tallahassee provide the best holdings of primary materials related to the home front. The Millard Caldwell and Spessard Holland papers at the archives and the papers of the State Defense Council are valuable sources.

Secondary Sources

Billinger, Robert D., Jr., "With the Wehrmacht in Florida: The German POW Facility at Camp Blanding, 1942–1946." *Florida Historical Quarterly* 58, no. 2 (October 1979):160–73.

Burran, James Albert III. "Racial Violence in the South During World War Two." Ph.D. dissertation, University of Tennessee, 1977.

Blum, John. *V Was for Victory: Politics and American Culture During World War Two.* New York: Harcourt Brace Jovanovich, 1976.

Dalfiume, Richard M. *Desegregation of the U.S. Armed Forces: Fighting on Two Fronts, 1939–1953.* Columbia: University of Missouri Press, 1969.

Davis, Jack. "'Whitewash' in Florida: The Lynching of Jesse James Payne and Its Aftermath." *Florida Historical Quarterly* 68, no. 3 (January 1990): 277–90.

Daniel, Pete. "Going Among Strangers: Southern Reactions to World War II." *Journal of American History* 77, no. 3 (December 1990):886–911.

Gannon, Michael. *Operation Drumbeat: The Dramatic True Story of Germany's First U-Boat Attacks Along the American Coast in World War II.* New York: Harper and Row, 1990.

George, Paul S. "Submarines and Soldiers: Fort Lauderdale and World War II." *Broward Legacy* 14 (Winter–Spring 1991):2–14.

Green, Barbara G. *The History of the Wainwright Liberty Ships and Tankers.* Panama City: Bay County Historical Society, 1978.

Hartmann, Susan M. *The Home Front and Beyond: American Women in the 1940s.* Boston: Twayne Pubs., 1982.

Hemphill, William Edwin. *Aerial Gunner from Virginia.* Richmond: Virginia State Library, 1950.

McGovern, James R. *The Emergence of a City in the Modern South: Pensacola, 1900–1945.* DeLeon Springs, Fla.: E.O. Painter, 1976.

Mickler, J. R. "Key West in World War Two." Key West: Public Information Office, 1945. Key West Public Library.

Mormino, Gary R. "G.I. Joe Meets Jim Crow: Racial Violence and Reform in World War II Florida." *Florida Historical Quarterly* 73, no. 1 (July 1994):23–42.

Napier, John Hawkins III. "Military Bases." In *The Encyclopedia of Southern Culture,* pp. 640–41. Chapel Hill: University of North Carolina Press, 1989.

Polenberg, Richard. *War and Society: The United States, 1941–45.* Philadelphia: Lippincott, 1972.

Rea, Robert Right. *Wings of Gold: An Account of Naval Aviation Training in World War II.* Tuscaloosa: University of Alabama Press, 1987.

Rogers, Ben F. "Florida in World War II: Tourists and Citrus." *Florida Historical Quarterly* 39, no. 1 (July 1960):34–41.

Shofner, Jerrell H. "Forced Labor in the Florida Forests." *Journal of Forest History* 25 (January 1981):14–25.

Sikes, Bob. *He-Coon: The Bob Sikes Story.* Pensacola: Perdido Bay Press, 1984.

Sitkoff, Harvard. "Racial Militancy and Interracial Violence in the Second World War." *Journal of American History* 58, no. 3 (December 1971): 661–81.

Sosna, Morton. "More Important than the Civil War? The Impact of World War II on the South." In *Perspectives on the American South,* edited by James Cobb, 4:145–63. New York: Gordon and Breach, 1987.

Tindall, George B. *The Emergence of the New South, 1913–1945.* Baton Rouge: Louisiana State University Press, 1967.

Waldeck, Jacqueline Ashton. "How Boca Won the War." *Boca Raton* 37 (Winter 1988):140–47.

Wynne, Lewis N., ed. *Florida at War.* Saint Leo, Fla.: Saint Leo College Press, 1993.

19 Florida Politics in the Twentieth Century

David R. Colburn

"We're a southern state and damn proud of it," a resident of Taylor County commented in 1993 as he sat in his pickup truck, but 300 miles to the south a resident of Dade County looked thoroughly bewildered when asked what it meant to be a southerner. For much of its history, Florida has been two states—one that extends south from the Georgia border to Ocala and that has identified with the South and its racial and social traditions and another south of Ocala whose heritage has little association with the South and that views the state as part of a national and, indeed, international economy. To understand Florida politics in the twentieth century, one has to be aware of this schizophrenia.

Linked closely to the Deep South for most of the nineteenth century, Florida continued to share many characteristics with its regional neighbors through the first half of the twentieth century. Much of its population in the nineteenth and early twentieth centuries, for example, came from Alabama and Georgia, both of which border Florida, and from South Carolina. These migrants re-created the southern culture of their former states in north Florida and undertook economic activities that reinforced social and political ties with their southern neighbors. Florida joined readily with the others in seceding from the Union in 1861 and participating in the bloody war for independence in order to secure its southern economic, social, and cultural values. Memories of the Civil War and Reconstruction were burned irrevocably into the

344

minds of Floridians from 1876 through the first half of the twentieth century.

By joining the Confederacy, Florida was forced to share the costs of the conflict and the burden of military Reconstruction. It was a painful period for Floridians, and they remained isolated from the national mainstream and mired in rural poverty for much of the late nineteenth and early twentieth centuries as a result of this decision.

Florida's leaders did not accept the results of the Civil War gracefully. At every stage in the Reconstruction process, they took steps to preserve many of the traditions of the past. And in the aftermath of Reconstruction, they established a caste system, at first informally and then through law, that permeated the entire society, denying African Americans the rights promised them during Reconstruction. This Jim Crow system imposed a subservient status on African Americans until well into the second half of the twentieth century. The ramifications of this racial system had a profound impact on state politics during this era.

The costs of civil war and the commitment to segregation hobbled Florida and the entire region for decades, but Florida's frontier-like environment shaped its social and economic character and its politics in a manner different from the rest of the region during the first forty years of the twentieth century. In 1900, Florida had the smallest population of any southern state, less than half that of the next smallest, and most of the state was undeveloped and often inaccessible wilderness. As recently as 1940, Florida had more open acreage than any other state east of the Mississippi River. Political leaders recognized the critical importance of a development program if Florida was to prosper, but the state lacked the capital to spur development and population growth. The only resource political leaders had to barter was land, and they did just that by granting large sections of land indiscriminately in order to encourage ambitious and wealthy men to develop the state and to make it accessible to others. This frontier experience and the commitment to growth and development made Florida and its politics quite different from those of its southern neighbors.

The state's geography was a second aspect of its uniqueness. Its population was isolated and fragmented by enormous distances that stretched from as far as Key West to Pensacola—approximately the same road distance as that from Pensacola to Chicago. Tampa was as far from Miami as New York from Boston, and travel was so difficult that few passed from one city to the other. Even in the early twentieth century, Florida's southern region was closely linked to the Caribbean, and people from the islands moved freely to south Florida. Cubans settled in the Tampa Bay area around the turn of the century, where they established a substantial cigar industry. Other immigrants, including Italians and Greeks, also settled in the southern part of the state. Few residents of north Florida would have recognized the Tampa Bay area as part of their state. Tampa's ethnic and racial diversity took root in its early years and contributed to the creation of a dynamic society in which multiculturalism, labor organizations, and social unrest dominated for much of the early twentieth century.

A third feature shaping Florida's politics and its southern uniqueness was its economic diversity. The state escaped the "curse" of cotton, a dependence on a one-crop economy and the oppression of tenant farming. Although Florida remained a poor state up to World War II, its economy varied significantly from cotton, tobacco, timber, and turpentine in the north to citrus, phosphate mining, cattle ranching, and tourism in the south. Florida thus never had the same commitment to a "southern way of life" that so influenced its southern neighbors.[1]

Florida's geographic and economic distinctiveness shaped its politics in often unusual ways. In examining southern politics prior to World War II, political scientist V. O. Key, Jr., was the first to recognize Florida's differences. Describing its politics as "every man for himself," Key attributed Florida's political development to its geography and the immigration of newcomers, both of which factionalized its politics and discouraged political cohesion. Key reasoned that because of these differences and the fact that Florida had a relatively small black population which constituted a majority in only three small counties, Florida would be the first southern state to develop a viable two-party system. Without the threat of a black majority, Key wrote, the ability of Democrats to play the race card would diminish in time and allow for the reemergence of the Republican Party.[2]

Little did Key realize at the time that the Florida Democratic Party would dominate state politics every bit as thoroughly and for nearly as long as it did in those southern states with large black populations. For approximately ninety years, from the post-Reconstruction period to the late 1960s, all statewide elections were effectively decided within the Democratic Party. The general election, during which Democrats seldom bothered to campaign, only confirmed the decisions of the party primary.

Had Key misjudged Florida? In one sense, his hypothesis was probably correct. The race card never had the same impact on Florida that it did on such southern states as Mississippi, Georgia, Alabama, and South Carolina, where the size of the black population, and therefore its perceived threat to white domination, served as a constant source of political concern.

What Key failed to appreciate fully was the political fragmentation created by the massive population growth in Florida, and the impact it would have on the development of a two-party political system. In the post-Reconstruction era, most Floridians lived within fifty miles of the Georgia border, and this region of the state was able to capitalize on its population majority to dominate the state legislature and to establish an apportionment system that ensured its control until the late 1960s. North Florida's dominance was aided, ironically, by the massive flow of newcomers into the state beginning in the 1940s. With an average of nearly 1.8 million people arriving each decade from 1940 to 1990, and most of them settling in south Florida, the region south of Ocala quickly came to have a majority of the state's inhabitants. The concerns of the newcomers focused chiefly on local matters and not on securing and holding statewide political control. Moreover, these new residents were not unified in their own political values and aspirations. For example, many from the Northeast had been lifelong Democrats, and they felt reasonably comfortable, at least initially, within Florida's Democratic Party.

In 1990, U.S. Senator Bob Graham, a native of Miami, described what he called the "Cincinnati factor" in state politics. In Graham's view, these folks had moved to Florida but remained Cincinnatians for all practical purposes. For example, they returned to Cincinnati at least once a year to visit family and friends; often sent their children to colleges in Ohio; subscribed to a Cincinnati newspaper; voted only to oppose new taxes, which they had resented when they lived in Cincinnati; and, at the end of their lives, had their remains shipped to Cincinnati for burial.

The consequence was that the culturally and economically homogeneous north Florida was able to maintain direction of the state Democratic Party and through it control of state politics. Key saw this fragmentation taking place even in the 1930s, but he underestimated its long-term consequences for the Democratic Party and Florida politics.

As Florida entered the twentieth century, its politics remained little different from those of the nineteenth century. The racial and cultural traditions of the antebellum era and the events of the Civil War and Reconstruction defined the mental outlook and social relations of most of its citizens and ensured the loyalty of white Floridians to the Democratic Party. Racial tensions in Florida remained at or near the surface during the post-Reconstruction era as native whites reasserted local rule and blacks attempted to secure equality. The rise of the Farmers Alliance movement in Florida, the secret affiliation between white and black farmers in the 1890s, and Florida's leadership in the national Populist crusade would seal the fate of black Floridians but not in quite the manner they had hoped or envisioned. Democratic fears about an alliance between white and black farmers led to a ferocious backlash in which traditional Democratic leaders enacted a poll tax, grandfather clause, and multiple-ballot law to prevent blacks and whites from ever joining forces again at the polls. These same Democrats then adopted a series of segregation ordinances in the late nineteenth and early twentieth centuries that prevented whites and blacks from being educated or socializing together, so that racial understanding and cooperation could not continue or develop further.[3]

The Democratic counterattack against Populism was devastating; it not only destroyed the movement in the state, but it also constructed a racial caste system in which blacks were denied their rights of citizenship and equality. The poll tax had a profound impact as well on the ability of white farmers to participate in Florida's electoral process. The $2 tax was often more cash than white or black farmers in the state had in a week (in some cases a month), a sum that few could afford. The poll tax not only decimated the ranks of black voters, it also did much the same for poor white voters. By the turn of the twentieth century, the Democratic Party had fallen securely into the hands of social and economic elites who strengthened their political position when needed by paying the poll taxes of those who agreed to support them.

The party and indeed state politics were heavily influenced by these north Florida elites, most of whom were very conservative on issues of race, social matters, and economic reform. While this group dominated state politics, they would not always control it. Religion, class, and race were three factors that, in combination, would occasionally challenge their leadership.

By 1901, without the threat of black voters or the independence of rural, white voters, the Democratic Party thoroughly dominated state politics, but this dominance made it difficult for the party to keep personal ambitions within the traditional party structure. In 1901, party leaders opted to abandon the nominating convention and party platform as a vehicle for controlling the selection of candidates for particular offices. This change persuaded most politically ambitious Floridians to stay within the Democratic Party by allowing as many as were interested to campaign for various state offices through the new Democratic primary system. Once Democratic voters had cast their ballots in the primary, then all Democrats would rally around a particular candidate in the general election against the Republican opponent.[4]

This structural change worked well in preventing the creation of a multiplicity of parties, but it did not prevent the Democratic Party from splintering into a variety of factions that allied with certain individuals or machines. Little unity existed within the party other than a commitment to the racial caste system and to economic development. Those who were sympathetic to the policies of Republican President Theodore Roosevelt (1901–9) or with the probusiness, conservative Republican leadership in the U.S. Senate kept their views to themselves and ran as Democrats if they wanted to win political office in Florida. The Democratic Party in Florida thus represented a broad mix of political and economic views, which further promoted factionalism.

Throughout the period from 1900 to 1940, state politics were dominated by a few central issues. National developments, especially those that occurred within the Democratic Party, occasionally impacted on state politics in significant ways throughout this era from the age of progressivism to the New Deal. Race was never far from the forefront of state politics and played a particularly prominent role throughout the era from 1900 to 1924 and from the post–World War II era to 1970. Last, economic development dominated the concerns of state politicians and Floridians generally. They did not always agree on how that development should occur and various strategies for economic growth would divide them, but Florida Democrats were committed to developing their state so that rural poverty would not continue to define its future and theirs.

At the beginning of the twentieth century, Florida politics felt the influence of the progressive movement that came to play a prominent role in national Democratic and Republican parties. Shaped by a variety of forces that sought to make government more responsive to the needs and concerns of voters, especially white Anglo-Saxon Protestants, the national progressive movement took many different forms. In Florida, the administrations of Governors William Jennings (1901–5) and Napoleon Bonaparte Broward (1905–9) adopted the rhetoric of the progressives to limit the influence of the railroad and corporate land interests in the state's development. Both men were committed to state development and to a state-planned and -directed drainage program for the Everglades, but both also emphasized the needs of Floridians over the aims of railroad owners and land developers.

During his campaign for governor, for example, Broward repeatedly attacked the railroad and corporate interests in Florida and their efforts to exploit various sections of the state. The resentment in Florida toward the railroad interests, in particular, grew out of the belief that much of the prime real estate in Florida was being usurped by the railroads. Farmers also felt that railroads discriminated by charging them much higher rates to ship their goods to market to offset the reduced rates they granted to large citrus and industrial interests. Many native Floridians saw railroad owners as interlopers or, even worse, as northerners who sought to enrich themselves at the expense of the state and its citizens.[5]

Development and who would determine its course in the state constituted one of the two dominant issues in the first decade of the twentieth century. Governors Jennings and Broward carried the fight on behalf of the citizens of the state, but their efforts were hampered by the state's inability to pay the costs of developing the Everglades or any other area. Florida was simply too poor to be able to convince investors that it could guarantee the bonds for such a project. Jennings and Broward also encountered strong opposition in the legislature to their efforts to have the state play a greater role in this process for these reasons and also from probusiness elements who saw no conflict of interest between the needs of business and of the public.

For the first decade of the century, progressives like Jennings, Broward, and Broward's successor, Albert Gilchrist (1909–13), controlled the governor's office, but because of their limited ability to carry out their economic reforms and sharp divisions within the legislature, they gradually yielded power to more entrenched, conservative forces in the state. Progressivism was never as strong in Florida as it was elsewhere, although the city manager and commission forms of government did spread to local communities throughout the state. Nevertheless, the movement never had the impact it did in states like Wisconsin, New York, and Ohio. Florida's brand of progressivism lacked the economic resources to transform its political promises into policy. The state's progressives also faced strong opposition from forces that were allied with or sympathetic to the efforts of railroad magnates like Henry Flagler and of land developers like Hamilton Disston. The opponents of progressivism and even some of its allies believed that a cheap land policy and private development, even in areas as environmentally sensitive as the Everglades, were essential to the state's emergence from poverty. At this stage in Florida's development, environmental concerns took a distant second place to concerns about economic growth and expansion of the population. Florida's flirtation with progressivism was thus a short-lived affair, and by 1912 political power had fallen into the hands of probusiness spokesmen. World War I sealed the fate of progressivism in Florida, as it did in the rest of the nation, focusing attention on events overseas and on domestic affairs related to the war.

Race constituted the second major feature of progressivism in Florida. Like their southern neighbors, white Floridians saw no contradiction in their efforts to strengthen democracy and to deny equal rights to African Americans. The progressive movement in Florida was a white man's movement, and it sought to protect their rights against the power of railroads and land developers and also against the black man. White Floridians easily carried two banners, one for progressive reform and the other for segregation. Black Floridians resisted these efforts, but with limited resources and few allies they gradually succumbed to the pressures of segregation. Florida adopted most of its statewide segregation ordinances in the early twentieth century, and the local laws were firmly in place by 1910.[6]

The election of southern-born Woodrow Wilson as president in 1912 and the onset of World War I had a twofold impact on Florida and on the South generally. First, with Wilson's election, the South felt that it had been redeemed, and its sense of regional alienation began to diminish. Second, the gradual involvement in the war effort and the social dislocation that resulted from mobilization caused considerable consternation in the South over race relations. Having recently imposed segregation, white southerners by 1914 were in no mood to have this system altered. By contrast, black southerners viewed the war as an opportunity to cast off the oppressive blanket of segregation by demonstrating their patriotism.

Whites in Florida had mixed feelings about black participation in the war effort. Grove owners, lumber and turpentine interests, and those businessmen generally dependent on a large supply of cheap, black labor did not want blacks going off to war. But others worried that if only whites were conscripted, black men would greatly outnumber the remaining white men and thus constitute, in their minds, a major threat to the security of white women.

Not surprisingly, in this context the war years had a tumultuous effect on Florida's race relations, so much so that whites resorted to legal and extralegal violence during those years and the immediate postwar period to maintain prewar racial patterns. Black soldiers who had experienced the liberating effects of living and training in many northern communities and in Europe, where they found they could move around with much more freedom than in the South, looked forward to the postwar period and the freedom and opportunity they felt they had earned.

Racial patterns in the South were additionally complicated by the massive migration of African Americans to the Midwest and Northeast beginning around 1910 to escape the oppression of segregation and the economic havoc created by the boll weevil's devastation of the cotton crop. They were also drawn to the North by the promise of economic opportunity and greater freedom. Over 40,000 black Floridians joined 283,000 African Americans from other southern states in the migration to Chicago and other midwestern and northeastern cities where a shortage of labor had created great demand for workers. Labor agents from northern industries and railroads descended on the South in search of black workers. The Pennsylvania Railroad, for example, brought 12,000 to work in its yards and on its tracks, all but 2,000 of whom came from Florida and Georgia.[7]

The response of Florida's whites to the massive departure of black residents was mixed. Initially, whites ignored or expressed satisfaction with this exodus. Up to the turn of the twentieth century, white Floridians had seriously discussed sending local blacks to a foreign country or to a western region of the United States. During his term as governor, Napoleon Broward proposed that Congress purchase territory, either foreign or domestic, and transport blacks there where they could live separate lives and govern themselves.

As the massive exodus of African Americans continued from the northern counties of Florida during the war years, Governor Park Trammell (1913–17) and his successor, Sidney J. Catts (1917–21), essentially ignored it. Trammell, no friend of black Floridians, had disregarded the lynching of twenty-nine blacks when he was the state's attorney general and twenty-one lynchings during his governorship. Catts had been elected on an anti-Catholic and antiblack platform. Once in office, he publicly labeled black residents as part of "an inferior race," and he refused to condemn two lynchings in 1919. When the NAACP complained about these lynchings, Catts denounced the organization and blacks generally, declaring, "Your Race is always harping on the disgrace it brings to the state by a concourse of white people taking revenge for the dishonoring of a white woman, when if you would . . . [teach] your people not to kill our white officers and disgrace our white women, you would keep down a thousand times greater disgrace."[8]

Catts changed his tune when white business leaders, especially in the

lumber and turpentine industries, began to complain that the continued outmigration of blacks was having a devastating effect on labor
availability and labor costs in Florida. Suddenly Catts began to urge
blacks to stay in Florida and called for unity and harmony among the
races. Few black citizens listened to him or were intimidated by threats
of violence. The migration continued to escalate as a quiet protest
against racial conditions in the South.

During the early 1920s, white Florida gradually suppressed the aspirations of its remaining black population. Its governors played a willing
hand in this process. They defended their actions by asserting the inferiority and dependence of the black race and received ample encouragement from the writings of anthropologists and popular authors who
claimed that scientific evidence documented black inferiority. Black citizens, however, resisted efforts to reimpose segregation by whatever
means were at their disposal. In Ocoee, black residents marched to the
polls in an effort to vote, only to be physically assaulted and to have
their homes and property seriously damaged.[9]

The white commitment to maintaining segregation knew few
bounds, however. In Perry and Rosewood, blacks were killed and their
property destroyed following alleged assaults upon white women.
When blacks in Rosewood tried to defend themselves against a white
mob, their public buildings, churches, and homes were burned to the
ground, six were reported murdered, and all were chased from the
community in January 1923, never to return.[10] The promise of the war
years and the great migration had been completely snuffed out in
Florida by 1924, and state leaders were willing accessories in this
process.

Although governor of Florida during this era, Catts was more than
just another conservative white Democrat. He was a political maverick
who had stepped down from the pulpit to capture the governorship in
1916 on a platform that denounced the Catholic church, corporations,
and alcoholism. He broke the cycle of Democratic governors who had
risen through the party ranks or who had family connections with
prominent Democratic leaders. Catts was neither, and he played upon
white concerns about ethnic, racial, and religious differences and hostility to corporate power to mobilize a large political following. With
support from many Floridians of modest means, Catts took steps to protect the interests of white farmers and workers and to improve public
education. His challenge to traditional Democratic leadership in the
state was unwelcomed, and the party acted to avoid his like again by
passing a resolution that blocked any person from voting in the

Governor Sidney J. Catts (1917–21) is shown here (*seated, left front*) with his family on the governor's mansion steps. A resident of Florida only five years when he announced for governor, Catts campaigned in the rural counties as an anti-Catholic demagogue. Yet his administration was characterized by numerous progressive programs, including penal reform, support for organized labor, and improved status for women. And his official stance toward Catholicism was conciliatory (his executive secretary was Catholic, and his son Rozier, with his father's blessing, married a Catholic).

Democratic primary who opposed a candidate because of his religious views. How they proposed to enforce it was not mentioned.[11]

Although Catts and his allies remained political factors throughout the 1920s, the Democratic Party returned to the hands of party stalwarts in 1920 with the election of Cary Hardee (1921–25), who took office just in time to bask in the prosperity of the economic boom in south Florida. The economic development and population expansion that Florida had long sought began to stir, and Florida's leaders turned their backs on Catts and his allies and eagerly embraced the new investors. Growth was so dramatic that Florida's political leaders did little more than ride the fast-moving roller coaster. Towns sprang up along the coast and in what were formerly swamp-like areas. Floridians and people from around the country rushed to become part of Gold Coast development. Unfortunately, like all roller coasters, Florida's economy suddenly lurched downward in late 1925, and Floridians were ill equipped and ill prepared to do anything about it. Buoyed by the new wealth, state leaders had done little to regulate speculators or to restrain the massive expansion.

Florida became a metaphor for the boom and bust years of the 1920s, and no state experienced the highs and lows any more thoroughly. By the time the stock market collapsed in the fall of 1929, Florida was already mired in four years of depression (see chapter 17).[12] The financial collapse paralyzed political leaders and left the state unprepared to meet the crisis. Governor Doyle Carlton (1929–33) attempted to counter the political ineptitude by urging the legislature to raise taxes to reduce a state deficit of $2.5 million and to assist counties in paying off their bonds. He also sought a gasoline tax to pay for roads and to keep schools open. But the governor's tax plan encountered stiff opposition from representatives whose counties had small debts and who felt they were being forced to pay for the sins of those with large debts. Fistfights broke out in the legislature as members debated the governor's proposals and the economy continued to worsen. At one point Carlton, totally exasperated, pleaded with legislators, "If the program that has been offered does not meet with your liking, then for God's sake provide one that does."[13]

Carlton's successors, David Sholtz (1933–37) and Fred Cone (1937–41), refused to follow Carlton's controversial lead and instead urged economy in government. Both blamed Florida's problems on irresponsible leadership and called for a return to fiscal restraint, balanced budgets, and sound business principles. Decimated by the state and national depression, Florida looked to the federal government more than most states did for assistance. With nearly 30 percent of the population unemployed and state governors offering little hope or vision, voters in 1932 embraced the Democratic candidate for president, Franklin D. Roosevelt, with a sense of desperation, hoping that his election would provide Florida with much-needed federal assistance.

Roosevelt's election and his New Deal programs provided the lifeline that kept Florida afloat during the 1930s. The Agricultural Adjustment Act, in particular, provided crucial assistance for financially desperate farmers and grove owners. Roosevelt's buoyant attitude and his ties to the South through his home in Warm Springs, Georgia, gave encouragement to the region and to Florida in particular. Governor David Sholtz cast the fate of his administration entirely with the New Deal and his personal relationship with Roosevelt. The results secured Florida a safety net that halted the downward spiral of state and personal finances. Despite Roosevelt's leadership and aid from the federal government, however, Florida continued to suffer greatly during the depression, and as late as 1939 no end seemed in sight.[14]

By the beginning of World War II, Florida had seen its population expand to 1.5 million, but much of the state was sparsely settled. Orlando, for example, was a town of fewer than 40,000 people, and much of the southwest coast of Florida stood relatively undeveloped. Ft. Myers had a population of only 10,600. Despite the brief boom of the 1920s, Florida had changed remarkably little from 1900. The Democratic Party still had a hammerlock on state politics, and representatives from north Florida controlled both houses of the legislature. Black Floridians still suffered under the oppression of segregation, and the depression had taken a devastating toll on black family life. Only the small assistance that flowed from New Deal agencies and passed through the hands of white farmers and citrus owners eventually found its way into their pockets and kept them from being completely impoverished. The state still depended on agriculture and the lumber business for most of its economic vitality, much the same as it had in the first decade of the century. Florida's political and economic leaders sought growth under nearly any conditions, especially after more than a decade of depression. The state remained predominantly rural throughout this period, although Miami had expanded to rival Jacksonville as the largest city in the state, with a population of just over 100,000. By the end of the 1930s, Floridians still saw themselves as a rural, agricultural people with conservative political and social views. The depression had curtailed their optimism about the future of their state and confidence in state political leadership. Much of this was about to change, however, as Florida and the nation entered the new decade and as the international crises in Europe and Asia threatened to change their lives at home and abroad forever. Indeed, the coming of World War II would finally end the state's long economic depression and launch an era of dramatic growth.

Although Florida's economic development was probably inevitable given its semitropical climate, its lengthy and languorous coastline, and its lush vegetation, the state's revitalization commenced in the 1940s with massive federal expenditures in Florida and the migration of 2,122,100 men and women into Florida for military training. The federal government opened major military bases throughout the state to meet the demands of its navy and air force in particular, and tens of thousands of laborers poured into the state to work on base construction and in shipyards in Jacksonville and Tampa. The arrival of service personnel, workers, and their families led to the dramatic expansion of cities from Miami to Jacksonville to Pensacola and, perhaps as important, provided federal funds to build modern transportation facilities to connect the cities.

The gradual use of air-conditioning and the introduction of effective mosquito control during this period made the state even more appealing to new arrivals and awakened some to its potential development. The nearly five months of summer had made Florida almost intolerable to all but the hardiest of souls, but air conditioning and pesticides suddenly made the summers bearable. The rest of the year had always been appealing to the rich; with new roads it now became accessible to the middle class.

Led by Governor Spessard Holland (1941–45), Florida worked closely with the Roosevelt administration and the War Department to secure federal funds for Florida. The war gave the state a much-needed economic boost, and its leaders moved quickly to capitalize on the changes. Holland's successor, Millard Caldwell (1945–49), dramatically expanded activities of the Florida Department of Commerce to attract new business and visitors into the state. Commerce Department employees seemed to take particular pleasure in sending photographs of beautiful young women, scantily clad and lounging around a pool or at the ocean, to northern newspapers in the dead of winter. On a more serious note, Caldwell and his successors also began a series of trips to the North and Midwest in an effort to recruit more business. These trips expanded in subsequent administrations to include foreign countries as Florida sought to internationalize its economy and its tourism. The state modernized its roads to accommodate increasing automobile traffic, and Caldwell's successor, Fuller Warren (1949–53), pushed through a fence law to keep the cattle from crossing the roads, killing the tourists, and damaging their cars.

Florida's sales pitch to prospective business interests and residents was essentially the same throughout the period from 1945 to 1980 and differed only slightly from that used before the war. Emphasizing low taxes, a healthy environment, cheap land, and a probusiness political climate, state agencies, led by the governor's office, appealed to tourists and investors throughout the nation but especially to those east of the Mississippi. The prosperity of the war years, air-conditioning, and good roads were instrumental in making the appeal successful. During the 1940s, nearly 400,000 people moved to Florida, despite the dislocation and lack of permanence created by the war effort in five of the ten years. Florida had been discovered once again, but unlike the 1920s, this time its discovery would not be short lived.

The potential social and political upheaval threatened by Florida's population growth had not escaped the attention of legislative leaders from northern Florida. Efforts to reapportion the legislature suddenly became much more significant, but few such proposals ever made it to the floor of either chamber in the 1940s and 1950s. At the same time, efforts by Governor Caldwell and his successors to streamline state government through reorganization met with consistent legislative opposition. Even with a governor like Caldwell who shared their own political and social convictions, rural legislators were reluctant to allow the governor's office to strengthen its hand at the expense of the legislature. These same legislators understood, too, that with the growth of south Florida, the ability of north Florida to control the governor's office in the future was limited at best.

The war also created new opportunities for 500,000 black residents of Florida, and the war propaganda had given many hope that racial change would be forthcoming in the wake of the war. The length of World War II, in contrast to the twenty months of U.S. participation in World War I, and the resulting social and geographic dislocation had mobilized the black community behind racial reform in ways the country had not seen (see chapter 18). While Florida whites and their state political leaders basked in the postwar boom, they kept a wary eye on racial developments and sought to do what they could to maintain a continuation of race relations as they had been in the prewar era. Governor Caldwell and his successors, Fuller Warren and Dan McCarty (1953), did what the federal courts required of the state, but they stonewalled implementation at every turn. Caldwell, for example, persuaded the legislature to adopt a Minimum Foundation Program for the public schools. Such legislation was common in the South in the postwar period and had two purposes. One, quite legitimate, was to strengthen the educational system in the region through increased funding so that southern states would be more competitive in recruiting new business and its native population would have more economic opportunities than had been available to them. The other aim, however, was to upgrade the black schools in the region so that the federal courts could not charge that public education in Florida was unequal. This ploy required a very substantial investment from southern states because black schools had fallen into such disrepair from lack of funding during the depression, but southern states, and Florida particularly, were willing to do so in order to avoid integration.[15]

In the postwar era, local leaders and law enforcement officials, often in cooperation with white militants, also took steps to make sure that segregation barriers remained intact. County sheriffs assisted grove owners and lumber and agricultural interests in seeing that black veterans shed their uniforms and returned to work in the groves and fields. Deputies often disciplined blacks who expressed dissatisfaction with wages and working conditions. They also systematically repressed black desires for equality and greater freedom. When black residents persisted in their protests, they were arrested and placed in county jail, where they were beaten until they agreed to return to work or to conform to segregation customs. As an example to others in Florida, Klan leaders and allies in Orange County murdered Harry T. Moore, state leader of the NAACP, and his wife in their homes on Christmas Eve 1950 for conducting a statewide campaign to register blacks to vote in Florida during 1949 and 1950. Governor Caldwell and Attorney General J. Tom Watson generally ignored acts of violence and intimidation against black citizens and against those involved in NAACP activities. The FBI led the inquiry into Moore's death and found that there was a widespread network of local officials, police, and militant whites operating throughout central Florida to suppress the rights of blacks.[16]

The efforts of political leaders in the state to control racial developments were undermined not only by the federal courts but also by their own efforts to diversify the state's economy and increase its population. Business leaders and residents came predominantly from the Northeast and Midwest and had no intention of having their interests jeopardized by a commitment to a long dead southern past. Businessmen and tourist officials insisted that their operations be conducted in a stable environment. All this worked against the efforts by the rural, north

Governor Fuller Warren (1949–53), one of Florida's most charismatic orators, addresses an audience at the 1947 Forest Field Day in Taylor County.

Florida–dominated legislature to preserve segregation. By the late 1940s and throughout the 1950s, battle lines were drawn between proponents of traditional southern values and those who sought to build a "new" Florida. Ironically, the notion that "we have seen the enemy and he is us" was especially true in Florida as racial and social traditions were steadily eroded by development policies embraced by political leaders.

The issues of race and reapportionment were inextricably linked in the 1950s. Legislative leaders from north Florida believed that not only their political dominance but their way of life was threatened by reapportionment. They understood correctly that south Floridians did not have the same commitment to the state's racial traditions that they had and that those residents would readily cast these traditions aside if they felt their economic prosperity threatened. The war over reapportionment thus had even greater significance than was first apparent.

By 1950, as Florida continued to grow dramatically and as the legislature remained unreapportioned, 13.6 percent of the state's population elected more than one-half of the state senators and 18 percent of the population elected more than half the members of the House of Representatives. Governor LeRoy Collins (1955–61), who was elected with substantial backing from the urban regions of the state and with especially strong support from south Florida, made legislative reapportionment one of his top priorities. As the battle unfolded, rural legislators formed the Pork Chop Gang and "took a blood oath to stick together, and did that on all legislation," especially on reapportionment. Collins introduced reapportionment in each legislative session, only to see it blocked by rural legislators, who dominated the senate leadership and held nearly a majority of the seats in the house.[17]

If Collins, south Florida legislators, and residents of that region had any hope of winning this fight, their plans were set back by the emergence of the civil rights movement. When the Supreme Court issued its *Brown v. Board of Education of Topeka* edict on 17 May 1954, few in Florida were prepared for such a decision. Pork Chop elements in the state legislature quickly seized the lead, denouncing the decision and drafting proposals of resistance. Representatives from south Florida also criticized the Court's pronouncement, but they found themselves and their state being led by north Florida politicians who militantly rejected any compromise.

Locked in a struggle to win the governorship in a special election at the time of the Court's pronouncement, Collins announced his commitment to segregation. As a business progressive, however, Collins was not an extremist. Indeed, he sought to create an environment that would help the state diversify economically and understood that racial militancy could crush his modernization program. Moreover, as a Florida native, Collins was not anxious to see the ambitions of his state and its future ruined once again. Still, he was not prepared at this point to accept desegregation, and he joined with other southern leaders in opposing the Court's decision. Richard Kluger noted in *Simple Justice*

Senator Claude D. Pepper greets some of his Florida constituents in the 1940s. A vigorous advocate of President Roosevelt's New Deal, Pepper brought many millions of federal dollars to Florida during the depression and war years. In his last years, as a member of the U.S. House of Representatives, he became the nation's staunchest advocate for senior citizens.

that Florida "submitted the most extensive and spirited brief" criticizing the implications of the Court decision on public education.[18]

Collins pursued a variety of measures that were designed to preserve school segregation but also sought to avoid racial extremism. His plans faced strong challenges from north Florida legislators, who countered with proposals to close down the schools if desegregation occurred, open a private school system, and enact an interposition resolution to block implementation of the Court's decision. Collins, however, was able to keep the racial militants at bay so that he and Florida gained a reputation for racial moderation, and tourists, new residents, and new businesses continued to stream into the state. Although Florida was only one of four southern states with virtually no integration by 1960, the national press continued to portray Florida as a progressive state because of the leadership provided by Collins and because his counterparts in Arkansas, Mississippi, and Alabama pursued extremist policies.[19]

Collins also found that he had strong allies for his moderate approach in the business community and among south Floridians generally. Few among these recent arrivals had a serious commitment to segregated schools and a segregated society. It was this attitude that made north Floridians all the more determined to block reapportionment, maintain control of the legislature, and ensure that Florida would perpetuate segregation. A special legislative committee, created in 1956 and chaired by former governor Charley Johns (1953–55), not only investigated the NAACP as an alleged "communist organization" but also sought to ensure conformity of thought in the state's public schools and universities.[20]

The efforts by north Floridians to continue to hold on to the reins of power in the state took on a note of desperation in the 1960s. Without the political skill of a LeRoy Collins in the governor's chair and with Florida continuing to be a seedbed of change as a result of massive population growth, a burgeoning tourist economy, and an expanding civil rights movement, Governors Farris Bryant (1961–65) and Haydon Burns (1965–67), both of Jacksonville, together with rural, north Florida legislators, pursued efforts to maintain the status quo. Attempts to stymie desegregation took on a harder edge, and both Bryant and Burns used the state police and the National Guard to preserve segregation against local civil rights protests and the national campaign conducted by the Reverend Martin Luther King, Jr., in St. Augustine. Florida's reputation for racial moderation slipped badly during the first half of the 1960s.[21]

Ironically, as Burns fought to block school desegregation, he led a statewide effort in 1965 to bring the Walt Disney Corporation to Florida. Disney and the other tourist operations that opted to follow Disney's new theme park in Orlando would further undermine racial extremism and the social instability that accompanied it. Above all, these businesses insisted on a secure environment in which to conduct their operations.

Although the state's economic development program steadily eroded its commitment to a segregated past, there was no clear sign that political leaders were prepared to abandon Florida's racial heritage until the federal government intervened. Washington removed the civil rights issue from state control by adopting the Civil Rights Act of 1964 and the Voting Rights Act of 1965. The Federal District Court followed in 1967 by ordering the implementation of the principle of one person, one vote in Florida and dismantling opposition to reapportionment with one stroke of the pen. The world of the Pork Choppers had collapsed, and with it the southern cause that they had so vigorously championed. In contrast to what happened in the Reconstruction era of nearly a century earlier, this time the federal government did not renege on its promises to black Americans. Although few white leaders would have acknowledged it in the sixties, federal officials had done Florida an enormous favor by removing racial extremism and rural domination from its politics.

The changes mandated by the federal government and courts were traumatic for Florida and for the South generally, but it was not immediately obvious what impact they would have on state politics. The state and national reforms, and especially the removal of race from around the neck of state politics, allowed a fresh breeze to blow over the entire region.

Without a race-based politics and without a legislature dominated by rural north Florida, the state began to address important issues that had been ignored for years in the battle over segregation and, in the process, to revisit political loyalties that had gone unchallenged during the twentieth century. The most immediate impact of these developments was the adoption of a new Constitution in 1968 which recognized the Court-ordered reapportionment in 1967, effectively gave legislative control to south Florida, and completely overhauled the old Constitution of 1885. The document strengthened the hands of the governor by allowing him to serve two consecutive terms, consolidating the number of executive departments, and granting him budgetary responsibilities. At the same time, however, it formally recognized the cabinet as a constitutional body and granted certain cabinet officers authority over the consolidated executive agencies. These changes, together with the Legislative Reorganization Act of 1969, which led to annual meetings of the legislature (as opposed to the previous biennial meetings) and the creation of permanent legislative staffs, effectively counterbalanced the new powers of the governor's office.

Florida's demographics continued to change dramatically in this period, with nearly 500 new residents entering the state each day in the 1960s and 1970s. What was once a frontier-like state became the largest and most urban state in the region. In the process, Florida's demographic features began to resemble more closely those of the Sunbelt states of Texas, Arizona, and California than those of the traditional South. Florida's economy became increasingly dependent on housing construction, high technology manufacturing, and tourism, although agriculture and to a lesser extent the phosphate industry and cattle ranching still played prominent roles. The migration of Latin peoples into southeast Florida from Central America and the Caribbean also expanded the state's influence into the Caribbean basin and Central America, enabling Miami to become one of the principal banking and financial centers of the region. By 1975, Florida was looking less and less like a southern state.

A critical component of Florida's population expansion in the post-1960 era was the infusion of retired people and Cubans into the state. Florida's elderly, who today constitute nearly 25 percent of the population—the highest in the United States—made heavy demands on the state's social and medical services, while simultaneously pressuring state politicians to limit new tax initiatives and other revenue measures that might adversely affect their fixed incomes. Thus, they supported programs to aid the infirm and to protect the elderly from crime but resisted new spending for other social programs, education, and families. They have had a profoundly conservative impact on state politics because they are so well organized by the American Association of Retired Persons and because they vote in much higher percentages than other segments of the population.

Cuban Americans, who fled Communist Cuba in 1959 and settled in Dade County, made a rapid and remarkably successful adjustment to American life (see chapter 21). Their middle-class status and the size of the Cuban community in south Florida facilitated their economic advancement and also made them a political force in Dade County and in Florida generally. Because of their opposition to Fidel Castro and communism, they focused their attention primarily on foreign affairs, but they were also strong advocates of an unfettered American capitalism. Beyond these concerns, they have been generally conservative on social programs and issues of race. The size of this community and its particular agenda have combined to add a further ethnic dynamic to state politics. Cubans mimicked the ethnic activism of Jewish Floridians, who actively pursued support for the state of Israel throughout this period. This ethnic dynamic has marginalized racial concerns which had dominated Florida politics for much of the nineteenth and twentieth centuries.[22]

The Republican Party, which had been making slow but steady gains in the postwar period, benefitted considerably from the growth in the number of retirees and Cuban Americans. In 1966, the party captured the governorship in a stunning development, after having failed to challenge seriously for the office since 1900. The election of 1966 and Republican Edward Gurney's defeat of former governor LeRoy Collins for the U.S. Senate in 1968 reflected the expansion of an electorate that was not committed by racial and historical ties to the Democratic Party and by public dissatisfaction with President Lyndon Johnson's Great So-

Governor LeRoy Collins, whose administration (1955–61) was perhaps the most en-lightened and successful in modern Florida history, promoted New South values of business pragmatism, social harmony, and governmental reform. During his first years in office, which directly followed the U.S. Supreme Court decision of 1954 ending racial segregation in the nation's schools, he adopted a moderate stance that prevented defi-ance of the court. On his death in 1991, the state house of representatives unanimously named him "Floridian of the Century."

ciety programs. Collins and Democratic gubernatorial candidate Robert King High were characterized by their opponents as liberal, free-spending Democrats, a charge that would continue to resurface in the post-1965 era and that would lead state Democrats to distance them-selves as far as possible from the national Democratic Party.

The 1966 and 1968 votes did not mark a trend in Florida politics, but they did indicate that Democratic control was no longer a certainty. The election of Claude Kirk as governor in 1966 and Gurney's senatorial success resulted from voter belief that they were the more conservative candidates and thus more likely to preserve the political and social traditions of the past. It was not insignificant that Floridians quickly dumped both men once they realized that these traditions could not be retained, and they did not turn back to the Republican Party until the 1980s. The party also suffered a setback in state politics by its nomination and election of these two weak candidates. Kirk, who came across as a political buffoon, and Gurney, who was accused of political corruption, reinforced the traditional view that Republicans in Florida were political mediocrities. As late as 1979, no statewide political office was held by a Republican, and only 26 percent of the seats in the legislature and three of fifteen congressional seats were held by Republicans.[23]

Despite these developments, the Republican Party gradually emerged as a viable second party in the 1960s. Its achievements were principally the result of the new population mix, with many voters who had been registered Republicans elsewhere. The party also began to make gains among former Democrats who had moved to Florida to escape the high taxes and cost of living in their home states. The emergence of a new national Republican Party under Barry Goldwater, Richard Nixon, and, most important, Ronald Reagan won a strong following among Florida voters with its emphasis on smaller government and lower taxes. This conservative Republican agenda also had considerable appeal among traditional, conservative Democrats in Florida, most of whom felt little affinity with the social programs of the Democratic Party. By 1968 Floridians were voting Republican in every presidential election except 1976, when the candidacy of native southerner Jimmy Carter brought Florida back to the Democratic fold.

Although the Republicans' initial power was centered in south Florida, from the southwest coast to the Orlando area, and along the southeast coast from Vero Beach to Ft. Lauderdale, its influence gradually spread throughout the state during the Reagan presidency. By 1990 the party had become so influential that it even constituted a powerful force in north Florida, a region where residents would have turned over in their graves before voting Republican in the period before 1960.

By 1994, the Democratic Party still had a slight edge in the number of registered voters, but the Republican Party was narrowing the gap rapidly, as nearly every new voter joined its forces. For the first time in the twentieth century, Republicans seized power in the state senate. Republicans also hold one of the two U.S. Senate seats and more than half of the Florida seats in the U.S. House of Representatives. Whether the Republican Party becomes the dominant party in Florida politics remains to be seen, but the momentum is clearly on its side. Moreover, the social policies of the national Democratic Party up to 1994 remained at odds with the interests of most Florida voters.

The demise of race as an issue in Florida politics also focused the attention of voters on important state issues that had long gone unattended. Despite the bumptious nature of his governorship, Claude Kirk (1967–71) reawakened Floridians to the fragile nature of the state's environment and, with the backing of a citizens' group, Florida Defenders of the Environment, led an official effort to stop the construction of the Cross-Florida Barge Canal. Offered as a way to link east and west Florida commercially and also to make Florida a hub of sea traffic passing from the Gulf of Mexico to the Atlantic and back, the canal quickly lost support when Floridians became aware of the potential damage to their drinking and recreational waters if a major shipping accident occurred.

The environmental movement reflected the increasing influence of south Florida in state politics. It was this region of the state that suffered most under a laissez-faire approach by rural, north Florida political leaders, as unrestricted state growth jeopardized their supply of fresh water and their quality of life. Environmental activism reached its apogee under Governor Reubin Askew (1971–79) with adoption of the Oil Spill and Pollution Control Act in 1970 and the Environmental Protection Act in 1971. Aided by a strong economy, Florida legislators went even farther in 1972, adopting the Land and Water Management Act, the Water Resources Act, and the State Comprehensive Planning Act, which provided the framework for state development and environmental protection in subsequent years. Florida also began a land acquisition program under Askew to preserve some of the most sensitive and endangered lands.

The effort to protect Florida's environment, however, has often found itself subject to the state's economic development. State leaders have historically chosen development over the environment and often used the environment to facilitate economic expansion. This traditional response has continued to influence state politics, especially in north Florida where population and economic expansion have been relatively limited. But even in south Florida, the environment has often been jettisoned in times of recession, as happened in 1991 along the Gold Coast when environmentalism was perceived to be hampering economic recovery from the severe recession in 1990 and 1991.

While the modernization of the state and the abandonment of race

Reubin O'Donovan Askew (*right*) served two terms as governor, 1971–79. The sedate, judicious former state senator from Pensacola was the first to be elected to two full terms. His administration was characterized by many progressive initiatives, including a Sunshine Law that required financial disclosure by all state officials and a state income tax on corporations. He is shown here at the capitol on 14 April 1976 honoring Pensacola-born Air Force General Daniel "Chappie" James, the highest ranking African American in the armed forces.

and a gerrymandered legislature have markedly improved the nature and quality of Florida politics, significant problems continue to challenge Florida's leadership. The dramatic expansion of the state's population, with nearly one-fourth of its residents being over sixty-five, has caused the needs of the state in 1995 to appear overwhelming. In thirty short years, Florida went from being the thirtieth state in size to the fourth, and projections indicate that it will be the third largest in the year 2000. Education, the environment, roads, water, crime, not to mention the medical and social needs of the elderly, children, and poor, challenge state leadership in ways that Florida has not previously experienced. Both gubernatorial and legislative staffs have expanded dramatically in recent years in an effort to address these problems.[24]

Even with reforms in the state bureaucracy and the legislature, Florida is overstressed in meeting its needs in large measure because the state had attracted its many new residents and businesses by offering low taxes and small government. The state has continued to remain a haven for people seeking to avoid paying personal income taxes. A significant number of military personnel, for example, claim residence through a post office box in order to enjoy the state's considerable tax advantages. The consequence has been dramatic for state-funded programs. In 1992, for example, Florida ranked last in the nation in funding for higher education. In the same year, it was unable to staff two newly constructed prisons, because it lacked the revenue to pay for the staffs. Like most other states, Florida found itself bedeviled by Medicare and Medicaid costs that threatened to bankrupt its finances. Moreover, the accelerating rate of violent crime has begun to undermine the state's tourist economy and its economic development as both Europeans and other Americans questioned the risks of vacationing in and moving to Florida.

Hurricane Andrew, which hit south Florida in August 1992, was only the most visible sign that there was trouble in paradise. Highly publicized tourist murders in the fall of 1993 confirmed the fact. These two developments not only highlighted but seemed symptomatic of the state's worsening social, environmental, and economic problems. Crime, poverty, educational concerns, and racial and ethnic tensions all conspired to threaten the quality of life in Florida and to dismantle the Florida dream.

The dream faced further erosion in recent years at the hands of the two political parties which waged a titanic struggle for control of the state. The pressures of this political battle and the potential stakes involved have pushed the social, environmental, and economic needs of the state to the background. The consequences for the state and its citizens have been nearly as damaging to its development and future as were the forces of race and political gerrymandering of an earlier era.

Notes

1. V. O. Key, Jr., *Southern Politics in State and Nation* (New York: Alfred A. Knopf, 1949), pp. 86–87.
2. Ibid., pp. 82–105.
3. Jerrell H. Shofner, "Florida and Black Migration," *Florida Historical Quarterly* 57, no. 3 (January 1979):267–88.
4. David R. Colburn and Richard K. Scher, *Florida's Gubernatorial Politics in the Twentieth Century* (Tallahassee: University Presses of Florida, 1980), pp. 61–62.
5. See Samuel Proctor, *Napoleon Bonaparte Broward: Florida's Fighting Democrat* (Gainesville: University of Florida Press, 1950).

6. See Jerrell H. Shofner, "Custom, Law, and History: The Enduring Influence of Florida's 'Black Code,'" *Florida Historical Quarterly* 55, no. 3 (January 1977):277–98.

7. John Hope Franklin, *From Slavery to Freedom: A History of Negro Americans,* 4th ed. (New York: Alfred A. Knopf, 1974), p. 350.

8. Colburn and Scher, *Florida's Gubernatorial Politics,* p. 222.

9. John Higham, *Strangers in the Land: Patterns of American Nativism, 1860–1925* (New York: Atheneum, 1965), pp. 149–57; Papers of the NAACP, pt. 7, Anti-Lynching Campaign, 1912–55, Lynching—Ocoee, Florida (Series A: Anti-Lynching Investigative Files, 1912–53, reel 9, group 1, ser. C, Administrative Files, Box C-353, Microfilm, 1987, University Publications of America). Also see Lester Dabbs, Jr., "A Report of the Circumstances and Events of the Race Riot on 2 November 1920 in Ocoee, Florida," Master's thesis, Stetson University, 1969.

10. "A Documented History of the Incident Which Occurred at Rosewood, Florida, in January 1923" by Maxine D. Jones, Larry E. Rivers, David R. Colburn, R. Thomas Dye, and William W. Rogers (submitted to the Florida Board of Regents, 22 December 1993), 93 pages.

11. Wayne Flynt, *Cracker Messiah: Governor Sidney J. Catts of Florida* (Baton Rouge: Louisiana State University Press, 1977). Also see Colburn and Scher, *Florida's Gubernatorial Politics,* pp. 66–67.

12. Colburn and Scher, *Florida's Gubernatorial Politics,* p. 190.

13. Ibid., pp. 191–92.

14. Ibid., p. 193.

15. Ibid., pp. 244–47.

16. James Clark, "Death Found Suspects Before Justice," *Orlando Sentinel,* 11 October 1992, and "Klan Once Had Strong Grip," *Orlando Sentinel,* 17 October 1992.

17. William C. Havard and Loren P. Beth, *The Politics of Mis-Representation: Rural-Urban Conflict in the Florida Legislature* (Baton Rouge: Louisiana State University Press, 1962), pp. 50, 62; also see Colburn and Scher, *Florida's Gubernatorial Politics,* pp. 173–77.

18. Richard Kluger, *Simple Justice: The History of Brown v. Board of Education and Black America's Struggle for Equality* (New York: Alfred A. Knopf, 1976), pp. 724–25.

19. See David R. Colburn, "Florida Governors Confront the *Brown* Decision: A Case Study of the Constitutional Politics of School Desegregation, 1954–1970," in *An Uncertain Tradition: Constitutionalism and the History of the South,* edited by Kermit L. Hall and James W. Ely, Jr. (Athens: University of Georgia Press, 1989), pp. 326–55. Also see Tom R. Wagy, *Governor LeRoy Collins: Spokesman of the New South* (Tuscaloosa: University of Alabama Press, 1985).

20. See Steven F. Lawson, "The Florida Legislative Investigation Committee and the Constitutional Readjustment of Race Relations, 1956–1963," in Hall and Ely, eds., *Uncertain Tradition,* pp. 296–325.

21. David R. Colburn, *Racial Change and Community Crisis: St. Augustine, Florida, 1877–1980* (New York: Columbia University Press, 1985), pp. 104–9, 178, 187–88.

22. See Raymond A. Mohl, "Miami: The Ethnic Cauldron," in *Sunbelt Cities: Politics and Growth Since World War II*, edited by Richard M. Bernard and Bradley R. Rice (Austin: University of Texas Press, 1983).

23. See Edward Kallina, *Claude Kirk and the Politics of Confrontation* (Gainesville: University Press of Florida, 1993), and Mark Stern, "Florida's Elections," in *Florida's Politics and Government*, edited by Manning J. Dauer (Gainesville: University Presses of Florida, 1980), pp. 73–91.

24. For further insight into the modern period in state and local government, see Robert J. Huckshorn, ed., *Government and Politics in Florida* (Gainesville: University of Florida Press, 1991).

20 The African-American Experience in Twentieth-Century Florida

Maxine D. Jones

On 31 March 1994, nineteen African-American legislators in Florida utilized black political clout, perhaps for the first time in the twentieth century. Sensing that a bill to compensate victim families of the Rosewood massacre in 1923 might be defeated in the House of Representatives, the Black Caucus decided to play hardball by putting pressure on Governor Lawton Chiles. Even though Chiles supported the measure, the Black Caucus believed that he should use his influence more actively to secure votes for passage. They threatened to withdraw their support for the governor's health-care package unless he lobbied more vigorously for their piece of legislation.

The House passed the Rosewood Compensation Bill on 4 April 1994 by thirty-one votes, and four days later the Senate voted twenty-four to sixteen in its favor. The Black Caucus's shrewd tactical move guaranteed the passage of a measure that had come to represent to thousands of black Floridians an acknowledgment for past wrongs and hope for the future of race relations. It also symbolized the distance traveled and the political strength African Americans had gained since the turn of the century. In 1900, the 230,730 African Americans in Florida were politically impotent and voiceless. During Reconstruction and for a brief time afterward, black males had joined the Republican Party and had actively participated in politics by both voting and holding office. White Floridians, however, curtailed the black vote, first through violence and economic intimidation and later through legislative means. A

Table 1. Florida Legislative Black Caucus, 1992–94

Rudolph Bradley	House	Manatee/Pinellas
Larcenia J. Bullard	House	Dade
Beryl D.Burke**	House	Dade
James Bush, III	House	Dade
Cynthia Moore Chestnut	House	Alachua/Marion
Muriel Dawson	House	Broward
Willye F. Dennis Clayton	House	Duval
Josephus Eggelltion	House	Broward
Addie L. Greene	House	Palm Beach
James T. Hargrett	Senate	Hillsborough/ Manatee/ Pinellas/Polk
Anthony C. Hill, Sr.	House	Duval
Betty Holzendorf	Senate	Duval
Douglas L. Jamerson***	House	Manatee/Pinellas
Daryl L. Jones	Senate	Dade/Monroe
Alfred J. Lawson*	House	Gadsden/Leon
Willie Logan, Jr.	House	Dade
Matthew Meadows	Senate	Broward
William H. Turner	Senate	Dade
Lesley Miller, Jr.	House	Hillsborough
Alzo J. Reddick	House	Orange

* Chair   ** Co-chair
*** Appointed commissioner of education

poll tax and a multiple-ballot-box law enacted in 1889 effectively reduced the number of black voters and rendered the Republican Party powerless in the state.[1]

Thus, when Florida's first primary law was passed in 1897, African-American voting strength had already been seriously diminished. The adoption of the Democratic white primary further ensured the exclusion of the majority of blacks from the political process in state elections. Some African Americans were permitted to register as Republicans and independents and to vote in general elections. According to historian Hugh Price, approximately 20,000 blacks Floridians were registered voters in 1944—all Republicans. But even that limited right could not always be fully exercised. When blacks voted in the general election in Ocoee (Orange County) in November 1920, violence erupted. Sections of the black community were burned, several blacks were beaten and killed, and hundreds were forced to flee the area never to return. Nevertheless, blacks continued to fight for their right to cast ballots.

A family portrait by Vansickel Studios in Gainesville, 1900.

Threats and intimidation directed against them sometimes backfired. The Ku Klux Klan in Miami paraded through the black section of the city, burned crosses, and hanged an effigy of a black man in May 1939 in its efforts to keep blacks from the polls. Those threats, however, had the opposite effect as more blacks than ever before turned out to cast their votes in Miami. African-American women, who had secured the right to vote in 1920, joined their men in exercising their limited rights to participate in the electoral process. Eartha White gave encouragement and served cool refreshments to the long line of black women waiting to register to vote in 1920 in Jacksonville. She also directed the Negro Republican Women Voters in 1920 and served as state chairperson of the National League of Republican Colored Women in 1928.

It was not until the U.S. Supreme Court outlawed the white primary in *Smith v. Allwright* (1944) that blacks in Florida and across the South could register as Democrats and vote in state primary elections. Black voter registration significantly increased in the following years. Before 1944 few blacks were permitted to register as Democrats in Florida, but 106,420 were registered as such by 1950. Conversely, the number of black registered Republican voters decreased from an estimated 20,000 in 1944 to only 9,725 in 1950. Although no longer hampered by the poll tax or the white primary, only 37.5 percent of the state's adult blacks were registered to vote by 1956. Racism and social customs still prevented many blacks from exercising their rights.

As late as 1952 several Florida counties with a majority black population had few registered voters. For example, even though they represented almost 50 percent of the population, no blacks were registered to vote in Madison County. But 586 African Americans bravely marched to the Madison County courthouse in 1954 where they were finally allowed to register. Five hundred and fifty-eight of them registered as Democrats. Similar conditions existed in other counties, including Gadsden, Flagler, and Jefferson.

A strong belief that placing the right people in office could improve conditions for African Americans encouraged organizations and individuals to work incessantly to increase the number of blacks voters. Voting leagues were organized across the state, and the National Association for the Advancement of Colored People (NAACP) actively sought to convince African Americans of the importance of voting. Black Floridian Harry T. Moore, of the NAACP and the Progressive Voters League, played a major role in augmenting the number of black registered voters. From his base in Brevard County, Moore canvassed the county and the state. By 1950 over 50 percent of the blacks in Bre-

Table 2. African Americans in the
Florida Senate, 1982–92

Arnette E. Girardeau	1982–92
James T. Hargrett	1992–
Betty S. Holzendorf	1992–
Daryl L. Jones	1992–
Matthew Meadows	1992–
Carrie P. Meek	1982–92
William H. Turner	1992–

Table 3. African Americans in the Florida
House of Representatives, 1970–94

Rudolph Bradley	1994–	Anthony C. Hill, Jr.	1992
Corrine Brown	1982–92	Betty S. Holzendorf	1988–92
Larcenia J. Bullard	1992	Douglas L. Jamerson	1989–94
Beryl D. Burke	1992–	Daryl L. Jones	1990–92
James C. Burke	1982–92	Joe Lang Kershaw	1968–82
James Bush, III	1992–	Alfred J. Lawson	1982
Gwendolyn Sawyer Cherry	1970–79	Willie Logan, Jr.	1982
Cynthia Moore Chestnut	1990	Carrie P. Meek	1979–82
Bill Clark	1982–92	Lesley Miller, Jr	1992–
Muriel Dawson	1992–	John Plummer	1980–82
Willye Clayton Dennis	1992–	Darryl Reaves	1990–92
Josephus Eggelltion	1992–	Jefferson Reaves, Sr	1982–90
Donald G. Gaffney	1986–87	Alzo J. Reddick	1982–
Arnette E. Girardeau	1976–82	Mary L. Singleton	1972–76
Addie L. Greene	1992	John Thomas	1978–86
James Hargrett	1982–92		

vard County were registered. In addition to encouraging blacks to exercise their right, Moore also challenged the racist infrastructure of the state by demanding equal salary for black teachers and denouncing lynching and the inhumane treatment of black prisoners. Moore was murdered on Christmas day 1951 when his home was bombed.

The movement to expand the African-American voting populace was long, laborious, and dangerous, but the efforts of such men as Harry T. Moore, C. K. Steele, and Edward Davis eventually paid off. The Democratic Party was the party of choice for most African Americans. Voter figures in October 1962 showed 176,820 blacks as registered Democrats and 14,843 as Republicans; twenty years later 483,388 blacks were registered as Democrats and 16,146 as Republicans. By

Florida's first African-American Supreme Court justice, Joseph W. Hatchett, of Pinellas County, poses with his family prior to taking the bench for the first time, 2 September 1975. Hatchett resigned from the Court four years later in order to accept an appointment to the Federal Court of Appeals.

1992, a total of 521,328 registered black voters gave voice to the views of more than 1.5 million African Americans in Florida.[2] Aided by redistricting and an unprecedented numbers of blacks going to the polls, black Floridians were now represented at all levels of government. In 1968, Joe Lang Kershaw became the first black elected to the state legislature since Reconstruction and Gwendolyn Sawyer Cherry the first African-American female in 1970. Carrie P. Meek and Mary Littlejohn Singleton followed in Cherry's footsteps. In 1982, Meek became the first African-American woman elected to the Florida Senate. In 1992, Meek, Corrine Brown, and Alcee Hastings became the first African Americans since Reconstruction to represent Florida in the U.S. House of Representatives.

Blacks have also been appointed and elected to high nonlegislative offices. Governor Reubin Askew appointed Jesse J. McCrary secretary of state in 1978, and in 1994 Governor Chiles named former legislator Doug Jamerson to be Commissioner of Education. Two African Americans have served on the state Supreme Court. Governor Askew appointed Joseph Hatchett to the high court in 1975 and Governor Bob

Table 4. Population of Florida, 1900–1990

Year	Total Population	White	Black
1900	528,542	297,333	230,730
1910	752,619	443,636	308,699
1920	968,470	638,153	329,487
1930	1,468,211	1,035,205	431,828
1940	1,897,414	1,381,986	514,198
1950	2,771,305	2,166,051	603,101
1960	4,951,560	4,063,881	808,186
1970	6,789,383	5,724,464	1,041,535
1980	9,746,324	8,184,855	1,343,134
1990	12,937,926	10,749,285	1,759,534

Graham selected Leander Shaw to serve on the court in 1983. In 1990 Shaw became the first African American to sit as Chief Justice of the Florida Supreme Court. By 1994 African Americans in Florida had made great strides in their effort to participate fully in the political process.

The economic and social position of black Floridians remained static for much of the twentieth century. Forced to live in a segregated and unjust society, blacks were frequently subjected to lynching and mob violence. Between 1900 and 1917 approximately ninety black men and women were lynched in the state. Their "misdeeds" ranged from insulting a white woman, to a refusal to give up land, to alleged rape and murder. Mob violence in Perry (Taylor County) in December 1922 and Rosewood (Levy County) in January 1923 resulted in the loss of lives as well as substantial property damage. Whites were responsible for more than fifty lynchings between 1918 and 1930. The brutal lynching of Claude Neal in Jackson County in 1934 drew the attention of the nation. Rarely were those responsible prosecuted. Black Floridians knew their place in society, and few dared to step outside of it.

African Americans eked out livings as best they could. Forced out of traditionally "Negro jobs," they found it increasingly difficult to succeed economically. Black men especially had difficulty finding employment in urban areas. Thus large numbers of black men and women were relegated to agricultural, unskilled, and semiskilled labor. In 1910, farm workers aged ten and older numbered 47,953 males and 18,330 females. Approximately 43,729 African-American men and 12,440 women were gainfully employed as agricultural workers in 1930. Twenty years later 30,432 nonwhite males (19.9 percent) and 15,596 women (15.9 percent) age fourteen and over were paid farm laborers. These figures do not include unpaid family workers or those who managed or owned farms. African Americans sixteen years and older earning their living as farm laborers numbered 17,673 men and 10,108 women in 1970, and approximately 21,676 men and 3,747 women worked as farm workers and in related occupations in 1990.

Not all black men worked on the land. More than 6,000 in 1910 and 9,219 in 1930 worked in saw and planing mills. Substantial numbers also labored on steam railroads, and as lumbermen, craftsmen, wood choppers, porters, and servants. There were 1,530 African Americans employed in 1910 as longshoremen and stevedores, 1,882 in 1930, and 1,155 as late as 1970. Between 1940 and 1990 the bulk of black men found employment as truck drivers and in construction, manufacturing, transportation, communication, and other public utilities.

Few women remained in agriculture as more and more found work as domestics, personal servants, and service workers. More than half of the gainfully employed black women in Florida worked as personal or domestic servants in 1930. Almost 60,000 out of 97,994 black women fourteen years old and above were employed as private household or service workers in 1950. The trend between 1960 and 1990 varied only slightly, as black women continued to dominate service occupations. While classifications changed and the percentages declined, according to the 1990 census an estimated 115,614 black females were employed in service occupations. More than 10,000 worked in private households, 23,595 in food service occupations. Another 29,610 women in 1990 earned their livelihood by cleaning offices and buildings.

While the majority of African Americans labored in unskilled jobs, there was always a black professional class and significant gains were made in the size of this group after the turn of the century. There were eighty-three African-American physicians and surgeons in Florida in 1910, ninety-six in 1930, but only eighty-eight in 1940 (eighty-five male and three female). Several African Americans practiced medicine in Ocala (Marion County) in 1935, among them R. S. Hughes, W. P. Wilson, and N. H. Jonus. Carrie E. Mitchell Hampton also had a medical degree and her husband, L. R. Hampton, was one of at least two African-American dentists in Ocala in 1935. The black community in Jacksonville was served by five dentists, one chiropractor, and ten physicians in the late 1950s. Between 1940 and 1970, the number of African-American doctors in the state grew by only twenty-seven, but a significant increase took place between 1970 and 1980. In 1980 there were 323 black male and 152 female physicians in Florida. Ten years later, more than 1,200 blacks were identified as health diagnosticians,

A. Philip Randolph was born in Crescent City in 1889. Educated in Jacksonville and New York in the 1920s, he organized the Brotherhood of Sleeping Car Porters, an all-black AFL union. As a result of his leadership Pullman porters' working hours were cut, pay was increased, and working conditions were improved. During World War II and afterward, Randolph worked to end racial discrimination in defense factories and in the military. In 1963 he organized and directed a march on Washington that became the largest civil rights demonstration in the nation's history. He died in 1979.

Table 5. Negro Population in Florida
1900–1990

Year	Male	Female	Total
1900	120,199	110,531	230,730
1910	161,362	147,307	308,669
1920	167,156	162,331	329,487
1930	215,148	216,680	431,828
1940	252,799	261,399	514,198
1950	293,137	309,964	603,101
1960	432,107	448,079	880,186
1970	498,695	542,956	1,041,651
1980	636,961	705,727	1,342,688
1990	839,189	920,345	1,759,534

which included doctors, dentists, veterinarians, optometrists, and podiatrists. Pharmacists, lawyers, dentists, nurses, accountants, chemists, drafters, engineers, and photographers were and remained a part of Florida's black professional class, but teachers have traditionally made up its majority. From the 916 employed in 1910 to the more than 22,000 in 1980 and 47,321 in 1990, they have been the backbone of the middle class.

Business owners also contributed to the development of a strong and diverse middle class. Thriving black business districts existed in several Florida cities, including Jacksonville, Tampa, Miami, and West Palm Beach, and proprietors across the state organized Negro Business Leagues. If nothing else, the practice of segregation guaranteed black business owners a clientele and several businesses prospered. Blacks owned and operated funeral homes, florist shops, rooming houses, restaurants, insurance companies, and newspapers. The *Tampa Bulletin*, owned and edited by Mr. and Mrs. M. D. Potter, was one of several African-American newspapers in Florida. Others included the *Florida Star* and the *Tattler*, both located in Jacksonville, the Tampa *Florida Sentinel*, and the *Miami Times*, edited by H.E.S. Reeves. Newspapers serving the African-American community in 1994 included the *Miami Times*, the Jacksonville *Sentinel*, the Tallahassee *Capitol Outlook*, and the St. Petersburg *Weekly Challenger*.

In 1958, Jacksonville boasted numerous black-owned businesses, including two photography studios, twelve nightclubs, five realty companies, fourteen restaurants, and more than 100 beauty shops. Abrams L. Lewis provided insurance to thousands of black Floridians as one of the founders and later president of the Afro-American Insurance

Company, which became a flourishing venture. When he died in 1947 the company was valued at approximately $1.5 million, and in 1975 the company was worth $10 million. Unfortunately, integration took a major toll on black businesses. When blacks gained the right to frequent shops, theaters, and stores that had previously refused to serve them, black businesses experienced a sharp decrease in their earnings and many were forced to close. There has been a revival of sorts in the nineties, as some African-American entrepreneurs are seeking not only to regain black customers but also to attract a white clientele. These business owners continue to search for their niche.

As a group, African Americans in Florida have always wanted their piece of the American dream. Owning land or a home has always been important to the black community. About 20,916 black families in 1910 (27.7 percent) and 30,160 in 1930 (27.3 percent) owned their homes. And although not deemed of much value—52.1 percent of the homes owned by blacks in 1930 were valued at less than $1,000—many of these families managed to keep their property for generations.

Most African Americans had rented their homes, and during the depression the federal government began to construct housing units which would improve conditions for thousands of black Floridians. Complexes were constructed in Jacksonville, Miami, West Palm Beach, and other Florida cities. By 1942, Miami had three federal housing projects, including Liberty Square. The Durkeeville Housing Project in Jacksonville and Dunbar Village in West Palm Beach were welcomed by those who resided in slum areas. While the federal government helped to improve the living conditions of many black Floridians, numerous negative consequences accompanied the move toward housing large numbers of people in small areas. Many residents of the projects felt hemmed in and frustrated, and unfortunately some of the housing units became the breeding ground for poverty, crime, and drugs. The perplexing problems of the inner city remain. White flight and the desertion of business establishments from urban areas have contributed to the loss of jobs and a reduction in the quality of services and education provided to those trapped in inner city areas. The frustration and helplessness felt by thousands of African Americans in Florida often resulted in violence and crime. Riots in Miami and Tampa in the 1980s gave young blacks an arena in which to vent their anger and outrage at a system they considered racist, insensitive, and unsympathetic.

Education had always been extremely important to the black community, not only in Florida but across the United States. In education, many blacks believed, rested the future and hope of a scorned people.

Even though the education provided to blacks in Florida at the turn of the century was inadequate and remained so for decades, blacks took every opportunity afforded them. The disparities between black and white schools were myriad, in facilities, supplies, student load per teacher, expenditures per student, length of school year, and teacher salaries. For example, in 1901 the average student load per white teacher was thirty-nine; it was seventy-nine per black teacher. The average salary for black teachers in Gainesville in 1935 was $562, for white teachers $970. The assistant supervisor of schools in Duval County in the 1940s complained that black schools were overcrowded, lacked equipment, had half-day sessions, and occupied buildings in disrepair. He deemed many schoolhouses unfit for their intended use. While its intent was not really to equalize black and white schools, the adoption of the Minimum Foundation Program by the Florida legislature in 1947 resulted in making education and teacher salaries more equitable. According to J. Irving Scott, the Minimum Foundation law "accomplished more for the Negro, within the framework of segregation, than any other education legislative act in the state."[3]

This measure improved conditions but not enough, so community leaders, teachers, and parents challenged the inequities. Teachers filed salary inequity suits during the 1940s in Escambia, Duval, Brevard, Palm Beach, and Hillsborough counties. With African-American attorneys such as S.D. McGill representing them, and with the support of the NAACP and the Florida State Teachers Association, they met with some success. Teachers and parents confronted school boards in St. Johns, Palm Beach, Marion, Broward, Dade, and Hillsborough counties over allowing black schools to close so that students could harvest vegetables and fruits. In some of these areas students attended school for three months, left to pick vegetables for a couple of months, and then returned for three more months of school. Black students attended school for only four months in some counties. Noting that white schools were not closed during the vegetable harvesting season, the Palm Beach County Teachers Association successfully challenged the custom. Opposition from parents and community leaders helped end the so-called Strawberry Schools by the late 1950s. Many of the apparent educational disparities disappeared with school desegregation in the 1960s and 1970s, but white flight and the disintegration of inner cities resulted in widespread inequities in many public schools.

Until 1958 the only institutions in the state open to blacks seeking higher education were Florida Agricultural and Mechanical University (FAMU), Bethune-Cookman College, Florida Memorial, and Edward

Waters College. Established by the Florida Legislature in October 1887 as the State Normal College for Colored Students, FAMU has emerged as the premier historically black college in the state. Under the leadership of Frederick S. Humphries, who became the eighth president in 1985, FAMU experienced unprecedented growth and in 1993 was second only to Harvard in attracting National Achievement Scholars. The institution is also well known for its School of Business and its band, "the Marching 100."

Bethune-Cookman College in Daytona Beach was founded and headed by one of Florida's most famous citizens, Mary McLeod Bethune. Bethune merged her Daytona Literary and Industrial Training School for Negro Girls in 1923 with the all-male Cookman Institute in Jacksonville and served as the school's president until 1943. The college proudly carries on her legacy. The African Methodist Episcopal Church founded Edward Waters College in 1883, and in 1941 the Southern Black Baptists merged Florida Memorial in Live Oak (1879) with St. Augustine's Florida Normal Collegiate Institute (1892). The small school relocated to Miami from St. Augustine in 1968. Although small, these two institutions along with FAMU and Bethune-Cookman have produced many of Florida's African-American educators, leaders, and role models for the black community.

Until 1958 graduate programs and professional schools in Florida were closed to blacks. Those desiring to become lawyers, doctors, and engineers had to leave the state for training, since such programs did not exist at FAMU or any of the other black institutions. In fact, the State Board of Control sometimes assumed tuition costs for African-American students who attended graduate and professional schools in other states. In 1949, however, five black students—Virgil Hawkins, William T. Lewis, Oliver Moxey, Benjamin Finley, and Rose Boyd—challenged the state law that prohibited them from attending white state institutions. They sought unsuccessfully to enter the University of Florida's law, pharmacy, agriculture, and engineering programs, and all challenged the unfavorable decisions in court. But it was Virgil Hawkins's courage and persistence that overshadowed the others, and he pushed his appeal to the fore. Refusing to accept money to attend law school out of state and, even though the Board of Control established a law school at FAMU, Hawkins continued to seek admission to the University of Florida. For nine long years he fought a system that denied him access to equal education.

Hawkins defied the Board of Control, the Florida Supreme Court, and law school officials and continued to file petition after petition in

Dr. Mary McLeod Bethune, president of Bethune Cookman College in Daytona Beach, is shown at her desk in this photograph by Gordon Parks in February 1943. Daughter of former slaves in South Carolina, Dr. Bethune founded the Daytona Literary and Industrial Training School for Negro Girls in 1904, which merged with the Cookman Institute of Jacksonville in 1923. Until her death in 1955, she was Florida's best-known African-American educator.

state and district courts as well as in the U.S. Supreme Court. Finally, on 18 June 1958, federal district court Judge Dozier De Vane ordered the University of Florida graduate schools opened to qualified blacks. The university, however, determined that Hawkins did not meet its admissions requirements and refused to admit him. Even though Hawkins did not personally benefit from his struggle, other African Americans did. The University of Florida Law School admitted African American George H. Starke for the fall semester 1958.

In black communities the only institution that was considered more important than the school was the church. The church provided refuge from a cold, racist, and indifferent world. It was probably the only institution where blacks could seek solace, occupy leadership roles, make decisions, and maintain organizational control without interference from whites. There were 2,882 black churches in Florida in 1926, ranging in denominations from Seventh Day Adventist to Roman Catholic. A majority of African Americans were members of the Baptist and the African Methodist Episcopal churches. Traditionally, the church offered spiritual guidance to the black community, but because of the unusual circumstances of its parishioners it provided much more. Black congregations relied on their ministers for political and legal advice as well as for welfare and social services. African-American ministers have always exerted great influence in the communities they served.

Because of segregation, the black church was for a time the only institution that provided clubs, associations, and social activities for African Americans. Black men and women held positions in national and district church conventions among the various denominations. Eventually blacks began to organize their own secular clubs and organizations, which gave them a social outlet and an opportunity to communicate with people of common interests. Fraternities and sororities, such as Alpha Phi Alpha and Sigma Gamma Rho, were open only to the college educated, thus limiting membership. Black women formed women's and civic clubs and various circles. The Ever Ready Workers Civic Club was active in West Palm Beach, and in Jacksonville the Criterion Matrons Club and the Junior Service League engaged in charitable work and community uplift. The Florida Federation of Colored Women's Clubs brought many of these groups under one umbrella. Purely social clubs were also popular.

Masonry gained a strong foothold among African Americans in Florida, especially in Jacksonville. The Most Worshipful Grand Lodge established in 1870 in Jacksonville was the first organized for blacks in the state. By 1942 their temple, a five-story brick building at the corners of Broad and Duval streets, was valued at half a million dollars. Other fraternal and secret societies included the Household of Ruth, Eastern Star, the Daughters of Calanthe, the Knights of Pythias, the Lily White, and the Protective Order of Elks. Several of these were benevolent and burial associations providing sick and burial benefits to members.

Recreational facilities for African Americans in Florida were lacking and restricted until integration. Community leaders lobbied for playgrounds so that children could have safe areas for play. When white city officials refused the request of Tallahassee civil rights activist Robert Perkins, Sr., to build a park in a black community in 1955, he persuaded them to do so by taking two truckloads of African-American youth to play in a city park reserved for whites. Segregated branches of the YMCA and the YWCA gave African-American youth supervised recreation. Scouting for boys and girls also filled a void in the black community. Florida's beaches, known the world over for their beauty, were generally off-limits to blacks or they were segregated. American Beach on Amelia Island, owned by the Afro-American Life Insurance Company, became a favorite playground for African Americans. Blacks also

Zora Neale Hurston left the all-black town of Eatonville, near Orlando, where she was born, to pursue an education and a writing career in New York City. With books such as *Mules and Men* (1935), *Their Eyes Were Watching God* (1937), and *Dust Tracks on a Road* (1942), she became a luminary of the Harlem Renaissance group of writers and dramatists in 1930s. Though her last years were spent in poverty as a domestic servant in Fort Pierce, where she was buried in an unmarked grave in 1960, her name and books have since achieved international fame.

enjoyed St. Augustine's Butler Beach which was owned and developed by African American entrepreneur Frank B. Butler.

The civil rights movement in Florida, while not as violent or as publicized as in Alabama or Mississippi, brought fully as much change, and Florida's moderate white leadership kept the state from becoming a bloody battleground. FAMU students in Tallahassee initiated a bus boycott and protested segregation in the capital city's business establishments in the 1950s and 1960s, but the movement took center stage in St. Augustine in 1964 when blacks challenged the rigidly segregated and racist community of that city. Historian David R. Colburn concluded that the 1964 demonstrations and their resulting violence in St. Augustine played a deciding role in the passage of the Civil Rights Act of 1964. Emboldened by militant blacks across the South, black Floridians vigorously took issue with a government that not only discriminated against them but also generally ignored them.

Although slow and reluctant, change gradually came to Florida. Schools and colleges were desegregated; blacks gained the right to vote and secured genuine political power. They were protected in their rights to frequent business establishments and to live where they wished. Overt racism is less, and African Americans make daily contributions to Florida politically, economically, and socially. Black Floridians in 1900 hardly dared to dream of the freedom blacks enjoy in 1995. Yet, in some ways blacks in Florida are not that much better off; some would say that their present state is even worse than it was at the turn of the century, since, with integration, many of the strengths of the black community were diluted or lost altogether. Residential segregation is still entrenched; poverty is rampant; the black family is suffering; and a large segment of the population remains voiceless and invisible.

Notes

1. The state poll tax was repealed in 1937, and the Australian ballot replaced the multiple-ballot-box law in 1895.
2. Rolls showed 479,423 Democrats, 25,862 Republicans, 26 Libertarians, 22 Populists, and 15,995 with no party affiliation.
3. Scott, *The Education of Black People in Florida*, pp. 12–13.

Bibliography

Button, James. *Blacks and Social Change: Impact of the Civil Rights Movement in Southern Communities*. Princeton: Princeton University Press, 1989.

Colburn, David R. *Racial Change and Community Crisis: St. Augustine, Florida, 1877–1980.* Gainesville: University of Florida Press, 1991.

Cooper, Algia R. "Brown v. Board of Education and Virgil Darnell Hawkins: Twenty-Eight Years and Six Petitions to Justice." *Journal of Negro History* 64, no. 1 (Winter 1979):1–15.

Ingalls, Robert P. *Urban Vigilantes in the New South: Tampa, 1882–1936.* Knoxville: University of Tennessee Press, 1988.

Jones, Maxine D., and Kevin McCarthy. *African Americans in Florida.* Sarasota, Fla.: Pineapple Press, 1993.

Jones, Maxine D., Larry E. Rivers, David R. Colburn, R. Thomas Dye, and William W. Rogers. "A Documented History of the Incident Which Occurred at Rosewood, Florida in January 1923." Submitted to the Florida Board of Regents, 22 December 1993.

Neyland, Leedell W. *Florida Agricultural and Mechanical University: A Centennial History, 1887–1987.* Tallahassee: Florida A&M Foundation, Inc., 1987.

———. *Twelve Black Floridians.* Tallahassee: Florida Agricultural and Mechanical University Foundation, Inc., 1970.

Padgett, Gregory B. "C. K. Steele and the Tallahassee Bus Boycott." Master's thesis, Florida State University, 1977.

Poore, Caroline Emmons. "Striking the First Blow: Harry T. Moore and the Fight for Black Equality in Florida." Master's thesis, Florida State University, 1992.

Porter, Gilbert, and Leedell W. Neyland. *History of the Florida State Teachers Association.* Washington: National Education Association, 1977.

Price, Hugh. *The Negro and Southern Politics: A Chapter of Florida History.* New York: New York University Press, 1957.

Rabby, Glenda A. "Out of the Past: The Civil Rights Movement in Tallahassee, Florida." Ph.D. dissertation, Florida State University, 1984.

Scott, J. Irving. *The Education of Black People in Florida.* Philadelphia: Dorrance and Company, 1974.

U.S. Census Bureau. Censuses, 1900–1990.

Waters, Roderick D. "Gwendolyn Cherry: Educator, Attorney and the First African-American Female Legislator in the History of Florida." Master's thesis, Florida State University, 1990.

21 From Migration to Multiculturalism: A History of Florida Immigration

Raymond A. Mohl
and
George E. Pozzetta

Although blessed with abundant natural resources and available land, Florida has struggled for most of its long history to attract people to its borders. As late as 1860 Florida had a population of only 140,423 (77,746 whites, 61,745 slaves, and 932 free blacks). These residents were clustered heavily in a thin band of settlement along the northern tier of the state. Until late in the nineteenth century, in fact, most of Florida existed in a frontier-like condition of virgin wilderness. The development of the state's lands, industries, and urban centers accordingly lagged behind other sections of the nation, a fact that many residents attributed directly to a lack of immigration.

Modern-day Florida responds to very different types of population problems. Present-day residents of the state, who number more than 14 million, now debate proposals to limit population growth and discuss various strategies to curtail resource consumption. Increasingly burdened by the costs associated with refugee and immigrant influxes from the Caribbean and Latin America, and concerned about the social tensions engendered by multiculturalism, the state no longer worries about attracting newcomers. Rather policymakers anxiously question whether Florida should continue to welcome new arrivals at all.

To understand how Florida has fluctuated between such curious extremes, it is necessary to comprehend the state's multifaceted encounter with migration, immigration, and settlement. A scrutiny of this history reveals that the many efforts

391

to stimulate population movement to the state—and occasionally to repel it—varied over time and represented vastly different interests. Large landowners, for example, frequently devised schemes to populate unused land with settlers, and employers sought differing means to ensure adequate and appropriate labor supplies for the state's economic development. Civic boosters similarly produced lavish plans to procure productive citizens for their communities. Superimposed over all of these initiatives were the strategies of the ordinary migrants themselves, who often ignored the grand schemes of others and followed their own routes to a better future.

Vast acreages of undeveloped land and the need for resourceful settlers were two great motivating forces behind early human migration to Florida. Representative of these attempts was the celebrated, if ill-fated, New Smyrna colonization experiment begun in 1768. Bolstered by a 20,000-acre land grant, a visionary London physician named Dr. Andrew Turnbull boldly transported 1,500 Greek, Italian, and Minorcan indentured servants to a site along the Atlantic coast of Florida to clear virgin forest for an indigo plantation (see chapter 8). Within several years, the endeavor failed because of mismanagement and disease; the settlers drifted away, and Turnbull moved to Charleston to practice medicine. Both the Spanish and British governments made generous grants of lands to other individuals during their colonial administrations, hoping to stimulate substantial migration, but these schemes generally produced results no better than the New Smyrna venture.

During the early years of statehood, Floridians were less concerned with questions of immigration and settlement than with the problems associated with the emerging sectional controversy and slavery. As the Civil War unfolded, Florida was forced to devote all of its energies to the urgent demands of the conflict, leaving little opportunity for other initiatives. The immense dislocations caused by the war, however, did set the context for a postwar period in which migration and population growth became one of the state's major concerns.

Faced with the formidable problems of reconstruction and development, many Floridians looked to the future convinced that what the state most needed was a rapid augmentation of its population. As the official publication of the state Grange emphatically proclaimed, "Unquestionably Florida's greatest need is immigration; next to immigration we need capital."[1] Unlike other southern states, however, Florida labored under special burdens. The peninsula was greatly underpopulated, having by far the fewest residents of any of the former Confederate states; in 1900, for example, Florida counted slightly more than a half million inhabitants, while Georgia and Alabama totaled 2,216,000 and 1,829,000, respectively. Such a small population in relation to the state's vast land area meant a pronounced lack of development as defined by urban areas, transportation facilities, cultural amenities, and industry. Many Floridians believed that the state's deficiencies could most easily be erased by acquiring a class of industrious immigrants to populate unused lands, provide a stable labor force, and infuse the state with new ideas and energies.

Adding urgency to the desire for immigrants during this period was a pervasive white discontent with the black labor available in the state. In the years after the Civil War, many employers worried about the frequency with which former slaves exercised their new rights and deserted the plantations and farms. Other Floridians reflected the racist attitudes of the time by claiming that without the coercive powers of the slave system, even those blacks willing to remain on jobs would be unreliable, lazy, and unproductive. The *Tallahassee Semi-Weekly Floridian*, for example, concluded in 1865 that a majority of citizens believed "negroes will not work on the plantations in a manner that will pay for the necessary investment of capital."[2] Even more troubling, many whites firmly maintained that blacks lacked the mental capacity to be trained for diversified and intensive farming or to use new farm machinery. Racist thinking reached such extremes that some white Floridians became convinced that under conditions of freedom, the black race itself was retrogressing toward barbarism and would die out.

However unrealistic, the lesson of these varied messages was clear—for Florida to tie its future development to black labor would only result in ruin. Anxious Floridians urged that if a fraction of the increasing tide of European immigration then flowing into America could be diverted to the state, all problems would end. The dilemma was how to define and implement a suitable immigration policy to achieve this end. Over the course of several decades, proponents of foreign immigration attempted several initiatives, but their efforts were marked by acrimonious debate and deep division, and ultimately immigration promoters were not able to fashion an effective solution.

The state agency most directly involved with immigration matters was the state Bureau of Immigration, which directed public efforts to advertise and promote Florida to prospective immigrants. Tracing its roots to the Constitution of 1868, the bureau aggressively attempted to stimulate foreign settlement during its short life span. It published and distributed throughout Europe promotional pamphlets such as *The Florida Settler* (1877) and a newspaper called the *Florida Immigrant*

(1877–79) and generally attempted to coordinate immigration efforts prior to being abolished by a cost-conscious legislature in 1891.

More active and effective immigration activities emanated from private interests. During the late nineteenth century, railroads, farm groups, real estate companies, wealthy landowners, mine operators, and industrialists directed an impressive volume of literature about Florida to distant parts of the globe. In August 1881, representatives from all parts of the state met in Jacksonville to discuss ways of coordinating these efforts. One enthusiastic delegate explained that when God selected a home for humans, He put them "in that zone which embraces Florida.... Florida should be the other Eden—the center of the world's glory!" The assembly resolved that each county should establish immigration associations to collect and publish information on their attractions in "the different languages of European countries ... and that said pamphlets be distributed among the masses of said European countries."[3]

Although early publications issued an open invitation to all types of foreigners, Italian immigrants received special attention in these campaigns. The prevalent perception of Florida as the "Italy of the South" and the common view that Italians excelled in citrus horticulture combined to make them appear particularly desirable. In 1873, citrus developer Henry S. Sanford explained that they were "a most valuable class of immigrants ... intelligent and industrious, accustomed to orange and vine culture, and to a warm climate."[4] A similar enthusiasm for Chinese workers swept the state in these years, based on reports of their industriousness and skill in gardening. Promotional efforts attracted only insignificant numbers of Italians and Chinese, however, and when Florida turned away from supporting immigration in the first decade of the twentieth century, these two groups ironically came to be regarded as the least acceptable newcomers.

The drive to acquire foreign immigrants collapsed for several reasons. Since many Floridians supported foreign immigration as means of replacing blacks, they assumed that the new arrivals would be content merely to change positions with the former slaves. Unsatisfactory crop lien and sharecropping arrangements thus characterized the fate of many immigrants who worked in agriculture. Even worse, peonage exploitation was a common circumstance in turpentine camps, railroad construction projects, and naval stores operations. News of these conditions quickly spread outward and considerably dampened enthusiasm for Florida among potential immigrants.

The attitudes of Floridians themselves similarly underwent transformation. Slowly in the 1890s and then with increasing speed after 1900, the state's earlier policy of open welcome turned to a position of resistance to foreign settlement. Florida had become engulfed in the rising tide of nativist sentiment sweeping the nation. Concerns over the effects of introducing foreign religions, alien political ideologies, and potentially disturbing new "racial" strains came to the surface. By 1910, most Floridians believed that if the state were to retain its racial integrity, preserve its unique "American" character, and protect its cherished institutions, it now had no room for foreign immigrants.

Even during the turn against immigration, however, there were interests in the state that pursued active settlement campaigns involving foreigners. The colonial-era dream of establishing entire colonies of immigrant settlers found adherents during the modern period, and a variety of promoters pursued colonizing plans. Immigrant colonies appealed to landowners and financiers on several grounds. This mode of settlement disposed of large tracts of land in one transaction and enhanced the value of adjacent property substantially. Moreover, this tactic seemed to offer the best prospects of permanent residence, since newcomers could more easily perpetuate familiar customs and ease the difficult transition to new homes.

The Florida record of modern colony settlement contained instances of both success and abject failure. One effort to bring fifty Scottish settlers to Sarasota in 1885 floundered when the new arrivals found not the thriving community promised to them but rather a "swampy wilderness" and a few scattered buildings. They soon abandoned their plans. Similarly, in 1893, approximately 500 Danes purchased land at White City in St. Lucie County, only to learn shortly after arriving that their on-site manager had died and the group's financial agent had sold them land he did not own and absconded with their money. This venture, however, was rescued at the last moment by the Florida East Coast Railway (FEC), which provided emergency supplies and financial backing.

It was no accident that the railroad was on hand to assist. The company owned vast tracts of land and supported its own active immigration bureau for many years. The settlement of Dania by Danish immigrants in 1898 grew out FECR operations, as did a 1904 venture to establish a Japanese colony called Yamato near present-day Boca Raton. In the case of the Japanese, several years of successful pineapple farming raised expectations of a large-scale movement of people. By 1907 the FEC had established a rail station at Yamato, and several hundred industrious immigrants worked the land. A devastating attack of

In 1913 three members of the Japanese colony of Yamato near present-day Boca Raton posed for the camera outside what had once been their prosperous pineapple planta-tion. A blight destroyed the crop in 1908, and, owing to cheaper, earlier maturing rail-transported pineapple exports from Cuba, the plantation never recovered.

pineapple blight in 1908 ruined the colony's hopes, however, and most settlers returned home disillusioned with Florida's prospects.

As promoters and state officials vacillated over the wisdom of at-tempting to attract foreigners, immigrants themselves were often pur-suing strategies of their own and independently creating centers of for-eign settlement. The movement of Greeks to Tarpon Springs, for example, was guided by the business enterprise and vision of John Cocoris, a Greek immigrant who saw rich possibilities in the Florida sponge industry. Some Greek spongers had worked in Key West during the 1890s, using the "hook" method of harvesting from boats. But when huge beds of sponges were found in the Gulf of Mexico off the coast of Tarpon Springs, Cocoris recognized that the Greek method of collecting, which involved deep-water diving with special suits, would yield greater results. After initial harvesting successes in 1905, a steady flow of Greek immigrants came directly to Tarpon Springs, eventually dominating by force of numbers the small community's institutions and culture.

Two three-year-old cousins of Greek descent pose in colorful Greek military costumes at Tarpon Springs on 6 January 1947.

There were two instances in this period of large-scale migration resulting in urban settlement capable of sustaining a full range of viable ethnic institutions and an enduring immigrant culture. The first of these occurred in Key West, where expatriate Cuban and Spanish cigar workers and manufacturers fled Cuba after 1868 and established a cigar-making center. Some 5,000 exiles soon labored in Key West's factories, organizing effective labor unions and community institutions. Key West was quickly eclipsed, however, by a cigar-making rival located to the north in Tampa.

During the years 1885–1924 thousands of Cubans, Italians, and Spaniards came to the small coastal village of Tampa and transformed it into a thriving industrial center. Drawn primarily by the cigar industry

Cubans, Spaniards, and Italians came to West Tampa and Ybor City, east of Tampa, to work in the hand-rolled cigar industry. At the Cuesta Rey factory in West Tampa in 1929, these men and women silently rolled coronas, perfectos, and panatelas while *el lector* (the reader) on a raised platform (*right*) read to them in Spanish from newspapers, novels, and political tracts.

brought to Tampa by Spanish industrialist V. M. Martinez Ybor, the immigrants quickly made the city into the nation's leading center for the production of high-quality, hand-rolled cigars.

Settling in what was initially the separate community of Ybor City, the "Latins" of Tampa created a rich associational life that included immigrant labor unions, foreign language newspapers, ethnic fraternal clubs, radical political organizations, and a thriving theater. Multistory marble and granite mutual aid club buildings gave impressive physical evidence of the commitment to immigrant cultures and the communities that these people manifested. So, too, did the extraordinary medical cooperatives established by Latin immigrants that provided subsidized medical care with an efficiency and low cost that remain remarkable to this day.

No inquiry into the impact of immigrants on Florida during these years would be complete without a recognition of the role played by transient foreign workers. Isolated work gangs of Italians, Greeks, Chinese, Portuguese, Spaniards, and many others crisscrossed the state, laboring in plantation fields, drainage operations, and construction sites.

The FEC, for example, regularly recruited work crews from far afield in its construction projects, hiring immigrant workers through labor agents located in major northeastern cities. The building of the famous overseas Key West extension (completed in 1912), for example, depended heavily on the work of foreign laborers, many of whom came from the Caribbean. In other economic sectors, such as sugarcane harvesting, the seasonal influx of migrant workers from the Bahamas and other locations became a long-term economic strategy that annually brought large numbers of foreigners into Florida.

Actually, a distinctive Bahamian presence had already been established in Key West by the mid-nineteenth century. Bahamian fishermen, shipwreck salvagers, and Indian traders, according to one Bahamian writer, regarded Florida "much as another island of the Bahamas."[5] By the 1830s, black and white Bahamians were beginning to migrate to the Florida Keys, especially Key West. Facing meager economic prospects at home, Bahamian blacks especially found better employment opportunities in Key West. By the 1890s, Bahamians made up about a third of the population in Key West, where they worked primarily in sponging, turtling, and fishing. A large majority of Key West blacks trace their ancestry to Bahamian origins. Ironically, those Bahamian origins might be traced back even farther to Florida, as several thousand slaves were brought to the Bahamas by British Loyalists who fled East Florida after the American Revolution.

The black Bahamian migration to Florida intensified after the establishment of Miami in 1896. Like other Caribbean islanders, Bahamians pursued a "livelihood migration" involving temporary labor elsewhere and a later return to the home island. The building up of Miami at the turn of the century created new opportunities for Bahamian migrant workers, who were attracted to the city for the same reasons that European immigrants poured into the industrial cities of the Northeast and Midwest at the same time—better jobs and higher wages. As one Bahamian migrant remembered it, perhaps overoptimistically, "Miami was a young Magic City where money could be 'shaken from trees.'"[6] Bahamians who returned to the islands enticed others to follow with exaggerated tales of their fame and fortune in the "promised land"—a familiar theme in immigrant literature. The introduction of regular steamship service between Miami and Nassau by the early twentieth century made the trip to Florida cheap and convenient. According to Bahamian population studies, 10,000 to 12,000 Bahamians left the islands for Florida between 1900 and 1920—about one-fifth of the entire population of the Bahamas.

In Florida, Bahamian newcomers found work in building construction, as railroad laborers, and as stevedores on the Miami docks. The emergence of Miami as a tourist center provided job opportunities for Bahamian women, especially as maids, cooks, and laundry and service workers in the city's new hotels and restaurants. Large numbers of Bahamians also worked in the citrus industry and as field hands in south Florida agriculture. Many came as migrant laborers during the harvest season, returning to the islands each summer. In the years before effective federal regulation of immigration, Bahamian blacks moved easily and often between south Florida and the islands.

The Bahamian presence in Miami and south Florida was proportionately large. By 1920, Miami's population stood at 29,571, one-quarter of them foreign-born. More than 65 percent of Miami's immigrants—4,815 individuals—were blacks from the West Indies, mostly Bahamians. They comprised 52 percent of all Miami's blacks and 16.3 percent of the city's entire population. By 1920, Miami had a larger population of black immigrants than any other city in the United States except New York. As agriculture expanded along Florida's Atlantic coast, Bahamians responded to new work opportunities. As a result, by 1945, the Florida state census reported more foreign-born blacks living in Palm Beach County (5,597) than in Dade County (4,609).

For thousands of Bahamians from the 1890s to the 1940s, the widespread perception of economic opportunity was too strong to resist. But the Bahamians routinely encountered racial segregation and discrimination in Florida. Racial confrontations involving Bahamian blacks and white policemen were not uncommon in Key West, Miami, and Jacksonville. The British Foreign Office and the governor of the Bahamas often protested police brutality and other forms of racial discrimination directed against Bahamians in Florida, generally without result. Unaccustomed to harassment and racial barriers, Bahamians in large numbers in Miami, Key West, and West Palm Beach joined the Universal Negro Improvement Association, the black nationalist movement led by Marcus Garvey.

As was true of Latins in Tampa, Bahamians built flourishing ethnic communities in Florida, especially in Key West and in Coconut Grove and Overtown, two major black neighborhoods in early twentieth-century Miami, where they established businesses and laid the foundations for churches and a vibrant organizational life. The permanence and stability of these neighborhoods, along with strong links to the islands, contributed to cultural maintenance and an enduring sense of nationality. Bahamian drum rhythms, dance and song traditions, folk-lore, and foodways had a powerful impact on native black communities in south Florida. Although nominally Episcopalian in religion, the Bahamians retained a strong adherence to the Afro-Caribbean cult of *obeah*. To both Key West and Miami, the Bahamians brought a distinctive architectural style typified by two-story wooden frame houses with wide, two-tiered, balustraded porches designed to take advantage of ocean breezes. Following British and Bahamian traditions, Florida Bahamians regularly celebrated Guy Fawkes Day and other holidays, including, during the early decades of the twentieth century, the monarch's birthday. Unfettered Bahamian migration ended with World War II, when the agricultural labor supply came under governmental regulation. But enough Bahamians had settled permanently in south Florida in earlier decades to sustain the growth of cohesive communities held together by a strong sense of nationality and cultural distinctiveness. To this day, some sections of black Miami and Key West have retained the indelible atmosphere of the Bahamas.

Bahamian migration to Florida was paralleled by early Cuban migration to Key West and Tampa. Florida's human connection to the Caribbean intensified as the twentieth century progressed. In retrospect, it is somewhat prophetic that the achievement of Cuban independence (1898) and the founding of Miami (1896) coincided at the end of the nineteenth century. The era of the Spanish-American War represented the first phase of that magnetic pull that has linked Miami and Havana as the twin cities of the Caribbean for much of the twentieth century. Key West, Tampa, and New York continued to be the centers of Cuban exile life in the United States through the 1920s, but Miami was already beginning to emerge as a convenient place of political exile for Latin American revolutionaries, dissidents, and dictators. For example, Porfirio Diaz, the Mexican dictator for thirty-five years between 1876 and 1911, was living in Paris in 1913 when the *Miami Metropolis* reported that he would be setting up an exile establishment in Miami. Diaz died in France before getting to the Magic City, but the idea of exile in south Florida remained fully alive for others. By the late 1920s, more than 1,000 Cuban exiles, mostly young, radical university students opposed to the dictatorial regime of Gerardo Machado, had set up an exile headquarters in Miami. With the success of the 1933 Cuban Revolution, anti-Machado exiles in Florida returned home, with the blessing of the *Miami Herald*, which editorialized prophetically in 1933 that "Miami's gates will always be open to Cubans, should the time ever come again when they need a refuge."[7] Actually, that time came rather quickly, since ousted Machado supporters immediately took up new places in Miami exile.

It had become a natural pattern. Harry Guggenheim, U.S. ambassador to Cuba in the early 1930s, noted at the time that Cuban exile leaders went to New York and Washington to solicit financial and political support, but the chief point of exile had already become Miami, where, he said, "The rank and file of emigrés and followers of the junta concentrate, since they can live more easily in Florida's sunshine."[8] Older communities of earlier Cuban immigrants were still thriving in Tampa and Key West, numbering about 7,400 and 1,600, respectively, in 1930. But a new Cuban exile community began to emerge in Miami during the 1930s; by 1940, Miami had over 1,100 Cuban-born residents, a colony that gradually grew larger over the next two decades. Militant anti-Batista Cuban exiles were active in Miami in the 1950s, including Fidel Castro himself. Cuban-born workers, especially women, made up a large portion of the garment workers in Miami's needle trades in the early 1950s. Even before the success of Castro's revolution in 1959, a concentrated area of Cuban settlement had begun to take shape in Miami's center, and the neighborhood was already being called "Little Havana." So the exiles who flowed out of Cuba in such astonishing numbers during the 1960s and 1970s were only the latest in a long line of Cubans who historically sought refuge in Florida.

Despite the concentration of Latins in Tampa and of Bahamians in Key West and Miami in the early twentieth century, Florida had not yet become a major destination for immigrants to the United States. In 1930, for instance, the foreign-born made up about 12 percent of national population; by contrast, Florida had just under 70,000 white and black immigrants at the time, or about 4.7 percent of the state's total population. According to the 1930 U.S. census, more than half of those immigrants lived in the Tampa, Miami, and Jacksonville metropolitan districts. In addition to English, the most popular mother tongues of Florida's urban immigrants in 1930 were Spanish and Italian in Tampa, German, Yiddish, and Arabic in Jacksonville, and German, Yiddish, and Spanish in Miami. Despite small numbers of foreign-born, urban Florida was already displaying some ethnic and cultural diversity by the 1930s.

Over the next thirty years, immigration statistics for Florida converged with national patterns. By 1960, for example, the proportion of immigrants in Florida's population had increased marginally to 5.5 percent. For the nation as a whole, the immigrant proportion had declined

In 1912, two Norwegian women at Davenport, in Polk County, displayed the dresses of their native land.

In October 1958, at Masaryktown, in Hernando County, Florida citizens of Czechoslovakian origin participate in a traditional dance of their homeland.

to 5.4 percent of total population, reflecting the restrictive legislation of the 1920s. The foreign-born proportion for most of Florida's cities and counties hovered at or below the state average. But there were some dramatic exceptions, such as Miami Beach, where 33 percent of the city's population was foreign-born in 1960—mostly East European Jewish immigrants who had retired to Florida from the northeastern states. Demographically speaking, Dade County appeared as an oddity in the 1960 U.S. census, with 113,000 foreign-born—over 40 percent of the state's total—whose mother tongues included German, Polish, Hungarian, Russian, and Yiddish, as well as English and Spanish. Pockets of immigrants clustered in other parts of Florida, too. Tarpon Springs, with many Greek immigrants, was almost one-quarter foreign-born. The foreign-born made up 14 percent of the population of Lake Worth, a small city in Palm Beach County where Finnish immigrants began settling in the 1930s. Jacksonville had a minuscule foreign-born population in 1960, but the city had long been home to several thousand Syrian-Lebanese people, a multigenerational ethnic community that grew to over 25,000 by the 1990s. Surprisingly, Canadian immigrants, largely a post–World War II phenomenon, comprised the largest foreign-born group in the Orlando, Jacksonville, Tampa–St. Petersburg, and Fort Lauderdale–Hollywood metropolitan areas. Finally, Dade

County already had over 50,000 Hispanic immigrants in 1960, reflecting the early surge of Cubans just before and just after the fall of Batista in 1959.

The success of Fidel Castro's Cuban Revolution in 1959 permanently altered Florida's demography. The migration of Cuban exiles to the United States forms one of the most compelling and fascinating chapters in the history of American immigration. Over the course of thirty-five years, more than 800,000 Cuban exiles arrived in the United States, the majority of whom remained in Florida, especially the Miami area. They came to the United States in several waves over three decades, an erratic migration flow dictated by the state of U.S.–Cuban relations at any particular time. This relationship also dictated the form of the exile movement. At various times, the Cubans have arrived in Florida by airlift, boatlift, travel through third countries, or as escapees on small boats and rafts. American policymakers, beginning with the Eisenhower administration, encouraged the exile migration in order to destabilize and discredit Castro's communist regime. To a large degree, however, Castro controlled the timing and methods of migration, periodically opening and closing the doors and permitting the exodus of dissidents to defuse internal economic or political problems. Humanitarian considerations had little to do with the Cuban migration on either side. Rather, as one recent Cuban-American scholar has suggested, "the refugees became a prime weapon in the political war between the United States and Cuba," and Miami became a "front line in the Cold War."[9]

The great exodus of Cuban exiles to Florida reflected disenchantment with the outcome of the Cuban Revolution. The earliest exiles were ideological opponents of Castro, primarily the business and professional classes unhappy about the expropriation of property and the redistribution of wealth in socialist Cuba. Later exiles were more likely to have been initial supporters of the Cuban Revolution whose zeal had been eroded by pragmatic experience in the new Cuba. Federal policy opened the gates to the anticommunist Cuban exiles, who entered the United States without immigration quotas or restrictions. Most of these newcomers entered through Miami, which became one of the nation's chief immigration ports after 1959.

The federal government established a Cuban Refugee Program and a Refugee Emergency Center in 1960 to handle the processing and resettlement of the exile Cubans. These agencies provided the exiles with an unprecedented variety of social services, educational programs, medical assistance, and job training; by the mid-1970s, more than $1 billion had been spent by the federal government to assist Cuban resettlement in the United States. The refugee center also coordinated private aid from numerous religious and voluntary agencies, such as the Catholic Archdiocese of Miami, which played an important role in Cuban refugee resettlement. Tens of thousands of Cuban exiles were resettled throughout the United States, but a large number eventually returned to the Miami area. By the 1980s, more than 60 percent of all the Cubans in the United States resided in the Miami metropolitan area.

The arrival of the Cuban exiles in the 1960s initiated several decades of remarkable economic, political, and social change in south Florida. Given the professional and business backgrounds of the first-wave exiles, the enormous amount of resettlement assistance they received, and their concentration in a single city, it is not really surprising that the Cubans have adjusted well and prospered in their new home. They created a thriving ethnic community in Miami's Little Havana, in Hialeah, and in other sections of the Miami metropolitan area. After an initial period of adjustment, the initial wave of Florida Cubans generally became successful economically, creating an enclave economy that has encouraged Spanish-language maintenance and provided jobs for a steady succession of Cuban newcomers. Later Cuban arrivals may not have been as successful, but statistical evidence gathered by the U.S. Census Bureau demonstrates that the Cubans collectively have more education, better jobs, and higher incomes than the U.S. Hispanic population generally. Most observers would agree that the Cuban presence has been largely responsible for the recent emergence of Miami as an important center of international banking, trade, and tourism.

U.S. foreign policy toward Cuba remains a passionate issue in Cuban Miami, but as the exiles increasingly came to view south Florida as a place of permanent settlement, they put down roots and became citizens and voters. Although exile politics persists in powerful and volatile ways, Miami's Cubans have become new players in the old game of ethnic politics. They have adjusted to life in the United States, but they have also held tenaciously to old-country language, culture, customs, religion, and foodways. Recent political controversies over bilingualism in south Florida have heightened Cuban ethnic identity and the sense that language and culture should be maintained. Second-generation Cuban-Americans may be assimilating more quickly, but the constant infusion of new waves of Cuban exiles (such as the 1980 Mariel boatlift that brought 125,000 to south Florida) has tended to strengthen Cuban cultural maintenance in the new land. In Dade County, where the 1990 census reported the population to be 45.1 percent foreign-born, 49.2 percent Hispanic, and 53.3 percent non-English-speaking at home, it

Two Cuban families, those of mechanic Oreste Ortega (*seated, foreground*) and of ex-Castro captain Armando Rodríguez (*standing*), enter a U.S. Coast Guard boat at Key West on 11 April 1961 after a night escape from Cuba in the open boat shown in rear.

has been difficult to ignore the cumulative impact of the Cuban exile migration over three decades.

Since the 1970s, the immigrant Cubans increasingly have shared exile space in Florida with two other refugee communities in the Sunshine State—Haitians and Nicaraguans. Political repression, violence, and poverty in Haiti over several decades have triggered a large exile migration to Florida from that beleaguered Caribbean island. The rise of François "Papa Doc" Duvalier to power in Haiti in 1957 stimulated an early exodus of the country's professional and business elites, mostly to New York City, Montreal, and a few other northeastern cities. Miami's Haitian community was initially small; the 1960 census reported only a few hundred Haitians living in Dade County. Haitian exile patterns changed dramatically by the mid-1970s, as Haiti's urban workers and rural peasantry began an exodus of their own to the United States, mostly in clandestine fashion by small boat, either directly to Florida or by way of the Bahamas, where tens of thousands of Haitians have temporarily settled. The magnitude of this Haitian migration was brought home first to Floridians in 1980, when more than 25,000 Haitian boat people washed up on south Florida beaches. The massive immigration of Mariel Cubans was occurring simultaneously, and the parallel nature of the Haitian and Cuban exile migrations focused attention on the important place of Florida in the political economy of the Caribbean.

Federal policy on Haitian exiles has been controversial in south Florida. Haitian newcomers have received a less than enthusiastic welcome, especially when compared to the treatment accorded Cuban exiles. U.S. policy generally rejected Haitian appeals for political asylum, as the Immigration and Naturalization Service (INS) sought to return the exiles to Haiti, interdict them at sea, or discourage their departure from Haiti. During the 1980s, thousands of Haitian exiles were officially detained at the Krome Refugee Center west of Miami while awaiting deportation hearings. By contrast, Cuban exiles who arrived in the United States went free immediately under the provisions of the Cuban Adjustment Act (1966), which granted them permanent resident alien status. The INS and the U.S. Congress have never completely resolved the double standard in American immigration policy—one that welcomed mostly white exiles from Cuban communism but rejected black refugees from a totalitarian regime in Haiti.

The ongoing immigration of Haitian exiles has begun to reshape the ethnic structure of south Florida. Initially, the Haitians settled heavily in the Edison–Little River section of Miami, an older, inner-city residential area that soon was being called "Little Haiti." By the 1980s, Haitians had also begun moving north into Broward and Palm Beach counties, mostly into a corridor of older and low-income housing that stretched along Interstate 95. Substantial Haitian communities have now emerged in Fort Lauderdale, Pompano Beach, Delray Beach, Boynton Beach, Lake Worth, West Palm Beach, and Riviera Beach, as well as in agricultural communities such as Pahokee, Belle Glade, and South Bay on Lake Okeechobee. Although accurate statistics are hard to come by, the three large counties of south Florida may now be home to as many as 200,000 Haitians and Haitian-Americans.

In Florida, the Haitian newcomers have been confronted with the traditional immigrant task of adjustment and accommodation. They lack the self-sufficient enclave economy created by the Cubans, and they have entered the low end of the labor market, mainly in marginal service jobs and unskilled work in construction, landscaping, and the like. Several thousand Haitians have found work as cane cutters in rural South Florida's sugar industry, and other thousands have joined the migrant farm worker stream that ranges up and down the eastern seaboard. They have a strong work and education ethic, and a variety of public school and community school programs has facilitated their acquisition of English-language skills.

Despite their problems with the INS, Florida's Haitian exiles have begun to build new ethnic communities with important institutional and cultural attributes. Premigration Haitian culture remains a powerful ingredient of community life. Haitian dress, food, music, and art are prevalent in Miami's Little Haiti and in the other Haitian communities. Frequent festivals and celebrations perpetuate the homeland flavor. The extended family structure serves important functions, ranging from facilitating the chain migration process to providing job recruitment for newcomers. Haitian Catholic parishes, with French- and Creole-speaking priests, provide a form of religious continuity. Like the Cubans, the Haitians have mixed organized religion with folk religion of African origins. Haitian voodoo includes a mélange of music, magic, ceremony, ritual, natural medicine, and animal sacrifice. An indelible part of Haitian immigrant culture, the informal voodoo rites are commonly practiced even by those belonging to organized churches.

The Florida Haitians have also maintained their identity through political organization. A powerful brand of exile politics testifies to the Haitians' intense interest in the fate of their homeland, even as an increasing number of the exiles become U.S. citizens and voters. Miami politicians cannot ignore a concentrated bloc of more than 10,000 Haitian voters in Dade County. The continuing odyssey of the Haitian boat people suggests the magnetic lure of Florida for the politically oppressed and poverty-stricken peoples of the Caribbean.

A second new Florida exile community emerged after Nicaragua's Sandinista revolutionaries overthrew dictator Anastasio Somoza in 1979. By the mid-1980s, 75,000 opponents of the leftist Sandinistas had established an exile base in Dade County. The Nicaraguans found Miami, with its large population of anticommunist Cubans, a hospitable and convenient place of refuge. Much like the Cubans in the early days of their exile in Florida, the Nicaraguans initially hoped to return home; they supported the contra fighters in Central America, and organized a powerful lobby, the Nicaraguan American Foundation, to influence U.S. foreign policy and protect the interests of the new Nicaraguan immigrants. By 1988, worsening economic and political conditions in Nicaragua coincided with a temporary loosening of U.S. immigration policy toward Central America, resulting in a further exodus of Nicaraguan exiles who trekked overland through Mexico to Texas and then came to Miami by bus. By the end of the year, several hundred Nicaraguans were arriving in Miami each day, and the press was widely predicting that as many as 100,000 additional Nicaraguans would be arriving within the next year. A peaceful transfer of power took place in Nicaragua in 1990, when the contras put down their arms and the U.S.-backed Violeta Chamorro surprisingly defeated the Sandinista government at the polls, thus short-circuiting the newest migration stream to Florida. By that time, however, the south Florida Nicaraguan community had swelled to 150,000 or more. During the following year, perhaps as many as 25,000 Miami Nicaraguans went back home, but many of those soon returned to Florida in disillusionment.

What began as a temporary exile migration eventually resulted in a new and seemingly permanent immigrant community in Florida. It was a rerun of the Cuban exile migration. The earliest Nicaraguan exiles adjusted quickly, as Spanish language use was beneficial rather than detrimental in Miami. Many Nicaraguans had business and professional backgrounds, and a new surge of immigrant entrepreneurialism began in the early 1980s. The Cuban enclave economy absorbed many other newcomers from Central America, although one recent study also contended that many Nicaraguan professionals had been "proletarianized" and worked in low-skill, low-wage jobs in Miami. The Nicaraguans (or Nicas, as they are called in Miami) settled heavily in Sweetwater and Fontainebleau Park, communities on the western fringes of the Miami metropolitan area; in keeping with a now-established Miami tradition, this section of Dade County quickly earned the appellation "Little Managua." Later migrations of working-class Nicaraguans settled initially in an older, inner-city section of Miami now called "Little Nicaragua." Streets in Little Managua bear the names of famous Nicaraguans, and shopping center signs resemble those in the homeland. By 1990, the Nicaraguans had become the second largest Hispanic group in Dade County. They had also replaced Cubans as the largest single group of foreign-born students in the Dade County schools.

The Nicaraguan migration intensified the modern ethnic transformation of Dade County. Like earlier exiles from Cuba and Haiti, the Nicaraguans have a strong cultural identity. Communal institutions such as the Catholic parishes in Sweetwater and Little Havana, as well as family service organizations such as the Centro Asistencia Nicaraguense and La Divine Providencia, provide an important focus. Numerous Nicaraguan business and professional associations have been formed. Nicaraguan restaurants and street-corner groceries and bakeries have sprouted by the hundreds in the Miami area. The Nicas have their own radio programs and *periodiquitos*. Musical activities and religious festivals celebrating patron saints from Nicaraguan hometowns provide the newcomers with a sense of identity and community. *La*

Purisma, the major religious holiday among the Miami Nicaraguans, celebrates Catholicism and the Immaculate Conception of the Virgin Mary. Nicaraguans also have established several baseball leagues in Miami, keeping alive the sports tradition of that baseball-mad nation. Exile politics remained strong throughout the 1980s. The contra opponents of the Nicaraguan Sandinistas were headquartered in Miami, but the full spectrum of political opinion eventually came to be represented in Florida. Many exiles adhered to no political ideology but came to Miami to escape the military draft or avoid the civil war in Nicaragua. The transition to ethnic politics in Miami had only just begun in the early 1990s, but by the end of the decade the Nicaraguan newcomers will have become a powerful voting bloc in local political affairs.

The heavy attention devoted to the Nicaraguan and Cuban migration to south Florida has tended to obscure a wider pattern of recent immigration, especially Hispanic immigration, to Florida as a whole. Both the foreign-born and the Hispanic populations of Florida have been rising rapidly over the past few decades. Between 1960 and 1990, Florida's immigrants increased from 5.5 percent to 12.9 percent of total state population; Florida had about 272,000 immigrants in 1960, but about 1.7 million in 1990—a 525 percent increase over thirty years. Florida's Hispanic population has also been increasing at a rapid pace, from about 400,000 in 1970 (when the U.S. Census first began reporting data on Hispanics) to about 1.6 million in 1990. Not only has the state's Hispanic population more than quadrupled in twenty years, but the rate of growth has outpaced that of any other state over the same period. One final statistical measure also emphasizes the degree to which modern Florida has been changed by thirty years of new immigration: just over 2 million Florida residents, or about 16 percent of the state's population, speak a language other than English at home. About half of those non-English speakers live in Dade County, but the other million are spread throughout the state, especially in the big metropolitan counties—Broward, Palm Beach, Hillsborough, Orange, and Pinellas.

The Latinization of Florida generally has been attributed to the massive exodus of Cuban exiles to south Florida since 1959. This is only partially true. Cubans did form a majority of all Florida Hispanics in 1970 and 1980, but by 1990 other Hispanics considerably outnumbered Cubans. During the twenty-year period to 1990, the proportions of Mexicans, Puerto Ricans, and other Hispanics all grew more rapidly than did Florida's Cuban population. For example, the number of Mexicans in Florida—about 20,000 in 1970—grew by over 600 percent to

150,000 in 1990. The other Hispanic category, which includes Central Americans and South Americans, increased by 360 percent to 1990. Of the thirteen Florida counties with the largest percentage of Hispanic population in 1990, only in two—Dade and Monroe—did Cubans outnumber other Hispanic groups. In big urban counties such as Hillsborough, Pinellas, Duval, Broward, and Palm Beach, the other Hispanic category dominated. In the Orlando area and in several smaller central Florida counties Puerto Ricans predominated, and in six rural agricultural counties—Hardee, Hendry, Collier, Okeechobee, DeSoto, and Glades—Mexicans outnumbered all other Hispanics combined.

County-level U.S. Census data, then, suggest that two important and largely hidden demographic trends had begun to emerge as early as the 1970s: the statistics suggest the diffusion of the Hispanic population throughout the state, and they reveal the rapid diversification of Florida's Latin population, as groups other than Cubans came to predominate in areas outside south Florida. In Dade County, Nicaraguan exiles speeded the diversification of the Hispanic population during the 1980s, as did tens of thousands from Colombia, Venezuela, Panama, El Salvador, Mexico, Peru, Argentina, the Dominican Republic, Brazil, and other Latin nations. These newcomers have also settled in substantial numbers in Florida's other urban centers.

The Latinization process, moreover, has now extended to Florida's rural areas, where over a thirty-year period Hispanic immigrant workers have largely replaced African Americans in the farm labor force. For instance, Mexicans now make up about one-quarter of the population of Hardee County, an agricultural area once known as the cucumber capital of the world. Miami's Little Havana is well known as a center of Hispanic life and culture in Florida, but a visit to Wauchula, Bowling Green, or Zolfo Springs—Hardee County's chief towns—provides unmistakable visual and cultural evidence that the Latinization process has spread to the agricultural center of the state. The most popular holiday in Hardee County now may be Cinco de Mayo, a Mexican national holiday, during which Aztec dancing, music, and folk culture are celebrated by these new Floridians. In Indiantown, a small agricultural community in Martin County, the big holiday is the festival of San Miguel Acatán, the patron saint of some 5,000 Maya Indians, exiles from civil war in Guatemala, who have settled there. Perhaps another 5,000 or more Mayans reside in agricultural and farm-worker communities stretching from Immokalee to Homestead. In the rural north Florida town of Quincy, a still growing community of as many as 1,000 Salvadorans quietly sprouted during the 1980s, attracted through chain migration to work in nurseries, tomato-packing plants, and the lumber industry. As these examples demonstrate, the Latinization of Florida has spread far beyond Miami's Little Havana, and the Hispanic newcomers to the state represent a broad spectrum of Caribbean, Central American, and Latin American nations. Cuban and Nicaraguan and Salvadoran, Aztec and Maya—these newcomers and others suggest the powerful brand of multiculturalism that is beginning to reshape the social, cultural, and economic life of modern Florida.

The ethnic transformation of modern Florida is not simply a consequence of Hispanic immigration. More than 2,500 Soviet Jewish emigrés had concentrated in Dade County by the early 1990s. In the three large south Florida counties, 120,000 Jamaicans cluster in places called "Jamaica Hill," "Beat Street," and "Little Jamaica" in North Dade, Miramar, Lauderdale Lakes, Lauderhill, West Palm Beach, and Boynton Beach. Rarely heard from most of the year, thousands of south Florida's Trinidadians emerge publicly every October for their carnival, an extravagant parade on Miami's Biscayne Boulevard noted for its festive costumes and colorful marching bands, followed by a week of partying. French-Canadian tourists—almost 400,000 in 1992—still descend on south Florida and the Tampa Bay region every winter, but tens of thousands have purchased condominiums and mobile homes and become nearly permanent Florida residents. Lake Worth's "Little Finland" continues to maintain its cultural identity, partially through a recent direct migration of younger Finns to Florida. Florida's big urban areas, it should be clear, are now more culturally diverse than ever.

Mirroring national patterns, Asian immigrants emerged as the fastest-growing foreign-born group in Florida during the 1980s. The 1990 census reported 152,000 Asians in Florida, almost triple the number in 1980, and it is likely that these official census statistics represent a considerable undercounting. The largest groups in 1990 were Filipinos, Chinese, and Asian Indians—over 30,000 each—with smaller numbers of Koreans, Vietnamese, Japanese, and Thais. Almost two-thirds of Florida Asians live in the seven large metropolitan areas of Miami, Jacksonville, Tampa, Orlando, St. Petersburg, and Broward and Palm Beach counties. More than 7,300 Filipinos have settled in Jacksonville, for instance, drawn there initially by their tradition of service with the U.S. Navy. Hialeah may be 88 percent Hispanic, but it also has become home to more than 1,000 Asians, many of whom shop at the Saigon Supermarket, run small businesses and restaurants, and attend cultural events sponsored by the South Florida Buddhist Association and the Vietnamese Veterans Association. More than 17,000 Asians now reside in Broward County, many of them clustered in a Lauderdale Lakes neighborhood called "Little Asia," where Vietnamese and Chinese signs outnumber English on storefronts and strip shopping centers. A weekly Korean newspaper published in Miami and with news bureaus in Jacksonville, Tampa, and Orlando gets mailed to more than 3,000 Korean households in Florida. The *Florida Chinese News,* also published in Miami, has a circulation of 10,000, but it competes with three other Chinese-language papers in south Florida. Ten separate Chinese organizations in Miami sponsor an annual Chinese New Year Festival. After the crushing of the Chinese democracy movement in 1990 at Tiananmen Square, only Haitians and Cubans outnumbered Chinese refugees in detention at Miami's Krome Refugee Center. Chinese, Korean, and Japanese language schools serve immigrant children in Coral Gables, Miami, Fort Lauderdale, and Boca Raton. In West Florida, beginning in 1975, Vietnamese fishermen and shrimpers began settling in Pensacola and Panama City, where they applied energetic ethnic entrepreneurialism to a sleepy Gulf Coast industry.

Among the Asian immigrants, no group had a faster growth rate during the 1980s than Asian Indians, and more than one-third, or about 12,000, of them lived in Dade and Broward counties in 1990. Most are professionals or small business proprietors who have found economic success in America but cling to old country cultural ways. The Florida Hindu Parishad in Oakland Park, for instance, provides religious services and cultural activities for over 300 Hindu families. In Boca Raton, the South Florida Association of Indians regularly celebrates India's Independence Day. The Florida Muslim Alliance, based in Orlando, and a weekly newspaper, *The Muslim Chronicle,* published in Broward County, provide a cultural focus for Pakistanis in Florida. The Islamic School of South Dade offers classes in the Muslim religion and Urdu, the language of Pakistan. In 1993, the Bangladesh Association of Florida sponsored the first Bengali Cultural Festival in Pompano Beach in celebration of the Bengali New Year. Although they are not counted in the 1990 census, more than 5,000 Bangladeshis are said to reside in Palm Beach County alone. Florida may be thought of as a center of Hispanic immigrant life and culture, but considerable immigration during the 1980s brought diverse new Asian communities to the state.

Thus has Florida become a multicultural state with few parallels elsewhere. Early in its history, Florida had difficulty in attracting the European immigrants who poured into the northeastern and midwestern cities. With its historic connections to the islands and nations to the south, however, Florida had already become an immigrant destination for Cubans and Bahamians in the late nineteenth century. But since the 1960s, with revolutions and coups in Cuba, Haiti, Nicaragua, and elsewhere, Florida has exercised its magnetic attraction for exiles, refugees, and immigrants from the Caribbean and Latin America. Now wealthy businessmen and professionals from Venezuela and Argentina find themselves sharing immigrant status in Florida with peasant farmers and urban workers from Haiti, Mexico, and Guatemala. Immigration reform in the 1960s has also had an impact on Florida over time, especially noticeable in the rising numbers of Asian immigrants throughout the state.

The arrival of overwhelming numbers of newcomers in a relatively short thirty-year period has been accompanied by vigorous debate and controversy. State and business officials sought new immigrants in the late nineteenth century to stimulate the Florida economy, but this positive stance toward immigration largely had been reversed by the end of the twentieth century. Florida's political leaders and businessmen no longer yearn for new immigration. Instead, they have demanded stronger federal enforcement of U.S. immigration laws and more federal financial assistance to cope with the new demands that exiles, refugees, and illegal immigrants have placed on the state's schools and social services. Floridians have expressed special concern about the state's illegal or undocumented immigrants, who according to a 1992 INS report may number as many as 345,000. Consequently, by the mid-1990s, Florida voter initiatives revealed growing public support for a constitutional amendment, similar to that approved in California, that would curtail state services to illegal immigrants.

Floridians generally have expressed concern about rising ethnic and racial tensions touched off by the heavy immigration of recent years. Cubans and native-born black Americans have been engaged in a long-running competition in the Miami area over jobs, housing, and government assistance. Violence directed against Asians in Broward County and against Vietnamese fishermen in West Florida reflect a new late-twentieth-century nativism. Haitians, Mexicans, Guatemalans, and others suffer the consequences of racism and economic discrimination. For better and for worse, by the 1990s Florida was in the midst of dramatic demographic change, with all it entailed for the social, cultural, economic, and political life of the state. With the Caribbean Basin still in turmoil, Florida will continue to offer hope and opportunity for the exiles, refugees, and immigrants of the future. Like California and New York, Florida provides a glimpse of what multicultural America will be like in the twenty-first century.

Notes

1. *Florida Agriculturist,* 19 January 1881.
2. *Tallahassee Semi-Weekly Floridian,* 1 December 1865.
3. Jacksonville *Florida Dispatch,* 7 September 1881.
4. Tallahassee *Weekly Floridian,* 14 January 1873.
5. Larry Smith, "Coconut Grove: Bahamian Roots in Florida," *Nassau Tribune,* 12 October 1977, clipping file, Miami-Dade Public Library, Miami.
6. Ira De A. Reid, *The Negro Immigrant: His Background, Characteristics and Social Adjustment, 1899–1937* (New York: Columbia University Press, 1939), p. 184.
7. *Miami Herald,* 16 August 1933.
8. Harry F. Guggenheim, *The United States and Cuba: A Study in International Relations* (New York: Macmillan, 1934), p. 176.
9. Felix Roberto Masud-Piloto, *With Open Arms: Cuban Migration to the United States* (Totowa, N.J.: Rowman and Littlefield, 1988), pp. 2, 42.

Bibliography

Boswell, Thomas D., and James R. Curtis. *The Cuban-American Experience: Culture, Images, and Perspectives.* Totowa, N.J.: Rowman & Allanheld, 1983.

Burns, Allan F. *Maya in Exile: Guatamalans in Florida.* Philadelphia: Temple University Press, 1993.

Cruz, Arturo J., and Jaime Suchliki. *The Impact of Nicaraguans in Miami.* Coral Gables: Graduate School of International Studies, University of Miami, 1990.

Grenier, Guillermo J., and Alex Stepick. *Miami Now: Immigration, Ethnicity, and Social Change.* Gainesville: University Press of Florida, 1992.

Miller, Jake C. *The Plight of Haitian Refugees.* New York: Praeger, 1984.

Mohl, Raymond A. "Black Immigrants: Bahamians in Early Twentieth-Century Miami." *Florida Historical Quarterly* 65, no. 3 (January 1987):271–97.

———. "Florida's Changing Demography: Population Growth, Urbanization, and Latinization." *Environmental and Urban Issues* 17 (Winter 1990):22–30.

———. "Immigration Through the Port of Miami." In *Forgotten Doors: The Other Ports of Entry to the United States,* edited by M. Mark Stolarik, pp. 81–98. Philadelphia: Balch Institute Press, 1988.

———. "Miami: New Immigrant City." In *Searching for the Sunbelt: Historical Perspectives on a Region,* edited by Raymond A. Mohl, pp. 149–75. Knoxville: University of Tennessee Press, 1990.

———. "On the Edge: Blacks and Hispanics in Metropolitan Miami since 1959." *Florida Historical Quarterly* 69, no. 1 (July 1990):37–56.

Mormino, Gary R., and George E. Pozzetta. *The Immigrant World of Ybor City:*

Italians and Their Latin Neighbors in Tampa, 1880-1980. Champaign-Urbana: University of Illinois Press, 1987.

Portes, Alejandro, and Alex Stepick. *City on the Edge: The Transformation of Miami.* Berkeley: University of California Press, 1993.

Pozzetta, George E. "The Chinese Encounter with Florida, 1865–1920." *Chinese America* 2 (1989):43–58.

———. "Foreign Colonies in South Florida, 1865–1910." *Tequesta: The Journal of the Historical Association of Southern Florida* 34 (1974):45–56.

———. "Foreigners in Florida: A Study of Immigration Promotion, 1865–1910." *Florida Historical Quarterly* 52, no. 2 (October 1974):164–80.

———. "A Padrone Looks at Florida: Labor Recruiting and the Florida East Coast Railway." *Florida Historical Quarterly* 54, no. 1 (July 1975):74–84.

22 The Big Change in the Sunshine State: A Social History of Modern Florida

*Raymond A. Mohl
and
Gary R. Mormino*

In an astonishingly brief span of 150 years, Florida has passed from Old South to New South to Sunbelt South. In the process, and particularly in the twentieth century, Florida has experienced extraordinary and momentous changes. The population has grown dramatically, shifting markedly in composition and character along the way. Changing patterns of race and ethnicity, and of migration and immigration, have begun to create a new, multicultural Florida. Small towns, barrier islands, orange groves, and farmland have sprouted into great cities, towering at the center and sprawling at the edges. Technology and development have wrought enormous transformations upon the land, reshaping and reordering the way Floridians live, work, and play. An economy formerly based almost exclusively on agriculture and tourism has crossed over into the postindustrial age; agriculture and tourism remain important, but Florida has also developed a more diversified service economy that employs over 30 percent of the labor force. Once perceived by Americans as a balmy, dreamlike, semitropical paradise, Florida's newest image has incorporated fears stimulated by race riots, massive immigration, environmental destruction, and high crime rates. In virtually every aspect of life, big changes in the post–World War II era have transformed the old Florida, creating a powerful new Sunbelt juggernaut.[1]

Perhaps more than anything else, demographic change has served as a catalyst for the emergence of modern Florida. When admitted to the union in

1845, Florida boasted a population of only 69,000 residents. By contrast, the 1990 census heralded Florida as the nation's fourth largest state, home to over 14 million people. To put this growth in perspective, on a busy weekend Orlando's Magic Kingdom now attracts more tourists than the number of people who resided in the entire state a century and a half ago. In fact, the state's population has been growing rapidly since the nineteenth century—never less than 29 percent a decade for a century and a half. During some decades population growth was particularly dramatic: over 51 percent during the boom years of the 1920s, over 78 percent during a second boom period in the 1950s, and over 43 percent during the 1970s. And throughout the twentieth century Florida's population has grown at a rate considerably faster than the rate of growth for the nation as a whole—usually two, three, or four times as rapidly. Since 1970, only California and Texas have recorded higher numerical population increases than Florida. Despite the ebb and flow of the national economy, changing immigration patterns, and shifting internal migration flows between Snowbelt and Sunbelt, Florida has remained at or near the top of the population growth charts for many decades.

When Floridians cheered the coming of statehood in 1845, few residents south of Tallahassee heard the huzzahs. If a metaphor could describe the state of the mid-nineteenth-century state, it would be as a frontier. For Florida, the term *frontier* meant both place and process: geographically, vast portions of the peninsula lay remote, forbidding, inaccessible, and unsettled; experientially, the frontier mindset typified by Indian wars, open ranges, environmental disregard, and rampant individualism endured well into the twentieth century. In many respects, as late as the 1920s, Florida remained the last great frontier in the eastern continental United States.

Until the 1920s almost half of the state's small population resided in the northern tier of counties stretching from Jacksonville to Pensacola. South Florida—broadly defined as the vast area south of an imaginary line drawn between Tampa and Melbourne—remained virtually uninhabited. On the eve of the Civil War, only about 7,000 people had settled in south Florida (Key West excepted). Dade County, which then included also the future megacounties of Broward and Palm Beach, numbered a scant 83 persons in 1860. Even as late as 1900, less than 5 percent of the state's total population resided in south Florida. Despite rapid population growth in the first half of the twentieth century, not until the 1950s did Florida achieve a population density (51.1 persons per square mile) that exceeded that of the nation at large (50.7). So the image of Florida as a frontier, with vast open spaces and scattered development, matches the reality of the state's settlement patterns well into the twentieth century.

The peopling of Florida necessitated dramatic shifts to the south from population centers in the Panhandle and northern Florida. As late as 1880, three of every four residents still resided in the northern tier of the state, chiefly Middle Florida, the region between the Apalachicola and Suwannee rivers. The 1920s saw the inexorable population movement of new settlers to south Florida. In 1930, following the Florida boom, six in ten Floridians resided in central and south Florida. Since World War II, the population buildup of central Florida and along the Gold and Gulf coasts has been supercharged.

On the eve of statehood, a handful of sparsely populated towns had taken hold in Florida, chiefly Pensacola, Apalachicola, Tallahassee, St. Augustine, Jacksonville, Fernandina, Tampa, and Key West. While small in population and periodically wracked by virulent epidemics of yellow fever, antebellum cities served as vital centers of commerce, communications, and culture. Size was disproportionate to influence, but visitors were not always impressed by Florida's future urban prospects. Writing about Florida in the mid-1850s, for example, British traveler James Stirling observed in *Letters from the Slave States* that "here, in this poor Slave State, all is silence and stagnation; no cities are rising on the riverbanks."[2]

There was little in Florida's history up to 1880 that hinted at the state's future as one of the most populous and heavily urbanized regions in the nation. Only 10 percent of Floridians were urban dwellers in 1880. Buoyed by an influx of Bahamian "Conchs" and Cubans, refugees of the Cuban Ten Years War, Key West with 9,890 inhabitants stood as Florida's largest city. Only Jacksonville and Pensacola boasted populations greater than 3,000 persons in 1880.

A century later, Florida's status as one of America's most urbanized states is well entrenched, with fully 90 percent of Floridians classified as urban dwellers. Among the large states, only California currently has a higher percentage of urban population than Florida. Big cities like Miami, Tampa, and Jacksonville dominated Florida's urban profile for most of the twentieth century, but during the 1980s smaller cities such as Fort Pierce, Fort Myers, Bradenton, and Sarasota soared in population. During that decade, ten of America's twenty fastest growing metropolitan areas were found in the Sunshine State—a number that offers some measure of the dramatic development of Florida since 1945. Growth continues to cluster along the coasts; only two of the fast-track metro areas—Orlando and Ocala—are located in the state's interior. Naples, in particular, merits attention as a new Florida boomtown. One of Florida's most isolated locales, Naples exploded in the 1980s as a new retirement haven and tourist center, coming a long way since it was described in 1929 in the *Florida Highways* magazine as "only a hamlet with two hotels."[3] The relentless march of urbanization has had a tremendous impact on the creation of contemporary Florida, full of excitement, diversity, and danger.

No less dramatic than the sheer record of urban growth has been change in the composition of Florida's population. In temperament and profile, Florida was a slave state in 1845, solidly secure in the Deep South. African-American slaves constituted the greatest source of labor and wealth, evidenced also in their numbers. Between 1845 and 1880, African Americans comprised nearly half of Florida's population. Not until the 1920s did the proportion of black residents fall below one-third. Historically, the greatest concentration of African Americans was in the Black Belt, or Middle Florida. In Leon, Gadsden, Jefferson, and other northern counties, blacks outnumbered whites.

The growth of urban south Florida dramatically altered the racial and demographic profile of the state. The decades following World War I are critical to understanding the roots of modern Florida. The "Great Migration" of African Americans affected Florida but in ways different from the rest of the South. Like the South, an exodus, principally from the Black Belt, carried thousands of African Americans from Florida to more promising urban centers in the North. Unlike the South, which witnessed a hemorrhage of blacks and whites for the next half century, Florida actually attracted new black and white migrants. Whereas the number of blacks in Georgia and Alabama failed to increase between 1910 and 1950, in Florida the African-American population actually doubled over the same forty-year period. During this sustained great migration, African Americans from north Florida, Alabama, and especially Georgia sought new opportunities in the growing cities of Miami, Tampa, St. Petersburg, Jacksonville, and Orlando. During every decade between 1880 and 1960, Florida was the main destination of blacks migrating from Georgia. This migration has been largely unnoticed because of the overwhelming numbers of white migrants arriving in Florida simultaneously.

Adding to the ethnic and cultural diversity of a growing black population, substantial migration of blacks from the Bahamas to Key West and Miami occurred between the 1880s and 1930. In 1920, for instance, Miami's population of 29,500 included about 5,000 black immigrants from the Bahamas. Ironically, given the city's later immigration experience, the black islanders made up over 65 percent of Miami's foreign-born population. In 1920 and 1930, New York was the only American city with a larger population of black immigrants than Miami. Key West and Jacksonville also received Caribbean migrants during the century's early decades, although fewer than Miami.

While black migration and immigration made Florida more culturally diverse, demographic changes were redefining modern Florida in other ways, ironically making it the least southern state in the Deep South. Changes came swiftly in the twentieth century. Today, Florida is often described as a state where everyone is from some other place. Such was not the case a century ago. In 1880, an astonishing two-thirds of the state's population were born in Florida. Large numbers of transplanted Georgians and Alabamians also resided in Florida, giving the state a southern demographic profile.

A half century later, the great demographic transition was under way. By 1930, half of Florida's residents were born somewhere else, an indication of the large migration of new residents from the Midwest and Northeast. The proportion of population native to Florida (and the Deep South) has continued to dwindle, so that by 1990 only about 30 percent of Floridians claim native status. In central and south Florida, the percentage of newcomers is even more dramatic. Inclusion of hundreds of thousands of winter residents adds further to the demographic differential between native and newcomer, mostly along the Gold Coast and the Gulf Coast. But some of the interior rural counties of south Florida, such as Hardee, Hendry, Glades, and DeSoto, retain high proportions of Florida-born residents and thus differ markedly from their urbanized neighbors.

Florida's exploding growth in the twentieth century stems almost entirely from new waves of migrants, not from a high birth rate. Whereas a century earlier Florida's new births matched the high rates of other southern states, since the 1920s the state has registered the lowest birth rate of any southern state. Beginning after World War II, and especially in the 1970s and 1980s, commentators noted a salient theme in the demographic profiles of several counties, including Pinellas, Sarasota, Charlotte, and Pasco: annually, more deaths than births were being recorded. According to the 1990 census, the number of residents in Charlotte County aged zero to sixteen equals those residents seventy-five and over. The aging of the Sunshine State has become one of modern Florida's most pronounced social trends. In a telling bit of social criticism, Florida has been lampooned as "God's Waiting Room."

Ironically, Florida's state song, written by Stephen Foster in the nineteenth century, is "Old Folks at Home." But the phenomenon of growing old in America is a recent trend. Relatively few Americans lived to enjoy retirement prior to the twentieth century. The positioning of Florida as home to large numbers of elderly Americans stemmed from several political, social, and economic developments: improved medical care, a national Medicare program, Social Security, improved pension plans, and air-conditioning. Inflated housing prices in the Midwest and Northeast provided retirement capital for those who packed up for the move to Florida. The pattern first became apparent by the 1940s and 1950s as tens of thousands of Jews from the Northeast retired to Miami and Miami Beach and midwesterners chose St. Petersburg. Postcards of senior citizens lounging on green benches made St. Petersburg a symbol of old age in America.

Soon developers and entrepreneurs began providing new housing for retirees on a massive scale—high-rise, ocean-front condominiums and gated golf-course communities for the wealthy, sprawling tract houses for the middle class, enormous apartment complexes and mobile-home parks for the less well-to-do. The retired and aging new Floridians often lived in retiree developments with names like Sun City Center, Leisure City, Leisureville, Leisure Lakes, Golf Village, Serenity, and Century Village. The "graying of America," the increasing longevity of retirees, has had important consequences for Florida, whose population has been aging faster than that of any other state.

The graying of Florida has come swiftly and dramatically. In 1880, the median age of Floridians stood at eighteen, one of the nation's lowest; by 1990 the state's median age was thirty-six, the nation's highest. Most striking, a century ago about 2 percent of Floridians were older than sixty-five; by 1990 the figure had surpassed 18 percent and was still growing. In some Florida counties, the proportion of elderly doubled the state average. Charlotte, Highlands, Pasco, and Sarasota counties ranked among the top five counties nationally in percentage of population sixty-five and older. The 1990 census revealed that of the nation's 435 congressional districts, only seven contained populations with a median age above forty; all were in Florida. Topping that list, Charlotte County's median age stood at just under fifty-four in 1990.

The image of Florida as a relaxing, sunshine-filled paradise for retirees was a powerful one. Throughout the four decades after 1950, a thousand retirees were moving to Florida each week, representing a staggering transfer of financial capital and emotional commitment. The state's over-sixty-five population increased 70 percent during the 1970s and 40 percent during the 1980s. When the first Social Security checks arrived in the mailboxes of retirees in 1940, Florida claimed about 2,500 beneficiaries, about the same number as Delaware. By the 1990s, that number had skyrocketed to almost 3 million. Florida's invisible economy rests on a pillar of Social Security and pension checks. The aging of the now-middle-aged baby-boom generation will have a powerful impact on Florida, as that demographic cohort reaches retirement age early in the twenty-first century.

The history of modern Florida can be viewed as a dizzying set of migrations involving individuals, families, and groups over time. Thousands of Georgians—black and white—rushed to the promising frontiers of Florida during Reconstruction, during the 1920s boom, and during the flush times of World War II. Immigrants from the Caribbean worked as spongers in Key West, laborers in Miami, and cigar makers in Ybor City. During World War II, several thousand temporary workers from Jamaica, Barbados, and the Bahamas picked tomatoes in Belle Glade, harvested potatoes at Hastings, and cut sugarcane at Okeechobee. In the postwar era, tens of thousands of ex-servicemen who had trained at bases in Florida returned to pursue their tropical dreams. Huge numbers of Jews and Italian Americans trekked to Florida in the decades after the depression and the war. New migrations of Cubans, Haitians, and Nicaraguans have revolutionized the demographic profile of Dade County in the past three decades, with spillover effects on nearby Monroe, Broward, and Palm Beach counties. Annually thousands of Finns make the winter trek from the northern Midwest and Canada to Lake Worth. Throughout the 1980s, well over a million Canadians spent at least a day in Florida, many of them establishing semipermanent colonies at Dunedin and Hollywood. These multiple and ongoing migrations contribute to the difficult task of comprehending a common history for the peoples of Florida. Ironically, migration provides a unifying theme in their history.

The migrations have contributed to a firestorm of social change in Florida. Such population growth over a compressed period of time is unparalleled in the American South. The population of Florida in 1845, just under 70,000 residents, barely equaled the population of Rhode Island in 1790. On the eve of Pearl Harbor, Florida's population of 1.9 million ranked it the least populated state in the Southeast. Even Arkansas outranked Florida in 1940. Since World War II, Florida's population has grown more than sixfold. Between 1970 and 1990, as the nation's population grew by 21 percent, the South's population soared by 40 percent, much of the growth the result of surging gains in Texas and Florida. Between 1970 and 1990, Arkansas, Louisiana, Mississippi, Alabama, and Kentucky achieved population gains averaging about 17 percent; Florida's recorded growth over the period was 90 percent. Only Texas at 46.5 percent came close to rivaling Florida's growth. Demographers predict no letup in the relentless surge of new population in Florida. One can only imagine what Florida will be like in the year 2050, when, according to one projection, the state's population will hit 47 million!

The dazzling pace of population growth has produced cataclysmic and catalytic change in modern Florida. The ecological relationship of man and land, between human groups and the geographical environment, has become increasingly unbalanced and destructive. Over time, man and machine, population growth and economic development, have taken their toll, transforming Florida, altering and reshaping the landscape, and reconfiguring the ways Floridians lived and live. In 1845, Florida's sylvan forests, lush lands, and superabundant waters must have seemed limitless. Over 30,000 lakes, rivers, and springs graced the state. The last century has witnessed a concerted private/public effort to dredge, ditch, dike, and dam the waters. Curiously, for a state where visionaries often invoked the metaphor of Florida as a land of dreams, the evidence suggests that most developers and dream makers sought to transform the land into something else. Florida beaches became seawall fortresses. Lagoons became Venetian canals. The natural Everglades sawgrass country, drained and ditched, became gigantic farms producing vegetables and sugarcane. Pine scrub and palmetto country were transformed into theme parks or sprawling housing developments and mobile-home parks.

The diverse ecosystem known as Florida was often found to be too hot, too wet, and too inaccessible. The history of the Everglades parallels Florida's historical rush, with tragic consequences. Seen in 1845, the Everglades presented a majestic yet disturbing portrait: Here seemed to be untouched nature, a perfectly functioning system of water and land, flora and fauna. The Kissimmee River drained slowly southward, the region's wetlands filtering the waters, feeding the 750-square-mile liquid heart of the system, Lake Okeechobee. The lake served as a great shallow saucer, overflowing to feed the complex environment of sawgrass, prairie, and hammock. In the words of Marjory Stoneman Douglas, it was "a river of grass."

Yet, even in the nineteenth century one could detect ominous signs of change. At the conclusion of the Second Seminole War, about one hundred Seminole Indians were refugees in the Everglades. They were

A cabbage farm at Hastings in 1947. Florida's second-ranked industry after tourism by mid-century was agriculture, which in 1950 contributed $401 million to the state's growing prosperity—an increase of 300 percent over 1935. The various soils of the peninsula and Panhandle produced 104 different commercial crops, more than were grown in any other state. Most farmers owned the farms they managed. Truck and vegetable crops, harvested by resident and migratory workers, were shipped in ever increasing tonnage to northern winter markets. Sugarcane brought in $9 million in south Florida; tobacco was a leading field and crop in the northern and western counties. Commercial ornamental horticulture was a new and thriving agribusiness, producing chrysanthemums, gladiolas, lilies, orchids, roses, cut green foliage, ferns, and potted foliage plants for interior decoration of Florida's and the nation's profusion of new homes. By the 1990s agriculture would gross $6 billion a year.

reluctant and unwilling new residents, victims of a U.S. government willing to spend millions of dollars and thousands of lives to liberate Florida's lands for new settlers. A government with such resolve could later marshal its awesome resources to straighten rivers, drain wetlands, cut canals through oolitic limestone, and change the very life of the Glades.

Generations of politicians and entrepreneurs, bewitched by visions of agricultural empire, surveyed the immense region, but the transformation did not begin until the 1880s when developer Hamilton Disston began clearing his central Florida swamplands. "Water *will* flow downhill," prophesied engineers. Developers promised that the reclaimed Everglades would become a paradise for small farmers, but, ironically, the virgin lands turned out to be a bonanza not for rugged yeomen farmers but for corporate agribusiness. Few small farmers but thousands of migrant farm workers have toiled in the steaming Everglades throughout the twentieth century. From Zora Neale Hurston's *Their Eyes Were Watching God* (1937) to Edward R. Murrow's *Harvest of Shame* (1960), artists and journalists have attempted to portray the poignancy of the lives of migrant workers.

The most dramatic chapter in the history of the Everglades occurred after World War II. In 1947, President Harry Truman dedicated 1.4 million acres of the Everglades as America's newest national park, yet the following year Congress passed a multimillion-dollar appropriation bill to convert much of the southeast Everglades into new farmland. New levees and pumping stations permitted massive profits, while the federal government provided generous subsidies to sugar growers. In 1918, farmers harvested only a few hundred acres of Everglades sugar; by the early 1990s, nearly a half million acres of glade mucklands were given over to it. The combination of agricultural pollution and the drinking water demands of millions of new Floridians has proven calamitous. Many predict a dire future for the dying Everglades. Others admit that the River of Grass is not dying but is already dead.

The sad fate of the Everglades is only one example of the ecological consequences of Florida's modern growth-at-any-cost mentality. For generations, developers and politicians looked to Washington for the funding of a cross-state barge canal. The controversial project, opposed by south Floridians, would link Yankeetown on the Gulf Coast to the St. Johns River on the East Coast. Authorized but never funded by the New Deal, the canal project made political, if not environmental, sense to Lyndon B. Johnson's Great Society in the 1960s. Making a beginning on the project, engineers succeeded in diverting the Ocklawaha River and creating new lakes. However, Richard Nixon pulled the plug on the idea, perhaps listening with one ear about cost overruns and the other about ruination of the underground aquifer.

An examination of a map of the Florida peninsula explains the irresistible appeal of a cross-state canal. Napoleon Bonaparte, who appreciated the significance of distances, once asserted that Italy was too long

For nearly five decades, since the publication of her 1947 classic *The Everglades: River of Grass,* Marjory Stoneman Douglas (*left*), shown in her Coconut Grove home, has been the most eloquent and enduring defender of the Everglades, Florida's last frontier, and the greatest roadless wilderness in the United States. In 1993, in recognition of her environmental activism, she was awarded the Presidential Medal of Freedom. Marjorie Carr of Gainesville (*right*) founded Florida Defenders of the Environment in 1969 to oppose construction of the Cross-Florida Barge Canal, which, Carr argued, would both destroy a large part of the scenic and sensitive Ocklawaha River and threaten the underground freshwater aquifer. As a result of her efforts, on 17 December 1976, the Florida Cabinet formally recommended to Congress that canal construction be halted, and that subsequently was done.

to be a country. Florida, cursed by businessmen and mariners, was a long state. Geographically the largest state east of the Mississippi—recent calculations boosted the Sunshine State over its rival, Georgia—Florida boasts 65,758 square miles of land mass and 3,800 miles of tidal shoreline. The state capital, Tallahassee, lies only 20 miles from the Georgia border but 500 miles from Miami. The creation of modern Florida has been in large measure a struggle to overcome the tyranny of distance.

Indeed, modern Florida has been transformed by new transportation technologies that shortened distances, speeded development, and promoted tourism. In 1845, anyone wishing to traverse the peninsula faced daunting and generally uncomfortable options. One might travel by horseback or stagecoach in some areas, by canoe or sailboat in others, primitive means untouched by the transportation revolution unfolding in the northern states. By the time of the Civil War, steamboats were plying the Apalachicola and St. Johns rivers, but Florida had only 400 miles of railroad track in place and remained last among the Confederate states in railroad mileage.

By the end of the century, however, railroads crisscrossed the peninsula, reaching Pensacola and even distant Miami. Beginning in 1880, a great surge in railroad construction began to open up new areas for settlement, tourism, and economic development. Total railroad mileage in Florida surpassed 3,500 in 1900, and it nearly doubled to about 6,000 miles by 1930. Great railroad magnates such as Henry M. Flagler and Henry B. Plant rushed Florida into the twentieth century. Flagler's transportation and hotel empire eventually extended from St. Augustine to Key West, leaving in its wake the new or rejuvenated cities of Daytona Beach, Palm Beach, West Palm Beach, Fort Lauderdale, and Miami. Before his death in 1913, Flagler pushed his railroad all the way to Key West, an engineering marvel of the time.

On Florida's west coast, the iron messiah made and unmade cities. Cedar Keys, in 1880 one of Florida's most promising cities, was connected by rail to Fernandina on the East Coast north of Jacksonville and was blessed with rich nearby cedar forests, as well as lumbermills, fine wharfs, and steamship connections to New Orleans, Key West, and Havana. Yet it was devastated by Henry Plant's decision to select Tampa as a rail hub for his growing empire. A village of only 720 residents in 1880, Tampa prospered with the coming of the railroad in 1884. By 1885, Tampa was linked by rail to Jacksonville, but in a greater sense, like many emerging Florida cities, it was becoming part of a complex modern economic and transportation system. Cigar manufacturers in Tampa, lumber companies in the Panhandle, commercial fishermen in Fernandina, cattlemen in central Florida, orange growers in Polk County, and truck farmers in Dade County all belonged to an expanding integrated system of railroads and steamships, markets and schedules.

Technology pierced the Florida interior. The steamboat and then the railroad opened markets and spurred growth in such places as Sanford, Orlando, Mount Dora, Leesburg, Gainesville, and Ocala. Yet technology could be capricious. Just as new developments such as the railroad and cotton processing doomed the once thriving seaports of Apalachicola and St. Marks, so new technologies such as electrification and the automobile threatened the primacy of the railroad. Where once cities relied upon "natural advantages"—a seaport, river, or crossroads—electrical generating plants with their spinoff technologies (streetcars and telephones) reorganized and reshaped American cities. Above all, perhaps, the automobile brought a flurry of big changes to the Sunshine State.

The motor car altered the roadside landscape, introducing the familiar trinity of the gasoline station, diner, and motel. Introduced by Henry Ford in 1907, the Model-T helped reduce distances, socially and geographically, between rural and urban Florida. Farmers and rural families drove to town on Saturdays, accentuating the importance of downtowns with their attendant attractions of department stores, movie theaters, and other entertainment. The automobile also democratized tourism in the 1920s, enabling middle-class "tin can tourists" to share Sunshine State attractions and amenities that had been the exclusive domain of the wealthy.

The building of highways and roads to serve the automobile accelerated the development of modern Florida. In 1906, when it had fewer than 300 automobiles, the state had only a handful of paved highways. As one travel writer put it in 1918, "it was an exceedingly troublesome matter to get an automobile down into the central part of the state."[4] Prior to 1916, road building in the United States was in the domain of county government. Given the travail of distances and the inequitable capacities of counties to pay for highway construction, road building in Florida in the nineteenth and early twentieth centuries was a haphazard and many-splintered thing. During the Progressive Era, a popular idea known as the Good Roads Movement swept through the South: Good roads spelled progress and prosperity. The crisis of World War I crystallized the national movement for efficient transportation. The federal government now sought state participation in road building, helping to subsidize state efforts. The famous Dixie Highway linking Florida with Chicago stands as a testimonial to new-found resources for road construction.

By the 1920s, Florida's good roads movement began to achieve some successes. With one eye on the tourist trade, road builders began laying asphalt that connected the state's cities and linked them with highways leading north. By 1925, a half million tourists were arriving annually in Florida by automobile, and by 1930 Florida had over 3,200 miles of paved highways. Even working-class Americans, driving their Fords and Chevys down the Dixie Highway or across the Tamiami Trail or (after 1938) over the Overseas Highway to Key West, could take their families on a Florida vacation by the seashore. As the state road department's official magazine, *Florida Highways,* noted enthusiastically in 1930, "Florida's magnificent system of highways is creating a somewhat nomadic tribe of tourists" who were "now roaming all over the state."[5] By 1950, over a million cars a year were entering Florida for tourism and recreation. The bus and the truck also contributed in important ways to stimulating tourist traffic and economic growth.

The construction of the Tamiami Trail illustrates the impact of modern transportation upon a region. The dream of an east-west highway artery across south Florida had existed for decades, but its implementation lay beyond the financial means of individual counties. Beginning in the late teens, and aided by the geopolitical lobbying of land developer Barron G. Collier and Miami business interests, the dream took hold. The Tamiami Trail was an engineering marvel of the time. When it was finished in 1927, cars and trucks could travel on modern roads from Tampa to Miami (hence the name Tamiami). It had social costs, however. The Seminole Indians, who prior to the 1920s had lived in semi-isolation, now confronted modernity. Soon dugout canoes and subsistence living surrendered to airboats, bingo, and alligator wrestling. A tourist economy offered the Seminoles a new and different life-style. Hunters enjoyed easy access to the bounties of Big Cypress country and quickly depopulated the wildlife of the region. When Winchesters and Remingtons failed to kill, Fords and Chevrolets often added to the toll. The Tamiami Trail proved ruinous to the Florida panther, unaccustomed to on-beam prestolites, ironically developed by Carl Fisher, the chief promoter of Miami Beach in the early twentieth century.

Subsequent highway construction, especially the Sunshine State Parkway (now called Florida's Turnpike), in the 1950s and early 1960s and the interstate highway system in the 1960s and after dramatically enhanced mobility in Florida. Interstate 95 on the east coast linked Miami and south Florida directly to the northeastern states. Interstate 75 connected Tampa with the Midsouth and the Midwest. Interstate 10 pushed across the northern tier of the state from Jacksonville to Tallahassee and Pensacola and beyond to New Orleans. Interstate 4 traversed a theme-park corridor from Busch Gardens in Tampa through the Disney landscape of Orlando to Daytona Beach on the Atlantic Coast. These new highways launched tourism to lofty new levels and opened up areas of the state to business and residential development. Typically, a new stretch of I-75 between Tampa and Naples has propelled the incredible spurt of recent growth in southwest Florida, now the fastest growing part of Florida. Truck traffic on the interstates further undermined the declining railroads, the technology that originally made Florida accessible.

Linked to the interstates, new central-city expressways in Jacksonville, Miami, Orlando, Tampa, and St. Petersburg had important consequences. They tore through established neighborhoods and uprooted entire communities—especially African-American communities—in the drive to speed automobile traffic in and out of the downtowns. Daily rush-hour traffic jams in Tampa and Miami made these highways less like expressways than slow-moving parking lots. But the new auto arteries did trigger a rapid spatial reorganization of urban populations, as white residents moved to the suburbs and African Americans pushed out of redeveloped inner-city areas to newer, formerly white, "second ghetto" neighborhoods. In Florida, as elsewhere, the interstate highway network had both positive and negative effects.

The automobile had still other consequences. Some observers have recently noted that new and dynamic business and commercial centers—new configurations of urban life called "edge cities"—have sprouted distant from traditional downtowns. Miami, Orlando, and Tampa all have developed such edge cities, usually at interstate highway interchanges or near large international airports. In part, they evolved because the automobile promoted the decentralization of urban business and the deconcentration of city people. Older metropolitan areas such as New York, Chicago, and San Francisco developed with mass transit, so their building and population patterns reflected high levels of residential density. By contrast, Florida's metropolitan areas grew up in the automobile age and thus are settled out rather than up, revealing relatively low density rates as well. Recent and expensive attempts to persuade Floridians to give up their automobiles, notably in Miami and Jacksonville, have not been encouraging. South Florida's Tri-Rail system, a commuter rail system linking West Palm Beach with Miami, and Miami's new above-ground transit system known as Metrorail have attracted few regular riders, as most urban Floridians prefer the privacy of their cars, even at the expense of daily traffic jams.

By the late twentieth century, commercial air transportation had come to rival the automobile in importance. Indeed, aviation technology has had a bigger impact on Florida than on most other states. Florida boasted the world's first regularly scheduled air-passenger service, the short-lived St. Petersburg–Tampa Airboat Line established in 1914. During World War I, U.S. naval air stations were established in Pensacola, Miami, and Key West. Before the end of the decade, regularly scheduled air service carried passengers from Key West, Miami, and Palm Beach to Cuba and the Bahamas. In the 1920s, the U.S. Congress laid the foundations for the national air transportation industry by subsidizing airmail service. Aviation entrepreneurs in Florida quickly seized the opportunity, and soon three major airline companies emerged in the state: Pan American Airways and Eastern Airlines in Miami and National Airlines in St. Petersburg. By the 1930s, these and other airlines, using the newly developed DC-3 airliner, were carrying tens of thousands of passengers monthly to Florida from U.S. and Latin American cities. Increasingly after mid-century, commercial air travel supplanted rail and auto transportation as a mainstay of Florida's tourist economy.

The novelty and excitement of aviation had come to be an essential ingredient in Florida's national image by the 1930s. Beginning in 1929, Miami provided the annual setting for the All American Air Races, seen by millions on newsreels at movie theaters. By the 1930s the *Miami Herald* was carrying a regular aviation column called "Wings Over Miami." Goodyear blimps based in Miami became a common sight in the air over south Florida's Atlantic coastal beaches during the thirties and after. This consciousness of aviation's importance intensified during World War II, when the federal government, induced by Florida's good year-round flying weather, located air training bases all over the state.

Thus, Florida entered the postwar era with a strong sense of the importance of air travel. Business and political leaders quickly came to realize that aviation stimulated tourism, economic activity, and population growth. The Miami International Airport emerged as one of the nation's leading airports in passengers and air freight, especially as a gateway to Latin America. Several airlines selected Miami as a center for aircraft overhaul and maintenance operations, with important spillover effects: by 1960, Eastern Airlines, with over 7,000 workers, had become the leading employer in the Miami metropolitan area. By the 1980s, an estimated 160,000 workers, or about one-fifth of the Miami labor force, were directly or indirectly employed in airport and aviation activities. Major new airport expansion and construction since the 1970s highlighted the degree to which airports have become elaborate image-boosting entry points, much like the opulent urban railroad stations of the late nineteenth century.

Technology not only revolutionized the way we traveled; it affected profoundly the way we lived, worked, played, even slept. Air-conditioning has become so omnipresent that we forget how recently climate control arrived in Florida. We also take for granted the manifold changes resulting from this new technology. Floridians, of course, had

In 1959, a Pratt and Whitney engineer monitors a jet engine test in Palm Beach County. The fifties marked the beginning of a dramatic increase in the number of industries that took root in Florida. In addition to Pratt and Whitney these included Martin Aircraft, Sperry Rand, IBM, Maxwell House, Anheuser-Busch, and Disney World. The last-named corporation opened the Magic Kingdom in 1971 and Epcot Center in 1982, which together would draw more visitors each year than Florida had residents.

always been keenly—and physically—aware of the importance of passive cooling. Southern architecture studied the science of passive cooling: wide verandahs, high ceilings, cross ventilation, louvered jalousies, the central breezeway, and chinaberry trees to cast shade. The riddle of removing humidity went unsolved until a nineteenth-century Apalachicola physician experimented with a steam-driven ice-making machine. John Gorrie's hospital patients, stricken with yellow fever, improved in the mechanically produced chilled air, establishing an early precedent for twentieth-century air-conditioning.

In 1929, Willis Carrier introduced the modern, prototype air conditioner. Still, air-conditioning for most urban Floridians in the 1930s and 1940s meant a visit to the movie theater or department store. Trains and buses bringing travelers to Florida were air-conditioned by the end of the 1930s, and a few hotels had air-conditioned ballrooms by the early 1940s, but otherwise tourists had the privilege of sweating in the semitropical heat just as the Florida natives did. The end of World

War II, however, with its rush of accumulated savings and applied technology, allowed the introduction of affordable window air-conditioning units. Houses and apartments, motels and shops, began sprouting the boxy window units in the 1950s, and the new technology was cooling planes and cars by the end of the decade. Air-conditioning augured a New South, celebrated by historian Raymond Arsenault as "the end of the long hot summer."[6]

Air-conditioning had a gradual rather than a sudden impact on sweltering Florida summers. As late as 1960, only 18 percent of all Florida households had air-conditioning, and only a scant 2 percent of African-American households. The decade of the 1960s ushered it in on a massive scale, as homes utilizing climate control increased to 60 percent by 1970, to 84 percent by 1980, and to over 90 percent in the nineties. By 1980, moreover, almost half of Florida's African-American households had adopted air-conditioning. Certainly, the ubiquitous whirring of the central air unit made Florida more attractive year-round to retirees.

Florida homes that once obeyed the environmental imperatives of a tropical climate—"hot air rises and water may"—took on new forms, materials, and functions. Low ceilings, concrete-block walls, and entertainment centers replaced high ceilings, thin, wooden walls, and front porches. Air-conditioning permitted Floridians to orient lives around schedules no longer dependent upon summer afternoon storms or seasonal change. Schools, which once began classes in late September or October, now begin in late August—just as in Philadelphia and Chicago. Floridians, who like other southerners had historically maintained a close association with the land, now became more detached from the natural world, cruising in air-conditioned cars to climate-controlled malls and offices, to domed stadiums, to housing developments with disassociated names such as Cypress Bend or Clear Lake. Air-conditioning allowed Floridians to keep their sunshine and "cool it" at the same time twelve months a year. Florida's fantastic trajectory of population growth in the decades after 1950 would almost certainly have flattened out without the introduction and widespread adoption of air-conditioning. Tourists, who once regularly abandoned Florida between June and December, found that a controlled temperature means no seasonal boundaries. Once a six-month industry, tourism became a year-round business.

Tourism first attracted attention in the years following the Civil War, when small numbers of winter visitors arrived in Fernandina and Jacksonville. Many found their way on steamships up the St. Johns River and along the crooked Ocklawaha, destination Silver Springs. But if the

1870s belonged to charming stern-wheelers and glass-bottomed boats, the 1880s and 1890s unleashed a decade of conspicuous consumption in the building of elaborate Florida hotels—the Ponce de Leon, the Royal Poinciana, the Bellview Biltmore, and the Royal Palm. The Gilded Age had arrived in Florida, traveling the rails of Henry M. Flagler and Henry B. Plant.

The 1920s unveiled a new Florida with new forms of pleasure. New freedoms generated by economic prosperity and inventive genius created a national consumer culture. The symbols of the era—Ford Flivvers, Palm Beach, Coral Gables, Miami Beach, the Tamiami Trail—underscore the interlocking destinies of tourism and economic health. Tourism was the oxygen for Florida's boom. "All of America's gold rushes," noted journalist Mark Sullivan in his classic *Our Times* (1935), "all her oil booms, and her free-land stampedes, dwindled by comparison . . . with the torrent of migration pouring into Florida."[7]

The promise of Florida, the dreams of the good life under sunshine and palm, on golf course and sandy beach, melded into compelling and romantic images. Dreams could be packaged into residential lots and tourist parks, gated developments and mobile-home communities. Historically, American cities evolved by developing commerce, industry, and transportation, but Florida cities such as Daytona Beach, St. Petersburg, and Miami Beach sold themselves, promoting their beaches, salt air, endless sunshine, and the Florida dream. St. Petersburg appealed to sedate middle-class midwesterners, while Miami Beach attracted a nouveau riche crowd interested in fishing, golf, polo, jai alai, horse racing, and gambling. America's middle classes, the "tin can tourists," validated the Florida dream. Even Chicago gangster Al Capone, a frequent visitor, proclaimed Florida "the Garden of America."[8]

Postwar Florida came to embody and in turn radiate the values of American culture: youth, leisure, consumption, mobility, and affluence. Tourism figured prominently in this midcentury culture. Television enhanced the image of Florida as the Sunshine State. Most Americans were familiar with the Miami-based TV shows of Arthur Godfrey and Jackie Gleason, both of whom shared an affection for the good life in the Sunbelt before that concept had been invented. Dozens of glamorous new hotels went up on Miami Beach in the 1950s, including the extravagant and glitzy beach-front Fontainebleau. The publicity machine, one journalistic account noted in 1964, was "like a huge ballyhoo generator that never shuts down. Its output voltage is always there, waiting to stun the unwary."[9] Not surprisingly, tourism began hitting new peaks in the postwar era. In 1933, officials estimated that about a million tourists arrived in Florida. By 1940, they numbered 2.8

million, and that number increased exponentially to 5 million in 1950, 20 million in 1980, and 40 million in 1990. A $32 billion industry by the mid-1990s, tourism became, truly, the bedrock of Florida's economy.

These raw statistics provide sparse insight into the character of the dynamic tourist economy and its vast impact on the landscape. In the halcyon 1950s, Florida's top tourist attraction was Marineland, near St. Augustine. In 1956, Miami and Miami Beach sparkled as the crown jewels of tourism, attracting nearly one-quarter of the state's visitors. The opening of Disney World in 1971, however, inaugurated a dramatic new chapter. By the 1980s, it had become the world's greatest tourist attraction—over 20 million tourists a year and a total of one billion by 1994. Disney's fantasy landscape meshed perfectly with the modern culture of leisure and consumption. The surging growth of the Orlando area over the past twenty-five years has been based largely on the appeal of Mickey Mouse, but Busch Gardens, Sea World, and Universal Studios lure an additional 16 million visitors annually. "Theme parks" and "attractions" have created artificial worlds of elaborately contrived environments where tourists "experience" Thunder Mountain but rarely appreciate the real Florida. More people have experienced the pirates of the Caribbean than live in the United States today!

Rivaling tourism as a driving force behind Florida's postwar growth was retirement. The same palm tree, golf course, sunshine, and beach imagery that attracted tourists worked to bring retirees as well. Postwar guidebooks with can-do titles paved the way. George and Jane Dusenbury's *How to Retire to Florida* (1947) was typical—not inspiring but offering practical advice sought by millions. A. Lowell Hunt's *Florida Today: New Land of Opportunity* (1950) informed readers that "you don't have to be rich" to retire to Florida,[10] a message with an impact. The construction industry boomed during the 1950s and 1960s, working overtime to provide tract houses and condominiums for new Floridians. The tin-can tourists of the 1920s and 1930s, with travel-trailers hitched behind their cars, had a postwar counterpart: the mobile-home retirement village. They were fast, easy, and cheap, although rarely mobile. By 1980, Florida had more mobile homes than any other state, and by the 1990s over 12 percent of Florida's population resided in 760,000 mobile homes. The "amenities factor" underlay much of Florida's late-twentieth-century appeal to migrating and retiring Americans, as well as to tourists and vacationers.[11]

A final aspect of Florida's amenities can be found in sports and recreation. In the late nineteenth century, fishing and hunting opportunities in Florida attracted wealthy adventurers from the United States and Europe. Alligator and bear hunting, camping and fishing, formed the stuff

A part of hotel row on Miami Beach in April 1959. The hundreds of white sun-splashed hotels, both Art Deco and contemporary, became Florida's best-known architectural features in the years before the erection of the rocket gantries at Cape Canaveral and the Magic Kingdom turrets at Disney World. Described as the American Riviera of the leisured masses, Miami Beach attracted visitors not only to a year-round balmy surf but to 500 swimming pools, elegant shops on Collins Avenue, and a myriad of restaurants, cocktail lounges, and show bars. Since the mid-1980s the beach has enjoyed a second boom of tourism and night life.

of such first-person accounts as James A. Henshall's *Camping and Cruising in Florida* (1884) and Charles E. Whitehead's *The Camp-Fires of the Everglades, or Wild Sports in the South* (1891). As Florida became more established in the early twentieth century, sporting activities became more tame—golf, tennis, polo, horse racing, yachting, and other recreations that appealed initially to the upper crust of Florida visitors. For the retirees at mobile-home parks, there was always shuffleboard. By the late twentieth century, golf and tennis had become democratized and almost ubiquitous; virtually every condominium and apartment complex around the state had its own tennis courts and swimming pools. Palm Beach County had more golf courses per capita than any other county in the nation. But spectator sports now rival tennis and golf, suggesting that many Floridians prefer their recreation in more sedentary forms. Modern Florida has come to be defined by big-time college football, by professional football teams in Miami, Tampa, and Jacksonville, by the Florida Marlins National League baseball team and a new major league team in St. Petersburg, and by professional basketball, hockey, and soccer franchises. Sports have become an integral aspect of the Sunshine State's culture of leisure and consumption.

Sports, retirement, and tourism have all had important places in recent Florida history, in helping to shape its image and in propelling its economy. The agricultural sector, too, remains a significant economic force—a $6 billion industry that provides jobs for one out of six working Floridians. But in the years after World War II, powerful new forces of change began to emerge. The war itself had a tremendous impact. Military training facilities, air bases, naval bases, and major shipyards sprouted all over the state. Service personnel and their families migrated to Florida by the hundreds of thousands, and many thousands returned to live when the war was over. Miami, Tampa, Jacksonville, and Pensacola especially benefitted from military investment and enormous military payrolls. Huge federal wartime expenditures in Florida and throughout the Sunbelt produced essential new infrastructure, supported local economies, and stimulated construction and service industries. Heavy military and defense spending, as well as the new aerospace establishment at Cape Canaveral, continued to sustain Florida's urbanizing economy throughout the Cold War. By the 1980s, defense spending and military payrolls in Florida surpassed $15 billion annually. Underlying much of the nation's changing economic and urban pattern in the postwar era has been the redirection of federal resources through military and defense spending, and this "military remapping" of America had special salience for Florida in the second half of the twentieth century. With the end of the Cold War, however, the federal military-industrial complex, once so vital to Florida's defense industries and military bases, began to shrink.

The postwar federal presence was important, but a series of powerful economic changes also had a dramatic impact on post-1950 Florida. Scholars have begun to sketch the full dimensions of a long-term structural transformation of the American economy that dates back to the 1950s—a process of "deindustrialization" that has resulted in the dismantling and abandoning of much of the nation's increasingly obsolete industrial infrastructure. Taking the place of the aging Rustbelt factory industries are the dynamic new industries of the postindustrial economy—the high-tech, computerized information businesses and the more fully developed (and low-paying) service economy. The new American economy grew up around services provided by government, educational agencies, and financial services companies; it was spurred also by health care and medical delivery, food service, travel and entertainment, and retailing and consumerism. Fast food, motel chains, and car rentals, sprawling malls and shopping centers, lawn service and

No event in its history brought Florida more national and international notice than did the launch of Apollo XI from Cape Kennedy on 16 July 1969. The rocket and space vehicle enabled American astronauts Neil A. Armstrong (*left*) and Edwin E. Aldrin (*right*) to become the first humans to walk on the surface of the moon. At center of this photograph, taken beforehand, with the launch pad in background, is Michael Collins, pilot of the mission command module.

office temps, rent-a-maid and rent-a-nurse—these are some of the businesses that have emerged at the low end of Florida's late-twentieth-century economy, paralleling but hardly supplanting an older low-paid service economy centered on garment sweatshops, restaurant dishwashers, hotel maids, and migrant farmworkers.

There is a high end of the new service economy, as well. In the new information age, the high-tech and business service economy is no longer tied to older metropolitan centers of the Northeast or Midwest. With computer networks and other instantaneous communication, it has been possible for major corporations to relocate to Tampa, Miami, Boca Raton, or Orlando; costs are reduced for company and employees alike, and all benefit from Florida's low taxes, sunny climate, and enhanced amenities. Florida's new economy includes high-tech and computer companies in the state's "Silicon Beach" area stretching along the Atlantic coast north from Miami and in the Cape Canaveral area. The wondrous technological innovation of the late twentieth century—the personal computer—actually was developed at IBM's massive facility in Boca Raton. Major international trade and banking operations have clustered in Miami and Coral Gables since the early 1970s. Miami is not the Hong Kong of the West, but many business and civic leaders have aspired to enhance south Florida's place in the emerging global economy. Florida must continue to adjust and cope with the new technologies and global economic networks that will shape the twenty-first century.

New technologies and economies have helped to create modern Florida, but issues involving race relations and Caribbean immigration have had a more powerful impact in shaping national and world images of the state. Florida, in fact, has had a long and troubled history in the area of race relations. In the past, the legitimacy of its role as a "real" southern state was the subject of frequent debate, but the history of race relations in Florida leaves little doubt as to the answer. Florida's color line, drawn in exacting constitutional detail and cemented in everyday custom, extended across the state and across time for more than one hundred years after statehood in 1845. Jim Crow practices found easy acceptance even in Florida cities without southern-born populations, such as St. Petersburg, Miami, and Palm Beach. In tourist cities, leaders stressed the importance of maintaining a strict color line and docile black communities, making sure that blacks would serve but not be seen. When in Florida, northerners apparently adapted easily to southern racial customs and segregation.

Lynching, of course, loomed as the ultimate test of keeping blacks in their place. Historically, white Floridians vigilantly used the noose and the torch to control economic power and enforce race relations. Florida, not Alabama or Mississippi, led the South in lynchings in proportion to population. Lynchings were not confined to Jefferson, Levy, Marion, or Jackson counties in rural north Florida; Hernando, Pasco, Citrus, Polk, Hillsborough, and DeSoto counties recorded especially notorious acts of racial violence. Nor was the violence limited to isolated cases and individual victims. Attacks on entire black communities took place at Lake City, Ocoee, and Rosewood between 1912 and 1923. African Americans often fought back, as at Rosewood, or they organized boycotts of streetcars, as in Jacksonville and Pensacola between 1901 and 1905. In some cities, such as Miami and West Palm Beach, they joined Marcus Garvey's black nationalist Universal Negro Improvement Association in large numbers. Until the 1940s, poll taxes and white primaries kept them from the voting booth most of the time, but when possible (as in nonpartisan municipal elections in Miami), blacks turned out in force to exercise the franchise.

Enforcement of the Florida color line continued forcefully after World War II. In Miami, over a six-year period beginning in 1946, an active Ku Klux Klan regularly paraded, burned crosses, torched houses, and dynamited apartment complexes in an effort to keep blacks from moving into white neighborhoods. In 1951, in the small Brevard County town of Mims, the Klan dynamited the home of Harry T. Moore, a relentless civil rights activist and statewide leader of the NAACP, killing him and his wife. National magazines published articles in the 1950s with such titles as "The Truth about the Florida Race Troubles," "Florida: Dynamite Law Replaces Lynch Law," "Bigotry and Bombs in Florida," and "Bombing in Miami."[12] Big-city police departments in Miami, Tampa, and Jacksonville vigorously enforced the color line, often violently.

African Americans actively shaped the civil rights movement in Florida, even in the 1940s and 1950s before the national freedom struggle took off. A bus boycott in Tallahassee in 1956 inspired a wider civil rights movement in the state capital. Lunch-counter sit-ins led by the Miami branch of CORE in 1959 (a year before the more celebrated sit-ins in Greensboro, North Carolina) ultimately led to the desegregation of Miami's public accommodations and schools. But the civil rights movement was accompanied by racial conflict in the 1960s and after. Violent police behavior in the ghetto prompted Miami's Liberty City riot of 1980, and troubled police-community relations persisted in Miami and Tampa through the 1980s. Even as Florida became less southern, traditional patterns of race relations persisted. Urban uprisings in late-twentieth-century Miami and extensive media coverage of Florida's racial conflicts initiated new popular images of the state. Few were happy with either the broad outlines or the minute details of that image.

Immigration patterns since the mid-sixties have also dramatically re-cast Florida's image. Fidel Castro had a lot to do with the shape of Florida in the late twentieth century. The Cuban refugee exodus that began in 1959, episodic but relentless over time, has wrought big changes in south Florida. By the 1990s, close to one million Cuban ex-iles had made the journey across the Florida straits—by boat, by plane, by raft, even by inner-tube and sailboard. They and others are trans-forming Miami into the capital of the Caribbean and possibly of Latin America. The Cubans were followed by massive migrations of Haitians and Nicaraguans and smaller contingents from virtually every Carib-bean and Latin American nation. These migrations remade Miami and eventually all of south Florida. The demographic and cultural changes have been phenomenal, with few comparisons elsewhere. A sign of the changing times: in the new Miami more than 53 percent of the people speak a language other than English at home. The newcomers came in great numbers, they settled mostly in a single city, and their communi-ties were constantly being replenished by new waves of refugees. They maintained their old-country cultures to a great degree, developed their own brand of exile and ethnic politics, established their own en-clave economies, and competed vigorously with native Anglos and African Americans for economic and political power. The conflict be-tween blacks and Hispanics has been especially notable, and African Americans generally believe that they have been "displaced from main-stream opportunities by the newly arrived immigrants."[13] Older pat-terns of assimilation seemed not to apply in south Florida, which has emerged as a new multicultural cauldron and perhaps as a model for what Florida might become.

In reality, multicultural change has already spread far beyond Miami and south Florida to distant parts of the state. The Latinization of Florida is well under way. Large communities of Mexicans have settled in rural parts of central Florida, such as Hardee and Highlands counties. Puerto Ricans surpass all other Hispanic groups in metropolitan Or-lando. Hispanics from Central and South America outnumber Cubans and Puerto Ricans in the Tampa–St. Petersburg area. Guatemalans and

Salvadorans labor in agriculture and landscaping in north and south Florida. Jamaicans and other black islanders from the Caribbean have established large communities in Dade and Broward counties. Vietnamese fisherman have become an economic force in Pensacola and the Panhandle coastal region. Asians, primarily from India, China, Korea, and the Philippines, comprised Florida's fastest growing immigrant group in the 1980s.

For decades, Sunbelt states such as Florida, California, and Texas have been on the edge of a global migration of workers and refugees from poorer and less-developed countries and regions. Given the instability of the Third World, especially Latin America and the Caribbean, Florida's future will be tied even more closely to geopolitics and national foreign policy. A new "Columbian exchange" has taken place—an exchange that is happening now on the streets, in the schools, in the workplace, in the supermarkets, even in politics in some places. Ethnically and socially, the new Florida will be more multicultural, more ethnically and linguistically diverse, more Catholic, and Latin than the old and ever more different from the rest of the South. In many ways, Florida offers a glimpse of what America will become. Reconciling increasing numbers of senior citizens with new immigrants and established citizens will be a great challenge. New tensions in race relations in the post–civil rights era and new waves of exiles and refugees from the south have unalterably transformed Florida and have altered the way people at home and abroad perceive the Sunshine State.

The dizzying pace of new immigration and the challenges the immigrants pose suggest that big change has its costs. In fact, the rapid growth of Florida since midcentury should not be interpreted entirely as a success. For example, modern Florida has been a developer's dream but an environmentalist's nightmare. Dense urban development along the Atlantic and Gulf coasts has destroyed much of the tropical allure of old Florida and has left millions of residents vulnerable to hurricane damage. Urban sprawl has been gobbling up rich agricultural land in south Florida, and the builders and developers seem unstoppable. In central Florida, periodic freezes have damaged citrus crops and forced orange growers to move farther south, leaving abandoned grove lands to suburban Orlando developers. Urban development has been encroaching on the edges of the Everglades for many decades, threatening the underground aquifer that serves as a water supply for 5 million people in south Florida. Overdevelopment in the Florida Keys has produced a polluted paradise, killing off remaining live coral reefs and threatening marine life. The paving of paradise continues unabated.

Among Florida's other problems, the massive surge of immigrants has created ethnic and social tensions, especially in metropolitan Miami. Rioting and racial conflict have become common events in Miami, Tampa, and other Florida cities. By the 1980s, Florida had the highest crime rate in the nation, and for a time Miami had an unenviable reputation as the drug and murder capital of the United States. Crime, drug dealing, and random violence increasingly shape public images of Florida as "the lost paradise."[14] Recent killings of foreign tourists have badly damaged the state's attractiveness to visitors. If Florida had an edenic charm and appeal in the late nineteenth century, little of that natural and innocent quality remains at the end of the twentieth.

All of these problems have been magnified by a weakly developed public sector—a political and governmental system that routinely avoids important action addressing the state's social problems. As the state's voters have become more Republican and less Democratic, the state legislature regularly mimics the political gridlock that has characterized the nation's capital in recent decades. Political leaders in both parties seem more interested in low taxes than needed public investment in education, social services, infrastructure, growth management, or environmental protection. Boasting a relatively high per capita income, Florida has no income tax and relies almost entirely on a sales tax, tourist taxes, and a state lottery to support state government activities and services. Few state leaders seem ashamed that Florida ranks at the bottom of all fifty states in per capita support for higher education, or that the state's public schools are badly overcrowded and notoriously undersupported, or that Florida ranks high among the states in the number of prison inmates per capita. New prison construction, in fact, has been given higher priority by state leaders than building new schools, supporting higher education, protecting the environment, or providing mandatory health insurance. High social service demands, especially among the young and the elderly, are met only minimally by governmental programs. Getting beyond the tourist imagery, there are many shadows in the Florida sunshine.

Florida today, like the rest of the United States, struggles with uncertainty. Several major trends, each carrying the weight of history, have converged. The big changes that we have outlined—demographic change, technological innovation, shifting economic patterns, troubled race relations, and waves of new immigration—have brought us to our contemporary condition. And those same forces of change will still be at work shaping the Florida of tomorrow.

Notes

1. The organizing principle for this essay, focusing on big changes or "the momentum of change," has been adapted from Frederick Lewis Allen, *The Big Change: America Transforms Itself, 1900–1950* (New York: Harper and Brothers, 1952).
2. James Stirling, *Letters from the Slave States* (London: J.W. Parker, 1857), p. 227.
3. Frank F. Rogers, "The State of Florida and Its Highways," *Florida Highways* 6 (May 1929):5.
4. Nevin O. Winter, *Florida: The Land of Enchantment* (Boston: The Page Company, 1918), p. 369.
5. "Florida Highways," *Florida Highways* 7 (March 1930):34.
6. Arsenault, "The End of the Long Hot Summer: The Air Conditioner and Southern Culture."
7. Mark Sullivan, *Our Times*, 6 vols. (New York: Scribner's, 1926–35), 6:647.
8. "Paradise Regained," *Fortune* 13 (January 1936):35.
9. Cleo and Mesouf, *Florida: Polluted Paradise*, p. 2.
10. A. Lowell Hunt, *Florida Today: New Land of Opportunity* (New York: Scribner's, 1950), p. 72.
11. Edward Ullman, "Amenities as a Factor in Regional Growth," *Geographical Review* 44 (January 1954):119–32.
12. Joe Alex Morris, "The Truth about the Florida Race Troubles," *Saturday Evening Post*, 21 June 1952, pp. 24–25, 50, 55–58; William S. Fairfield, "Florida: Dynamite Law Replaces Lynch Law," *The Reporter* 7 (5 August 1952):31–34; "Bigotry and Bombs in Florida," *Southern Patriot*, 10 January 1952, pp. 1, 4; Nathan Perlmutter, "Bombing in Miami: Anti-Semitism and the Segregationists," *Commentary* 25 (June 1958):498–503.
13. Frank Soler, "Thoughts from a Wounded Heart," *Miami Mensual* 5 (August 1985):11.
14. Brian Duffy, "Florida, Paradise Lost: The Sharp Decline of the Sunshine State," *U.S. News and World Report*, 11 October 1993, pp. 40–53.

Bibliography

Arsenault, Raymond. "The End of the Long Hot Summer: The Air Conditioner and Southern Culture." *Journal of Southern History* 6, no. 4 (November 1984):597–628.

———. *St. Petersburg and the Florida Dream, 1888–1950*. Norfolk, Va.: Donning Company, 1988.

Bernard, Richard M., and Bradley R. Rice, eds. *Sunbelt Cities: Politics and Growth since World War II*. Austin: University of Texas Press, 1983.

Blake, Nelson M. *Land into Water—Water into Land: A History of Water Management in Florida*. Tallahassee: Florida State University Press, 1980.

Bouvier, Leon F., and Bob Weller. *Florida in the 21st Century: The Challenge of Population Growth*. Washington: Center for Immigration Studies, 1992.

Carr, Patrick. *Sunshine States: Wild Times and Extraordinary Lives in the Land of Gators, Guns, and Grapefruits.* New York: Doubleday, 1990.

Cleo, June, and Hank Mesouf. *Florida: Polluted Paradise.* Philadelphia: Chilton Books, 1964.

Derr, Mark. *Some Kind of Paradise: A Chronicle of Man and Land in Florida.* New York: William Morrow, 1989.

Dietrich, T. Stanton. *The Urbanization of Florida's Population: An Historical Perspective of County Growth, 1830–1970.* Gainesville: Bureau of Economic and Business Research, University of Florida, 1978.

Dodrill, David E. *Selling the Dream: The Gulf American Corporation and the Building of Cape Coral, Florida.* Tuscaloosa: University of Alabama Press, 1993.

Douglas, Marjory Stoneman. *The Everglades: River of Grass.* New York: Rinehart, 1947.

Fjellman, Stephen M. *Vinyl Leaves: Walt Disney World and America.* Boulder, Colo.: Westview Press, 1992.

Johnson, Charles S. *Statistical Atlas of Southern Counties.* Chapel Hill: University of North Carolina Press, 1941.

Miller, Randall M., and George E. Pozzetta, eds. *Shades of the Sunbelt: Essays on Ethnicity, Race, and the Urban South.* Westport, Conn.: Greenwood Press, 1988.

Mohl, Raymond A. "Florida's Changing Demography: Population Growth, Urbanization, and Latinization." *Environmental and Urban Issues* 17 (Winter 1990):22–30.

———. "The Pattern of Race Relations in Miami Since the 1920s." In *The African American Heritage of Florida,* edited by David Colburn and Jane Landers, pp. 326–65. Gainesville: University Press of Florida, 1995.

———. "Race and Space in the Modern City: Interstate-95 and the Black Community in Miami." In *Urban Policy in Twentieth-Century America,* edited by Arnold R. Hirsch and Raymond A. Mohl, pp. 100–158. New Brunswick, N.J.: Rutgers University Press, 1993.

———, ed. *Searching for the Sunbelt: Historical Perspectives on a Region.* Knoxville: University of Tennessee Press, 1990.

Moore, Deborah Dash. *To the Golden Cities: Pursuing the American Jewish Dream in Miami and L.A.* New York: Free Press, 1994.

Mormino, Gary R., and George E. Pozzetta. *The Immigrant World of Ybor City: Italians and Their Latin Neighbors in Tampa, 1885–1985.* Urbana: University of Illinois Press, 1987.

Portes, Alejandro, and Alex Stepick. *City on the Edge: The Transformation of Miami.* Berkeley: University of California Press, 1993.

Rothchild, John. *Up for Grabs: A Tramp Through Time and Space in the Sunshine State.* New York: Viking, 1985.

Smith, Charles U., ed. *The Civil Rights Movement in Florida and the United States.* Tallahassee: Father and Son Publishing, Inc., 1989.

U.S. Commission on Civil Rights. *Confronting Racial Isolation in Miami.* Washington: U.S. Government Printing Office, 1982.

Contributors

Charles W. Arnade is Distinguished Service Professor of International Affairs at the University of South Florida and author of *The Emergence of the Republic of Bolivia* and *The Siege of St. Augustine in 1702.*

Canter Brown, Jr., is Consulting Historian and Contributing Editor, Florida Supreme Court History Project, Tallahassee, and author of *Florida's Peace River Frontier* and *Fort Meade, 1849–1900.*

Amy Turner Bushnell is Associate Professor of History at the College of Charleston and a Research Associate of the American Museum of Natural History. She is the author of *The King's Coffer: Proprietors of the Spanish Florida Treasury, 1565–1702,* and *Situado and Sabana: Spain's Support System for the Presidio and Mission Provinces of Florida.*

David R. Colburn is Professor of History at the University of Florida. He is the author of *Racial Crisis and Community Conflict: St. Augustine, Florida, 1877–1980,* coauthor of *Florida's Gubernatorial Politics in the Twentieth Century* (with Richard K. Scher), and coeditor of *The African American Heritage of Florida* (with Jane Landers).

William S. Coker is Professor Emeritus of History at the University of West Florida. He is author or editor of fourteen books, including *Indian Traders of the Southeastern Spanish Borderlands: Panton, Leslie & Company, and John Forbes & Company, 1783–1847* (co-authored with Thomas D. Watson).

Robin F.A. Fabel is the Hollifield Professor of Southern History at Auburn University, Alabama. He is the author of *Bombast and Broadsides: The Lives of George Johnstone and The Economy of British West Florida, 1763–1783,* and the editor of *Shipwreck and Adventures of M. Pierre Viaud.*

Michael Gannon is Distinguished Service Professor of History and Julien C. Yonge Professor of Florida History at the University of Florida. He is the author of *Rebel Bishop, The Cross in the Sand, Operation Drumbeat,* and *Florida: A Short History.*

John H. Hann is Site Historian at San Luis Archaeological and Historic Site in Tallahassee and author of *Apalachee: The Land Between the Rivers, Missions to the Calusa,* and *A History of the Timucua Indians and Missions.*

Maxine D. Jones is Associate Professor of History at Florida State University. She is coauthor, with Joe Richardson, of *Talladega College: The First Century* and coauthor, with Kevin McCarthy, of *African Americans in Florida.*

Jane L. Landers is Assistant Professor of History and a member of the Latin American and Iberian Studies Center at Vanderbilt University. She is the author of *Florida: The World Around Us* and coeditor, with David R. Colburn, of *The African American Heritage of Florida.*

Eugene Lyon is Director of the Center for Historic Research at Flagler College. Author of *The Enterprise of Florida* and *Richer Than We Thought,* he is a frequent contributor to *National Geographic.*

John K. Mahon was a member of the Department of History at the University of Florida from 1954 to 1982, serving as chairman in 1965–73. He has written numerous studies of Florida's Indian wars, most notably *History of the Second Seminole War.*

Jerald T. Milanich is Curator in Archaeology at the Florida Museum of Natural History, University of Florida. He is the author of *Archaeology of Precolumbian Florida* and *Florida Indians and the Invasion from Europe;* coauthor, with Susan Milbrath, of *First Encounters: Spanish Explorations in the Caribbean and the United States, 1492–1570;* and coauthor, with Charles Hudson, of *Hernando de Soto and the Indians of Florida.*

Raymond A. Mohl is Professor of History at Florida Atlantic University. He is the author of *The New City: Urban America in the Industrial Age, 1860–1920, Urban Policy in Twentieth-Century America,* and numerous scholarly articles on the racial and ethnic history of modern Florida, especially Miami.

Gary R. Mormino is Professor of History at the University of South Florida. He is coauthor, with George Pozzetta, of *The Immigrant World of Ybor City* and coeditor, with Ann Henderson, of *Spanish Pathways to Florida, 1492–1992.*

Susan R. Parker is Historian for the Historic St. Augustine Preservation Board, Florida Department of State and coeditor of *Clash Between Cultures: Spanish East Florida, 1784–1821.*

George E. Pozzetta (1942–94) was Professor of History at the University of Florida for twenty-three years. A renowned authority on immigration history and ethnicity, he coauthored, with Gary R. Mormino, *The Immigrant World of Ybor City.*

Samuel Proctor is Distinguished Service Professor Emeritus of History and Director of the Oral History Program at the University of Florida. Author of *Napoleon Bonaparte Broward, Florida's Fighting Democrat,* he was editor of the *Florida Historical Quarterly* from 1963 to 1993 and acting editor in 1994–95.

William W. Rogers is Distinguished Teaching Professor of History at Florida State University. He is the author of *Outposts on the Gulf: A History of St. George's Island and Apalachicola from Early Times to World War II, The One-Gallused Rebellion: Agrarianism in Alabama, 1865–1896,* and other monographs in Florida, Alabama, and Georgia history.

Daniel L. Schafer is Professor of History at the University of North Florida. Author of numerous journal articles on African-American and Florida history, he recently published *Anna Kingsley*.

Jerrell H. Shofner is Professor of History at the University of Central Florida. Author of numerous books, including *Nor Is It Over Yet: Florida in the Era of Reconstruction, 1863–1877*, he became editor of the *Florida Historical Quarterly* in 1995.

Brent R. Weisman is Assistant Professor of Anthropology at the University of South Florida. He is the author of *Like Beads on a String: A Culture History of the Seminole Indians in North Peninsular Florida* and *Excavations on the Franciscan Frontier: Archaeology at the Fig Springs Mission*.

Credits

The photographs, maps, and engravings included in this volume have been provided courtesy of the following people, collections, or publications:

Harper's Weekly, 25 April 1885, engraved by T. de Thulstrup, frontispiece.

Information from Jerald T. Milanich, p. 3.

Florida Division of Historical Resources, Department of State, Tallahassee, p. 10.

William H. Sears and the Florida Museum of Natural History, p. 13.

Information from Jerald T. Milanich. Map from David Hurst Thomas, *Columbian Consequences,* vol. 2, *Archaeological and Historical Perspectives on the Spanish Borderlands East* (Washington: Smithsonian Institution Press, 1990). Courtesy of Smithsonian Institution Press, p. 28.

Information from Eugene Lyon, p. 47.

Center for Historic Research, Flagler College, p. 53.

Diocese of St. Augustine Archives, Mandarin, p. 65.

Bureau of Archaeological Research, Department of State, Tallahassee, p. 89.

Information from John H. Hann. Maps by Charles Poe. Courtesy of Bureau of Archaeological Research, Department of State, Tallahassee, pp. 84–85.

Photographic Collection, Florida State Archives, Tallahassee, pp. 103, 110, 135, 138, 147, 148, 155, 161, 209, 211, 223, 235, 238, 245, 254, 256, 258, 270, 271, 274, 279, 281, 283, 292, 295, 296, 313, 315, 318, 320, 321, 325, 327, 334, 335, 354, 360, 362, 366, 369, 375, 378, 381, 386, 388, 396, 397, 398, 403, 404, 407, 426, 434, 438, 440.

Archivo General de Indias, Seville, Spain, p. 119.

William S. Coker, pp. 120, 131, 152.

National Maritime Museum, Greenwich, London, p. 140.

Brent R. Weisman, p. 185.

Neg. #327045, Department of Library Services, American Museum of Natural History, p. 194.

Photo by Harry M. and Jacquelyn G. Piper. Courtesy of Brent R. Weisman, p. 198.

National Anthropological Archives, Smithsonian Institution, p. 202.

P.K. Yonge Library of Florida History, p. 242.

Special Collections, Rare Books and Manuscripts Collection, University of Florida, p. 388.

Photo by David Godfrey (Carr). Courtesy of Photographic Collection, Florida State Archives, Tallahassee, p. 428.

Index

Page numbers in italics refer to illustrations.